GOTHIC RIFFS

Anon., *The Secret Tribunal.* Courtesy of the Sadleir-Black Collection,
University of Virginia Library

GOTHIC RIFFS

*Secularizing the Uncanny
in the European Imaginary,
1780–1820*

Diane Long Hoeveler

THE OHIO STATE UNIVERSITY PRESS
Columbus

Copyright © 2010 by The Ohio State University.
All rights reserved.

Library of Congress Cataloging-in-Publication Data
Hoeveler, Diane Long.
Gothic riffs : secularizing the uncanny in the European imaginary, 1780–1820 / Diane Long Hoeveler.
p. cm.
Includes bibliographical references and index.
ISBN-13: 978-0-8142-1131-1 (cloth : alk. paper)
ISBN-10: 0-8142-1131-3 (cloth : alk. paper)
ISBN-13: 978-0-8142-9230-3 (cd-rom)
1. Gothic revival (Literature)—Influence. 2. Gothic revival (Literature)—History and criticism. 3. Gothic fiction (Literary genre)—History and criticism. I. Title.
PN3435.H59 2010
809'.9164—dc22
2009050593
This book is available in the following editions:
Cloth (ISBN 978-0-8142-1131-1)
CD-ROM (ISBN 978-0-8142-9230-3)

Cover design by Jennifer Shoffey Forsythe.
Type set in Adobe Minion Pro.

∞ The paper used in this publication meets the minimum requirements of the American National Standard for Information Sciences—Permanence of Paper for Printed Library Materials. ANSI Z39.48-1992.

9 8 7 6 5 4 3 2 1

This book is for David:
January 29, 2010

Riff: A simple musical phrase repeated over and over, often with a strong or syncopated rhythm, and frequently used as background to a solo improvisation.

—OED

- CONTENTS -

List of Figures		xi
Preface and Acknowledgments		xiii
Introduction	Gothic Riffs: Songs in the Key of Secularization	1
Chapter 1	Gothic Mediations: Shakespeare, the Sentimental, and the Secularization of Virtue	35
Chapter 2	Rescue Operas" and Providential Deism	74
Chapter 3	Ghostly Visitants: The Gothic Drama and the Coexistence of Immanence and Transcendence	103
Chapter 4	*Entr'acte.* Melodramatizing the Gothic: The Case of Thomas Holcroft	136
Chapter 5	The Gothic Ballad and Blood Sacrifice: From Bürger to Wordsworth	163
Chapter 6	The Gothic Chapbook: The Class-based Circulation of the Unexplained Supernatural	196
Epilogue		229
Notes		237
Works Cited		253
Index		277

- LIST OF FIGURES -

Frontispiece:	Anon., *The Secret Tribunal* (1803)	ii
Figure 1	Francisco de Goya, *The Sleep of Reason Produces Monsters* (1799)	7
Figure 2	John Thurston, *King Lear: O my dear father* (1805)	65
Figure 3	Handbill for *Camille* (1797)	81
Figure 4:	Handbill for *Le Moine* (1797)	84
Figure 5	Lithograph, *Robert le Diable*, Act II, Scene IV: Bertram to Alice: "Oui! Tu me connais!" (1831)	90
Figure 6	Musical score by Thomas Busby for the last act of *A Tale of Mystery* (1801)	159
Figure 7	Anon, Title page from *Tales of Wonder* (1801)	209
Figure 8	Anon, Frontispiece from *Tales of Wonder* (1801)	211
Figure 9	Frontispiece, M. E. L. D. L. Baron De Langon, *L'Hermite de la Tombe Mystérieuse, ou le Fantôme du Vieux Château*, vol. 1 (1816)	233

- PREFACE AND ACKNOWLEDGMENTS -

> We never saw more interest excited in a theatre than was expressed at the sorcery-scene in the third act [of Coleridge's gothic drama *Remorse* (1813)]. The altar flaming in the distance, the solemn invocation, the pealing music of the mystic song, altogether producing a combination so awful, as nearly to overpower reality, and make one half believe the enchantment which delighted our senses.
> —Thomas Barnes, review of *Remorse* in the *Examiner* (January 31, 1813)

The cover of this book, Pieter Breughel's epic canvas *The Battle of Carnival and Lent* (1566), depicts the denizens of an early modern European village engaged in a variety of activities that would have occurred on that specific day of transition including, off in the upper left corner, gawking at a public performance of the popular carnival pantomime *Valentine and Orson*. This 1489 French legendary tale concerns the adventures of noble twin brothers who have been separated at birth, one of them raised in the wild by a she-bear, the other brought up as a prince at court. This tale was so popular that it was first transformed into a street play and then chapbook form, in which it spread throughout European culture for three hundred years. In 1794 it was adapted as a melodrama by Thomas Dibdin, who altered the plot in a significant way. He has the two brothers meet by accident in the forest as adults, the cultivated Valentine serving wine to the bear-mother so that she dies, leaving Orson desolate (I.v). It is no coincidence that *Valentine and Orson* was typically performed by traveling troupes on the cusp of the religious calendar, during that period when carnival excess becomes Lenten penance and abstinence. In telling a tale that foregrounds a variety of transitions (from rural to urban; from "raw" to "cooked"), the play literally makes the maternal forest home of Orson a place of *das unheimliche*.¹

Its resurgence in popularity during this period can be seen as illustrating the "civilizing" and secularizing processes that Natalie Davis and Mikhail Bakhtin (1968) have associated with the early modern European carnival and the development of urban centers in Breughel's period.² As Charles Taylor has more recently noted, the carnival is but one manifestation of the "need for anti-structure" or what he calls ritualistic public displays of controlled chaos being "brought into a new founding of order" (47). For Taylor, who employs the theories of Victor Turner and Arnold van Gennep, the carnival gradually extended beyond a few days to become an "unofficial zone" in which the imagination was given free rein and where a "public imaginary" could flourish in the spheres of art, music, literature, and theater (52). Initially, these public performances of the "human code of complementarity" put forward the notion that all of us are members of a "communitas, fundamentally equal" and living in dependent coexistence with each other, the weak with the strong and all protected by an omnipotent deity (49–50). But gradually the productions of the public imaginary began to display the very processes by which European society acted out its ambivalent rejection of its earlier structuring principles, that is, its allegiance to God, king, priest, and patriarch. This earliest form of secularization, the secularization of public spaces, continued until the final stage of secularization could emerge, that is, internal transformations in subjectivity and the ability to embrace simultaneously multiple and contradictory belief systems. This book analyzes how those transformations in interiority and conscience were staged and culturally disseminated through a variety of popular gothic productions (operas, dramas, melodramas, ballads, and chapbooks), while at the same time examining how the gothic itself was a secularizing mode that shaped a number of art forms and had multiple points of presence in popular European culture.

Although *Valentine and Orson* is not generally considered part of the gothic canon, there are a number of gothic tropes in the work, particularly the death of the doubled bear-"mother" and the rescue of the biological mother Belisanta from a giant, and so I am interested in positioning this one particular work, and its transmutations through different literary forms, as representative of the larger argument of this book. What I would call the secularizing agenda of the gothic imaginary (as well as the interrelated and mediating genres of sentimentalism and melodrama) arose and flourished during this particular period, roughly the mid-eighteenth century through the early nineteenth century, throughout Britain, France, and "Germany" because all three developing nation-states were assailed by religious, political, and social changes that they were ill equipped to accommodate so quickly.³ In particular, the world of early modern Europe, a society dominated by the religious calendar and the festivities that we see depicted in Breughel's painting, was a culture thoroughly informed by traditional religious beliefs. Religious liturgies, texts, and doctrinal beliefs had been embraced and practiced for close to two thousand years and had functioned persistently for this culture as both its structuring principle and bulwark. The role of religion and what we might recognize as its more popular manifestations, superstition and magic, in the daily lives of Western Europeans were effectively undercut by the forces of secularization that were gaining momentum on every front, particularly by 1800. It is clear, though, that the lower class and the emerging bourgeoisie were loath to discard their traditional beliefs, and we can see their search for a sense of transcendent order and spiritual meaning in life in the continuing popularity of gothic performances, as well as May Day celebrations, Halloween, Christmas harlequinades, and the highly stylized and almost ritualistic theatrical productions based on fairy tales or myths, all events that demonstrate that there was more than a residue of a religious calendar or a "thirst for the Sacred" (Brooks, 16) still operating in the public performative realm.

In addition, the gothic aesthetic emerged during this period as an ideologically contradictory and complex discourse system, what I am calling a secularizing of the uncanny, a way of alternately valorizing and at the same time slandering the realms of the supernatural, the sacred, the maternal, the primitive, the numinous,⁴ and *das unheimliche*.⁵ Defining *das unheimliche* is frequently done by contrasting it with *heim*, literally meaning, as Freud reminds us, a home or secure space, and in Grimm's *Dictionary* a place "free from ghostly influences." Typically, theorists of the uncanny conceive of it as a repetitive, disturbing, haunting figure that intrudes into a largely secular domain, so that a culture in which religion still thrives does not organize itself much around the uncanny as a category (Royle 2003; Punter 2007). But the uncanny is not a strictly modern trope; certainly it was not invented by Freud or Ernst Jentsch, just labeled by them (Gentile, 24). The uncanny has always existed as Sophocles well knew, and it seems to be a manifestation of the doubleness at the heart of secularization itself, of what Charles Taylor has called the coexistence of the immanent and transcendent in modern Western consciousness itself. Because this culture could not turn away from God, it chose to be haunted by his uncanny avatars: priests, corrupt monks, incestuous fathers, and uncles. The gothic was, in fact, extremely effective at keeping alive all of the *ne plus ultra* of the supernatural (ghosts, witches, necromancy, exorcism, the occult, and the devil). The repetitious trappings of the uncanny and animism (magical thinking) continue to permeate the reading materials and theatrical performances that lower-class and newly bourgeois citizens attended in Britain, France, and Germany, but they did so in performances that sometimes explained away the supernatural in favor of the codes of the Enlightenment: reason, order, and clarity, and sometimes they did not.

There is no question that the bourgeoisie of Enlightenment Europe sought to embrace the secular codes of modernism as they understood them: self-control, commercial enterprise, education and the values of literacy, nationalism, legal rights, and civic values like "virtue" and "reason," and increasingly the novel developed to reify this ethos. As Angela Keane has claimed, "Novels stood to Protestant, Whiggish progressivism as romance stood to regressive, Catholic feudalism. . . . [Therefore] the later part of the eighteenth century produced a new, if ambivalent fascination with the pre-modern epistemology and its cultural and political signs, not least its national signs" (24). The gothic imaginary, however, is a distinctly hybrid genre, neither purely a novel form nor purely a romance. Able to assume different shapes and accomplish contradictory ideological work, the gothic could be Protestant (Sage) as well as Catholic (Purves) at the same (confusing) time. It also could present a "pre-modern epistemology" at the same time it denounced such nonsense. For David Punter, "the code of gothic is thus not a simple one in which past is encoded in the present or vice versa, but dialectical, past and present intertwined, each distorting each other" (1980, 418). In a similar manner, I would argue that the process of secularization that occurs in the gothic is not a simple forward-moving trajectory that we would recognize as the Enlightenment project, but more of an oscillation in which the transcendent and traditional religious beliefs and tropes are alternately preserved and reanimated and then blasted and condemned by the conclusion of the work.[6] The gothic aesthetic anxiously splits, then, between an evocation of the religious and feudal past and a glimpse of the almost present secular, between the importance of the pre-capitalist human community (Brueghel's vision) and the newly modern individual in the public sphere.

Literary critics have tended to focus their attention on the gothic as a primarily British phenomenon, taking cursory glances at France and Germany only sporadically and apparently grudgingly. But the recently discovered library in Corvey Castle, North Rhine-Westphalia, Germany, and the bibliography of its holdings reveal that there was extensive borrowing and interaction between British and German gothicists, while many British titles from this period that can no longer be found in England are available in the German collection.[7] Similarly, by focusing on England and France, Cohen and Dever have identified what they call a "cross-Channel zone of literary culture [that] produced a vision of the universally emotive human subject abstracted from national difference and historical specificity" (20). Additionally, Marshall Brown has criticized the "monoglot" tendency in Anglo-American discussions of the gothic, arguing that the "romantic gothic was a common enterprise developed by an international community of writers" (1). Peter Mortensen has also challenged what he called the "somewhat narrow construction of the gothic genre" that has been operative in the writings of Anglo-American critics by calling for a "more complex intertextual and transcultural exchange" between national productions. Mortensen claims that writers of the gothic should be understood as "participants in an international dialogue," "allies instead of opponents, united in their aim of appropriating, absorbing, and counteracting the sexually arresting and politically threatening fictions inundating Britain from the continent towards the end of the eighteenth century" (2005, 271).

It is folly, for instance, to overlook the fact that earlier eighteenth-century London was dominated by a German-speaking court and contained a sizeable German colony, but by the 1790s Germany had replaced France as the despised and demonized other, and German gothics were accused of promulgating political radicalism, religious fanaticism, and sexual licentiousness. In Germany, English gothic works were increasingly seen as immoral influences, while in many ways France continued to serve as a conduit between both German and British gothics, translating and adapting both traditions. A more conservative British culture feared what it considered to be the dangerous religious enthusiasms and politically revolutionary ideas that were being disseminated through translations of French and German writings. As Robert Miles sees it, England and, I would claim, Germany viewed the Protestant Reformation as "unfinished business," and so the gothic became popular because it displayed "the deformities of Catholicism[, and] held them up to the reader for the purposes of Protestant delectation." But, as Miles notes, "anti-Catholicism is frequently a screen for national concerns," meaning that for him the gothic is actually much less concerned with religion per se and much more focused on anxieties about the new sources for political and social legitimacy, or the lack of them, in a society that had suspended the Divine Right of Kings and had no plausible replacement on hand (2002, 84). In postrevolutionary France, of course, anxieties toward England and the German states were all the more intense, with the added complication of Napoleonic censorship and military aggression during the Empire period. In the German principalities, we can see fear of political violence oscillating with an incipient drive toward nationalism, all of this complicated by Protestant and Catholic factionalism.

PREFACE AND ACKNOWLEDGMENTS

Although it has long been standard to claim that one of the defining features of the gothic is its persistent use of the "explained supernatural," it is in fact more accurate to recognize that explaining away the supernatural in the gothic discourse is another way of privileging its talismanic force. Many scholars (i.e., Abrams, Rabkin, Peckham [1951], Todorov, R. Jackson) have identified what they have called the "natural supernaturalism" or the "naturalized Gothic" of the period, but no one (to my knowledge) has analyzed the performative gothic as one of the major modes of easing the transition from a religiously inflected culture to a secular one. Although it has long been a critical truism that the gothic is "anti-Catholic" and anticlerical, this book will argue that the issue of religion's uncanny presence in the period's literature is much more complex and conflicted. Yes, the "whiggish" gothic aesthetic is anti-Catholic, but in its bid to establish a (false) pedigree for itself, it is also nostalgic, reactionary, and in thrall to the lure of an earlier feudal, aristocratic, and Catholic past.

There is no question that contemporary British writers recognized the power of the gothic to seduce its readers with ambivalent and confusing messages. The satirical poem *The Pursuits of Literature* (1797) written by the anti-Jacobin T. J. Mathias recognizes that "LITERATURE, *well or ill-conducted,* [is] THE GREAT ENGINE, *by which all civilized states must ultimately be supported or overthrown*" (162; his italics). Writing a year later, Dr. Nathan Drake acknowledged the intense vogue for the gothic among all classes of readers: "all were alive to the solemn and terrible graces of the appalling spectre. . . . Of all the various kinds of superstition which have in any age influenced the human mind, none appear to have operated with so much effect as the Gothic. Even the most enlightened mind, the mind free from all taint of superstition, involuntarily acknowledges its power" (II:137). Such sentiments reveal that the gothic was understood to be a powerful ideological discourse-system that kept specters and apparitions of the sacred as well as the demonic alive at the same time that it castigated the failings of institutionalized religion.[8] As a major component of the secularizing process, the gothic aesthetic anxiously looked both backward and forward at the same time, torn between reifying the past and anxiously embracing a future it could not quite envision.

When I was writing the preface to *Gothic Feminism* in 1998, I was somewhat facetiously ruminating on what then appeared to be the gothic and melo-

PREFACE AND ACKNOWLEDGMENTS

dramatic contortions of my own life. Suffice it to say that the last decade has been no different. Family, friends, colleagues, and graduate students have supported as well as celebrated with me through this period, and it is my pleasure to acknowledge them here: first of all, my beloved and loving family, David, John, and Emily Hoeveler, Vince and Kathleen Long, Charlie Hoeveler, and the extended Thornburgh clan. I have also had constant support from friends like the Cazhillac family, Julie Darnedier, Ben Franklin, Frank Hubbard, Shoshana Milgram Knapp, Cathy Miller, the Perkins family, Angela and Don Pienkos, and Pascale Sardin. My colleagues Amy Blair, John Boly, Sarah Cordova, John Curran, Tim Machan, Krista Ratcliffe, and Albert Rivero have supported and encouraged me over the past twenty years. My graduate students Amy Branam, Ellen Letizia, William Lofdahl, Margaret McCann, Tenille Nowak, Amy Raduege, Debra Ripley, Donna Schuster, Wendy Weaver, and Mark Zunac have been devoted in their kindnesses to me as well. I would also like to thank my dean, Dr. Jeanne Hossenlopp, for her professional support.

Several sections of this book were originally presented at conferences held by the International Conference on Romanticism and the North American Society for the Study of Romanticism. Both professional organizations have been instrumental in my intellectual growth, and I would also like to acknowledge the collegiality and friendship I have received for many years from these scholarly communities, a diverse group of very kind and very smart people: Stephen Behrendt, Marshall Brown, Fred Burwick, Jeff Cass, Jeff Cox, Nora Crook, Bill Davis, Michael Eberle-Sinatra, Susan Allen Ford, the late Fred Frank, Michael Gamer, Marilyn Gaull, Nancy Goslee, Jerry Hogle, Gary Kelly, Greg Kucich, Maurice Lévy, Harriet Kramer Linkin, Kari Lokke, Mark Lussier, John Mahoney, Jerry McGann, Larry Peer, David Punter, Marjean Purinton, Alan Richardson, Donelle Ruwe, Sheila Spector, Judith Wilt, and Anne Williams. I am particularly grateful to David Collings, Gary Dyer, Regina Hewitt, Robert Miles, Franz Potter, Doug Thomson, and Miriam Wallace for reading drafts of this work at various stages and offering helpful advice and encouragement.

I am also immensely pleased to be able to thank Marquette University for awarding me the Way Klingler Sabbatical Fellowship for 2007–2008, and the Way Klingler Senior Humanities Fellowship for 2009–2011. This generous support allowed me to conduct research in Britain and France and gave me the time to complete the writing of this book, as well as to begin my next book, on anti-Catholic gothic chapbooks. I am also honored to have been awarded the Faculty Achievement Award from Marquette's Alumni Association of Women and endowed by Nora Finnegan Werra.

Those funds helped to support my research travels throughout the summers of 2007 and 2008. For specialized help, it is my pleasure to thank Jack Zipes for fairy-tale arcana; Julius Ruff for French dates; Norbert Besch, Olivia Gatti-Taylor, and Susan Vida Muse for help with German and Italian translations, and finally Victor Hugo Murillo and Robin Graham for word-processing assistance. I am also indebted to Joan Sommer at Marquette University's interlibrary loan office, and the librarians and curators who assisted me at a variety of libraries: the Huntington Library, the British Library, the Victoria and Albert Theatre Collection-Blythe House-London, Cambridge University Library, the Bodleian Library-Oxford, the Centre for the Study of Early English Women's Writing-Chawton, the Folger Shakespeare Library-Washington, DC, the Sadleir-Black Collection at the University of Virginia, Bibliothèque Nationale-Richelieu, and Bibliothèque-musée de l'Opéra-Paris.

Finally, I would like to thank the two anonymous readers for the press who offered valuable and astute readings of the manuscript. Sandy Crooms and Eugene O'Connor, and the editorial staff at The Ohio State University Press were, once again, a joy with whom to work. I am also indebted to the editors of the *Wordsworth Circle, Papers in Language and Literature, Romantic Circles,* and the *European Romantic Review* for permission to republish material originally printed in different versions in those venues.

I have dedicated this book to my husband, David, on the occasion of our thirty-eighth wedding anniversary. We met in 1968 when we were both students at the University of Illinois-Urbana. It is my good fortune that more than forty years later he is still my best and most patient friend.

- INTRODUCTION -

Gothic Riffs
Songs in the Key of Secularization

> Memory, a wan misery-eyed female, still gazing with snatches of the eye at present forms to annihilate the one thought into which her Being had been absorbed—& every form recalled and fixed—In the effort it seemed to be fluttering off—the moment the present form had been seen, it returned—She fed on bitter fruits from the Tree of Life—& often she attempted to tear off from her forehead a seal, which Eternity had placed there; and instantly she found in her Hand a hideous phantom of her own visage, with that seal on its forehead; and as she stood horror-struck beholding the phantom-head so wan & supernatural, which she seemed to hold before her eyes with right hand too numb to feel or be felt / itself belonging to the eye alone, & like a distant rock in a rain-mist.
> —from *Notebooks of Samuel Taylor Coleridge*, II:2915 (October–November 1806)

I.

When James Joyce mused that history was a nightmare from which he was trying to awake, he was also resuscitating one of Western culture's primary gothic tropes. Further, he certainly was not saying anything that Coleridge or Keats had not already observed about the gothic hag they represented as Mnemosyne, Moneta, or "Memory," a figure whose numbness alternates with postures of impotent and aghast shock at what she has been forced to witness. Coleridge's vision of Memory haunted not only his own consciousness, but, I will argue, European society at large. As the embodiment of a nightmarish past that could only uncannily recur in increasingly horrific manifestations, Memory is the mind that haunts itself with its own increasingly hyperbolic and compulsively violent reenactments of the past. This representation of the gothic maternal in agony recalls the death of Valentine's "bear-mother," but this mother's forehead bears a seal that reminds us of the legacy of gothic textuality that presented to its readers the violent images of revolutions and counterrevolutions that were occurring in their midst, of changes that were happening so quickly that their participants were almost speechless to record their painful contortions in a series of gothic narratives. In some ways we can read Coleridge's Memory as an avatar of what Freud labeled as the uncanny, *das unheimliche* (1919), a representation of the ambivalent attraction to and rejection of the primitive feudal past of Europe, the animistic heritage of "magical thinking" found in Catholicism, or in Coleridge's case, to his own past as well as the origins of his creativity. Strange and yet familiar, the uncanny is most frequently associated in Freud's essay with the mechanisms by which that which is most familiar to us—our families, our homes, and our own bodies—suddenly seem strange or possessed by a force that we do not recognize and cannot control.

The gothic secularized the uncanny by making traditional religious beliefs and values both familiar and strange, both immanent and transcendent, both minimal and powerful at the same time. And in many eerie and uncomfortable ways, the master narrative that was being constructed by Coleridge in 1806 was not so very different from the one that forms the basis of our political and religious experiences in the early twenty-first century. On September 11, 2001, American citizens were rudely awakened to the realization that the processes of modernization and secularization, long taken for granted throughout most of America, were in fact still contested in other areas of the world. This event, to have such serious repercussions for so many people across the globe, has caused a number of scholars to produce a series of recent studies that ruminate on how Western society became "modern," and how that concept can be understood as connected to the convoluted processes of secularization.

Until the publication of David Punter's *Literature of Terror* in 1980, the gothic novel was routinely read as a reaction against the Enlightenment. Given the very long vogue of rationality during the eighteenth century, the turn to the irrational in literary works was seen as natural and predictable. On much the same grounds, the gothic was understood to be a reaction against secularization: hence its resurgent interest in the supernatural and the return of sectarianism (as witnessed by the genre's investment in anti-Catholicism). *Gothic Riffs* is the first study to be written in the aftermath of Charles Taylor's *A Secular Age* (2007), a work that turns our customary understanding of secularization on its head. The usual interpretation of the secularizing process—dubbed "subtraction stories" by Taylor (22)—is that either religion in "public spaces" diminished during the origins of modernity (called "secularization 1" by Taylor), or that "religious beliefs and practices" declined (called "secularization 2"). Taylor argues that both of these approaches are inadequate because, while there is certainly less religion in modern Europe, this is not a universal feature of the Western experience (the United States being the prime counterexample). Nor is it true to say that the separation of the public and religious spheres is rigorously observed. Taylor argues instead that while the creation of a Western "secular age" is indeed historically unique, its defining feature is not a diminution in religion, but a change in the "background" of the public "imaginary" (13). Using Heidegger and Wittgenstein, Taylor defines "background" as the prephilosophical understanding that conditions thought by being universal, within culture, and invisible to its citizens (13). During the Enlightenment there was a unique change in this "background," one that asserted for the first time that human beings have the choice as to whether they locate the experience of "fullness" in the quotidian realm of everyday life or in the transcendent and spiritual, or in some other construction that allowed them to simultaneously embrace both worldviews. For Taylor, the final stage of secularization can be understood as a matter of personal choice as to whether one locates supreme value in the supernatural and transcendent, in mundane "human flourishing," or in a "cosmology" that combines the two (a locus that he calls "secularization 3" [2–4]). As Taylor observes, "[T]here has been a titanic change in our Western civilization. We have changed not just from a condition where most people lived 'naïvely' in a construal (part Christian, part related to 'spirits' of pagan origin) as simple reality, to one in which almost no one is capable of this, but all see their option as one among many" (12).[1]

For Taylor, this transition in subjectivity occurred when the concern for and emphasis on earthly "human flourishing" replaced the high value that had been placed on accumulating "merit" in an afterlife: "I would like to claim that the coming of modern secularity in my sense has been coterminous with the rise of a society in which for the first time in history a purely self-sufficient humanism came to be a widely available option. I mean by this a humanism accepting no final goals beyond human flourishing, nor any allegiance to anything else beyond this flourishing. Of no previous society was this true" (18). Taylor also argues that, paradoxically, this modern secular mindset was largely fostered in the eighteenth century by religious reforms and enthusiasms—what he calls "Providential Deism"—an argument supported by modern historical opinion, which tends to see schools of French rationalism, for instance, as the exception during an eighteenth century that was otherwise marked by a revival of religious feelings and beliefs (19). According to Taylor, this change of mindset—this fundamental alteration in the Western "background" (13)—did not happen by accident. On the contrary, it was the product of several newly invented cultural practices and technologies, and I would claim that some of these technologies can be seen in the development of the highly gothicized phantasmagoria, the melodrama, the chapbook, and the opera, all of which performed their cultural work by transforming that "background" through iteration and repetition. G. Graham has made a similar observation, noting that "the decline of Religion gives Art its greatest opportunity, to become the means by which humanity can enchant its own world" (143). And "enchant," as he reminds us, derives from the Latin *incantare*, or "to sing a magic spell over" (116).

But for Taylor, the work of the social imaginary is not a simple matter of "re-enchantment," as Max Weber has employed the concept. Instead, he argues that the development of "secularity 3" was based on "images, stories, legends" developed initially by an elite and then spread through the wider culture (172) through "new inventions, newly constructed self-understandings and related practices" (22). These cultural practices paradoxically revealed the uncanny doubleness at the heart of secularization 3, or what I will refer to as ambivalent secularization. That is, it was now possible to believe simultaneously in both the realms of the supernatural and the natural, the enchanted and the disenchanted, at the same (uneasy) time. For Taylor, this "repertoire of collective actions at the disposal of a given group of society" (173) actually encouraged the development of what he calls a "social imaginary" that advocated a sort of imaginative pluralism that in turn fostered the coexistence of the transcendent and the immanent realms:

> The great invention of the West was that of an immanent order in Nature, whose working could be systematically understood and explained in its own terms, leaving open the question whether this whole order had a deeper significance, and whether, if it did, we should infer a transcendent Creator beyond it. This notion of the "immanent" involved denying—or at least isolating and problematizing—any form of interpenetration between the things of Nature, on one hand, and "the supernatural" on the other, be this understood in terms of the one transcendent God, or of Gods or spirits, or magic forces, or whatever. (15–16)

Within the "background" of the popular cultural imagination, a variety of attempts were made to resolve the metaphysical split between the material and transcendent realms that had occurred during the Enlightenment period. One of its first explanatory challenges was the 1755 earthquake in Lisbon. While Rousseau saw the earthquake as a product of urban development and human hubris, others came forward to suggest purely natural causes as well as the laws that governed the immanent realm (Goldberg, 11–12). The disappearance of God as an explanatory mechanism was, of course, the subject of a good deal of debate but ultimately gave way to the rise of a growing conviction or anxiety that anything in the material world that could not be explained by recourse to either a beneficent God or to natural laws had to have its source in the continuing realms of the demonic and magical. This contentious intellectual "background" actually recalls Tzvetan Todorov's definitions of the fantastic, the uncanny, and the marvelous:

> In a world which is indeed our world, the one we know . . . there [can] occur an event which cannot be explained by the laws of this same familiar world. The person who experiences the event must opt for one of two possible solutions: either he is the victim of an illusion of the senses, of a product of the imagination—and the laws of the world then remain what they are; or else the event has indeed taken place, it is an integral part of reality—but then this reality is controlled by laws unknown to us. Either the devil is an illusion, an imaginary being; or else he really exists, precisely like other living beings—with this reservation, that we encounter him infrequently. (25)

And presumably only in the pages of fantastic literature. For Todorov, the "fantastic occupies the duration of this uncertainty. . . . The fantastic is that hesitation experienced by a person who knows only the laws of nature, confronting an apparently supernatural event" (25). Although he distinguishes the fantastic from the uncanny and the marvelous by claiming that they ultimately offer resolutions governed either by natural laws (the uncanny) or the supernatural (the marvelous), Todorov finally sees the uncanny as concerned with events that can be explained only by "the laws of reason, but which are, in one way or another, incredible, extraordinary, shocking, singular, disturbing or unexpected, and which thereby provoke in the character and in the reader a reaction similar to that which works of the fantastic have made familiar" (46).

The gothic imaginary arose within this impasse, in the growing confusion that existed between the realms of reason and faith, while the gothic aesthetic can be read on some levels as an epistemological attempt to explain how the immanent world of nature could have displaced the divine as an explanatory mechanism, but not the demonic. But rather than force people to choose exclusive allegiance to either the immanent order or the transcendent, the rise of ambivalent secularization actually allowed modern Europeans to inhabit an imaginative space in which both the material (science and reason) and the supernatural (God and the devil) coexisted as equally powerful explanatory paradigms. This uneasy coexistence of the immanent and the transcendent can be seen throughout the gothic corpus, particularly in those works in which a ghost speaks to warn and protect the living (the murdered Elvira appearing to her daughter in *The Monk* [1796]) or provides the missing clue to the dramatic mystery on stage or in the text (Evelina's two appearances to her daughter Angela in *The Castle Spectre* [1797] or the bleeding nun who haunts Lorenzo until she receives a decent burial in *The Monk*). Other examples include the devil who meddles very directly and disastrously in the affairs of the living (Cazotte's *Le Diable amoureux* [1772]; Lewis's *The Monk;* or Maturin's *Bertram; or the Castle of St. Alodbrand* [1816]; *and Melmoth the Wanderer* [1820]). All of these examples, in fact, illustrate the growing Protestant concern as traced by Nathan Johnstone, who has argued that during the English Reformation the concern of Protestants was to "emphasise the Devil's power of temptation, especially his ability to enter directly into the mind and plant thoughts within it that led people to sin.... Subversion was now the Devil's greatest threat—of the pious aspirations of the individual Christian, and of the godly nation as a whole" (2).

My argument is that the gothic needs to be understood, not as a reaction against the rise of secularism, but as part of the ambivalent secularizing process itself. Providing a satisfactory explanation for the popular gothic's fixation on formula has always been one of the main challenges facing its critics. By using Taylor, this study is able to account for the highly repetitive quality of the gothic (or what I am calling its "riffs"). The gothic is a site of endless iteration or what Katherine Hayles calls "remediation," "the cycling of different media through one another" (5), because it is a family of genres in which the cultural work of secularization is particularly intense. Following from Taylor's argument, this study reads the gothic as a member of a set of cultural practices invented to instantiate the rise of secularism, and therefore, it would be expected that it would be found in both high and low art forms across Europe and the West. If the old critical narrative was something like: where the supernatural once was, the secular now is or where the soul was, the mind now functions, the new story informed by Taylor would claim that the gothic is part of the way modern Western societies generate an ethos of intellectual, imaginative, and spiritual pluralism in an attempt to advance the goal of "human flourishing."

FIGURE 1: Francisco de Goya, *The Sleep of Reason Produces Monsters*, 1799. From *Los Caprichos*. Courtesy of the Bridgeman Art Library

INTRODUCTION

By way of historical background, it is important to note that by 1780 the "philosophic" movement in France had built an extremely strong case against religion as a species of "superstition" and the prop on which a corrupt political apparatus rested. Proponents of a variety of elite Enlightenment ideologies—scientific experimentation, mechanistic philosophy, materialism, Naturalism—challenged the now largely lower-class animistic conception of the universe that had been constructed on traditional Christian beliefs. In their attempt to establish a new society based on the realities of matter or the organic cycle of birth, growth, and decay, these epistemologies endorsed the scientific principle and the notion that the processes of life and matter occurred without recourse to a belief in spirit or the supernatural. But as various theorists of the decline of magic and superstition have noted, one cannot simply attribute the changes in beliefs that happened at this time to the success of the scientific revolution, the increase in urbanism, or the spread of various Protestant self-help ideologies. As Keith Thomas has concluded, "[I]f magic is to be defined as the employment of ineffective techniques to allay anxiety when effective ones are available, then we must recognize that no society will ever be free from it" (1971, 668). Indeed, as Thomas notes, explanatory supernatural theories were rejected by intellectuals throughout most of England well before effective techniques to explain medical and natural events were developed.[2] In many ways, this conflict is represented in stark visual terms by Goya's etching *The Sleep of Reason Produces Monsters* (1799), in which the uncanny gothic dream world of superstition, magic, and demons continues to exist only when the subject sleeps and his reasonable faculties are dormant (fig. 1). And it is precisely in this historical gap—between the decline of magic and the rise of science—that the gothic imaginary emerges.

Another possible way to approach the secularization thesis would be to ask, how did the West, at least ideally, evolve the values of universal human rights, suffrage, equality between the sexes, companionate marriage, and toleration of religious and cultural differences? One very persuasive explanation has been provided by Jürgen Habermas, who has argued that the development of what he called a textual society produced readers who were unified rather than divided into hierarchical social classes. The development of this broad-based literate public sphere was characterized by a print-based culture and literary texts that extolled the "whiggish"-bourgeois values of individuality, duty, loyalty, equality under the law, a public educational system, companionate marriage, and freedom of choice.[3] The public sphere, according to Habermas, originated as a way of defending the advances that had been made within the private sphere, so that the newer cultural practices instantiated in the Sentimental ethos found their public expression in literary societies, institutions of learning, and performative spaces such as the theater and opera house. But these social, political, and legal developments did not occur seamlessly or without a fairly contentious interaction with previous modes of largely religiously enforced patterns of behavior and thought, and this is where the vexed topic of secularization enters the discussion.[4] The contemporary French philosopher Jean-Claude Monod has sketched two dominant ways of understanding what secularization is and how it works:

> In effect, . . . if secularization signifies the *retreat of religion* as a dominant sphere and the reconstruction of institutions on a rational basis, it accords well with the belief that the present epoch opens a new perspective without precedent, and the belief according to which men are capable, and more and more capable, of "making" history. (Monod, 23; qtd. Pecora, 5; emphasis in original)

In this view, secularization is a type of modernity and, in fact, one of the "guiding-concepts," according to Monod, of modernity. But there is also another way of understanding secularization:

> If secularization designates essentially a transfer having consisted of schemes and models elaborated in the field of religion; if religion thus continues to nourish modernity without its knowledge, the theory of secularization constitutes a putting into question of the two fundamental modern beliefs. Modernity would live only as something consisting of a bequest and inheritance, despite the negations and illusions of auto-foundation. Modernity would then not be a new time, founded and conscious of its foundations, but would be only the moment where there is effected a change of plan, a *"worlding" of Christianity*. (Monod, 23; qtd. Pecora, 5; emphasis in original)

And so we are invited to return to Coleridge's representation of Memory as the "bequest" we have inherited from our predecessors, haunted and self-haunted by many indelible layers of historical residue that never disappear, but only shape and reshape before our startled eyes in increasingly uncanny formations.

It is also possible to suggest that the process of secularization is itself ritualized during this period, and if secularization "worlds" Christianity as Monod argues, it does so ritualistically *against* a previous notion of Christianity. In other words, the cultural work of constructing modernity at once expels certain features of an older practice and it does so in a ritualistic/

religious fashion, as if to borrow from that older practice. But exactly how does a cultural practice like literature ritualistically perform modernity? If modernity is itself produced by a vast cultural system of performances and narratives, is it not at once a religion and a counterreligion? As Hegel observed in a series of *Lectures on the Philosophy of Religion* that he never published, one way of locating the ethical life of a culture is to examine the "cultic images, rituals, songs and dances, sacrifices, and habits of worship" that they have developed. Those practices "then reciprocally shaped the thoughts and feelings of individuals, making them members of that culture by passing on to them a certain way of conceiving of God, humanity, and world" (qtd. Lilla, 181).

In much the same way I will argue that we can understand the European social imaginary by examining its performative cultural productions, almost ritualistic in the ways they have increasingly served as substitutive public religious practices. Whether performed on stage or presented through chapbooks or ballads, the gothic imaginary in Western Europe told a repetitious and fairly simple tale of familial and blood sacrifice and ritualistic social, political, and religious transformation. That is, in order to modernize, the newly bourgeois citizen of the secular city (the newly evolving nation-state) had to reject the archaic and superstitious beliefs of the past and embrace a brave new world of reason and "natural supernaturalism," a society in which the increasingly feminized and domesticated middle-class family replaced the hierarchical family proffered earlier by the church and king. The earlier, feudal, aristocratic, and ecclesiastical family/clan (or way of positioning and understanding oneself in a hierarchical cultural structure) was replaced during this period by a new political and familial structure—nationalistic, bourgeois, individualistic, personal, and conjugal—and it was in the oscillation and struggle between these two competing "families"—these two social, religious, political, and cultural formations—that the uncanniness and anxiety in the gothic imaginary was created.

To further clarify, my use of the term "imaginary" is initially indebted to Louis Althusser's notion that "ideology represents the imaginary relationship of individuals to their real conditions of existence." For Althusser, ideology does not "reflect" the real world but "represents" the "imaginary relationship of individuals" to the real world; the thing ideology (mis)represents is thus itself already at one remove from the real. In this, Althusser follows the Lacanian understanding of the imaginary order, which is one step removed from the Lacanian Real, or the primal world unprocessed by any psychic rationalizations. In other words, we are always within ideology because of our reliance on language to establish our "reality"; different

INTRODUCTION

ideologies are but different representations of our social and imaginary "reality" and not a representation of the Real itself (109–18). But Charles Taylor has recently adapted the term in ways that are more germane to my discussion here. For him, the "social imaginary" is

> something much broader and deeper than the intellectual schemes people may entertain when they think about social reality in a disengaged mode. I am thinking rather of the ways in which they imagine their social existence, ... [and this] is carried in images, stories, legends, etc., ... it is shared by large groups of people, if not the whole society, ... [and it] is that common understanding which makes possible common practices, and a widely shared sense of legitimacy. (171–72)

It is this social aspect of the gothic that is pursued here, rather than the psychoanalytical notion of the imaginary as the internalized image of the ideal, whole self situated around the notion of coherence rather than fragmentation. For Lacan, the imaginary is understood as the space that develops between the narcissistic ego and its self-created images. Instead, it is possible to look at works as performances that exhibit the relation between texts as cultural products and authors as social actors and producers of ideology, in short, the relation between the "inside" of genre and the "outside" of history.

By using a variety of largely forgotten gothic texts, "gothic collateral," so to speak, this book examines one aspect of the modernization process that occurred from roughly the outbreak of the French Revolution, through the chaotic period of the Terror and invasion threats in England, to the Napoleonic campaign and its aftermath. This large topic and this particular historical period have been the subject of debate for more than a half century,[5] and I enter the academic fray as something of a revisionist by focusing my attention on the gothic performative imaginary. But I argue here that the processes of modernization and secularization[6] actually evolved and advanced during the late eighteenth and early nineteenth centuries by appropriating and adapting the belief systems and subjectivities that were implicit in the conventions of three interlocking and performative modes that were extremely popular at the time: the sentimental, the gothic, and the melodramatic. And as for the concept of "the modern," I would define it as a temporal category, as a moment of coincidence or immediacy ("classical Latin *modo* just now" [OED]). For in analyzing the era's fascination with the "just now," we inevitably find ourselves confronting the period's coincident fascination with death, ruins, and apocalyptic imaginings, in short, with the gothic.

INTRODUCTION

This study also has implications for the literature that we now label as "romanticism," because it seeks to complicate the easy period designations and canonical status of this topic. By seeing the origins of "romanticism" in "gothicism," rather than the other way around, it is possible to demonstrate that literary culture in this period was not confined to armchair, "closeted" readers (presumably upper-class white male readers) extolling the beauties of the latest lyric offered by Wordsworth. In fact, British literary culture was a raucous, contested terrain fought over in rival theater productions, operas and burlettas, melodramas, popular gothic ballads, chapbooks, and novels, all of which Wordsworth and the other canonical male romantics seem to have enjoyed (despite their vehement protests).[7] I am certainly not the first to assert that the relation between gothic and romantic culture was fraught with ambivalence, class anxiety, and a fair amount of sour grapes. When Wordsworth's attempt at a gothic drama, *The Borderers,* failed, he simply found it much easier to blame the audience's jaded tastes than his own lack of dramatic skills.[8]

In fact, one of the premises of this book is that the canonical romantic movement has to be understood as much less original than it has been purported to be. Canonical male romantic poets borrowed from the popular literature and performances of their day, altering them by giving them an elite veneer that distanced their origins in more humble literary productions. I intend here also to advocate for the importance of recognizing the influence of popular, overlooked, marginalized literary productions ("riffs") on high, elite literary texts. My contention is that Wordsworth, Coleridge, Shelley, Keats, Byron, and Scott were much less revolutionary or original than they or later literary critics have claimed. A sort of cultural amnesia has occurred, allowing British and American critics to screen out their culture's debts to plebian, common literary and cultural texts, thereby giving them the illusion that elite literature (in league with reason, Enlightenment, and secular values) has "always already" existed. But the major romantic poets were enormously important in that they mainstreamed some of the most important modern ideals that writers like Thomas Holcroft (see chapter 4) could only glimpse and not yet fully articulate. In advocating for universal human rights, cosmopolitan ideals, literacy, companionate marriage, and the power of the imagination over the privileges of "blood," the canonical romanticists paved the way for the triumph of the ideology of individualism, interiority, and modern subjectivity as we know it today, but it is more accurate to recognize that these values were initially honed in the flood of gothic works that permeated European culture during this period.

Romanticism as well as gothicism can be understood, then, as distinctly modern, secular literary modes that evolved out of appropriating earlier and more dramatic genres, like sentimentalism, thereby ensuring their popularity and audience familiarity, but at the same time propagating a newer, modern consciousness that advocated imaginative pluralism or what Taylor calls ambivalent secularization, that is, intellectual openness to a variety of contradictory belief systems. In contemporary modern Western culture it is easy to take for granted a society in which women are not forced into dynastic or polygamist marriages with despotic tyrant-husbands, but such a threat was still actively present within the social imaginary of late eighteenth-century Britain, France, and Germany. This convention or trope became a powerful and persistent figure to be invoked and then ritualistically eradicated in the performances and productions of the gothic. That is, the historically "real" situation was less important than the ritualized, imaginary space that existed in gothic performances, all of which needed the representation of the tyrant-husband in order to reinforce evolving secular values (i.e., the acceptance of companionate versus arranged marriages and the triumph of "human flourishing"). Similarly, gothic "riffs" performed their major cultural work by (sometimes ambivalently) denouncing the privileges of the clergy, the aristocracy, and primogeniture, the legal disenfranchisement of women as heirs, and the fetishization of virginity. By repeatedly telling a few narratives that focused on core secular beliefs, the gothic enacted a wholesale reform of consciousness for the emerging bourgeois European citizen.

II.

> There was hardly a soul alive who did not experience more adversity in four or five years than the most famous novelist in all literature could have invented in a hundred. Writers therefore had to look to hell for help in composing their alluring novels, and project what everyone already knew into the realm of fantasy by confining themselves to the history of man in that cruel time.
>
> —Marquis de Sade, "An Essay on Novels"

As Sade goes on to observe in his overview of the novel, the contemporary gothic novel of his time was poised between the tactics of Ann Radcliffe or Matthew Lewis: either a writer could, as Sade observes, "develop the supernatural and risk forfeiting the reader's credulity," or "explain nothing and fall into the most ludicrous implausibility." Clearly, however, in both instances, Sade recognized that the presentation of the supernatural and the power of the transcendent were situated at the crux of the gothic imaginary. And behind the supernatural, Sade notes that the primary question raised is whether or not the culture should sustain or denounce its religious beliefs and traditions (13–14). Imagine, if you will, that cultural ideologies can be understood as operating much like a symphony does; there is a major melodic line, interspersed with *leitmotivs* and a variety of refrains, repetitions, crescendos, and reversals. In some ways, what I am describing is similar to Bakhtin's theory of the "heteroglossia" or "multi-voicedness" in textuality.[9] Heteroglossia enters a discourse through "authorial speech, the speeches of narrators, inserted genres, and the speech of characters." For Bakhtin, genres are performances or specific textual practices within a larger sociohistorical context and they are always responses to social utterances that have already begun. The discourses that emerge out of any genre are by necessity competing and often contradictory because they are responses to a society that is in flux and to a social reality that can always only be partially "real" and "unreal" to anyone at any given moment (1981, 264). Bakhtin has also argued that complex literature emerges during periods of "intense struggle," when a culture is suddenly deprived of its naïve absence of conflict, when moral systems are recognized as relative rather than unitary: "when boundaries are drawn with new sharpness and simultaneously erased with new ease; it is sometimes impossible to establish precisely where they have been erased or where certain of the warring parties have already crossed over into alien territory" (1981, 418). But discourses are, as Susan Wells has noted, "deeply implicated in relations of desire." In addition, they are concerned with "objects that have no being outside of the discourse, and are profoundly and unconsciously implicated in the temporality of the text" (145). Fredric Jameson has approached this same issue and stated that history does not "cause" genre in any simple way, but instead "shut[s] down a certain number of formal possibilities available before, and open[s] up determinate ones, which may or may not ever be realized in artistic practice" (148).

As anyone with a passing interest knows, the gothic bears strong affinities with the discourse of the Sentimental as it operated in the mid- to late eighteenth century, and certainly both genres relied on a fairly limited number of historical, mythic, ballad, and even biblical plots (see chapter 1). Very quickly, gothic novels became so popular that they were translated into operas (chapters 1 and 2), dramas (chapter 3), melodramas (chapter 4), ballads (chapter 5), and chapbooks (chapter 6) that circulated beyond the working or independent artisan classes and eventually to the emerging bourgeois reading public who seem by 1800 to have been their primary target audience. It is these cultural afterlives, so to speak, of the mainstream gothic novel that are examined here. In particular, I am interested in interrogating how and why a culture tells and then retells the same narratives in a variety of different media. Specifically, these works attempt to negotiate and mediate the reform of religious beliefs and rituals, the changing dynamics of companionate marriage, the contours of the new, more egalitarian family structure, the rights and responsibilities of women in a newly evolving capitalistic society, and finally, the implications of a society based on merit and financial status rather than birth ("blood") privilege. In short, the gothic's ideological agenda is primarily a "whiggish" attempt to expose and then relieve for its readers the anxieties produced in a new world in which neither a king nor a pope (nor their representatives) dominate the subjectivity or agency of the new bourgeois citizen. In many ways, the gothic and its "riffs" are the first truly modern discourses in which individuals stand in a sort of existential alienation in a universe of their own largely imaginary making.

We would, I think, agree that religious wars largely shaped the major political and dynastic events of the Renaissance and early modern periods, and we have a tendency to take for granted that those struggles led to the triumph of individualism, Protestantism, democracy, and the concomitant decline of the church's and the clergy's power and status. This "whiggish" version of history claims that the rise of Enlightenment ideology made possible the growth of capitalism, nationalism, and secularization, all of which privileged individualism and interiority, the private over the public display of spirituality, and the "closeted" reading of the word itself rather than its communal interpretation by a priest. But to transform a society in this way, to move it from an oral to a print-based culture, to uproot traditional ways of doing and living and being could not have been easy or painless. Such an upheaval leaves behind marks, what I could call the scars of modernization, and those wounds are what the gothic sought to trace, preserve, and alleviate to some extent in its own ambivalent manner. Thus in the gothic we have monks who keep coming back from the dead, or nuns who turn out to be our mother, or peasants who are actually princes. History is a rough beast, with little respect for the props—like religion and class and gender—that we have erected to explain why life appears to have a certain shape or character. When history displaces these constructions, there is change, and sometimes this change is of a radical and painful nature. So literature like the gothic arises as something of an alternative theology or therapeutic therapy, what I am calling the "secularization of the uncanny." This secularized quasi-religion performs its cultural work in a ritualistic manner and provides a variety of attempts to explain, soothe, and eradicate the pain of change by making sense of the wound.[10]

If the gothic can be understood as a form of secularized theology, then what is its object of worship? It would seem that the modern individual—

middle class, white, male, heterosexual, and capable of displaying an individualistic subjectivity and virtuous feelings and actions—is in fact the new social and cultural divinity. It would appear, in fact, that as paradoxical as it might seem, we are actually talking about the triumph of secular humanism when we are talking about who survives in the gothic textual universe. But exactly how and why did such a construction emerge and how was the gothic involved in spreading the ideal of secular humanism or what Taylor calls "human flourishing"? These are large questions, and in order to answer them it is necessary first to address the subject of subjectivity itself. Human beings can think of themselves only as human subjects, although the definition of what exactly constitutes the "human" has radically changed over the centuries, and for the last three hundred years or so, this definition has included a fair amount of machine as well as animal imagery. By providing a brief overview of the construction of this particular modern and cultural subject, it is possible to suggest some key issues and texts in the development of bourgeois subjectivity in late eighteenth- and early nineteenth-century culture.

First, as many critics of the period have noted, dazzling displays of personality dominate the canonical literary works of this period. The individual on the stage or on the page of literature, enacting a uniquely personal drama rather than a typological or formulaic one, seems in many ways to represent what we think of the newly emerging self of the gothic/romantic period. Romanticism, however, cannot be generalized about, much as we would like to be able to codify and limit its perimeters. To begin, it seems necessary to cite Friedrich Schlegel, who stated that human beings are characterized by their "terrible unsatisfied desire to soar into infinity, a feverish longing to break through the narrow bonds of individuality" (qtd. Berlin, 15), in other words, he reifies the transcendent tradition. And yet it is also necessary to cite René Chateaubriand, who claimed that his greatest delight was "to speak everlastingly of myself" (qtd. Berlin, 16), a being immersed in the quotidian realm of the senses and bodily desires. We are here at the paradox of the invention of the modern individual.[11] There is on one hand a desire for transcendence and the need to escape individuality, which can be seen in Keats, for instance, who dreams of merging into a nightingale's song or the figures on an ancient urn, or in Shelley, who seeks obliteration of the solipsistic psyche by union with his epipsyche. But, on the other hand, it is clear that the realm of the immanent was becoming increasingly more seductive. Individual rights, scientific and technological advances, and the battle cry of the revolutionary spirit were sweeping America and Europe, and such reforms demanded nations composed not of amorphous or interchangeable members of classes, but of unique individuals, all of them bringing their particular talents to an increasingly specialized capitalistic economy. This need to nurture the separate and unique individual was complicated by platonic residue, by the belief that none of us is whole apart from merger with another (the "communitas" depicted in Brueghel's painting).

We can see in gothics (like other romantic-era texts) an ideological split between what Habermas refers to (somewhat sweepingly) as the transcendent—the "pre-modern," paternalistic, providential, divine-right approach versus the immanence of "modernity's utilitarian, rationalistic replacement of the divine and authoritarian with the human and the secular" (1997, 39). In an era that was negotiating rival claims between an oral-based culture and a print-based one, the gothic embodies within itself a discourse system that is fractured between "singing" and "writing"; hence we have a number of operas and dramatic performances that align themselves with a chivalric, faith-based, feudal, and earlier oral-based clan system, while the novels and chapbooks move increasingly to a more modern, secularized, and legally inflected system of signification. Interestingly, the gothic ballad is a genre that attempts to straddle the two traditions, aligning itself at times with an earlier, providential "lifeworld" and the emerging modern and secular state. Habermas has claimed that the "form and content of Romantic art" can be found in what he calls the "absolute inwardness" of the human subject (1987, 18), while at the same time he asserted, not without challenge, that this period invented the "public bourgeois sphere" (1974, 49–55), a space in which the growing middle class could operate in an increasingly professionalized arena and where written discourse and a print culture dominated over oral testimony. The growing divide between the public and private spheres, and the concomitant dispute between dynastic/political and personal/individual concerns, can be seen by examining the evolution of a number of performative gothic texts, that is, gothic works intended to be performed on stage or sung rather than merely read in the "closet" of one's home.[12]

Building on the distinction between the "naïve" and the "self-conscious," Friedrich Schiller's terms from his essay "On Naïve and Sentimental Poetry" (1795), Taylor defines the two types of subjectivity that emerged during this period as the "porous" and the "buffered" selves. The "naïve" or "porous" self is one who is unprotected from the animistic forces of the cosmos, understands time in a nonsecular fashion, and sees an exact correspondence between the self and the cosmos. As such, the porous self lived unprotected from the world of "anima," demons, spirits, or any of the many cosmic and malevolent forces that could only be staved off through the use of magic, prayer, or luck (38). In contrast, the "buffered" self has created a "thick emotional boundary" between itself and the cosmos which allows it to oppose animistic forces. The modern "buffered" self understands time in a linear fashion, accepts the world as inert material substance that is subject to reason and human effort, and "takes a distance from, [and] disengages from everything outside the mind" (38). Here Taylor's sense of the "buffered" self intersects with Habermas's rise of the bourgeois public sphere, the triumph of a series of practices that create and nurture a historically new sense of the private (Miles 2010).

Using Taylor, it is possible to claim that there were at least two competing subjectivities within the gothic during this period. This first subjectivity was prone to hysteria, cried or prayed at virtually any opportunity, and was either seduced by demons or buffeted about by its own passionate and excessive emotions (in other words, was a continuation of the "porous" self and can be seen, for instance, in the actions of most of the characters in Matthew Lewis's *The Monk*). The second emerging subjectivity (largely existing within gothic texts like those written by Ann Radcliffe) was self-possessed under the most threatening circumstances, rational in the face of the most primitive superstitions, pious and habitually Protestant, and literate and committed to an often self-imposed educational program (a "buffered" self attempting to embrace the tenets of Providential Deism). But I do not want to suggest that the chronological transition between these two subjectivities was seamless or moved in a smooth historical trajectory. There was more than a little oscillation in these "selves," and the gothic at points was the locus of both "buffered" and "porous" selves interacting with each other in the same novel or on the stage at the same (confusing) time. It is actually more accurate to say that the modern individual is, in fact, at once troubled and assured, or in Taylor's terms, porous and buffered. This individual seems compelled to rehearse endlessly certain rituals in order to dispel or contain the uncanny, and evidently the ritual is necessary precisely because the uncanny constantly recurs. Hence we begin to hear of people who cannot stop reading gothic novels or attending the theater because something like an addiction has seized them.

As Miles (2010) has recently argued, Taylor helps us to read the Enlightenment and romanticism as "different phases in the history of mediation." For instance, in Miles's schema romanticism is less a transitional stage and more of a "cusp" that looks both forward and backward at the same time; it is a "bridge" between the earlier transitional period (Providential Deism) and modernity (as fully developed in ambivalent secularization). I would argue that almost identical claims can be made for gothicism, which is very similar to romanticism in its cultural work except that it presents us with a much more problematic and alienated human subject. Whereas the poetry of Wordsworth, Coleridge, Keats, Shelley, and Byron aimed largely for an elite or upper-bourgeois reading audience that was thoroughly invested in the public sphere, individualism, and interiority, the gothic met the needs of those who found themselves continually confronted by forces that they did not understand or could not control. They inhabited an imaginative landscape in which the human oscillated with its opposite, the nonhuman, the undead, the uncanny. Unable to embrace the brave new world of whiggish optimism, the lower classes found themselves haunted by a kind of undertone of doubt, an awareness that such a faith was unwarranted or at least not yet assured for them.

It is also necessary to recognize that the gothic arises at precisely the time when upper-class white males felt increasingly under siege by middle- and lower-class men, women's rights, political unrest, and the rapid economic, political, and social transformations of their society. Originally a socially and politically conservative genre, the gothic as a literary mode originated in the mind of Horace Walpole, a man haunted not simply by his own sexual otherness ("effeminacy" was the code word of the day for homosexuality), but more importantly by his illegitimacy (supposedly the youngest son of Sir Robert Walpole, the prime minister, Horace was widely rumored during his own life to be the bastard son of Lord Hervey, one of his mother's lovers).[13] So what began as a genre ostensibly based in the humanistic myth of the universal and privileged subject (the "buffered self") actually fissured to focus instead on the dark others who were buried within that partial and inherently false subject (the "porous self"). The gothic, in other words, is haunted by the bifurcation that plagues definitions of the self, as well as contradictory attitudes toward the body, agency, sex, class, and race. All of these avatars of indeterminacy were to appear on the margins of the major gothic texts in increasingly anxious formations. Thus Walpole's *The Castle of Otranto* (1764) redeems the politically dispossessed hero—after the appearance of the gigantic ghost Alfonso—as the rightful heir by the conclusion of the novel. Displaying what Marshall Brown calls a "half-religious sublime," Walpole's novel clearly straddles the "old rhetoric and a new psychology" (44), and his use of the supernatural was crude to say the least. Despite the absurdity of scattered body parts, gigantic helmets, breathing portraits, and statues that have nosebleeds, the popularity of Walpole's novel revealed a continuing hunger for the supernatural uncanny in the European imaginary, and, although the novel did not immediately spawn the popular outpouring of texts that would occur by 1798, it clearly presaged a new sensibility, or rather, the rebirth of an older one.

Walpole's novel concludes by reinstating class status and privileging birth and blood, but this ending was not possible by the time Matthew

INTRODUCTION

Lewis was writing his *Monk* (1796) and *The Castle Spectre* (1797). In addition to attempts to invoke something like a Burkean sublime, Lewis's works position doomed monks, devilish women, sexual nuns, and black slaves within its imaginary in order to complicate and challenge the upper-class white male's status and power in society. By the time Charles Robert Maturin's *Melmoth the Wanderer* (1820) and James Hogg's *Confessions of a Justified Sinner* (1824) were published, full-scale anxiety about a stable, universal-masculine subjectivity and "buffered self" had taken hold. The hysterically split and jeopardized male figure reached his final nineteenth-century British shape(s) in Robert Louis Stevenson's *The Strange Case of Dr. Jekyll and Mr. Hyde* (1886), Oscar Wilde's *The Picture of Dorian Gray* (1891), and Bram Stoker's *Dracula* (1897), all texts suffused with dread toward a masculine body no longer under rational control of the masculine mind.

III.

> Hail! Germany most favored, who
> Seems a romantic rendezvous;
> Thro'out whose large and tumid veins
> The unmixt Gothic current reigns!
> Much thou hast giv'n of precious hosts
> Of monsters, wizards, giants, ghosts:
> Yet, give our babes of fancy more
> Impart to novelists thy store!
> Till classic science dull monastic
> Dissolves in flood enthusiastic.
>
> —*The Age. A Poem* (1810), VII, ll. 407–16

Continuing our examination of fiction as the most dominant form of gothic subjectivity, we can also chart extremely similar developments in France by noting the transitions that occurred between the *roman noir* of the late eighteenth century and the *roman frénetique* in the 1820s and 1830s. Charles Nodier (1780–1844) coined the term *frénetique* and defined it himself by stating that it applies to those writers who "flaunt their atheism, rage and despair over tombstones, exhume the dead in order to terrify the living, or who torment the reader's imagination with such horrifying scenes as to suggest the deranged dreams of madmen" (qtd. Hale 2002, 78). The author of *Jean Shogar*, a Schilleresque tale of a noble outlaw, he also adapted Charles Maturin's gothic drama *Bertram* and Polidori's *The Vampyre* for the French stage (Kessler, xiv).

INTRODUCTION

Beginning with Jacques Cazotte's *Le Diable amoureux* (1772; one of the major French sources for *The Monk*), French works reveal a clear British and German pedigree, while they also in their turn influenced future gothic writings in both of those countries. The stark ideological bifurcation in French works between *noir* and *frénetique*, however, can perhaps best be demonstrated by contrasting the Marquis de Sade's gothic tales like "Eugène de Franval" and "Florville and Courval," both published in his *Crimes of Love* (1800), with the works of Joseph-Marie Loaisel de Tréogate. Sade's tales are filled with sufferings caused by incest, abduction, and murder in order to show that the random operation of a malignant fate is indifferent to the lives of individuals. In contrast, Tréogate's *Soirées de mélancolie* (1777) present moral tales that depict all manner of suffering as the way to achieve secular virtue in a world in which the divine is inscrutable if not absent. In neither case are the subjectivies buffered; these are works that continue to present the human subject as an object of events that they cannot control, let alone understand.

The French gothic was in many ways derivative and based on the earlier English graveyard school's immense popularity and influence. For instance, Jean Joseph Regnault-Warin's *Le Cimetière de la Madeleine* (1800) and Villemain d'Abancourt's *Le Cimetière de Mousseaux* (2 vols.; 1801) were both meditations on the senseless violence of the Revolution, the trauma of regicide, the "perversity" of the September massacres, and the consequent bloodshed that occurred as the nation attempted to democratize. Borrowing their structure and ambience from Edward Young's *The Complaint, or Night Thoughts* (1742, 1745), both works mix politics with domestic and sentimental situations much as did the earlier gothic works of Walpole, Clara Reeve, and Sophia Lee. As Dennis Porter has argued, French literature of this period reflected its society's "anxiety at the random, individual violence, of murder, rape, seduction, burglary, and street theft" (16–17). One of the most famous examples of this tendency can be seen in Charles Nodier's "Smarra, or The Demons of the Night" (1821), a concentrically layered tale within three other tales, all of them concerned with violence (infanticide, the guillotine), doubling, and the dream sequence as a "narrative of nightmare" (Kessler, xiv).

Henri de Latouche's *Fragoletta, ou Naples et Paris en 1799* (1829) illustrates another tendency to be found in French literature of this period, for it is an anti-Catholic political allegory in which the "heroine" turns out to be a hermaphrodite who has masqueraded as a man throughout the novel. Pétrus Borel, who styled himself the "lycanthrope," also took aim at both the Catholic Church and the Bourbon monarchy, accusing both of hypocrisy and repression. His *Campavert: Contes Immoraux* (1833) contains his most frequently reprinted short tale of horror, "Andreas Vesalius the Anatomist," about the famous sixteenth-century Flemish anatomist who dissected bodies in defiance of the Catholic Church's proscriptions. The tale presents an ambivalent depiction of secularized scientific advances, with the anatomist dissecting his wife's lovers and eventually her in his basement laboratory in a strange confluence of personal revenge and scientific ideals. On the political side, Borel's two-volume novel, *Madame Putiphar* (1839), attacks the sexual promiscuity and predatory hypocrisy of the *ancien régime*, specifically Louis XV and his mistress Madame de Pompadour.[14]

In Germany the gothic novelistic tradition was located in what came to be known as the genres of *Ritter-*, *Rauber-*, and *Schauerroman* (knights, robbers, and ghosts; or chivalry, banditry, and terror). Goethe's *Götz von Berlichingen* (1773; trans. Walter Scott 1799) and Christiane Naubert's *Hermann von Unna* (1788; trans. English 1794), a novel purporting to expose the workings of "secret tribunals" at the corrupt aristocratic court of the Emperors Winceslaus and Sigismond in Westphalia (see Murphy; Sweet; Hadley). There is no question that *Hermann* was extremely popular in Britain and has long been recognized as an important influence on Radcliffe's depiction of the Inquisition in *The Italian* (1797). In addition, James Boaden virtually plagiarized the work as his gothic drama *The Secret Tribunal* (Covent Garden, 1795), while a redaction of the novel appeared as an 1803 chapbook (see Frontispiece). Felicia Hemans later adapted the legend as the basis for her long narrative poem *A Tale of the Secret Tribunal* (comp. early 1820s; pub. 1845), citing Madame de Staël's *De l'Allemagne* (1813) as her source. In addition to "tribunal" novels, the German ballad was most frequently imported by British gothicists, Lewis himself transposing virtually wholesale a number of German ballads and novels into his own productions (see Conger). Walter Scott, writing in 1833, noted that Lewis was "the person who first attempted to introduce something like the German taste into English fictitious dramatic and poetic composition" (1932; IV:29), while Scott himself not only translated Goethe's *Götz*, but also drafted a Tribunal play "The House of Aspen," based on Veit Weber's *Sagen der Vorzeit* in 1799.

Friedrich von Schiller's *Der Geisterseher* (1789), translated into English as *The Ghost-Seer; Or, Apparitionist* (1795), was clearly influenced by Cazotte and was itself later the major Germanic source for both *The Monk* and *Melmoth the Wanderer*, as well as a number of German necromancer novels, most famously K. F. Kahlert's *Der Geisterbanner*, 1790 (*The Necromancer*, trans. Peter Teuthold 1794). *The Ghost-Seer* is a scathing portrait of the real-life Masonic charlatan, Count Cagliostro, a Sicilian who performed across Europe in the late 1780s as a fortune teller and séance leader and was eventually executed by the Inquisition in 1795. Rumored to be a member of the Illuminati, a revolutionary group of Freemasons who used a number of sensory tricks (magic lanterns, exploding powders) to gain power over their gullible victims, the Freemasons' aim was to assume control over the property of their bamboozled adherents (usually convents of easily duped nuns). By extension, fear of the Illuminati was based on the belief that they could use these same techniques on powerful "Princes" in order to gain power over nation-states. Schiller's short mystery was also supposedly modeled on yet another contemporary historical figure, the third son in line to the dukedom of Würtemberg, whose family was Protestant but who was himself rumored to be considering the idea of converting to Catholicism. *The Ghost-Seer* tells the tale of a young German prince driven by a mysterious monk first to religious skepticism, then to libertinism, and finally to murder in the religiously paranoid atmosphere of Venice. Raised in a strict Protestant society, the prince's naturally good feelings and impulses are corrupted so thoroughly that he easily falls prey to the superstitious mysteries and displays that the mysterious Armenian monk offers to him. *The Ghost-Seer* is almost a textbook study of the "explained supernatural," except that all of the supernatural powers of the so-called Incomprehensible Armenian monk are finally not explained fully, nor is the work finished. Influenced by the Schwabian piestism of his youth, Schiller focused on depicting God as a punishing force and his *Ghost-Seer* returns repeatedly to exploring the unfortunate connection between freethinking and damnation, skepticism and credulity (see LeTellier).

During the period 1787 through 1798 a series of gothic novels known as *Trivialromane* appeared under the general title of *Sagen der Vorzeit* ("Sagas of Olden Times"), written by Leonard Wächter using the pseudonym "Veit Weber." A representative title by Wächter is *Woman's Revenge; or The Tribunal of Blood* (republished in the 1840s in England by William Hazlitt's *The Romanicist and Novelist's Library* in weekly installments). Characterized by their use of the rationalistic demonic, these novels set their action in the medieval period and featured occultism, secret societies, demons, and the familiar cast of characters that were also popular in England under the Minerva Press imprint. Christian Spiess, who specialized in writing biographies of suicides (*Biographien der Selbstmörder* [4 vols., Leipzig, 1790] that were some of Thomas De Quincey's favorite reading material), also penned *Das Petermännchen* (1791), a work very typical of the indigenous German gothic. Folkloric and almost like fairy tales, Spiess's novels have been identified as part of the *Geisterromane* tradition (where the ghosts are real and act in human affairs), as well as the *Schicksalstragödie* tradition (tragedies of fate), where an ancestral curse dooms an entire family and the only survivor is fated to wander the earth until his ghastly mission is completed, this last trope being a variation on the Wandering Jew theme. Also relevant to the German gothic tradition were writers of the *Sturm und Drang* ("Storm and Stress") movement. Committed to celebrating the genius of Shakespeare and Ossian and embracing primeval energy as the source for all creativity, *Sturm und Drang* authors loosely associated with the movement, like Goethe, Schiller, and Gottfried Bürger (whose works were quickly translated into French and English and influenced Lewis's *Monk* as well as the ballads of Wordsworth, Coleridge, and Southey), challenged the established power of both the church and state in their works, advocating instead an exaggerated cult of feeling and a personal and individualized ethos that we would recognize as protosecular (see Pascal).

Schauerroman ("shudder novels") were another German specialty, or what Thomas Carlyle referred to as "bowl and dagger" works in which spectral nuns and outlaws fled across the Black Forest, which itself was filled with walking skeletons. One major practitioner of the genre was Joseph Alois Gleich (1772–1841), who published under the name "Dellarosa," and who wrote *The Torch of Death; or the Cave of the Seven Sleepers* and *Udo the Man of Steel; or, The Ruins of Drudenstein* (see Mulvey-Roberts). The major German gothicist, however, was E. T. A. Hoffmann, whose short fiction "The Sandman" (trans. English 1824; trans. French 1829) was most famously used by Jacques Offenbach as part of the source material for his opera *Les Contes d'Hoffmann* (Paris, 1881) and was also one of the literary inspirations for Freud's essay on "The Uncanny." Featuring a series of striking primal scene and castration fantasies, the work ends with Nathaniel committing suicide when he cannot escape a *doppelgänger* who apparently murdered his father and then created and dismembered his beloved Olympia, a mechanical doll he thought was human. Another of Hoffmann's gothic tales, "The Entail" (1817; trans. English 1824), explores a dark family secret (the usurpation of an estate two generations earlier) and the class warfare that haunts the Castle of Roderick von R——, driving away all its owners. Narrated by a visitor to the castle who spends his evenings reading Schiller's *Ghost-Seer* and serenading his beloved to the melancholy strains of *Ochi, perchè piangete* (O eyes, why weep you?), the narrator finally unravels the meaning of the mysterious ghost who haunts the castle by uncovering his identity as a servant who murdered the rightful heir two generations earlier. Hoffmann's novel *The Devil's Elixirs* (1816; trans. English 1824) also exploits the gothic implications of the *doppelgänger* and the self-haunted or divided psyche. Characters are doubled, personalities are split, events repeat, and the supernatural and material realms intersect in uncanny ways throughout this novel (see Cornwell, 113; M. Brown, 127–34). In fact, *The Devil's Elixirs* was so popular in England that it was redacted into *The Devil's Elixir; or, The Shadowless Man,* a musical romance in two acts by Fitzball and Rodwell (Covent Garden, 1829), as well as two different gothic short stories, "The Mysterious Bottle of Old Hock" (1825) and "Saint Anthony's Flask; or, The Devil's Wine!" (1830).

As this brief overview of French and German gothic fiction suggests, the genre can be read as one extended historical document, a series of texts that trace some of the traumatic effects of rapid cultural, social, religious, and economic change. As a species of literary ideology, the gothic both reflects those changes—puts them in front of its contemporary readers as well as us for public scrutiny—while at the same time it effects change by accomplishing the cultural work that ideology strives to do. By reading and seeing performed a number of gothic texts, the British public allowed itself to vicariously and bloodlessly experience the French Revolution, for these texts enact a symbolic parricide by presenting the destruction of a corrupt clergy, and establishing a new hegemony presided over by the bourgeois capitalist. Nineteenth-century British subjects never made the move to actually remove their king, although certainly they had cause (as periodic bouts of insanity do tend to impede one's ability to rule a country) and more than a few of them were placed on trial for "imagining" the death of the king (see Barrell, chap. 17). Instead, the majority of British citizens were content to flirt with the idea of revolution, settling for the vicarious and sublimated experience of reading about revolution in place of experiencing it. So the subject who is created in British gothic texts is a surrogate for the reader, a hero or heroine who undergoes what bourgeois Britons did not want to subject themselves to—real action, real blood, real guillotines. The situation was different in France, with a number of gothic works replaying the revolutionary trauma of the guillotined over and over again, while fragmentation and dismemberment, as well as conspiracies by secret societies (read: Illuminati and Jesuits) were the dominant themes in German gothic works (and note that "Germany" as a united nation at this point did not exist; tiny principalities clinging to feudal vestiges of power were still in political operation, at least minimally).

Europeans during the period 1780–1820 were engaged in that most perilous performance, becoming modern and slowly accepting a type of ambivalent secularization that their increasingly rationalistic and capitalistic cultures demanded of them (see Gilmartin). The French chose to clumsily and bloodily perform the work of modernization with a guillotine, while the Germans resisted unification until the 1848 revolution violently began a process of nationalization that would not be complete until 1871. The British had already killed one king in 1649, and they did not, it seems, want to relive that particular historical nightmare. Revolutionary violence did occur in England during the Gordon Riots of 1780 when attempts were made by the Protestant Association to demand the repeal of the English Catholic Relief Act (sometimes called the Papist Act) of 1778. Close to three hundred protesters were killed and the public was reminded again that it was Protestant religious enthusiasts who had been the cause of the English Civil War and now the Gordon ("No Popery") riots (Lord George Gordon, the leading Protestant zealot, converted to Orthodox Judaism in 1787). By the late eighteenth century, the fear of French Jacobins, Protestant extremists, Illuminati, and Jesuits combined to create an atmosphere of political and religious paranoia throughout Europe. As Miles notes, "pre-1794 Gothics tended to focus upon Catholic superstition as the enemy of reason and modernity, [while] the German Gothics fixed upon the blind enthusiasm that the Illuminati fostered through their 'supernatural' tricks," but "after 1794 the Gothic became a way of speaking the unspeakable," that is, revolution. Gothic works, postrevolution, demonize both religious extremists and political "conspiracies," equating Protestant Dissenters, Jesuits, Illuminati, and Jacobins as identical in their threats to "human flourishing," political progress, and social stability because of their equally extreme beliefs (2002, 55–56). Whether Britain could survive the processes of secularization and modernization without a bloody revolution was in doubt until April 10, 1848, when the Chartists failed to stage their massive demonstration in London. There would be no political upheaval in England as there had been in virtually every nation-state on the Continent, only more novels about the dire consequences of political upheaval—Brontë's *Shirley* (1849) and Gaskell's *Mary Barton* (1848)—being two of the most well known.

IV.

We talk of ghosts; neither Lord Byron nor Monk G. Lewis seem to believe in them, and they both agree, in the very face of reason, that none could believe in ghosts without also believing in God. I do not think that all the persons who profess to discredit those visitations really do discredit them, or if they do in the daylight, are not admonished by the approach of loneliness and midnight to think more respectfully of the world of shadows.

—Percy Shelley, August 18, 1816, qtd. Edward Dowden,
The Life of Percy Shelley, II:37–38

INTRODUCTION

If the "outside" of the gothic is concerned with political, social, and economic anxieties, the "inside" of the aesthetic speaks to spiritual, transcendental, and religious transformations. And it is in trying to negotiate the persistently oscillating landscape of politics and religion, history and psychology, that most literary critics of the gothic have found themselves stranded. In addition to ambivalently presenting revolutionary sensibilities, the gothic repeatedly enacts a religious hysteria that can be traced in the continual appearances of demons, ghosts, guilt, confessions, and imprisonments within abbey cells. The "background" of this hysteria can most accurately be located in the uncanny sectarian doubleness at the heart of Christianity itself, that is, in the conflict between Protestantism and Catholicism. The "killing" of Catholicism in England took more than two hundred years, and the gothic charts that eradication in all its convoluted and complicated moves. On this same issue, Allison Shell has observed that

> the central paradox in Freud's essay [on the uncanny] is how the genuinely unknown is not frightening at all, because uncanniness depends on a previous, outgrown familiarity. To many English Protestants of the late eighteenth century, nothing could have seemed more familiar, more superseded or more threatening than medieval Catholicism; and its growing legal toleration would perhaps, at both conscious and subconscious levels, have been almost as terrifying as seeing monks move back into the ruined abbeys. (52)

One of the most persistent tropes in the gothic is the exposure, punishment, and usually death of a corrupt duke or monk, and certainly in this repetitive action we can see ritualized the killing of a bad, illegitimate king (read: the legitimation of a *British* king) or the erasure of a God of superstition (read: the allegiance and fidelity to a *Protestant* God). The rationality and self-control that was so highly prized by Protestant individualism and Enlightenment ideology moves to center stage in the gothic, creating a new cultural ideal that chastised idolatry, superstition, hierarchy, and popery in all its forms. But one would hardly characterize the gothic as a uniformly consistent Enlightenment genre. In fact, numerous critics have seen in the gothic a series of nostalgic and ambivalent gestures, conflicted and contradictory poses, a mode of writing composed by authors who mixed piety with equal parts of political and social anxiety (see Baldick and Mighall, 211–21). For example, the Protestant Settlement of 1688, known as the "Glorious Revolution," allowed Britain to avoid another bloodbath on the order that it had experienced with the beheading of

Charles I. It also institutionalized Anglican Protestantism, complete with the requirement that one needed to pledge the Oath of Supremacy and Allegiance to the monarch as the supreme head of the Church in England in order to obtain a legal, governmental, or military position, and later even to attend university. But by requiring such a public oath, Anglicanism actually contradicted one of its main distinctions from Catholicism (see Sage, xix). Whereas Catholicism was accused of using the confessional to absolve the most heinous of sins, Protestantism insisted on the unmediated internalization of individual conscience (i.e., that no clergyman could absolve anyone of their sins, as this could only be done within the "closet" of one's own conscience). But how can a society be based on trust in each individual's conscience if, in fact, our own life experiences inform us all too clearly that evil (in the form of original sin) lurks in every bosom? Whereas the sentimental ethos clung to the notion of the "noble savage" or the inherent perfectibility of the untainted human subject, the gothic was willing to confront the inadequate explanations provided by Protestantism and Providential Deism to basic spiritual concerns: how to understand the persistent mystery of human cruelty, evil, corruption, and finally, death.

The issues of religion, the supernatural, and "God" take on the forms of atavistic mania in a number of gothic works, such as Hogg's *Confessions of a Justified Sinner* or Maturin's *Melmoth the Wanderer*, both published during the height of pamphleteering for and against the cause of Catholic emancipation in England. Hogg's *Confessions*, for instance, seems to be predicated on the distinction that David Hume makes between two kinds of superstition: Catholicism, where practitioners prostrate themselves to the authority of priests, and Protestant enthusiasts, who believe themselves saved and set themselves above human laws (76–78). *Confessions* satirizes these Protestant "enthusiasts" who, in their fanatical zeal, believe themselves to be the particular favorites of God and therefore above the law. The antinomian Calvinist doctrine of the sanctity of the internalized conscience allowed its believers to think that they were above both the laws of society and, in fact, even the Ten Commandments. The "saved" characters in this novel fancy themselves as answerable only to their own (rather peculiar) consciences. The novel also presents the devil, Gil-Martin, less as a supernatural being and more as a psychic projection of the hero, Robert Wringhim, or perhaps he is a being who only appears to assume an actual physical form because he is the material manifestation of Wringhim's religious mania.

Maturin, a Church of Ireland clergyman who was descended from Huguenots, was so invested in the anti-Catholic agenda that he published a tract entitled *Five Sermons on the Errors of the Roman Catholic Church*

(1824), while his *Melmoth* depicts a man who has sold his soul to the devil and then spends his expanded lifespan of 150 years trying to find someone else who will relieve him of his bargain. *Melmoth* reveals how clearly the gothic was committed, even if ambivalently, to charting the continuing power of the evils of the old world of Catholicism, communalism, feudalism, and the tenuous rise in its place of the Protestant subject, individual, modern, and secular. An epic work that contains five embedded narratives within the master narrative, *Melmoth* presents eternity, the soul, the devil, and the riddle of human suffering very literally and, one is tempted to observe, at the same time as components of an almost magical or performative belief system. At one point in the text, Monçada is tortured in a monastery by the temptations proffered by artificial demons and he exclaims, "When art assumes the omnipotence of reality, when we feel we suffer as much from an illusion as from truth, our sufferings lose all dignity and all consolation" (157). Shortly later, however, the narrator explains how that illusion has replaced truth when he notes, "In Catholic countries, . . . religion is the national drama" (165). But the publication date—1820—was late and by the time Honoré de Balzac wrote his satiric and ironic sequel to the novel, *Melmoth Réconcilié* (1835), the date was even later. France during the 1830s had been racked by anti-Catholic riots and attacks on Catholic churches that recalled those of the earlier Revolutionary period. Balzac's novel is in fact less a *hommage* than a bitter retort, suggesting how absurdly impossible it would be for a writer like Maturin, who had spent hundreds of pages depicting the horrors of the Inquisition and of scheming Jesuits attempting to steal a young man's inheritance, to ever be reconciled to such a monstrously corrupt institution (see Gaillard, Lanone, and Le Yaouanc).

Traces of an almost cartoonish Catholicism[15]—like the public deathbed confession, the belief that the dead can return as spirits (usually carrying blue lights) to demand vengeance or at least a decent burial, the notion that suffering is inevitable and serves a purpose in the cosmic scheme of things, or that the devil can assume the form of a beautiful young woman in order to trick people into losing their everlasting souls—continue to appear in gothic works as what I would identify as the residual uncanny, the persistently strange and yet seductive elements of this earlier system of belief in the transcendent. Once again, religion is the sign of the deviant uncanny in this culture. And when Europeans were not reading about the threats they were facing at home and abroad, they were packing theaters that staged adaptations of gothic novels, complete with ghosts, devils, and all manner of pyrotechnics, smoke and mirrors, designed to convince the populace that revolution and threats to father and fatherland could be confronted and then safely contained within the borders of ideology (see Evans; J. Cox).

The secularizing of the uncanny, then, is an ambivalent attempt by a modernizing, Protestant-inflected social imaginary to strip these atavistic practices of their power and, indeed, the magical properties that they still seemed to hold over the public imagination. But the process was bifurcated in its very origins by its ambivalence toward Catholicism, which was both "discredited and hollow," and at the same time "attractive" (Hogle 2008, 213). The otherness of Catholicism is inherent within the construct that was the Protestant imaginary, and the two systems overlap, intersect, and war with each other within the gothic aesthetic, creating an unstable genre, a confused and oscillating (uncanny) literary landscape. As Freud noted in his 1919 essay,

> an uncanny experience occurs either when infantile complexes which have been repressed are once more revived by some impression, or when primitive beliefs which have been surmounted seem once more to be confirmed. Finally, we must not let our predilection for smooth solutions and lucid exposition blind us to the fact that these two classes of uncanny experience are not always sharply distinguishable. When we consider that primitive beliefs are most intimately connected with infantile complexes, and are, in fact, based on them, we shall not be greatly astonished to find that the distinction is often a hazy one.

Analogously, within the gothic imaginary there is a fair amount of slippage between the primitive and infantile "Catholic" past that the European imaginary would like to repress or "surmount" and the modern, secular tropes of Protestantism that appear as liberatory and rational. In other words, in many of these gothic works there is an attempt to secularize the uncanny, but that attempt is a "hazy one," for the earlier beliefs hold such power that they frequently eclipse any modern or rational effort to displace or eradicate them. If Foucault (1970) is correct and power defines itself and spreads in culture through discourse systems, then the gothic became a powerful and popular discourse system because it spoke in the voice of the protosecularist, humanist, white bourgeois rational voice that advocated modernism, rationality, and immanence. But it also spoke in a more anxious, conflicted, ambiguous voice, a register that whispered and sometimes shouted that all attempts at rational self-possession were doomed to failure.

Finally, it is not possible to trace a neat progression in the gothic, charting an increasing investment in the immanent and rationalistic worldview taken by reforms in the political, social, and legal spheres and a concomitant decline in anachronistic, premodern, providential narratives. In fact, later gothic novels continue to present rabidly providential narratives and use antiquated legal and religious codes to prop up their adherence to a chivalric code of conduct. One need only think of *Melmoth the Wanderer, Confessions of a Justified Sinner,* or *Jane Eyre* (1847). Gothic fictions continued to be split in their presentations of flawed human subjects who attempt to move away from the constraining and antiquated vestiges of the past, as Melmoth does throughout *Melmoth the Wanderer* or as Heathcliff tries to do in Emily Brontë's *Wuthering Heights* (1847). Ironically, there is both a deep nostalgia and a genuine repugnance in gothic works toward the "old order," the premodern, oral, providential universe, for all its outmoded class privileges and corruptions. Or rather, it seems more accurate to say that the gothic is hopelessly fractured in its presentation of the bourgeois subject, caught between its allegiance to the modern, Protestant, and rational, and its nostalgic attraction to an earlier Catholic and aristocratic lineage that it wanted to maintain for itself. By holding on to a past that it had never historically possessed, the bourgeois subject gave itself a false pedigree that provided it with the sort of "gothic" history (complete with stained glass windows and carved walnut furniture) that it wanted at least imaginatively to continue to possess as yet another performative social imaginary within its repetoire. Odd as it may seem, the bourgeoisie appear to have been strangely reassured by the act of haunting themselves through the gothic. Isolated and vulnerable in their brave new world of modernity, these subjects reached out for something outside the self for authenticity and legitimacy, even if that something was not under their control and frightened them out of their wits. Longing for a tradition they never quite possessed, the middle class appropriated the gothic trappings of their culture with a vengeance (witness Keats's "Eve of St. Agnes" or Coleridge's "Christabel"), hoping that the veneer would become a reality, that they would inhabit again a landscape of chivalry with all its attendant fantasies of grandeur.[16]

In the final analysis, modern subjects would henceforth not locate their subjectivity in religion, politics, economics, or social class. Self-reflective and possessed of a fully autonomous but ambivalent consciousness, the modern subjects who emerged in late nineteenth-century textuality were individuals who acted out of the constraints placed, not on their minds, but on a discourse about the gendered construction of their bodies. Control of the body with its concomitant issues—fertility, wellness, aging, and death—became the new foundation on which modern individuals based their identities. Male subjectivity could no longer be located above and beyond the body if there was in fact no soul, and there could be no soul if there was no longer a universal belief in a supernatural religion. Men, in other words, became like women; they were feminized in their reduction to the merciless demands of the physical, decaying, corruptible body. Stoker's *Dracula* as well as Wilde's *The Picture of Dorian Gray* represent the final and late explorations of this British gothic subjectivity.

Clearly, Taylor's neat schema of porous and buffered selves begins to break down as we contemplate the fates of Dr. Jekyll or Jonathan Harker or Dorian Gray. Doesn't the notion of a buffered self, in fact, appear to be a phantom construction designed to shield the modern subject from an ominous threat, indeed, the ultimate threat? In throwing up such a construction, and ritualizing the buffered self's interaction with his environment through various gothic performances, isn't the modern individual simply displacing his anxieties from one region to another (from the world of anima to the realm of science)? Or perhaps what we see in the late gothics are subjects who are compelled to ritualistically enact the notion that they are threatened in both body and soul at the same time. In a society that could no longer hold out the comforts that accrue from an unquestioning belief in immortality, death becomes the ultimate gothic nightmare, the "Real" that so insults the narcissistic ego that it furiously creates an imaginary and uncanny "other" realm composed of ghosts and presided over by powerful secret societies that provide access to this denial of death. The gothic emerges as a desperate imaginative gesture and ritualized performance, a literary theology that attempts to shield its audiences from a glimpse of the unimaginable abyss into which one descends at death, a state that the subject cannot fully imagine because none of us can imagine ourselves dead, none of us can accept complete and personal nonbeing. To stave off the horror of such a notion, gothic texts, besides presenting their audiences with fantasies of immortality, alternately offered parables about the horrors of eternal life or everlasting youth. The two German vampire operas of 1828, Heinrich Marschner's *Der Vampyr* and Peter von Lindpaintner's *Der Vampyr*, as well as Stoker's *Dracula* present eternal life in a blood-glutted body as a diseased and horrific possibility, while *Dorian Gray* presents eternal youth and beauty only to curse it as a lie, a sexually deviant perversion. When subjectivity no longer could be positioned in a spiritual, internal, bodiless realm, then the body itself, the external and mortal ontological being, became the final gothic reality for both men and women.

To conclude by gazing on the supposedly immortal bodies of Dorian Gray and Dracula is to recall the interrelated problems of uncanniness and secularity. As I have argued, the process of secularization itself is already ritualized; it is already a religious practice. That is, the secular has its own inbuilt *telos,* its own origin and end, and that end is the creation of modern individuals successfully repressing their fear of death and inhabiting a desacralized (unhaunted by the past or the future of death) world. I began by claiming that the gothic would appear to be haunted by revenants of the past, but it is perhaps more accurate to say that these hauntings are present simply as part of the gothic's ritualistic secularizing performances, as presences that must be invoked or invented for the ritual to have efficacy, and then for these older presences to be recognized and then expelled. Perhaps modernity does not privatize religious faith so much as create a new universal "secular" faith in the individual and "this-world" happiness. The ritualized gothic performance is not so much interrupted by the uncanny, but in fact requires its presence in order to be efficacious.

The gothic, then, does respond to real political and social anxieties, as well as to spiritual traditions that present the terror of death in very stark terms to its audience. But this threat is not mystified in the gothic; on the contrary, gothic performances and productions are constructed precisely to weave this threat into the narrative and thus to account for how to withstand it. Thus, gothic is a ritualized performance of the "just now," while the hyperbole of, say, its language is one convention of its ritual. That is, the anxiety about death (or what we could call ritualized anxiety) is real, but the gothic ritual can operate only by using a set of tropes that eventually becomes an elaborate and highly repetitive discourse, a religion that operates through the invocation of anxiety. Analogously, David Collings has observed that "secular history can found itself neither by pretending to displace the sacred, nor by bracketing it, nor by differentiating sacred and secular authority, for in each case the secular remains vulnerable to an uncanny return of what the sacred once codified" (2007). It is precisely gothic's attempts to ritualize, contain, commodify, reify, or displace the sacred that this book will examine. While there may be no ultimate "outside" to literature's presentation of history, there is in these works a gothic interiority that continues to be haunted by its need to both claim and reject the symbol of the sacred and the past. There is, it would appear, finally, only Memory.

- CHAPTER 1 -

Gothic Mediations

Shakespeare, the Sentimental, and the Secularization of Virtue

They say miracles are past; and we have our philosophical persons, to make modern and familiar, things supernatural and causeless.

—Shakespeare, *All's Well That Ends Well,* III.iii

I.

The performative gothic and gothicized music accomplished a significant amount of cultural work during the late eighteenth century throughout Europe, and this chapter will examine that period by focusing on three major influences on the secularization of the gothic uncanny: the resurgence of Shakespeare as the premier author of the violent and supernatural; the destabilization of the notion of didactic virtue by Sentimentality; and the rhetorical classification or codification of the emotions as the source for a new concept of human subjectivity and spirituality. Along with the latter trend, there is a pronounced tendency during this period to structure erotic and filial affections in new, secularized ways, and, concurrently, to nostalgically present the father as a sublime figure who once presided over a lost time of innocent purity. By idealizing the bourgeois family as a secularized version of a religious community, complete with a divinely inspired *paterfamilias* and docile children-worshipers, the sentimental ethos prepared the imaginative way for the domestication and secularization of religious sentiments. And in constructing Sentimentality as a pan-European ethos that advocated universalist, progressive ideals like cosmopolitanism or the "feeling heart," the *coeur sensible*, that could emote in recognizably familiar ways across borders and classes, the secularizing imaginary attempted to ease the transition from a providential worldview to an individualized, modern one. As Jerome McGann has noted, sentimentality can best be understood as "the body in the mind," while the discourse of sensibility "emphasizes the mind in the body" (7). Both ideologies, however, were predicated on the belief that "no human action of any consequence is possible—including 'mental' action—that is not led and driven by feeling, affect, emotion" (McGann, 6). But finally the central question that needs to be posed is, how can a culture define "goodness" if transcendent religious beliefs and traditions no longer supply its citizens' codes of conduct? What does it mean to inhabit a "disenchanted" world?

It is necessary to note at the outset that another source of chronic instability in gothic criticism relates to the relationship between the gothic and the sentimental novel and sensibility in general. As many critics over the years have asked, is gothic to be understood as merely an offshoot of the literature of sensibility? Is gothic a debased form of the sentimental novel? Is it a derivative style spiced rather heavily with sex and death? Or does it use the codes of sensibility in productive ways? For critics like Elizabeth Napier and Terry Castle, the gothic's hackneyed uses of the conventions of sensibility are just another aspect of its popular and lower-class characteristics. Instead, this study argues that one of the ways that we can see the ambivalent secularizing process in action is by examining one of sentimentality's most dominant tropes, the damsel in distress or more specifically, the Cordelia figure who redeems her father. In these works the concept of human flourishing is shifted from a transcendental register (the fate of the holy family), to a mundane one (the fate of the bourgeois nuclear family), where the family politics in question are largely determined by the historical ascent of the middle class. Sensibility and sentimentality would be examples of cultural practices that served to entrench Taylor's notion of ambivalent secularization because both of them sought to advance the core beliefs of Providential Deism: "a sense of impartial benevolence, or purely human sympathy," and the embrace of the "ordering project" or the social control agenda, as well as the "dispelling of mystery" so that there could be a "kind of equilibrium between our goals and our moral abilities" (Taylor, 261). Within the framework of this background, the virtuous female is a figure of especial value because she embodies the virtues that define the bourgeois conception of the ideal form of mundane human flourishing.

To return here to Taylor's secularization theory, the romantic period is for him unique in human history because these crucial intellectual and spiritual "transitions" achieved their full modern expression around the beginning of the nineteenth century. During this period, human subjects began to assume that they had a choice between whether they would locate their humanity and happiness ("fullness") within the transcendental (the "era of naïve religious faith") or in the quotidian realms ("the self-conscious"). But because this choice was so stark, a middle ground emerged to ease the transition, and for Taylor this middle ground was the development of what he calls "Providential Deism," a compromise formation between traditional Christianity and the newly emerging secularism that was too extreme for all but the elite to embrace:

> My claim will rather be something of this nature: secularity . . . came to be along with the possibility of exclusive humanism, which thus for the first time widened the range of possible options, ending the era of "naïve" religious faith. Exclusive humanism in a sense crept up on us through an intermediate form, Providential Deism; and both the Deism and the humanism were made possible by earlier developments within orthodox Christianity. Once this humanism is on the scene, the new plural, non-naïve predicament allows for multiplying the options beyond the original gamut. But the crucial transforming move in the process is the coming of exclusive humanism. From this point of view, one could offer this one-line description of the difference between earlier times and the secular age: a secular age is one in which the eclipse of all goals beyond human flourishing becomes conceivable; or better, it falls within the range of an imaginable life for masses of people. This is the crucial link between secularity and a self-sufficing humanism. (20)

As I noted in the introduction, the gothic is one of the major sites of cultural work where ambivalent secularization is first instantiated through the iterations of the gothic in all its forms (rather than being simply a reaction against what Taylor calls secularization 1 or 2). My purpose in using Taylor is to resuscitate a gothic criticism that has lost its capacity to comment profitably on the gothic's obsessive interest in the transcendent. The supernatural has been tamed, in a sense rendered invisible, by a routine avoidance of the gothic's affinity with religion and by the almost routine incorporation of the supernatural into only one possible explanatory framework, Freud's narrative of the uncanny. While I would not dismiss Freud altogether (as some have done), I would like to nuance my analysis by also looking at other cultural and historical explanations for the gothic's continuing investment in the supernatural (in contrast to the focus on "romantic religion" by Ryan). It is necessary to begin by looking at that most uncanny of phenomena, ghosts.

In discussing the psychological origins of ghosts, Roger Money-Kyrle notes that they were most frequently believed to be ancestors, rulers, or sacrificial victims associated with the totemic beings worshiped by earliest humanity (75). The ghosts of Hamlet's father, Banquo, Julius Caesar, or the little princes in *Richard III* are the most obvious examples of the supernatural content in Shakespeare's works, and certainly these figures conform to what we know from anthropological studies on the origins of ghosts. Despite their superstitious content, or perhaps because of it, these works continued in popularity throughout the Enlightenment period in England and Germany. Voltaire mounted an extended attack on Shakespeare's "barbarous" productions, and much of Walpole's two prefaces to *The Castle of Otranto* consists of retorts to Voltaire in an attempt to justify the more spectacular devices employed by Shakespeare as a native British genius (see Hopes). In fact, Walpole's novel—as well as the gothic aesthetic itself—has been read by Emma Clery as an attempt to vindicate the Shakespearean ethos against Voltaire's attacks, for in presenting a universe in which the dead can return or at the very least step down from their portraits in order to exert a continuing influence over the affairs of the living, Walpole was reanimating much of Shakespeare's most controversial supernatural effects (1995, chap. 3) and presenting a textual universe in which the immanent and the transcendent uneasily coexisted.

Such a gothic worldview proffers a "re-enchanted" universe, a continuance of the uncanny and thereby reassures its audiences that a spiritual, "magical," and animistic presence is still active in their midst, despite increasingly vociferous Enlightenment claims to the contrary. Early gothic "riffs," like the sentimental operas and novellas, developed in conjunction with and as commentaries on the bifurcated subjectivities of "porous" and "buffered" selves that I traced in the introduction. In short, there was throughout Europe both anxiety and an increasing ambivalence about the reality of a spiritual dimension in a world that appeared to be increasingly understood through science, materialism, and reason alone. One of the results of this uncertainty about the existence of the spiritual was that the culture—heavily invested in mechanistic and rationalistic epistemologies—began to privilege the buffered self and the physical body as the primary sites of meaning in the world. But authors did not fixate on the body alone, rather they coupled their presentation of the body with a new focus on the power of the emotions, entities that could not be seen but only felt. By valorizing the emotions as "real," palpable presences, Europeans anxiously reassured themselves of the continuing existence of a nonmaterial realm, a "spiritual" world that came to be equated with the reality and physicality of the emotions (read: I suffer and feel pain; therefore, God exists). We can see a particularly apt example of this tendency by considering the scene in which Goethe's Gretchen asks Faust about his religion, and he replies simply: "Feeling is all" (qtd. Conger, 4).

But this intensely Christian anxiety, which reached a fever pitch in Edward Young's *The Complaint,* or *Night Thoughts on Life, Death and Immortality* (1742; 1745), as well as other offerings from the English graveyard school of poets, was quickly transformed into what Stephen Cornfold calls the "secular cult of sepulchral melancholy" (17), or what Patricia Spacks has referred to as "the sentimentalization of the supernatural" (89). Brooding on death and questioning the existence of an afterlife were not simply fashionable poses in these literary works, they were deeply felt expressions of the *zeitgeist* that permeated Europe and spoke to its obsession with nostalgia, futility, and a vague sense of doom (see Pfau). One of the most effective ways of confronting that pain and uncertainty was to exorcise it in cultural and performative works that wrote and then staged in very large letters their *angst*-filled scripts. Hence, a grandiose figure like James Macpherson's *Ossian* (1763) emerges to represent in a self-dramatizing and extravagant manner the sense of being out of step with one's times, of being the last of a dying breed, of being caught between two worlds, that of the ancient, bardic past with its acceptance of ghosts and manifestations of the supernatural (Taylor's "porous" self) and a new world that is coming into being and that repudiates such things as nonsense (the "buffered" self). *Ossian* is in many ways a textual manifestation of one of Scottish philosophy's major positions: "that passion and feeling are the basis of human action" (McGann, 35). Seeking to present poetry that functions as a form of magic, and that evokes an animistic, primitive world in which the body and spirit are one, Macpherson's bard was an early sentimentalist with a nationalistic agenda, and certainly he was appreciated by Napoleon for those very reasons. But attitudes toward Macpherson's *Ossian* were more typically ambivalent even in his heyday and can be best understood by contrasting the largely laudatory content of Wordsworth's poem "Written on a Blank Leaf of Macpherson's *Ossian*" to his dismissal of *Ossian* in his *Essay, Supplementary to the Preface* (1815):

> Yet, much as those pretended treasures of antiquity have been admired [the *Ossian* poems], they have been wholly uninfluential upon the literature of the Country. No succeeding writer appears to have caught from them a ray of inspiration; no author, in the least distinguished, has ventured formally to imitate them—except the boy, Chatterton, on their first appearance. (3:78)

CHAPTER 1

In ways that suggest the complexity of mediation, orality, and what she calls the "artifactual," Maureen McLane analyzes *Ossian* as that which "remains" after the necessary acts of cultural transmission and poetic mediation have occurred (2007, 235–40). Nevertheless, I want to begin by invoking the figure of the Ossianic bard because music, the fragment, and the oral "strain" became crucial components in Sensibility's dominant script, and as such, this chapter will focus on a few representative musical performances of sentimentalized trial and redemption.

Music erupted into the public sphere throughout Europe in the eighteenth and early nineteenth centuries in new religious, political, social, and cultural ways. As a number of literary genres increasingly sought to moderate religious and political reform and secularize and nationalize public and private consciousnesses, music was enlisted as a potent ideological and aesthetic force, a manifestation of the residue of a culture that still clung to the power of oral-based methods of communicating the reality of the spiritual. In short, "virtue" was put on trial during this period throughout Europe, and opera emerged to mediate the pain that occurred when a secularized notion of virtue emerged to displace a theologically based system of values and beliefs.[1]

First, it is necessary to define "virtue" as a concept and briefly trace its history as a public source of value. As J. A. G. Pocock has noted, virtue has traditionally been synonymous with "nature," "essence," or an "essential characteristic," but within the republican vocabulary it took on the additional meanings of "devotion to the public good," or "the relations of equality between citizens engaged in ruling and being ruled." Understood as *virtù* by Machiavelli, the concept also increasingly began to be understood as something like citizenship, "a code of values not necessarily identical with the virtues of a Christian," and was expressed instead in the notion of justice or "a devotion to the public good" (41–42). Distinguishing between abstract rights (*politicum* like equality, citizenship) and the right to bear arms and own property (*commercium*), Pocock argues that as "the universe became pervaded by law, the locus of sovereignty [became] extra-civic, and the citizen came to be defined not by his actions and virtues, but by his rights to and in things" (43). By the mid-eighteenth century, "the ideals of virtue and commerce could not be reconciled to one another" as long as virtue was seen as purely civic, and so virtue was redefined with the aid of a concept of "manners":

> The effect was to construct a liberalism which made the state's authority guarantee the liberty of the individual's social behavior, but had no intention whatsoever of impoverishing that behavior by confining it to the rig-

orous assertion of ego-centered individual rights. On the contrary, down at least to the end of the 1780s, it was the world of ancient politics which could be made to seem rigid and austere, impoverished because underspecialized; and the new world of the social and sentimental, the commercial and cultural, was made to proliferate with alternatives to ancient *virtus* and *libertas*.... Now, at last, a right to things became a way to the practice of virtue, so long as virtue could be defined as the practice and refinement of manners. (50)

In England the duel over the nature of virtue can be seen in the protracted and pre-gothic assaults on the heroines in the novels of Samuel Richardson, particularly his *Pamela*, 1740; *Clarissa*, 1747; and *Sir Charles Grandison*, 1753 (see Festa). Analogously, the pre-gothic novels of the French author Antoine-François (L'Abbé) Prévost (1697–1763) continued the development of Sensibility and Sentimentality in the European imaginary. Wildly popular in France and Germany, Prévost's novels (*Manon Lescaut*, 1728–31; and *Clèveland*, 1731–38) were quickly translated into English and had a strong influence on Sophia Lee's *The Recess* (1783–86) as well as on the novels of Charlotte Smith (see Foster).

The sweeping historical trajectory that Pocock charts here can be glimpsed in miniature by examining one nexus of interrelated texts: Giovanni Paisiello's *Nina* (1789) and Fernando Paër's *Agnese di Fitzhenry* (1809), as influences on as well as rewrites of Amelia Opie's sentimentally gothic novella *The Father and Daughter* (1801). All three of these works present the struggle of the heroines' virtue to assert itself against a force of paternal domination that is figured as an antiquated imperial power. In the heroines' struggles to control the possession of goods (family jewels in *Nina* and property in *Agnese*), the operas enact the performance of public virtue as it intersects with private trials and tribulations. Both operas also position the quasi-religious domestic space as the rightful habitation of the sentimentalized, virginal daughter who leaves such an abode only because her husband can rightfully replace her father in *virtù* and status.

The term "Sentimental" needs to be defined in the context of these operas, although clearly it is beyond the scope of this chapter to develop fully all of the permutations of its use in a variety of different national literary traditions.[2] The "Sentimental" in these operas embodies, as Schiller noted in his essay "On Naïve and Sentimental Poetry" (1795), the reflective, the self-conscious, and the "desire for an immediate sense of the organic wholeness of experience" (McGann, 120), as distinct from the simple, direct, or natural poetry of the ancient world (which he called the "naïve"). Another way of understanding the Sentimental privileges the authenticity of the emotions, combined as this action is with tropes of interiority and the use of objects that provoke memories and their association with identity or personal history (Howard, 65). As Howard notes, when we use the term "Sentimental" we can be understood to be suggesting that the work "uses some established convention to evoke emotion; we mark a moment when the discursive processes that construct emotion become visible" (76). Straddling the divide between the visible and the interior, the social and the natural, sentimental artists tend to construct cultural artifacts that portray humans as thinking and feeling beings, or rather, individuals who feel and live in their bodies as much as in their minds. Within the British tradition, the third Earl of Shaftesbury's *Characteristics* (1711) has been seen as the source for much of this ideology, but his class prejudices have recently been interrogated, as have those of such erstwhile followers as Francis Hutcheson, Adam Smith, Laurence Sterne, and Addison and Steele. As Robert Markley has noted, literary historians have attempted to understand Shaftesbury's formulation of sentimentality ("Shaftesburian benevolence") as either a manifestation of Latitudinarianism or deism, both vaguely secularizing systems that advanced the notion that self-sufficient virtue is the means by which manners rather than Providence dominated and controlled behavior in the public realm (211). As a blend of providentialism and morality, Latitudinarianism was the face of rational Protestantism during the eighteenth century, a way of rejecting the old superstitions and providing reasonable explanations or apologetics for God's order. It can also be understood as the transitional form of historical consciousness that Taylor calls "Providential Deism," brought about through three primary "anthropological shifts": the imposition of a "disciplined order on personal and social life"; the triumph of "purely human goods like human flourishing"; and the "dispelling of mystery" or magical thinking, like belief in the prospect of an afterlife (261). For Taylor, Sentimentality is the performative and imaginative face that Providential Deism takes as it promulgates its agenda throughout Western elite culture.

Adam Smith as well as Jean-Jacques Rousseau theorized that human benevolence and morality could only be understood by acknowledging an innate disposition to sympathy or empathy in human nature. For these theorists, emotions lead to manifest acts of virtue or, what Smith's *Theory of Moral Sentiments* (1759), a quasi-sociological study of the origins of morality, defines as the empathetic imagination: "By the imagination we place ourselves in [another person's] situation, we conceive ourselves enduring all the same torments, we enter as it were into his body, and become in some measure the same person with him, and thence form some idea of his sensations, and even feel something which, though weaker in degree, is not altogether unlike them" (9). There can be no question that by attending performances of operas such as *Nina* and *Agnese* audience members were forced into a participatory and empathetically imaginative posture. Given the hyperbole of the theatrical and musical action, the audience was virtually hurled into the emotional maelstrom being enacted on stage and thus participated in the empathetic display and reification of sentiment. The emerging bourgeoisie throughout Europe validated their newly assumed class status by learning what it meant to "feel" (rather than "be") middle class. Defining themselves in opposition both to the lower class and the aristocracy, the bourgeoisie appropriated a number of emotions that marked them as worthy of the privileges they were so quickly gaining. In particular, the proper emotions ascribed to this new class were self-control, order, loyalty, honesty, authenticity, deferentiality, and hard work. Like stylized poses, these emotional postures were defined and then challenged in any number of theatrical and operatic performances that the middle class attended. The final scene was generally characterized by a vindication of bourgeois values and emotions.

But the "buffered self" that embraced Providential Deism could not be suddenly or wholly embraced by a populace that was still invested in their earlier identities as "porous selves," open to magic, anima, and subject to being punished for their sins by an external being like the devil who was believed to have the power to act directly in human affairs. Sentimentality is that transitional bridge between the two selves in which remnants of the "porous" can still be glimpsed, particularly in staged performances of extravagant displays of emotional openness. As Raymond Stephanson has observed, sentimentality can be understood as a complex cultural reaction in which "the symptoms of nervous disorder or weak nerves (tears, physical agitation, fainting, etc.) now became important evidence of moral and social virtues" (284). In addition to Richardson's novels, perhaps the best evidence for this open display of the emotions can be seen in Henry Mackenzie's *The Man of Feeling* (1771), in which the hero cries almost continually in order to demonstrate his benevolence and sensitivity to others, that is, his secularized Christian virtues.

Adam Smith's *Theory of Moral Sentiments* defines what, for his age, was the ideal display of moral sentiment: a male aristocratic sufferer whose intense attempts at self-control in the face of great suffering cause tears in his immediate community. What Julie Ellison has called the "early cultural prestige of masculine tenderheartedness" (9) can be understood if we recognize that the culture at large was seeking to define what it meant to be not simply human, but also modern. There have been many recent studies of the emotions during this period in addition to Ellison, and another influential position has been put forth by Adela Pinch, who has argued that emotions are not located exclusively within the self, but are "vagrant" or "traveling," located "among rather than within people." Selfhood and emotions meet in "the social performative," the domain of "rituals by which subjects are formed and reformulated" (16, 167, 10). And, as Clery has noted, Shakespeare "had a very specific value for the romance revival [because] he was situated on the cusp between Gothic and enlightened times. His plays were believed to combine the benefits of Protestantism and Renaissance learning with ready access to the resources of popular folklore and Popish superstition, so conducive to the imagination" (2002, 30). During the Seven Years' War between England and France (1756–63), Shakespeare became something of a nationalistic talisman, with his dramas providing the master narratives for what it meant to be not only British, but also, in Harold Bloom's grandiose formulation, "human" (1998, 1–17).

II.

[Art] should move me, astonish me, break my heart, let me tremble, weep, stare, be enraged.

—Denis Diderot, *Salon de 1765*

But exactly how did this construction of the emotions intersect with the theater and opera, and specifically, with Shakespearean adaptations during the pre-gothic period? When David Garrick worked out his technique for portraying emotion on the stage ("passion animated"), he used Charles Le Brun's *Méthode pour apprendre à dessiner les passions* (1702), a treatise that was consistently referenced by both artists and actors during the eighteenth century and which was predicated on the essential correspondence between expressions on the face and the emotions within. According to Le Brun, there were only a certain number of emotions and to illustrate their expression was also to provide a "kind of descriptive inventory of the soul." Le Brun may have been the first to generalize about the emotions as if they constituted a field of scientific inquiry, but he was followed quickly by Charles Macklin, who thought that actors should have "philosophical knowledge of the passions" by knowing their "genus, species and characteristics as a botanist might those of plants" (qtd. Shawe-Taylor). Macklin was then succeeded by Aaron Hill, whose 1746 tract on acting was more like a taxonomy and claimed that there were "only ten dramatic passions," all of which had to be expressed in ten exactly stylized expressions. This inventory of the emotions suggests that the presentation of passion on stage required a highly stylized system of visual and codified mimic signs rather than verbal formulae. More than a century later, in 1871, the Haymarket Theater presented *The School of Shakespeare, or Humours and Passions*, which dramatized scenes from different Shakespearean plays, each representing a particular emotion, for instance, vanity, cruelty, revenge, ambition, greed (Schoch, xv). For this period, being able to generalize about anything meant to transform its significance from the individual into the realm of the universal.

In a similar manner, literary critics established criteria for judging character and motivation based on generalized assumptions about the consistency of personality or a sort of universal "humanity" that all people shared. Acting and criticism overlapped to the extent that the age was obsessed with defining, performing, and thereby controlling the emotions. Both efforts were at the same time attempts to work out a psychological and emotional inventory that ran parallel with—and in some way was complementary to—the scientific advancements and developments that were being made by such people as Erasmus Darwin and Charles Bell who believed that the emotions arose from an organic brain-body unit in predictable, species-specific ways (see Richards, Richardson, Reed, Micale). Feelings were presumed to be universal, and Adam Smith as well as David Hume made much of what they called the "natural capacity for fellow-feeling." But along with this celebration of the empathetic emotions were denigrations of excessive emotionality, and more specifically, superstition. Hume, for instance, famously stated that superstitious beliefs were based on "weakness, fear, melancholy, together with ignorance," while the suspension of disbelief, which resembles it emotionally, is based on the imagination (73).

In his *Essay on Taste* (1759), Alexander Gerard noted that music prompts an affective state that he called "a pleasant disposition of soul [that] renders us prone to every agreeable affection," while he also claimed that the highest topic of literature was the depiction of suffering because with suffering comes pathos, and "the pathetic is a quality of so great moment in works of taste, a man, who is destitute of sensibility of heart, must be a very imperfect judge of them" (qtd. Mullan 1988, 127). A few years later, Richard Hurd's *Letters on Chivalry and Romance* (1762) praised the poetry of "gothic romance" for its ability to "invent supernatural beings to suit its high purpose." William Duff in his *Essay on Original Genius* (1767) echoed Hurd's position, claiming that "the invention of supernatural characters and the exhibition of them, with their proper attributes and offices, are the highest efforts and the most pregnant proofs of truly ORIGINAL GENIUS" (his emphasis; qtd. Spacks, 94–95). This aesthetic reification of suffering combined with the use of the supernatural leads to the vogue we see beginning in the middle of the eighteenth century for a number of Shakespeare's more "supernatural" productions, but it also explains the veritable frenzy that was whipped up about "astonishment" and "fear" as aesthetic categories. It is almost as if the populace wanted to convince itself that it was still capable of intense emotions as well as imaginative transport, for to do so was to reaffirm their continuing investment in the transcendent, as well as their common humanity in the face of scientific assaults and growing religious doubts about the nature of the spiritual realm itself.

For William Duff and Elizabeth Montagu, Shakespeare was the only English writer who had successfully explored the realm of the supernatural, but operating behind these literary discussions was, as I mentioned above, the nationalistic cause of British supremacy, and then the even larger issue of trying to understand and codify psychological functions and aesthetic principles. And *Lear*, with its use of violent storms, an isolated and threatening heath, the cliff, blindness, madness and emotional excess, became the very embodiment of the sublime for the Enlightenment reading public. The gothic sublime employed the vocabulary of emotional hyperbole as well as the tropes of the mountainous crag, the heart-stopping abyss, or the moonlit ruin, but by this time it had become domesticated as pathos in novels like Jane Austen's *Sense and Sensibility* (1811), and tears became the coin of the realm for powerful men as well as fallen women. The various performances and the sustained critical and creative reading of Shakespeare's characters shaped not only European literary culture, but its emotional and national ones as well. Europeans—and by extension Americans—learned as a culture to understand and model acceptable private and public behaviors—emotional responses and civic responsibilities—by studying the fates of Shakespeare's characters.

Finally, it is important to note that there is no question that the growth of the Protestant habit of introspection merged with the institutionalization of Bardolatry during this period so that Shakespeare and the Bible became the ur-texts for the growth of the new European imaginary. Appeals to nationalism almost as a form of religion suffuse sentimental and domestic fiction, and the portrayal of the father and daughter begins to dominate the popular cultural imagination. Daughters replace wives and mistresses as the central focus of sentimental literature, while daughterly piety and devotion, displayed to an errant and undeserving father, becomes an allegory for the citizen's proper relation to an (unfortunately) mad ruler. Cato, in other words, is replaced by Cordelia as the cultural standard bearer, and it is her tears, not his, that signify in the new economy of the emotions.

Literary historians have traditionally been invested in believing that ideologies primarily spread through cultures by means of print media, and for many centuries we have deceived ourselves that male-authored, canonical poetry, preferably the epic or lyric, spread those ideologies most effectively and also most aesthetically. But increasingly, critics are recognizing that the ideologies that they detect within literary works have already been reflected, affected, adapted, and transformed through musical or other performative genres. This chapter will focus on how sentimentality and its valorization of *virtù* spread through one particular intersection of operas and literature: Giovanni Paisiello's *Nina* (1789), Fernando Paër's *Agnese de Fitzhenry* (1809), and Amelia Opie's novella *The Father and Daughter* (1801). Both of the operas furthermore spin in and out of ideological orbit with Samuel Richardson's novel *Pamela; or Virtue Rewarded* (1740–41), which in turn was quickly translated into French and German, rewritten by the Irish playwright Isaac Bickerstaffe as the comic opera *The Maid of the Mill* (1765), and adapted by François de Neufchâteau into the opera *Paméla* (1793). What I hope to suggest is that music and literature have collaborated in constructing a few fairly basic cultural scripts (domestic, familial, painful, and cathartic: recall Oedipus) that they then retell endlessly, continually readjusting the particulars to accommodate changing social, religious, and political conditions. Sentimentality as a value system, a potent ideology, and the artistic face of Providential Deism was spread throughout eighteenth and early nineteenth-century European culture not simply through novels, but also by being performed in opera houses from London to Naples. Certain aspects of Sentimentality, particularly the damsel in distress and the taming of the tyrannous father, were then adapted and transformed by the gothic as it sought to tell even darker tales about cultural transformation and the wages of modernization and secularization.

As Italian opera made its way into eighteenth-century London and Paris, it revealed its ability to provoke emotional responses in its audiences through highly stylized aesthetic spectacles that translated and staged potent ideological materials in a revolutionary age. And that ideological material—fear of violent change and its effects on what had been a stable class system—is largely the same content that was developed in the sentimental novels of Samuel Richardson, Prévost, Baculard d'Arnaud, and later Amelia Opie, and then in the sentimental operas of such adapters as Paisiello and Paër. These sentimental novels and operas most frequently took as their subjects the dysfunctions of the patriarchal family under siege, or the trials and tribulations of the seduced maiden and the abusive or betrayed father. They frequently employed, as Markley has noted, talismanic exchanges of money or property in order to reify the bourgeoisie's

CHAPTER 1

attempt to assert "the 'timeless' nature of a specific historical and cultural construction of virtue and to suppress [the] reader's recognition of the social and economic inequalities upon which this discourse of seemingly transcendent virtue is based" (210).

The Sentimental as an influence on the gothic presents cultural works that clearly attempt to mediate between members of a family who find themselves at odds over the shape and power structure of the newly evolving bourgeois society. In fact, sentimental operas, like later gothic dramas or melodramas, actually function as cathartic forms, public rituals in which the middle class haunted itself with its own act of imagined, fantasized revolution, usually depicted as some form of matricide or fratricide in a series of what we might see as social and political morality plays. André-Ernest-Modeste Grétry's sentimental opera *Lucile* (1769) is a case in point. Staging a wedding day celebration, the ensemble sings, "Where can one feel better than within the bosom of one's family?" while later the characters reply, "The names of spouse, of father, and of son, and of daughter, are delightful." With its heavy use of gnomic sentences and moral tags, *Lucile* reminds us that sentimental opera, like sentimental fiction, enacts Denis Diderot's recommendation to avoid intricacy of plot in order to "allow emotional expansion in the characters and similar responses in the readers or spectators. . . . Such ritual displays of emotion [within the domestic sphere] are often meant to show the power of human benevolence as a driving communal force between people both on and off stage" (qtd. Castelvecchi 1:141–43). They also place religious sentiments, which were once on display in the public church into the private, domestic space of the home, thereby transmuting religious practices and beliefs into filial, familial displays. As belief in a universal and traditional Christianity was breaking down, opera and literature stepped in to claim displaced religious sentiments for their own. And for this reason we can see the Sentimental as a mediating force between the transcendent and the immanent in the gothic and as participating in the larger secularist movement of a post-Enlightenment Europe.

III.

> Music which has not been heard falls into empty time like an impotent bullet.
> —Theodor Adorno, *The Philosophy of Modern Music*, 133

The Italian Giovanni Paisiello (1740–1816) epitomizes the sentimental strain in opera, which may explain the waning of his popularity by the 1820s. Rossini praised Paisiello's operas, however, by stating that "the genius of the simple genre and naïve gracefulness . . . realizes the most astonishing effects with the utmost simplicity of melody, harmony and accompaniment," while Mozart, who knew and admired Paisiello's works, once commented that "for light and pleasurable sensations in music [one] cannot be recommended to anything better" than Paisiello. For all the praise he received in his lifetime, including the patronage of Napoleon who called him "the greatest composer there is," Paisiello's best-known opera *Nina o sia la pazza per amore (Nina or the love-mad Maid)* has fallen on hard times (see Dent, Robinson). Winton Dean, for instance, has accused it of being "sentimental comedy at its worst. . . . Its sentimentality is to modern ears perfectly unbearable, and we cannot understand how the whole of Europe was reduced to tears by these infantile melodies" (111). First performed in London at King's Theatre on April 27, 1797, the opera was staged twenty times between its premiere and 1800.[3] Typically, it shared the bill with Elizabeth Inchbald's comedy *The Midnight Hour* and the farce *Love-A-La-Mode,* which made, as one reviewer put it, for a long night. Another review published a month after its opening noted: "If tears be indications of sensibility—abundant were the proofs Mrs. Billington [as Nina] afforded; from the melting versatility of her passions—the involuntary but irresistible sigh heaved in every tender-breast—her plaintive and expressive notes—spoke most powerfully to the heart, and every hand confirmed the plaudits she deserved" (*Illustrated London News,* May 17, 1797). Unlike a number of forgotten sentimental operas, *Nina* has had something of a resurgence in modern revivals, including one at the Zurich Opera House in 2002 (available on DVD).

As a *sentimentale* opera, as distinct from the other Italian operatic "mixed" genres of *semiserio* and *mezzo carattere, Nina* was a highly idealized portrait of how a family becomes virtuous after suffering has redeemed all its members of their excesses (read: sins). In the eighteenth-century Italian operatic tradition, the term *sentimentale* did not take on the negative connotations that the word assumed in England fairly early on: excessive, morbid, affected, or indulgent. Instead, within the Italian tradition the concept of *sentimentale* suggested the person who was ideally sensitive to understanding and feeling the highest emotions in harmony with their physical senses. These people were also capable of feeling compassion for others, or of possessing the quality of empathy, which marked them as practitioners of a new, humanized religion of the heart, "Sensibility." *Nina* portrays this new sensitivity on stage and, as such, the opera inaugurates not only a secularized religious spirit, but a new scientific interest in understanding insanity not as demonic possession, but as a treatable human response to trauma.[4]

The source for Paisiello's *Nina* was the version of the opera by the same name wrtten by Benoît-Joseph Marsollier and Nicolas Dalayrac, a one-act *opéra comique*, which premiered in Paris in 1786. That earlier opera itself was based, according to Marsollier and Dalayrac, on "an anecdote reported by our newspapers a few years ago, and already employed by François Thomas Marie de Baculard d'Arnaud in his *Délassements de l'homme sensible,* under the title *La Nouvelle Clémentine* (I:50–58; 1783)" (qtd. Castelvecchi 2, 93). The stories of Baculard D'Arnaud (1718–1805) were so prevalent and popular in France during this period that they originated their own literary term, "darnauderie," meaning to dwell in graveyards, mausoleums, or other sinister and uncanny landscapes. D'Arnaud's early works, like the twenty-four short stories in *Les Épreuves du sentiment (The Ordeals of Sentiment,* 1772–80), are filled with gore and horror and indicate that the gothic emerged in France very quickly after the first translation of Walpole's *Castle of Otranto* was published in 1767. Similar to the erotically intense works of the Abbé Prévost, D'Arnaud's earliest productions also included his translations of *Clarissa* (1767) and *Pamela* (1767). His later dramas and novels, however, are much more clearly in the newer *roman noir* category, gothic works characterized by a fixation on death: "funereal décor, tangible corpses, monastic villainy, extravagant victimization at the hands of close relatives, slimy catacombs, caverns, labyrinths, and an exquisitely cadaverous mise-en-scène were the leading features of his murky melodramas and dark novels of pain and death" (Frank 2002, 48).

Resoundingly popular throughout Europe, *Nina* exploited the motif of a young, beautiful, and virtuous woman suffering unjustly at the hands of a greedy aristocratic and patriarchal tyrant. Such a theme was particularly popular given the thunderous reception of the translation of Richardson's *Pamela* and its adaptation for the stage by Carlo Goldoni in 1753. In fact, Goldoni was in the audience for a performance of *Nina* and observed:

> [W]hen the opera of *Richard* [Sédaine and Gretry's *Richard Coeur-de-lion*] was withdrawn, it appeared difficult to supply its place with any thing which would be equally successful. This miracle was affected by *Nina, or the Distracted Lover;* and if the success of this piece did not surpass the preceding, it at least equaled it ... [because of the public's sympathy] for an unfortunate being without crime and without reproach. (*Memoirs* II:333)

By the autumn of 1788, *Nina* was being produced in Italy, thanks to an

Italian translation and libretto by Giuseppe Carpani, who staged the first Italian production in Monza. Paisiello set this version to music and first performed his *Nina* on the occasion of Queen Maria Carolina's visit to the new village of San Leucio, near the palace at Caserta, east of Naples.

Originally commissioned by King Ferdinand, the opera was to be performed at the opening of Ferdinand's "model village," San Leucio, a community of silk manufacturers who were to live in blissful harmony and productivity in a sort of protocommunist haven. The presence of a strong female queen in this Italian city-state, even one the size of the Kingdom of the Two Sicilies, in conjunction with the persecuted daughter-heroine of the piece, brings together two of the central tenets of Sentimentality as a political ethos: that is, the notion of the family as a microcosm of the nation, and of the parent as a deity of the city-state that is modeled on the family. Such a *topos* highlights the sentimental political ideology operating at the time: parents know best, and all subjects, like occasionally wayward children, need to obey their strictures and prop up the great chain of being that was the bourgeois patriarchal family and state.

Castelvecchi has provided the following summary of the source of Paisiello's *Nina*, the opera of Marsollier and Dalayrac:

> Nina and Lindoro [Germeuil in the French version] love each other, and are betrothed with the consent of Nina's father, the Count. Yet, when Nina's hand is requested by a wealthier suitor, the Count favours the latter, thus breaking the pact with Lindoro. A duel between the two suitors ensues; when Nina sees her beloved lying in his own blood, and her father asks her to accept as her spouse Lindoro's slayer, she loses her reason. The Count cannot bear the sight of his daughter's sorry state: he leaves Nina in his country estate, entrusting her to the benevolent care of the governess Susanna [Elise in the French version]. Nina—having lost all memory of the recent, tragic events—spends her days thinking of Lindoro and waiting for his return, surrounded by the affection and compassion of servants and peasants. On one occasion she falls into a delirium, and believes she sees Lindoro. Some time later the Count comes back, stricken with sorrow and remorse; but his daughter does not recognize him. When Lindoro, whom everyone thought dead, returns, the Count welcomes him with open arms, and calls him son. At first, Nina does not recognize Lindoro. Father and lover "cure" Nina by showing her that Lindoro is back and still loves her, and that she can marry her beloved with her father's consent. (2:92)

Somewhat anticlimactically for modern tastes, the opera stages only the events that occur after Nina's mental breakdown, providing the background in a long exposition that prepares us for the appearance of the mad Nina in the opera's first scene. As Castelvecchi notes, such a structure erases narrative complexity and instead puts its entire focus on the emotions of the principals: Nina, Lindoro, and the Count. This technique, lending itself to hyperbolic displays of madness, grief, confusion, and disorientation, became a staple of most eighteenth- and early nineteenth-century sentimental literature and theater. And such a device in this particular instance suggests that *Nina* needs to be "read" in many ways as a *tableau vivant,* with a few characters in a series of static, almost pantomimic poses, reciting the past and present actions in highly stylized, hyperbolic scenes. This technique reveals how closely sentimental opera remained in touch with its sources in the pantomimes of classical stories and fairy tales of the Boulevard Theatre in Paris, which themselves had a fragmentary, abrupt, and incomplete quality. As melodramas came to rely on the mute hero or the wound on the arm or hand as a token of identity, sentimental works depended on the blush, the sigh, the gasp, the interrupted speech, and the telling silence. Sensibility as an ideological discourse was predicated on the belief that the body spoke through tears and blood, and that such primitive, physical signifiers were more reliable than writing or print in conveying the truth of a person or a situation. As such, Sensibility and particularly sentimental opera reveal their alignment with the earlier oral-based cultural practices that a print-culture was slowly but surely displacing.

Further, it is necessary to emphasize that, unlike melodrama, which developed slightly later, there is no active villain operating in this opera. The Count, having seen the devastation that his greedy motives have had on his daughter's sanity, has already been reformed by the time the action begins on stage. Throughout Nina's interactions with Lindoro, whom she persists in not recognizing after his return, she continues to privilege her emotions above reason as a means to truth. When Lindoro arrives at the village to claim Nina, she fails to recognize him, instead thinking that he is a shepherd whom she questions about the dead Lindoro: does he know him, she asks? Nina is further confused that this shepherd knows so many details about the dead Lindoro. It is only when Lindoro shows her a ring that he had given to her as a souvenir of their "passionate embraces" and then kisses her that she is able to remember and then recognize him. But then Lindoro pretends not to recognize Nina, and she must produce a waistcoat that she had embroidered for him before he is able to accept her identity (in the 1790 version of the opera). In both versions of the opera the emphasis is on the physical talismanic object (either ring or waistcoat) that had been exchanged between the two lovers, foregrounding for the audience the importance of the body's purchase of sentimental currency. The doubled and quite extensive recognition scene between the lovers, such a staple of sentimental, gothic, and melodramatic literature, occurs literally over the bodies of both the heroine and Lindoro, or rather, over their bodies' remembrance and reenactment of sexual passion and bodily emotion.

I cite here the climactic duet performed in Act II during the recognition scene in order to point out its rhetorical investment in what I would call a pedagogy of *virtù*:

Lindoro:
Then, Lindoro took your hand:
He tightly held it to his bosom,
And in this same place,
I pressed on you, O my treasure,
My kiss of fire,
My soul—like this.

Nina:
You! . . . Heaven . . . ah, what a moment!
That which I feel in my heart,
I would like to explain to you,
Yet I know not how to explain it still.

In the Quattro that immediately follows, the Count and his servants observe:

Ah, it is taking a favorable course, oh God,
She is following the motives of her heart.
Quiet: she speaks in the language of love.

Immediately after the reconciliation of the lovers, Nina sings that she is now able to "talk about virtue," and she does so by sitting down to be transformed from the "mad" and suffering woman into the virtuous, controlled heroine. In order to convey on a performative level the transformation of Nina's character from "mad" to virtuous, the 2002 Zurich performance presents Nina (Cecilia Bartoli), whose hair had been disheveled and unkempt during her "mad" scenes, now sitting calmly while her maids carefully arrange her hair on her head. At exactly the point at which her hair is brought into control, Nina sings of *virtù*. We cannot know exactly how the performances of 1790 staged the same scene, but it is instructive to compare Nina's toilette scene with the presentation of Laurence Sterne's Maria de Moulines, perhaps one of the most famous "mad" women in sentimental fiction. In his *Tristram Shandy* (1760–67), Sterne first presented Maria sitting on the bank of a river with "her hair, all but two tresses, drawn up into a silk net, with a few olive-leaves twisted a little fantastically on one side" (529).

He revisits Maria in his *A Sentimental Journey* (1768) and this time presents Maria as driven mad by the desertion of her lover as well as the loss of her beloved goat: "She was dress'd in white, and much as my friend described her, except that her hair hung loose, which before was twisted within a silk net." As Maria cries for the loss of her father, lover, and goat, all of apparently equal value to her, the narrator wipes away Maria's tears

> with my handkerchief. I then steep'd it in my own—and then in hers—and then in mine—and then I wip'd hers again—and as I did it, I felt such undescribable emotions within me, as I am sure could not be accounted for from any combinations of matter and motion. I am positive I have a soul; nor can all the books with which materialists have pester'd the world ever convince me of the contrary. (II; chap. 64)

The valorization of the narrator's emotions reassure him that he has a soul, and that a spiritual dimension to life is just as valid as it was before the "materialists" "pestered the world" to the contrary. This passage is both comic and pathetic, ironic and sentimental in its presentation of the exchange and intermingling of bodily fluids, all the while the narrative voice protests the claims of the material. The scene, complete with authorial voyeur, handkerchief, dog, and disheveled hair was itself the subject of numerous popular engravings and at least three important paintings, one by Angelica Kauffmann, who in fact painted five versions of it. But it is the emphasis on Maria's hair, its earlier neat style contrasted to its later chaotic appearance, that performs in a very visual way the transition from sanity to madness, or, in Nina's case, from madness to sanity. Certainly it is fair to claim that the audiences of late eighteenth-century Britain and France would have recognized in Nina's performative gestures the similarity of her conduct to that of Maria de Moulines.

This pedagogy of *virtù* also is enacted in the opera through the presence of the townspeople throughout the action. The initial scene consists of a chorus of villagers retelling Nina's tragic story, providing a very public explanation for her current, lamentable state, which is also a very public spectacle: "Who can endure such pain? Our heart cannot, and melts into tears" (I:1). Like some Greek chorus, the townspeople of *Nina* witness and are instructed by the series of sentimental scenes that gradually enfold: the Count's frustrations with his daughter, his kindness toward Nina, Nina's sufferings and confusions, the reappearance of the long-lost Lindoro, and finally the reunions and reconciliations of Nina with her father and lover. Like a morality tale, the opera performs a pedagogy of public *virtù* for the townspeople, who are accepted by Nina and her father as extended family throughout the action.

The erasure of class differences is yet another bluff that this sentimental opera attempts to make, as it argues for the state as an extension of the family, thereby eradicating the appearance of class inequalities (and highlights the fact that the original premiere of the Italian version of the opera occurred at a totally constructed and artificial classless village of silk workers). An almost feudal notion of the father-Count ruling over his daughter-subjects is perpetuated by the opera, which performs its cultural work by suggesting that servants are just working members of an extended and happy family. But this is a political fantasy, as the ideological core of Sensibility actually works to enforce class distinctions as well as establish separate spheres for the genders. To some extent, this conservative core of the sentimental ethos was predicted by Robert Filmer's *Patriarchia* (1680), a quasi-religious attempt to demonstrate that absolute monarchy is the natural system of human social organization, and that the "fountain of all regal authority" is "the right of fatherhood" (7:10). But Filmer's rearguard defense of the patriarchy was already being replaced by new notions of the nuclear family, while male hegemony was also being transformed so that the family was no longer understood as a vertical line of descent from fathers to sons, but as a closed circuit of husband-wife-children. John Locke's *Two Treatises on Government* (1680–90) was an immediate attempt to refute the traditional conservatism of Filmer and instead offer a liberal attempt to shore up the claims of male authority by reinvesting power in the locus of "husband" rather than father, thus reasserting male dominance under the guise of a progressive ideology (see Gauthier). In a similar vein, Lawrence Stone has observed:

> In the late sixteenth and early seventeenth centuries, the restricted patriarchal nuclear family was modified by the loss of a sense of trusteeship to the lineage, by the decline of kinship and clientage, and by the concurrent rise of the power of the state and the spread of Protestantism. The most important consequence was the substitution of loyalty to state or sect for loyalty to lineage or patron. This weakened the diffuse affective network of kin and neighbours which had surrounded and sustained the loosely bound family structure, and tended to isolate the nuclear core. (653)

But by continuing to foreground the chorus of peasants as if they lived within the family and were actually members of a patriarchal family, *Nina* functions as a nostalgic discourse, persuading its audience members that a radical social and domestic transformation has not in fact occurred.

The issue of marital choice is also emphasized in the opera as Nina, the beleaguered heroine, goes mad, much like the later Lucia di Lammermoor in Donizetti's opera does (1835), when she is not allowed to marry the man of her choice. The contested nature of the increasingly popular companionate marriage, as well as the rights of women, is certainly at issue here. As Stone has noted,

> in France in the second half of the eighteenth century there was some intensive propaganda, both in writing and in art, in favour of the affective family type, free marriage choice, marital love, sexual fulfillment within marriage—the alliance of Cupid and Hymen—and close parent-child bonding. . . . Despite this, however, there is strong evidence that the practice of marriage arranged by parents for material advantages was reinforced by the legal code of both the *Ancien Régime* and Napoleon's Code Civil. (390)

European families at all class levels were undergoing tremendous changes in attitudes toward love, lust, and the need to procreate, and *Nina* enacts that familial transformation in a highly stylized, ritualistic manner for its audience. The opera also stages the vexed and contentious issue of the treatment of the insane by presenting a series of "mad scenes" in which Nina gives away family jewels to a variety of servants. We can recall here Foucault's discussion of the "disciplinary" society (1977) and the increased need during this period to define insanity in order to institutionalize it. But we can also recall what Markley calls a "theatrics of sentimentality" which relies on the actions of upper-class characters that must manifest signs of sentimental distress in order to display their moral worthiness, their right to possess the class status and privileges that they inherited at birth (220). By dispensing the family jewels, Nina in effect is performing her sentimental guilt, her rejection of her father's status, and her heightened awareness of class inequities.

These serious issues dissolve as the Count, motivated by simple and misguided greed, is reformed by witnessing the sufferings of his daughter and subjects. Later we are informed that the bloody duel that had precipitated Nina's mental crisis did not actually result in Lindorno's death, but only his wounding, and the piece ends happily, one might say magically, for all concerned. Given the date of this opera's initial performance in Paris,

1786, the political implications could not have been lost on a population that was beginning to agitate for reform (*Nina* was reprised on November 22, 1823, as a benefit at the Théâtre-Italien, Paris). The "happy ending" of this opera occurs not because the audience wanted to believe that they too lived in a nostalgic political-state that functioned as a family, but because the sentimental ethos demanded such a construction. In the sentimental universe, *virtù* became the most highly valued quality or characteristic of the bourgeois, secularized community, because this is clearly a public sphere in which private values must accommodate public sentiments just as public displays of emotions must conform to the reality of private relationships.

IV.

> The transgressive element in music is its nomadic ability to attach itself to, and become part of, social formations, to vary its articulations and rhetoric depending on the occasion as well as the audience, plus the power and the gender situations in which it takes place.
>
> —Edward Said, *Musical Elaborations*, 70

During 1801 a novella titled *The Father and Daughter, A Tale in Prose*, written by Amelia Opie (1769–1853), went through twelve editions, selling close to ten thousand copies. This fact alone tells us that Opie's didactic piece powerfully spoke to the beliefs, fears, sentiments, and prejudices of its culture. Opie was in fact so famous during her heyday that Thomas Love Peacock felt the need to satirize her as "Miss Philomela Poppyseed, the sleep-inducing lady novelist" in his *Headlong Hall* (1815). Walter Scott confessed that he cried over *The Father and Daughter* "more than I ever cried over such things," and Mr. Prince Hoare, editor of the journal *The Artist*, reported that he "could not sleep all night" after reading it (qtd. Ty, 135). Tears and pathos were precisely the reactions intended by Opie, and we might go further to claim that by depicting hyperbolic passions and unbearable grief in her male characters she was attempting to elicit emotional excesses and pity from her male readers rather than simply her presumed female audience. The issues here are not only sentimentality, subjectivity, agency, intention, or bourgeois control of the emotions, although all of these are important aspects in the evolution of the buffered self. Rather, the question is how a number of largely forgotten literary and musical texts based on Shakespeare's *King Lear* intersected to create the "buffered self" and what we now understand as modern, secularized subjectivity.

CHAPTER 1

In appropriating the cultural capital of Shakespearean narratives and domesticating them for an emerging middle-class reader, women writers like Opie actually positioned women as the dominant purveyors of personal morality and civic virtue. For instance, in 1832 Anna Jameson published *Characteristics of Women, Moral, Poetical, and Historical*, but what is most striking about this treatise is that the women she analyzes are not historical women, but heroines from Shakespeare's plays. In justifying her method, she claims, "We hear Shakspeare's [sic] men and women discussed, praised and dispraised, liked, disliked, as real human beings; and in forming our opinions of them, we are influenced by our own characters, habits of thought, prejudices, feelings, impulses" (I:xx). Jameson went on to note that she intended to analyze these fictitious heroines in order to find a way to talk about "the condition of women in society, as at present constituted, [for it] is false in itself, and injurious to them,— that the education of women, as at present conducted, is founded on mistaken principles, and tends to increase fearfully the sum of misery and error in both sexes" (I:viii). If Jameson could use Shakespeare's heroines as models for discussing the contemporary educational and social condition of women, it was because Shakespeare had by the late eighteenth century become an appropriated bourgeois cultural icon throughout Europe, celebrated as a middle-class poet who had bested the aristocracy of *belles lettres* and seized the right to pen immortal works about the folly of kings and aristocrats.

Strange as it may seem, analyzing Shakespeare's characters became one way of talking about modern culture, its aesthetic values, its construction of the emotions, and its conflicted political and domestic rearrangements. But it was also true that at least a vague familiarity with Shakespeare had become a sort of membership requirement in the new British empire; a passing knowledge of his plays and language became a crucial totemic aspect of the growing movement toward nationalization. As Michael Dobson notes, "By the 1760s Shakespeare is so firmly established as the morally uplifting master of English letters that his reputation no longer seems to depend on his specific achievements as a dramatist: a ubiquitous presence in British culture, his fame is so synonymous with the highest claims of contemporary nationalism that simply to be British is to inherit him, without needing to read or see his actual plays at all" (214). Or, as Jane Austen has Henry Crawford observe in *Mansfield Park*, "But Shakespeare one gets acquainted with without knowing how. It is a part of an Englishman's constitution." Or, it would appear, an Englishwoman's. (*Mansfield Park*, by the way, is yet another domesticated rewriting of the *Lear* narrative with the two foolish sisters hoisted on their own petards, while the

Cordelia character, embodied in Fanny Price, asserts her defiance of the patriarchy by refusing Henry Crawford as a husband.)[5]

But in addition to subjectivity and individuality, the development of the sentimental and the gothic occurred alongside, and we might even say, in tandem with the growing science of psychology. As we noted about Nina's insanity, the notion of demon possession as the cause for madness was replaced by an increasing investment in human (secular) explanations such as sudden shock to the nervous system or trauma as the likeliest causes of mental aberrations. One aspect of the secularization process occurs, then, when what had previously been supernatural now becomes psychologized, medicalized, and internalized. By looking at literary characters as if they were actual case studies for how the human mind and emotions operate during periods of stress, literary critics provided the first models for psychoanalysts, and we can recall here that Freud's essays on Sophocles' *Oedipus,* Shakespeare's *Hamlet,* Jensen's "Gradiva," or Hoffmann's "The Sandman" are blatant but later examples of this tendency. The earliest modern professional male literary critics—Samuel Johnson, Coleridge, Lamb, and Hazlitt—began their writing careers by analyzing characters in dramas, and most specifically, in Shakespearean works. As these critics fleshed out analyses of Shakespeare's major characters and their use of language, they were at the same time constructing a paradigm of what it meant to be a modern citizen, that is, of what it meant to be a constructive and empathetic member of both a family and of the state. The emphasis shifts in all of the popular adaptations of Shakespeare's dramas from the public to the private sphere, so that finally what we have of Shakespeare during this period is a series of dysfunctional family portraits, not studies any longer in failed royalty or kingship.

If Renaissance psychology had (crudely) framed itself around a theory of four "humours" maintaining a balance, then Enlightenment psychology would advance that notion one step further by internalizing one's "faculties" and categorizing and classifying the passions as so many elements on an empirical chart. But crucial to this new psychology was the role of the domestic emotions as moral touchstones in judging character. For instance, James Fordyce in his *Sermons for Young Ladies* (1766) writes: "The world, I know not how, overlooks in our sex a thousand irregularities which it never forgives in yours; so that the honour and peace of a family are, in this view, much more dependent on the conduct of daughters than of sons" (qtd. Marsden 1998, 21). Jean Marsden has drawn out the analogy here by observing that "the family acts as a type of the state, the dutiful daughter becomes the pattern of national honour: family drama becomes national drama, and the daughters of England stand responsible for the honour and peace of the nation." What is interesting about the sentimental and later the gothic, however, is that its operas and fictions consistently show the bond between father and daughter to be the "necessary pillar of patriarchy": "not only do these daughters uphold the familial power structure, they also reject or subordinate romantic love in favor of their filial piety" (17, 26, 22). If Shakespeare was "in the air," so too were religious, social, economic, and cultural anxieties about the place of women in the newly evolving European nation-state. Appropriating Shakespeare's characters, particularly his female characters, became a sort of cultural shorthand for depicting options available to women as either innocent victims (Cordelias) or vicious victimizers (Lady MacBeths).

In order to understand the proliferation of *Lear* narratives during this period, we need to appreciate the cultural anxiety that must have circulated in a powerful country that knew it was ruled by a king who periodically suffered from bouts of insanity. Consider that the "family" of England felt vulnerable to external assaults from its enemy, France, and besieged internally by the rebellion and defection of its most prestigious holding, the American colonies. This charged and anxious political situation was replayed allegorically in sentimental novels and operas as the seduction and insanity narrative. In fact, the private qualities of these stories are actually belied by their sheer public prevalence. But why would a culture need to retell compulsively the same story, and why would these revivals occur during the height of the king's madness and the attempts to impose a regency? The dominant ideology replayed for public consumption positions the vulnerable daughter as the emblem of embattled nationhood. And crucial in this construction of the new English national identity were the qualities of generosity and sincerity, exactly those traits that dutiful daughters were expected to display toward their families and their communities. The good daughter is the loyal Briton, willing to endure any slight for the pleasure of sitting in blissful obedience and deference at the mad father's feet. To be a Briton meant to assume a supine position, a subject-position of abjection and subjugation, a tolerant, indeed even groveling posture before absolute and unquestioned—and irrational—power. The ideological formula stated that domestic discord leads to political upheaval; the hierarchy of the state was duplicated in the hierarchy of the family, with the all-powerful and terrifyingly "other"/father as moral arbiter and final authority, no matter what his flaws. Father becomes quite literally fatherland, while the daughter—like Britain's beleaguered citizens—could only smile gamely through her tears.

By way of background, it is necessary to observe that the *Lear* that eighteenth-century British audiences would have known was Nahum Tate's anti-Whig version, not Shakespeare's. In 1681 Tate decided to rewrite Shakespeare's *Lear*, a play he considered to be a confused "heap of jewels, unstrung and unpolished" (Epistle Dedicatory). In addition to adding references to the Popish Plot, he also took it upon himself to eliminate the role of the Fool, to insert a love affair between Cordelia and Edgar, and to exclude the king of France as a character altogether. His most infamous transformation, however, was his addition of a happy ending in which Lear retires in order to hand his kingdom over to the happily married Cordelia and her husband, Edgar. In Tate's version Cordelia's cold comments to her father in the opening scene are the result of her love for Edgar and her desire to avoid a dynastic marriage arranged by her father. Cordelia becomes a pre-sentimental heroine whose virtuous love transforms the character of Edgar, so that, instead of a political drama, the audience has a good deal of familial and personal pathos to savor. Tate's Cordelia does not lead an army to rescue her father, as she does in Shakespeare's drama. Instead, she alternately cries and waits for Edgar to rescue her from her would-be rapist, Edmund (Marsden 1995, 36).

It is also important to note that Tate thought he was improving on Shakespeare when he increased Edmund's role in prominence, including Edmund's thwarted plan to rape Cordelia during the storm. This interpolated scene of virtue in distress was famously illustrated by Pieter van Bleeck's painting of Mrs. Cibber as Cordelia (1755), clinging to her maid Arante (also a new character) for support as she flees the lecherous advance of Edmund. This particular painting and numerous engravings of it became one of the most famous illustrations of Shakespeare's works during the late eighteenth century. Cordelia's rescue by Edgar concludes in a speech in which she lauds private love and virtue over Edgar's lowly public status and his lack of royalty. And so in spite of his Tory sympathies, Tate's version concludes by anticipating the bourgeois shift that would occur within the next century. For Tate, Cordelia is transformed into an almost-seduced maiden who is only too willing to forsake the corrupt aristocracy in favor of marrying a superior bourgeois British citizen, while Lear becomes a simple father who just needs to see his favorite daughter settled in a successful marriage so that he can retire and hand over his property (the country) to them. An article published in 1783 went so far as to see Cordelia as the "patron saint of the private sphere" because of her "propriety," "fine sensibility," and "softness of female character," all qualities praised as the marks of appropriate British bourgeois females (qtd. Dobson, 93).

David Garrick is the actor most associated with the portrayal of Lear throughout the eighteenth century, and, indeed, he played the role from

CHAPTER 1

1742–1776, over a thirty-four-year period. His revision of the *Lear* story downplayed the portrait of a pathetic Cordelia with an appeal instead to sympathy for a confused father and his devoted daughter. His stated intention was to draw "amiable tears" from his audience, rather than to make them miserable or titillate them with a threatened rape scene. And although Garrick made a number of attempts to restore some of Shakespeare's original language and plot to his 1756–76 versions of *Lear*, Tate's revision was actually kept alive on the British stage because of the increasing madness of King George III. Because his insanity made for more than a few awkward social and political moments, *Lear* was finally banned altogether from the London stage from 1811 to 1820. Indeed, the only caricature we have of King George as Lear was done by George Cruikshank in January 1811, just as the Regency Bill was being debated. Titled "King Lear and his Daughter," it depicts George with arms upraised in horror at the sight of a prone woman, meant to represent Cordelia, dead at his feet. The actual situation in the caricature is the death of George's youngest and favorite daughter, Amelia, in November 1810, an event that was believed to have sent her father into his final and irreversible insanity (Bate 1989, 85–86). But what is most interesting about this caricature—besides its sheer cruelty—is that it positions the king within his personal domestic space, as a father first, a monarch second. It also asserts that the reason for his insanity was not as a result of his political duties, but instead was caused by his disappointments and tragedies as a parent.

V.

> Music therefore quite literally fills a social space, and it does so by elaborating the ideas of authority and social hierarchy directly connected to a dominant establishment imagined as actually presiding over the work.
>
> —Edward Said, *Musical Elaborations*, 6

During the eighteenth century the British stage, like the French, was flooded with works that employed sentimental categories clearly derived from Richardson's tremendously popular and influential novels *Clarissa* and *Pamela*. The Irish playwright Issac Bickerstaffe (1733–?1812), for instance, adapted *Pamela* as a light comic opera with music by Samuel Arnold in 1765. With thirty-five performances at Covent Garden, Bickerstaffe's *Maid of the Mill* had to be "divested of the coarse scenes and indecency of the original" (Kavanaugh, 365), but it was so popular that it was credited with bringing comic opera back into popularity in London after *The Beggar's Opera* (1728) fell out of fashion. The conventions of sentimentality are a curious mixture, then, of musical forms, literary genres, displaced religious sentiments, and conservative political and social sympathies all bound up in a strikingly visual manner, suggesting the high-toned, moral origins of the genre. The demonization of the libertine-seducer who threatens the sanctity and order of the domestic sphere became a dominant, indeed a compulsive, impulse throughout the century, and certainly it is possible to read this trope as a nationalistic allegory in which French innovations (libidinal, sadistic, voyeuristic) invade and pollute a native British tradition. But it is also possible to read this repeated refrain as expressing to some extent the anxiety that occurred when the Hobbesian image of natural man, with all his rationalistic philosophies and animalistic desires, confronted a beleaguered and besieged Christian sensibility. The seduction of Clarissa concerns not simply her body, but her soul, and that was what was of most concern to the ethos of Providential Deism.

The Sentimental, then, is an ethical system that seeks to shore up the faltering claims of the *paterfamilias,* primarily through exerting control of the family's bloodlines, and validating the daughter's choice of a husband (in conformity with the father's wishes). In sentimental operas and fictions the dominant threat is the unsuitable secret marriage, the disputed inheritance, or the seduction plot, while in early gothic works dynastic, public, and political issues figure more prominently. Moving Shakespeare's royal personages out of the palace and into domestic hearth and home was actually the major strategy of Amelia Opie when she rewrote the *Lear* story as *The Father and Daughter.* Coincidentally, Opie shared with David Garrick a distinct fascination with visiting insane asylums. We are told by her biographer that when she was not attending murder trials, she was visiting insane asylums in Norwich and London (see Macgregor). An astute student of human passions in extreme situations, her sentimental novella traces the history of the motherless Agnes Fitzhenry and her devoted father, a successful businessman. Adored by her father and worshiped by the community, Agnes falls prey to a seducer, who persuades her to elope with him. Thinking they are on their way to be married in London, Agnes is pregnant before she knows it, and her lover has disappeared in order to marry—at the request of his corrupt aristocrat father—a woman with a larger estate. Thus far, the plot is a virtual copy of *Nina,* with the heroine Agnes being replaced in the affections of her lover by a wealthier woman, thus doubling the victimization of the damsel in distress. Seduced by a wealthy aristocratic man, Agnes is powerless against his family, reminding us of Ellison's observation, that "as sensibility's social base becomes broader, its subject paradoxically becomes social inequality. Sensibility increasingly is defined by the consciousness of a power difference between the agent and the object of sympathy" (18). Class inequities provoke our sympathy for Agnes, but the father's humiliation stirred the strongest emotions in Opie's readers. The loss of his daughter's virginity as a piece of valuable property that the father himself rightly possessed was what most incensed the contemporary male readers of this text.

The climactic recognition scene between father and daughter occurs after Agnes returns with her illegitimate son, Edward, to her birthplace, and encounters a chained madman roving around in the woods, claiming that he is there to visit his daughter's grave:

> At the name of "father," the poor maniac started, and gazed on her earnestly, with savage wildness, while his whole frame became convulsed; and rudely disengaging himself from her embrace, he ran from her a few paces, and then dashed himself on the ground in all the violence of frenzy. He raved, he tore his hair; he screamed and uttered the most dreadful execrations; and with his teeth shut and his hands clenched, he repeated the word father, and said the name was mockery to him. (Opie, 93)

The hyperbolic display here, the frenzy, the gnashing of teeth, and the "violence of frenzy," all of these actions would have been seen as expressions of pure mania of the sort that had recently been codified by the new medical theories of Jean-Étienne Esquirol (1772–1840) and Philippe Pinel (1745–1826) in France. In addition, Mr. Fitzhenry's behavior codes emotional excess as dangerous and unacceptable in the newly bourgeois British citizen. And to cause such extravagance of feeling, indeed madness, in another person, and that person being one's father, would have been read as an unforgivable breach of decorum in the new middle-class emotional economy. Agnes must pay for her error and she does so promptly: as her father gazes on her with "inquiring and mournful looks," Agnes begins to cry, "tears once more found their way, and relieved her bursting brain, while, seizing her father's hand, she pressed it with frantic emotion to her lips" (94). The father is led by Agnes to shelter in an insane asylum that he himself built in his prosperous days, before the ruination of his business which was brought about by his depression over his daughter's disastrous elopement. Here Agnes patiently serves as his attendant, while he spends his days obsessively sketching charcoal drawings of her tomb on his wall. His madness consists in telling Agnes that his daughter—standing directly in front of him—is dead. This delusional mania would have been recognized by Opie's contemporary readers as an idée fixe, a type of monomania,

FIGURE 2: John Thurston, *King Lear: O my dear father* (1805).
Courtesy of the Folger Shakespeare Library

or what Lennard Davis describes as obsession, the new face of insanity that had evolved when the "humors" theory of madness was replaced: obsession was a fixation on "a single idea, passion, or train of thought" that is "not dependent on humors or thoracic organs" but is produced by "some vague combination of ideas and 'nerves'" (69; also see Scull).

After seven years of such penance, Agnes is rewarded finally with her father's recognition of her, quickly followed by the father's death and then Agnes'. They are ultimately buried together in the same grave, the one the father had been designing on the wall of his cell. It is no coincidence to see the sudden profusion of sentimental prints of Cordelia and Lear produced and disseminated at this time as a response to the popularity of Opie's work. The earlier, pre-Opie depictions of Cordelia focus on her dead body or, as Bleeck portrayed her, victimized and fleeing. In contrast, after the publication of Opie's novella, we begin to see engravings like John Thurston's *King Lear: O my dear father* (1805), depicting a very maternal Cordelia comforting and cradling her father in her arms, very reminiscent of the death scene in Opie's novella (see fig. 2).

The climactic pathetic scene, in which father and daughter both recognize each other for the first time since her disgrace and the last time before both of their deaths, is dramatically framed by Opie with the use of an aria adapted from Handel's oratorio *Deborah,* and transformed into a popular parlor song which the father and daughter sing to each other about paternal love and hope (Opie, 113). The use of the aria at this particular point in the novella is telling, for what it suggests is that at points of high emotional intensity we turn to staged musical recitals of our feelings, hence the distancing effect of the Handel piece at the precise moment when the emotional intensity overwhelms both father and daughter and, presumably, the reader. The libretto for the Handel oratorio was written by Samuel Humphreys and was based on the gruesome story of Jael in the Old Testament's book of Judges, chapter four. The Israelites, who have been in captivity for the past twenty years, have been told by the prophetess Deborah that Sisera, the Canaanite commander, would be assassinated by a woman. After the battle in which the Israelites are victorious, Sisera flees the battlefield and seeks sanctuary in the tent of Jael, wife of Heber. Jael accommodates him, but while Sisera sleeps she nails his head to the ground with a tent peg. The challenge for the librettist was to make this violent murder demonstrate the goodness of God. The passage that is cited by Opie comes in Act 3, scene 2:

Abinoam [the father's] recitative:
My prayers are heard, the blessings of this day

All my past cares and anguish well repay;
The soldiers to each other tell
My Barak has performed his duty well.

Barak [the son]: My honored father!

Abinoam: O my son, my son,
Well has thy youth the race of honor run.
Abinoam's air:
Tears, such as tender fathers shed,
Warm from my aged eyes descend,
For joy to think, when I am dead,
My son shall have mankind his friend.

In E flat major, the air employs the distinctive color of two solo flutes to soft strings and a pair of organs. This aria is generally considered a welcome moment of humanity in a relentlessly nationalistic, bellicose libretto, and like other such airs written by Handel, an accolade to good sons by loving fathers, beautifully composed, simple, lyrical, a touching rich bass aria considered by Dean to be "as beautiful as anything of its length (18 bars) in Handel's work." Dean points out that it was adapted from an earlier Chandos Anthem, but in this version the Israelite father weeps for joy in the knowledge that his son's future fame is assured because of his success in battle (228). Most significantly, however, *Deborah*, like *Lear*, presents an earlier patriarchal period of masculine warfare and domination that is actually sustained by the presence and power of women. Not seen as daughters or even wives, the women in this biblical narrative are either prophets or assassins.

Deborah was performed seven times in 1733, and then revived again ten times over the next fifteen years (Dean, 228). Dean tells us that the oratorio was revived many times in the twenty years after Handel's death (1759–79). We might legitimately ask, however, how would Opie know the aria if the oratorio had not been performed since 1779, at which time she would have been only ten years old? And how would she even have had the opportunity to see one of the revivals if she did not travel to London until she was an adult? Interestingly, Dean claims that "there is no record of favourite songs [from the oratorio] being sung at concerts" (237), which suggests that the air could not have circulated as a publicly performed concert song during the period. But such airs did not need large forces to perform, so could become parlor songs and therefore had wide popular distribution in private, home performances. We know, for instance, that

CHAPTER 1

Opie wrote lyrics for songs like "The Favorite Hindustani Girl's Song" with Robert Birchall (?1750–1819), a music seller, instrument dealer, and music publisher in London who also ran a musical circulating library that would have stocked popular songs (see "Birchall"). In addition, a W. Booth was lending songs and glees in April 1800 in Norwich, while William Fish, an oboe player and music teacher, opened a Musical Circulating Library in Norwich and had an extensive printed catalogue by 1817 (see Potter, 32; King). We have to assume that the aria would have been familiar enough to Opie and other middle-class Britons to allow her to quote lines from the piece in her 1801 novella. Strongly melodic and very direct in its emotions, these airs were the most popular and accessible music in Handel's oratorios and contributed to the perception that the biblical oratorios were actually sentimental dramas and nationalist panaceas (R. Smith, 244). One could argue, in fact, that Opie's deployment of Handel stands as the crucial mediating moment between a print-based economy and a competing oral-based culture. In the emerging market for printed sheet music to be performed in the home, we can glimpse how print and performance culture began operating in close conjunction with one another.

The use of the Handel piece further prepares us for Ferdinando Paër's later adaptation of the novella into an opera he entitled *Agnese di Fitzhenry* (1809), an opera that follows closely its source material in Opie, although the action in this version is set in Italy and the opera has a happy ending, with Agnese marrying Ernesto and moving in with her suddenly recovered father. Like *Nina*, *Agnese* centers on insanity caused within the family by the greed or lust of one family member, setting off an illness that metaphorically suggests the interconnectedness of all members within the familial circle. In *Nina* the daughter magically regains her sanity and the opera can conclude happily in marriage, but in Opie's novella the father gains his sanity only long enough to recognize the horror of his daughter's situation, his own shame, and to die almost immediately as a result. Clearly, Paër did not want to present such a conclusion to his operatic adaptation, so, like Nahum Tate revising Shakespeare's *Lear*, he tidied up the story and presented the happy ending that he knew his audience would demand. Even so, his light touch did not please everyone in the audience. In his *Life of Rossini*, Stendhal recorded his disgusted reaction to seeing a performance of Paër's *Agnese*:

> Even the remarkable popularity of the opera cannot shake my conviction that it is profoundly wrong for art to deal with purely horrifying subjects. The madness of Shakespeare's Lear is made tolerable by the most touching devotion of his daughter Cordelia; but I personally feel that there is noth-

ing to redeem the ghastly and pitiable condition of the heroine's father in *Agnese* ... [which] has always remained with me as a thoroughly disagreeable memory. (qtd. Commons, n.p.)

Agnese's libretto, written by Luigi Buonavoglia, adds a few touches of comic relief, primarily the director of the insane asylum, who treats the inmates as laughable and easily cured if they would just stop indulging their extreme emotional responses to a variety of life's typical events (Kimbell, 244). *Agnese* was famous for being the first opera to take its audience literally into a lunatic asylum and to depict in almost clinical detail the behavior of a madman. Was its blatant depiction of insanity a cheap attempt to exploit the sensibility of the era? Certainly visits to observe the inmates of Bedlam had become a sort of sport for people like Garrick and Opie, not to mention the general bourgeois population.

Paër, however, transforms the Handel aria, "Tears, such as tender fathers shed," and instead has Agnese play the harp and sing a favorite song so that her father will finally recognize her through her voice. And instead of using the Handel piece, taken as it was from a gruesome Old Testament story, Paër has Agnese assume the character of her namesake, St. Agnes, whose name means "the lamb," and who was, somewhat ironically, the patron saint of virgins and rape victims. At the climactic moment in the opera, Agnese sings a decidedly New Testament lament that figures the daughter as a lost lamb seeking for her father, the good shepherd: "If the lost lamb / Finds her good shepherd once more, / Grief quickly / Changes to joy; / With her harmonious bleating / She sets the hill ringing; / Nor from her face could you tell / How dismayed she has been. / So to her father / Return Agnese" (see "Ferdinando Paër"). The change in imagery is significant, in that the Old Testament patriarch is replaced in Paër by the father as a forgiving Christ-figure, a shepherd seeking his lost lambs, not a vengeful deity.

Although composed in 1809, Paër's *Agnese* was not performed in London until 1817, and was unfortunately competing directly with Mozart's *Don Giovanni* that particular season. Despite a fine production and enthusiastic reviews, the opera had only five performances before it was suspended "on account of some similitude which was thought to exist between the situation of Hubert [the father] and that of his majesty [George III's insanity]" (qtd. Fenner, 131). But what is most striking about the use of Handel in Opie and later in the popular melodramas writtten by Marie Therese Kemble (*Smiles and Tears; or, The Widow's Stratagem*, 1815) and Thomas Moncrieff (*The Lear of Private Life, or the father and daughter*, 1820), is that the music is used in all of these pieces at what we would recognize as the "moment of desire" in the text. The aria is used to frame what can be identified as the oedipal crisis of the narrative: the moment at which the father is forced to recognize his daughter as a sexual woman, an individual who has defied him and allowed herself to enter into an illicit passion with a seducer who has no intention of making her his wife. As a conservative denunciation of the father's loss of control over selecting a spouse for this daughter, Opie's work is similar to so many gothic texts of the period that are split and intensely ambivalent about companionate versus arranged/dynastic marriages. Susan Staves has noted, for instance, that Opie's novella needs to be read in light of the Marriage Act of 1753, which caused "an expression of anxiety about the weakening of older restraints on the independent behavior of children" (109).

The recognition scene is so excruciating to the father that he distances it by performing its pain in a stylized, almost ritualized manner, couching it in distinctly Old Testament biblical imagery. Such a move emphasizes Opie's emotional pathos in order to suggest that the sexual disgrace of the daughter is equivalent to the warfare between rival Old Testament tribes. To lose one's virginity is tantamount to losing national honor and one's standing as God's chosen people. One is reminded here of Žižek's response to the question, why do we listen to music? His answer:

> in order to avoid the horror of the encounter of the voice qua object. What Rilke said for beauty goes also for music: it is a lure, a screen, the last curtain, which protects us from directly confronting the horror of the (vocal) object.... [V]oice does not simply persist at a different level with regard to what we see, it rather points toward a gap in the field of the visible, toward the dimension of what eludes our gaze. In other words, their relationship is mediated by an impossibility: *ultimately, we hear things because we cannot see everything.* (1996, 93; emphasis in original)

What the music screens from view here is the father's fantasized vision of his daughter in the sexual act. The music blocks, in other words, a reversed primal scene so that what cannot be imagined or viewed by the culture at large is the daughter's seduction, the daughter's uncontrolled sexuality. It is interesting to note that the three most recent adaptations of the *Lear* narrative written by women, Jane Smiley's *A Thousand Acres* (1992 Pulitzer Prize winner), Elaine Feinstein and the Women's Theatre Group's *Lear's Daughters* (1987), and Margaret Atwood's novel *The Cat's Eye* (1988), all reveal patriarchal incest and physical abuse to be the dark secrets hidden in the father-daughter relationship. Although Freud sees the *Lear* narrative as concerned with the need to accept the intermingling of Eros with Thanatos, for contemporary women writers the *Lear* story was focused on the father's corruption of the virgin daughter as a metaphor for his rape of land, resources, and innocence.[6]

What I am suggesting is that Handel's oratorios were secularized when his arias were sung as popular parlor songs and eventually made their way into the sentimental novels of the day, as emotional touchstones of sorts. But *Lear* and indeed all of Shakespeare's dramas were also domesticated so that the national and dynastic issues that Shakespeare explored became transformed into popular novels and dramas that moved the action from the public to the private realm. The shifts that we see in the secularization and domestication of high cultural artifacts to popular ones says a good deal about the construction of the national as well as the secularizing agenda in this period. I think therefore I am seems to have been transformed into I cry therefore I am, or I suffer and feel emotion and therefore I am reassured that there is still a God. Experiencing intense emotions became a way of talking about one's "soul," one's "spirit." Provoking intense suffering and displaying that suffering in stylized, almost ritualized ways became the dominant mode for this culture to define personal and civic virtue, and to reassure itself that God still existed. Europeans were able to recognize their shared humanity only when they could see demonstrated intense guilt about failed filial duty, intense shame about sexual license, and intense grief about causing madness or suffering in one's family members.

VI.

On this planet at least the reputation of Shakespeare is secure. When life is discovered elsewhere in the universe and some interplanetary traveler brings to this new world the fruits of our terrestrial culture, who can imagine anything but that among the first books carried to the curious strangers will be a Bible and the works of William Shakespeare.

—Louis Marder

The gothic imaginary was clearly indebted to a large extent to the Sentimental and specifically, to the sentimental Shakespeare. Therefore, Sensibility was complicit in the bourgeois strategy of secularizing virtue even as it attempted to domesticate the public realm in imitation of some idealized private family presided over by wise fathers protecting dutiful daughters. Stories from the Bible, Shakespeare, and Greek or Roman mythology had to be radically recast as models for a population that clamored for tales of secular heroism, a populace that was now drawn to psychological dramas rather than allegorical depictions of spiritual journeys. The poetic psychomachias of Blake, Byron, Wordsworth, and Coleridge found their theatrical and operatic equivalents in the dramatic agonies of suffering daughters and guilt-ridden fathers, who in turn were metaphorical equivalents to a populace ruled by a tyrannical despot (in France) or a periodically insane king (in Britain). As Fredric Jameson notes, the "political unconscious" of a nation is revealed in its symbolic enactments of a social narrative, and the master narrative of these particular societies was repression, long-suffering, and acceptance of a flawed political system that was preferred over the chaos that could result from revolution. Sentimental drama and opera spoke to the "political unconscious" of bourgeois Europe because they enacted their own "mixed" and ambiguous feelings toward failed rulers and corrupt societies committed finally to only incremental change.

As late as 1837 *Blackwood's Edinburgh Magazine* stated the opinion that the fame of Opie's *The Father and Daughter* would endure "till pity's self be dead" (qtd. Jones, 290). Opie herself wrote that her aim in writing was to "excite profitable sympathies in many kind and good hearts and . . . in small degree enlarge our feelings of reverence for our species, and our knowledge of human nature, by shewing that our best qualities are possessed by men whom we are too apt to consider, not with reference to the points in which they resemble us, but to those in which they manifestly differ from us" (qtd. Ty, 58). We return, then, to the need to universalize about an intrinsic "human nature" that all people share and that is rooted in "feelings," emotions that are so real that they reassure us that we are not animals and in fact, that we also inhabit a spiritual realm in addition to the material world that our bodies negotiate. Staging or performing emotions became a way of asserting our shared humanity (read: quasi-divinity) and so Europeans learned a variety of acceptable emotional scripts (and all of the stakes were at fever pitch; these were, as we have seen, life or death scenarios), and demanded that they be performed on stage.

But standing alone, stripped and bare like Lear on the heath, was precisely what was too painful for most European citizens to witness. The moral of the *Lear* tale as rewritten by the sentimental ideology was that no one finally stood alone. All of us—even the insane and the disgraced—can be redeemed by the love of the members of our families and our communities. If we master the scripts and become "buffered" selves embracing the optimistic codes of Providential Deism, we will have the capacity to move into a new transitional cosmos that promises a modicum of control over the emotions and forces that had previously assaulted us to such an extent that we needed to believe in magic in order to protect ourselves. Louis Marder, an American literary critic writing in 1963 in anticipation of Shakespeare's quatercentenary celebrations and at the height of space exploration and expansionist optimism, stated unironically: "On this planet at least the reputation of Shakespeare is secure" (362). And certainly it is significant to note that *King Lear* was so widely known throughout European culture that Hector Berlioz could compose his Overture *Le Roi Lear* in 1831 and provide no explanation for the movements, assuming that his listeners knew the play so well they would be able to follow the sections (see MacDonald). Indeed, Shakespeare and the Bible have provided the master narratives on which Western civilization has been constructed. These texts have taught us what to feel, how to feel, and how to perform those feelings in ways that preserve the patriarchal family, and position all of us in one socially, hierarchically, and religiously inscribed role after another. And when we can enjoy the performance of a tender father who sheds tears for a disgraced daughter, then we have constructed a secular image of God as the most benign face of the patriarchy we can imagine.

CHAPTER 2

"Rescue Operas" and Providential Deism

Roaming through the lower halls of the Louvre, I contemplated the sculptures of the old gods. There they stood, with their expressionless white eyes, and in their marble smile, there lurked a faint melancholy, intimating, perhaps, a pale recollection of Egypt, the realm of death from which they sprang; or a painful longing for the life from which they have been expelled by other divinities; or perhaps also the pain caused by their deadly immortality.

—Heinrich Heine, *Die Romantische Schule* (1833)

I.

"Gothic opera" is very much a contested concept or at least one that has not been understood or fully appreciated in the attempt to construct a critical history of the gothic imaginary. Just how can we begin to limit a canon of "gothic opera" when opera itself is inherently extravagant, emotionally hyperbolic, and engaged in staging a dreamworld where magic and fantasy are employed to convey supposedly plausible events and characters? John Dennis's "An Essay on the Operas after the Italian Manner" (1706) makes this question plain when he observes that "[i]f that is truly the most Gothick, which is the most oppos'd to Antique, nothing can be more Gothick than an Opera, since nothing can be more oppos'd to the ancient Tragedy than the modern Tragedy in Musick" (qtd. Williams 2006, 126). According to this definition, all operas would be to some extent "gothic" in their display of "barbarous" or "medieval" customs and emotions, so clearly some parameters for the genre have to be established initially.[1] This chapter will analyze those operas that imported onto the European stage the performative gothic and in doing so will demonstrate Taylor's thesis that Providential Deism spread through cultural productions and advanced the belief that deism functioned as the necessary transition between Christian faith and anthropocentrism (262), a system of belief that paved the way for the rise of exclusive humanism. The most prolific of these cultural products are the gothically inflected rescue operas that were so popular throughout Europe. Tangentially, I will also examine a few representative operatic adaptations of gothic novels, as well as works that exploit gothic tropes, such as *Ossian,* and the Germanic operas *Der Freischutz* and *Robert Le Diable.*

In 1962 the musicologist Aubrey Garlington claimed that "between 1764 and 1802, some sixty or seventy works for the stage exhibiting 'Gothic' characterstics were produced, [while] eighteen sources that formed the basis for operas by English composers have been found" (51). But, as he himself admits, this number is inflated by including works that simply employ a castle as a setting or have bandits as characters. In fact, English music during this period has consistently been criticized for being "weak" and for having no influence whatsoever on Continental composers (Garlington, 63; also see Chancellor). And even more alarming, the British were so aesthetically insular that as the Italian opera made its way into eighteenth-century London it was greeted by outright hostility and contempt by intellectuals such as John Dennis, Jonathan Swift, Samuel Johnson, and numerous others.[2] As a wholly imported art form originating in southern Europe, and arriving fully developed with its own conventions already set largely in place, opera somehow had to find a way to adapt to British culture before it could be accepted by the public as a legitimate art and viable form of entertainment. That opera did survive—and thrive—in late eighteenth- and early nineteenth-century England, France, and Germany is due to the quality of the music as well as to the power of its librettos to translate and stage potent ideological materials in a revolutionary age. As Anne Williams has observed, it would be ridiculously easy to imagine Walpole's *Castle of Otranto* as an opera because gothic and opera share so many characteristics: both "have their origins in an intellectual project designed to initiate a cultural reform. Each is consciously designed as an act of restoration, spurred by their creators' partly unconscious sense that their culture was in a process of profound transition. Opera was an Early Modern phenomenon, Gothic a product of the waning years of the Enlightenment" (2000, 109). But more importantly, it was *opera seria* (serious opera) that Walpole attended in London, and it was the aesthetic principles of these operas that most influenced Walpole's composition of *The Castle of Otranto*. As Williams notes (2000, 114–15), Walpole's novel is, like *opera seria*, a *pasticcio*, a cutting and pasting of old forms into something new, "a hodge-podge of romance motifs," "ornamentation for its own sake," and a "structure always full of imitation, disguise, and travesty (operatic cross-dressing)."

Clearly, the gothic and the theatrical opera have been bound up with each other from the very beginning, and one of the ways to demonstrate the connection is to examine one of the most popular forms of opera during this period, little remembered today, the rescue opera. Very similar in plot to the earliest gothic novels and, in fact, frequently borrowing their settings, characters, and themes, rescue operas can be understood as sung gothic, or an oral and performative transmission of the gothic imaginary. These operas frequently focused on two themes: the secular, domestic, ritual sacrifice of a woman or the unlawful political imprisonments of innocent victims of tyranny. In both cases, the rescue operas staged elaborate releases of these victims only after their heroic efforts allowed them to prove their worth, hence the operas collaborate in promoting a secularizing bourgeois agenda of earning one's salvation through one's own efforts and thereby vindicating "human flourishing" as an ideal. Whereas God is frequently invoked and sometimes appears to settle disputes from on high, most of the action centers on a wily protagonist's efforts to free himself from a tyrannical oppressor. Providential Deism, in fact, is questioned and slowly set aside as an impractical and abstract system of belief in these operas. Instead, bourgeois heroes and heroines earn their salvations through their own efforts, not through divine intervention. Extremely popular throughout Europe from roughly 1780–1840, rescue operas deserve to be recognized as important performative ideological markers of the gothic imaginary.

To begin, rescue operas most frequently employ the theme of escape from unjust imprisonment. In fact, the endlessly repeated motif of capture and escape (from a tunnel, a burning tower, a labyrinth, a camp of pirates, or a boat of kidnappers) is so pervasive that the modern critic knows that it bears the weight of the opera's ideology. But this is precisely where the confusion begins. Are the capture and escape meant to embody a politically and socially conservative message and a direct warning to the protagonists of the opera, and, by extension, to the audience? Or is the message one of revolution and liberation from tyranny and injustice? Like the process of secularization itself, these operas look both backward and forward at the same time; they are both nostalgic and reformist in their presentation of a number of ongoing European debates about the nature of the divine, the proper role of the monarchy, the threat of violent revolution, the shock of sudden class transformation, the anxiety of changing gender roles within the family structure, and, finally, the construction of newly nationalistic countries that seek to justify the means they have each taken to modernize and secularize. The rescue operas can be understood, I would claim, as allegories of the secularization process itself in that public loyalties are put on trial in works that depict, in slightly varied ways, the same plot: to whom do the emerging bourgeoisie owe their loyalties: to church, state, or family, or some newly reformed and composite form of all three institutions? And which public institution deserves that loyalty because it guarantees the greatest promise of "human flourishing" for the newly secularized bourgeois citizen?

When Handel died in 1759 the *Universal Chronicle* printed an epitaph that saluted him as a musician "whose compositions were a sentimental language rather than mere sounds; and surpassed the power of words in expressing the various passions of the human heart."[3] As we saw in chapter 1, delight in and expression of strong emotions was seen in this era as a part of the human condition, and Handel's oratorios fit nicely into the three main compositional styles that had been defined earlier by Charles Avison in his *Essay on Musical Expression* (1752): the grand or sublime, the beautiful or serene, and the pathetic (devout, plaintive, or sorrowful). James Beattie observed: "Mere descriptions, however beautiful, and moral reflections, however just, become tiresome, where our passions are not occasionally awakened by some event that concerns our fellow-men" (qtd. Schmidgall, 37). The operas and oratorios of this period can be seen, according to Schmidgall, as a "series of passionate or affective vignettes" which appear to portray the actions and emotions of their characters in a piecemeal fashion. Schmidgall sees Handel as working in the "passion-based aesthetic" (37) of his time particularly in his airs, which attempt to express idealized versions of one of the passions of the human heart and therefore reveal the eighteenth-century bias toward generalizing and universalizing.

The assumption that passions or emotions are definite in character, concrete in form, and separable in the mind led Shaftesbury to claim that they, rather than reason, were the "springs of action." Shaftesbury categorized the passions in three ways: as "natural or social" affections directed toward the general welfare; as "the self or private" affections directed toward the individual's own good; or as the "unnatural" affections directed toward neither. In Germany this tendency to systematize led to the theory of *Affektenlehre*, the doctrine that explained how the passions could be portrayed in music, leading to the belief that dramatic music must deal with various specific human emotions in order to evoke a pathetic response in its audience (Schmidgall, 38–39). This brings us to the Germanic definition of "rescue opera," that musical attempt to translate onto the European opera stage the gothic ethos, complete with all its paranoia, claustrophobia, persecution mania, and ambivalence toward authority. General consensus has settled on Friedrich von Schiller's robber-rescue drama, *Die Raüber* (1781) as the first incarnation of the rescue opera. Varma has described *Die Raüber* as a work of "violent sensationalism and a formidable set of dramatic personae: banditti, monks, inquisitors, tortures and poison, haunted towers and yelling ghosts, dungeons and confessionals." For him, the play "demanded justice for the oppressed, freedom from any established social order" (33). Using the device of two competing brothers, *Die Raüber* inspired Coleridge's *Remorse* as well as a number of rescue operas (Burwick 2009, 173). Translated into French as *Les Voleurs* by Friedel and de Bonneville in 1785, the drama was then translated into English by Alexander Tytler in 1792 and seems to have influenced the first English opera with gothic features, Samuel Arnold's *The Banditti, or Love's Labyrinth* (1781; with John O'Keefe). From the beginning, *Die Raüber* was viewed as an amalgam of French revolutionary spirit and Germanic hyperbole, a drama that "seemed to epitomize everything that was menacing in recent Continental literature and politics" (Mortensen 2004, 155). After first reading it in 1794, Coleridge wrote to Southey: "My God, Southey, who is this Schiller, this convulser of the heart? . . . Upon my soul, I write to you because I am frightened. . . . Why have we ever called Milton sublime?" (qtd. Summers, 121). For Thomas Carlyle, the publication of *Die Raüber* marked the beginning "not only in Schiller's history, but in the literature of the world." Versions of *Die Raüber* quickly made their appearance in the European gothic imaginary in a number of guises: as Lamartellière's dramatic French adaptation, *Robert, chef des brigands* (1792), which Wordsworth may have seen when he was in Paris (Mortenson 2004, 155); as the extended interpolated tale in the middle of Lewis's *The Monk*; as *The Necromancer*, in *Der Geisterbanner* (1792), a translation of a German *schauerroman* by Karl Friedrich Kahlert using the pseudonym Lorenz Flammenberg; as Charlotte Dacre's conclusion to *Zofloya* (1806); and as Byron's "Germanic" melodrama *Werner* (1822).

But if it was not compelling enough to witness various versions of the feud between Karl and Franz Moor over the love of Amalia, the rescue opera also featured that tried and true public-pleasing staple: the damsel in distress. Rescue operas frequently depicted the young nubile woman trapped in a tower (sometimes burning) under threat of forced dynastic marriage for high dramatic effect. A popular French example is *Eliza ou le Voyage aux glaciers du Mont St. Bernard* (libretto by V. Reveroni, Saint-Cyr and music by Maria Luigi Cherubini), a work that is almost paradigmatic of the genre. First performed in Paris at the Théâtre Feydeau in 1794, *Eliza* is set in the Swiss Alps, the early action taking place in a monastery located at the pass of Mount Saint Bernard. The separated lovers are here named Florindo, a painter, and Eliza, forced by her father to enter into an engagement with an odious man she despises. In his desperation at this news, Florindo begs the rocks and glaciers to descend on him in order to blot out his misery. Found in the ice and snow by a monk, Florindo is consoled and taken to safety by him, while at the same moment, Eliza and her maid, Laure, are traveling through the mountains, taking advantage of the recent death of her father in order to find Florindo. Act two presents Florindo leaving the inn and determined to commit suicide because of his betrayal. Making his way to the "colline des morts" (hill of the dead), Florindo is caught in a storm, and, in the most sublime moment of the opera, swept away by an avalanche over the edge of a precipice. Rescued by the monk and servants who dig him out, Florindo is reunited with Eliza, who chastises him for doubting her faithfulness and love ("Plus de douleur et plus de larmes"). Anyone who has read Byron's *Manfred* (1816–17) will be struck by the many similarities in plot, character, and setting, although Byron's gothic closet drama does not conclude happily in the manner of this and all rescue operas.

Defining rescue opera musicologically and developing a clear and concise history for this genre have been fraught with difficulty. David Charlton has claimed that the term itself is anachronistic and of limited usefulness because it "plays false on three levels [of] the musical theatre that it purports to represent." First of all, the term *Rettung* ("rescuing") does not distinguish between works of different moral purposes or dramatic styles. Secondly, the term relies on a blanket notion of "rescue," but does not take into consideration all of the other moral actions involved. Thirdly, the term ignores eighteenth-century definitions of its own theatrical use. In summarizing all of the meanings for the term that have been proposed by musicologists as eminent as Winton Dean, Charlton claims that each one of these attempts at definition "fail to account for certain operas and tendencies" (1992, 169). For him, rescue operas are not part of what he calls "an authentic genre like 'opera buffa.'" Instead, the term was coined only in the late nineteenth and early twentieth century, and as a legacy of that Germanic movement that sought to label music by the use of one word (e.g., *Humanitätsmelodie*). Dyneley Hussey used the term "rescue opera" to describe Beethoven's *Fidelio* in 1927, while Karl M. Klob labeled these works "das sogenannte Rettungsoder Befreiungsstück" ("the genre of the so-called rescue or deliverance operas"), suggesting that the term had become useful as a means of connecting the German *Fidelio* to the French tradition. As Charlton observes, the term "rescue" is problematic in that it suggests a happy resolution, or the use of a *deus ex machina* to resolve complications much in the manner of *opera seria*. Yet the sudden reversals of fortune that occur in many of the rescue operas resemble less the *coup de théâtre* of classical theater which corresponded to the shifting alliances among royals and more to the *tableaux* style in which everyone is (re)united in and because of their desire to be happy. For my purpose it might be useful to draw the following analogy: the genre of *opera semiseria* is the musical equivalent of the literary genre of melodrama, while rescue opera is the staged correlative of the *roman frénétique/noir* or the gothic novel.

Most musicologists agree that the librettist Michel-Jean Sédaine (1719–1797) was the operatic founder of the rescue opera, and they cite the very successful *Richard coeur-de-lion* (1784; revived 1824; music by André Ernest Gretry) as the originator of the genre. It was in its genre as successful as Beaumarchais' *Mariage de Figaro* for the 1780s decade.[4] Claiming that he wrote light *opéras comiques larmoyants* in the Italian style, Sédaine particularly influenced René-Charles Guilbert de Pixérécourt (1773–1844), who in turn recognized his artistic paternity when he stated that melodrama was "musical drama in which the music is played by the orchestra instead of being sung" and was therefore known as "l'école de Sédaine perfectionnée" (the school of Sédaine perfected).[5] Sédaine's originality stemmed from his belief that drama should deal with political and moral issues and, in the rescue operas he explored the theme of "unjust detention." In each case the reasons for detention are different, and even though the plot emphasizes the excitement of the danger and tension found in the actual rescue, the underlying ideology avoided the simplistic moral categories of the popular melodramas dominating the French stage at this time.

By the 1790s rescue operas were extremely popular, both in Britain and France, and adaptations of popular gothic novels about victimization and persecution reached all classes in a variety of theatrical and operatic venues. There were hundreds of gothic novels and chapbooks written in England between 1764 and 1799, a large number of which attempted to defend the increasingly serious threats posed against the monarchy and aristocracy more generally in England. As I have noted, the gothic began as an ideologically conservative genre committed to shoring up the claims of primogeniture and inheritance by entail. Novels such as Walpole's *Castle of Otranto* (1765) and Clara Reeve's *Old English Baron* (1778) were concerned with such threats to "human flourishing" as unjust tyrants, impris-

FIGURE 3: Handbill for *Camille*, November 10, 1797.
Courtesy Bibliothèque-musée de l'Opéra-Paris

onments, escapes, disinheritances, wrongful claims on an estate, threatened assaults on virginal females, and the eventual triumph of the "true" aristocrat as rightful heir. The staged form of these plots stressed the dramatic effects, and, as the Terror's impact spread, gothic villains began to appear in increasingly horrific manifestations in both England as well as in Germany and France. For instance, in 1791, the sixteen-year-old Matthew Lewis spent the summer attending the opera in Paris, and then sent a letter to his mother about the profound effect that B. J. Marsollier des Vivetières's very popular and long-running *Camille, ou le Souterrein* had on him (see fig. 3):

> There is an opera, called "Le Souterrein," where a woman is hid in a cavern in her jealous husband's house; and afterwards, by accident, her child is shut up there also, without food, and they are not released till they are perishing with hunger. The situations of the characters, the tragic of the principal characters, the gaiety of the under parts, and the romantic turn of the story, make it one of the prettiest and most affecting things I ever saw. (qtd. Railo, 85)

Clearly, we have here a miniature reenactment on the operatic stage of the most gothic of interpolated episodes in Madame de Genlis's novelistic "letters on education," *Adèle et Théodore* (1782; trans. 1783), *The affecting history of the Duchess of C***, in which an Italian noblewoman is imprisoned by her husband for nine years before she is released, a motif that would appear fairly quickly in Radcliffe's *A Sicilian Romance* (1790) and its imitations (Eliza Parsons's *The Castle of Wolfenbach*, 1793, is only one of many). The use of the imprisonment and rescue motif seems to have originated in the private domestic sphere and then moved to the public, political realm in works that feature male aristocrats under siege by hostile, usually "revolutionary" forces.

The popularity of the British gothic as a genre was conveyed almost immediately to France, where translations and stage adaptations of the British novels were in vogue. But the influence worked both ways, because the first example of a British rescue opera was an adaptation of Sédaine's libretto and André Grétry's musical score for *Richard coeur-de-lion*, staged in London in 1786 and in Boston in 1787. *Richard coeur-de-lion*'s popularity is an example of what James Watt has called the "Loyalist Gothic," or politically reactionary gothics that extol Royalist or Tory values in the face of class upheaval, in this case, King Richard the Lionheart's rescue during the Crusades from an Austrian prison by his troubadour Blondel (42–69). *Richard*'s continuing popularity can be seen in the publication of an adaptation of the legend and opera, James White's three-volume gothic poem *The Adventures of King Richard Coeur-De-Lion* (London, 1791).

The most accomplished British musical composer of politicized rescue operas was Stephen Storace (1762–1796), whose successes at the Theatre Royal Drury Lane were based on such operas as *The Haunted Tower* (1789), *The Pirates* (1792), and *Lodoïska* (1794). Storace's operas have been called "pasticcios" by Eric White (224) because they "borrowed" a good deal of their musical numbers from earlier operas, as had long been the custom in an era in which notions of copyright were murky at best (see Kaplan). Storace's *Lodoïska* was his only attempt at composing a serious rescue opera, and he collaborated on the project with John Philip Kemble, an untried librettist who never again wrote another libretto. Based on the diary-like narrative *Les Amours du Chevalier de Faublas* (1787) by Jean Baptiste Louvet de Couvray, two competing operatic adaptations of *Lodoïska* were composed and produced in Paris within a few weeks of each other, one by Luigi Cherubini (1791, with Fillette-Loraux) and one by Rodolphe Kreutzer (1791, with Jean Dejaure). Set in Poland, Storace's version of the opera concerns the beautiful Princess Lodoïska who has been placed by her father in the Baron Lovinski's castle because the father has refused to allow her to marry Count Floreski. Meanwhile, a band of Tartars are preparing to assault the baron's castle, and Floreski and his servant Varbel align themselves with the Tartar leader, Kera Khan, in order to gain entry into the castle. Once inside, they, along with Lodoïska's father, are captured, but the Tartars burn the castle and free all of its captives. Because Floreski has managed to rescue Losoïska from a burning tower, her father relents and approves of their marriage. Although no score has survived, we do know from the libretto that music was performed throughout the battle scenes, and we also know that martial music was particularly popular with the lower class during this period, both in England and in France (see Girdham). As Garlington notes about this work, "[T]he music was considered completely useless when divorced from the stage, and was not included in the published score. Obviously, the music for these scenes was secondary in importance to the stage machinery" (54).

For a work that contrasts greatly in tone, Storace's *Haunted Tower* (1789) features a gothic setting during the reign of William the Conqueror, double disguises, interesting class conflicts, and a hero who dons his father's armor and is mistaken for a ghost. Based on a tale of usurpation of the Baron of Oakland's estate by his foolish relative, *The Haunted Tower* is almost a burlesque of gothic tropes: servants who use superstitious fears of the baron's ghost in order to drink their master's best vintages in the "haunted tower." For all of its gothic trappings, however, *Haunted Tower* (libretto by James Cobb) is more a romantic comedy in the tradition of Shakespeare. In discussing the play, Burwick has called it "an anti-Gothic comedy with all the trappings of a Gothic melodrama" (2009, 1919), while he has traced its origins to Sade's play *La tour enchantée* (1788), about a lecherous king who is murdered in a tower by his friend, a baron, after the king makes a derogatory remark about the baron's current lover (Burwick 2009, 178–80). Although we only have an 1810 transcription of Sade's play and not the original, we can note that Sade's play focuses on dynastic and aristocratic corruption, while Storace's centers on the treacherous rivalry between English barons after the Norman conquest under King William.

Storace's *The Pirates*, in contrast, is set in Naples and features a series of failed attempts at escape and rescue between Don Altador and his lover Donna Aurora, who is seeking to flee her guardian Don Gaspero de Merida, an evil pirate who intends to force her to marry his nephew, another evil pirate. Much of the action occurs "on the Road to Pausilippo, near Virgil's Tomb," perhaps the most gothic touch in the opera. Virgil's tomb would become something of a *locus romanticus* over the next decades, serving also as a central location in Germaine de Staël's *Corinne; or Italy* (1807).

The other most well-known example of a British rescue/gothic drama was *Blue Beard; or Female Curiosity!* (Drury Lane, 1798) by George Colman the Younger and the successful singer-composer Michael Kelly (Lewis's musical collaborator on *The Castle Spectre*). Their collaborative version, adapted from the French *Raoul, Barbe bleue* by Sédaine and André Grétry

CHAPTER 2

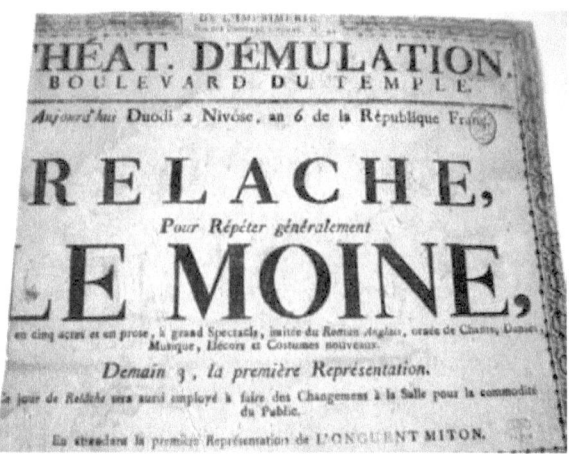

FIGURE 4: Handbill for *Le Moine*, November 22, 1797.
Courtesy of Bibliothèque-musée de l'Opéra-Paris

(1789), which itself was based on the actual history of depraved libertine Gilles de Rais (1404–1440), instead placed Blue Beard in Turkey and relied on references to Napoleon's campaign in Egypt. And if its political insinuations were not potent enough, this time the heroine has to escape from the harem of an accomplished wife-killer (G. Taylor, 94–95; also see Burwick 2009, 202–29).

It was a short step from the gothic novel to the rescue opera, with several versions of the same novel often appearing on stage within the same year. In fact, within a few years of the first translations of novels by Radcliffe and Lewis, French melodramatists were using all of the gothic devices at their disposal, hence there were bleeding nuns, *doppelgängers*, evil dukes, and eventually vampires all over the French and German stages. For instance, in 1798, François B. Hoffman and Nicolas Dalayrac adapted Radcliffe's novel *The Mysteries of Udolpho* (1794) as the "tyrant" rescue opera entitled *Léon, ou Le Château de Montenero* (Opéra Comique, 1798). And Pixérécourt, dubbed the "Corneille of the Boulevards" because most of his works were played on the boulevards that had replaced the old walls of Paris, turned the same novel into *Le Château des Appenins ou le fantôme vivant* (Ambigu-Comique, 1798), in which a menacing phantom appears at the end of Act III but is explained away, thereby employing the convention of the explained supernatural and transforming the ghostly apparitions of his source into hoaxes perpetuated on the gullible.

Pixérécourt adapted Lewis's *Monk* as the never-performed *Le Moine, ou la Victime de l'Orgueil*, while M.-C. Camaille-Saint-Aubin and César Ribié adapted the novel in 1797 as a *comédie en cinq actes* (see fig. 4), producing what Summers calls an "extravagant and grotesque farce," with a ballet interspersed between the dungeon scenes and Ambrosio whirled away to an inferno by a monstrous hippogriff (230). Attempts were made to shorten and revive the work as a tragedy in 1800 (as *Le Jacobin Espagnol* by Prévost) and as a melodrama in 1802 (an abbreviated version of *Le Moine*, directed by Ribié). Besides focusing on the plight of Ambrosio, there were also a number of adaptations that featured the tale of the bleeding nun exclusively, most famously *La Nonne de Lindenberg* by Cailleran and Coupilly (1798), the never-performed *La Nonne Sanglante* by Eugène Scribe and Germaine Delavigne (1838), and Charles Gounod's verion of *La Nonne Sanglante*, which saw eleven performances in 1854 (Williams 2006, 127; also see Gann; Baldrini; Killen). As Williams theorizes, the Gounod opera failed because the bleeding nun assumed an all too material presence, singing rather loudly in several scenes, so that what should have been a ghostly apparition from the transcendent realm instead became an uncomfortably material body and voice on the operatic stage.

Another distinct quasi-religious strand in the gothic can be seen in those works that reveal the continued imaginative investment made in the British Reformation. Depicting the events of the Tudor dynasty as an extended familial gothic drama, a variety of works arose to present Catholicism (personified in Mary, Queen of Scots) as the victim of the rapacious and lecherous Protestant tyrant (Elizabeth), thereby transferring personal and political histories into the realm of the uncanny. We can see how this impulse mutated into opera by placing Sophia Lee's novel *The Recess* (1783–86) and Rosetta Ballin's novel *The Statue Room* (1790) alongside Gioachino Antonio Rossini's opera *Elisabetta, Regina D'Inghilterra* (1815). *The Recess*, a gothic-historical romance that is actually vaguely sympathetic to Catholicism, focuses on two fictitious and secret daughters of Mary, Queen of Scots and owes a good deal of its theme and plot to L'Abbé Prévost's *Le Philosophe anglais, ou Histoire d'un Monsieur de Clèveland* (8 vols.; 1731–39), a novel about the life and adventures of one of Oliver Cromwell's illegitimate sons, raised in a remote cave by his mother so that he would not be found and killed by his hypocritical father (see Maxwell, 31–47). The two sisters in Lee's novel are similarly hidden in an underground cavern and system of tunnels beneath the ruined abbey of Saint Vincent in order to preserve their lives.

"Rosetta Ballin," the pseudonym of a female Catholic author, presents in *The Statue Room* yet another example of a counterfactual Reformation genealogy, this time predicated on the supposition that Catherine of Aragon was pregnant at the time of her divorce from Henry VIII and gave birth to a daughter named Adelfrida (see Dobson and Watson). This half-sister, like Mary Queen of Scots, is later held prisoner by Elizabeth, but somehow manages to marry the object of Elizabeth's affections, the Duke of Alençon, while he was supposedly courting Elizabeth. Yet another daughter is born, this one named Romelia, before Adelfrida is poisoned by her rival, the virgin queen (II:18). In the second volume of the novel, Adelfrida's daughter, Romelia, unsuccessfully attempts to assassinate Elizabeth by using a pistol: "the ball went through her hair and took off part of her crown" (II:135), is driven insane, and eventually commits suicide (II:136). Rossini's opera, with libretto by Giovanni Schmidt, focuses on the same religiously contentious period by creating a brother and sister, Enrico and Mathilde, the supposed children of Mary Queen of Scots, but living in disguise as shepherds. Mathilde secretly marries the Earl of Leicester, Elizabeth's favorite, and follows him to London in order to save their marriage from the untoward attentions of the lecherous Elizabeth. Mathilde very shortly finds herself in prison when Elizabeth learns of her true identity and she and Enrico, through a series of incredible events, find themselves saving Elizabeth's life and therefore having their lives spared by her.

In rewriting Tudor family history in a way that presented the Catholic Mary as an innocent victim of the rapacious and manipulative Protestant Elizabeth, gothic operas and novels actually seem to be mourning the loss of Catholicism as the state religion. Playing to overwhelmingly Protestant audiences, these operas shamelessly romanticize the "lost" Stuart tribe, the claims of ancient Scottish blood to the throne, and the clan-based ethos that undergirded an earlier way of life that the British bourgeoisie were not, it appears, quite so willing to thoroughly renounce. Or at least they wanted to appear nostalgically to mourn the loss of their earlier religious history, associated as it was with "porous selves," magic, superstition, and irrationality.

II.

> But still the heart doth need a language, still
> Doth the old instinct bring back the old names.
>
> —Samuel Taylor Coleridge, *The Piccolomini*, II.iv

As we have seen, it is impossible to focus on the gothic operatic stage in Paris or London in isolation, as there was as much artistic collaboration between the two countries as there was political angst and economic rivalry. While it is common to claim that the British imported melodrama from France (see Brooks 1976), just as they had earlier adopted opera from Italy, it is also possible to see a much more convoluted pattern of influences by shifting our gaze back to the mid-eighteenth century or so. All sorts of diversions moved across the English Channel in both directions, and there was in Paris a full-blown "cult of all things English" during the mid-eighteenth century (Rahill, 109). The availability of a growing number of translations of fictional and philosophical British and French texts encouraged the exchange of fashionable ideas and an examination of different sources of inspiration (see Streeter). Pixérécourt's favorite reading in 1793, for instance, was Rev. James Hervey's *Meditations and Contemplations Among the Tombs* (1746–47) and Rev. Edward Young's *The Complaint, or Night Thoughts* (1742–45), both works typifying what the French referred to as *le spleen anglais*.

In Paris, during the 1792 theater season, *Le Château du diable*, a four-act drama by Joseph-Marie Loaisel-Tréogate, was a huge success at the Théâtre de la Rue Martin. For many reasons, 1792 marks a turning point in the French Revolution and in the use of political representations and symbols. Along with the proclamation of the First Republic on September 21, the *Marseillaise* was composed and reached Paris on July 30; the name "Marianne" designated the Republic for the first time, and the female figure of Liberty with her Phrygian bonnet emblematized the nation; Louis XVI was imprisoned in August, tried in December, and executed on January 20, 1793. Three legal events transformed the French theater world during the Revolution. First, actors were granted the status of "citizen" in December 1789; second, in 1790 the Catholic Church, which no longer bestowed legitimacy upon the king, had to swear allegiance to the Republic's constitution; and third, the advent of the 1791 legislation of the National Convention broke up the Comédie Française's near monopoly of the repertoire which had limited smaller theaters to productions that differed little from the pantomimic, acrobatic, and trained animal entertainment offered at the fairgrounds on the outskirts of Paris. The abolition of state control of theater venues brought about a proliferation of new theaters that rivaled each other in the productions they presented to their newly formed audiences. Spectators were drawn in by the promise that the action would go beyond the excitement and fears of the events witnessed during the Revolution. With the multiple daily beheadings serving as a backdrop to street "performances," the excitement on stage had to surpass real disembodiments in order to successfully compete. The Boulevard du Temple in particular became popularly and humorously known as the "Boulevard du crime" because of all the staged abductions, murders, rapes and other heinous crimes committed on the theaters's stages (see Root-Bernstein). The theatrical world's freedom, however, proved to be short-lived. The Reign of Terror gradually reinstated modes of censure and censorship as certain dramaturges denounced the government's abuse of power and, early in the nineteenth century, Napoleon reinstituted the hierarchy of theaters and designated what sorts of spectacles could be performed on the various stages.

The new dramas—most of which changed their categorization (*comédie, tragi-comédie, opéra comique, drame, mélodrame*) depending on the venue of the particular performance—alluded frequently to current events but in a displaced manner (i.e., setting the story in other locales and times). The plots were borrowed from British literary successes as well as French literary and feudal histories even as the plays were enrolled by the state to promulgate didactically civic messages of *virtù* and republicanism. Rewritings of history that conformed to the new principles of the Republic were now the basis for many of the most popular spectacles, while anticlericalism guaranteed the popularity of many works that portrayed the supposed abuses perpetrated in convents and cloisters. Thus the origin of rescue operas is situated within the framework of popular agitation surrounding the dissolution of religious orders, as well as the reform movements that advocated the abolition of slavery and more liberal divorce legislation (Didier, 120).

After 1789, French operas increasingly took on the characteristics of popular melodrama, with a simple moral structure (the Manichean notion of good versus evil) and a conclusion that emphasized social and communal freedom rather than personal or individual redemption. The example already mentioned above of *Le Château du diable* follows this pattern. Consisting of equal parts melodrama and fairy tale, it charts the struggles of a young knight forced to penetrate a perilous castle filled with ghosts, ghouls, and all manner of sensual temptations. After many harrowing adventures endured while surviving his ordeal, the knightly hero learns that his fiancée's father, in fact, has staged all of these horrors in order to test his loyalty and courage.[6] Encouraged by the success of *Le Château du diable*, Loaisel-Tréogate went on to write a number of other popular pieces including, for the 1797 theater season, *La forêt périlleuse des brigands de la Calabre*, one of the most popular gothic dramas to play nightly to a packed house on the Boulevard du Temple. Overpopulated with banditti, the drama featured a beautiful heroine, Camille, and her devoted lover, Colisan, struggling against the evil machinations of an outlaw who kidnaps Camille and imprisons her in a cave where he threatens to starve her unless she becomes his mistress.[7] In his attempt to rescue Camille, Colisan stumbles into a secret passageway to the cave and eventually is forced to fight against his own rescuing party since his bandit captors have coerced him to join their party. This "robber" theme connects the French plays with not simply the Germanic gothics, but reveals the influence of such British gothic novels as Radcliffe's *A Sicilian Romance* (1790).

Something of a Franco-Germanic hybrid, *Robert Le Diable* was an extremely popular ("Grand") opera by the German-Jewish composer Giacomo Meyerbeer (Paris, 1831; libretto by Eugène Scribe and Casimir Dalevigne). Adapted from a tale taken from early French (1496; 1738) and Spanish (1627) chapbooks, as well as *Robert Le Diable,* a two-act French comedy by T. Dumerson and J.-N. Bouilly (Vaudeville, 1812), Meyerbeer's opera is set in the early eleventh century, and focuses on Robert, the child of Berthe, the Duchess of Normandy, and a devil who, in human form, seduced her. Driven from France for his monstrous deeds, Robert flees to Sicily where he attempts to kidnap the Princess Isabelle. When Robert is attacked by the princess's guards, he is rescued by the mysterious knight Bertram, who is actually his satanic father in disguise, and the two seek refuge in a military camp. Also living in the camp are Raimbaut, a bard from Normandy, and Alice, Robert's half-sister, who has come in search of Robert in order to deliver into his hands the last will and testament of their mother, Berthe.

Prone to gambling and alcohol, two prototypical aristocratic vices, Robert loses his wealth under the influence of Bertram and, even more disastrously, loses the chance to fight in single combat for the hand of Isabelle. Act III stages the most dramatic scene of the work on the gloomy rocks of St. Irene, Bertram's consultation with the demons of the underworld in a dark cavern. From this infernal chorus, Bertram learns that unless Robert freely yields to him by midnight of the next day, the power of goodness will remove him from Bertram's clutches forever. It is at just this moment that Alice stumbles into the cavern, clinging to a cross for protection, and promises not to warn Robert of his danger under threats to the life of her family. It was depictions of this particular scene, the sister clinging to the cross while under the threat of a demonic figure, that became the most popular in the opera. The recognition scene between separated parents and a child that was to become so crucial an element in the melodrama here is staged between the devil and the saving remnant, the divinely inspired sister. As he points menacingly at her, he demands her attention and recognition: "'Yes, you know me!'" Engravings of this particular scene proliferated throughout popular culture, and in fact, the representation recalls the cover of the earlier gothic British chapbook, *The Secret Tribunal* (see frontispiece). This persistent visual coding of the beleaguered but saintly female as the last and best hope for Christian salvation became

FIGURE 5: Lithograph, *Robert le Diable*, Act II, Scene IV:
Bertram to Alice: "Oui! Tu me connais!"
Courtesy of Bibliothèque-musée de l'Opéra-Paris

a potent and talismanic figure in a culture that was anxious about its own rapidly changing religious beliefs. As the population increasingly invested in the secular ideal of "human flourishing" apart from traditional religion's notions of eternal salvation, the social imaginary threw up before its eyes the threats and challenges posed by making such a decision. In *Robert le Diable* the devil is not dead; he is very much at the center of all the action. In fact, not only is God not dead, neither is Satan (see fig. 5).

Bertram's scheme to send his son's soul to hell involves Robert plucking a cypress branch from the tomb of Saint Rosalie, a violation of heaven's laws. This act concludes at the tomb where Bertram has gone to summon from their graves the spirits of debauched nuns who had been unfaithful to their vows in life. Considered the most gothic moment of the opera, the famous ballet of the ghostly nuns occurs as a *ballet blanc*, a performance that is meant to suggest another level of reality within the opera (see Guest and Jurgensen). In this ballet all the nuns, including Elena, the Mother Superior, engage in a passionate orgiastic dance designed to lead Robert to seize the magic branch. As he does so, the thunder rolls, lightning flashes, and hideous phantoms appear to present the cloister as a scene from hell. With the magical branch now at his disposal, Robert is able to enter the Princess Isabelle's bedroom and there he attempts once again to kidnap her. This scene is obviously indebted to the extremely similar myrtle branch episodes in *The Monk,* although the outcome in the opera is different. Through the power of her prayers, Isabelle breaks the hold of Bertram on Robert, and Robert destroys the magic branch, but this break is only temporary, as Robert once again falls under Bertram's influence when he loses a combat for the hand of Isabelle. In the dramatic conclusion to the opera, set in the cathedral of Palermo, Robert learns that Bertram is his father, that his rival for the hand of Isabelle is actually a knight under the control of Bertram, and that his mother's will consists only of the promise that she will continue to pray for him in heaven. Because Robert continues to waiver in pledging his allegiance to his devil-father until the cathedral chimes strike midnight, he is not doomed and instead Bertram plunges into a fiery chasm in defeat. The opera concludes with Robert's salvific marriage to Isabelle, the opera's ideology vindicating the belief that feminine purity and virtue have the power to redeem even the soul of one who is half-human, half-devil.

Robert le Diable was extremely popular in Restoration Paris, a startlingly late-gothic opera that performs almost reactionary political, religious, and cultural work. It was viewed much less sympathetically in London, where it was performed at Covent Garden in 1834.[8] Combining the gothic *topoi* of the debauched nuns, the satanic seducer, the magic branch, and the attempted desecration of a virgin, the work reminds one on several occasions of Lewis's *Monk,* except, of course, for the happy ending found by Robert and Isabelle. Written by a practicing Jew, the opera works to reaffirm the tropes of the Catholic Church and the absolute reality of the devil. But, given the late date of the opera, perhaps this is not so strange. France had invited the Bourbon Louis XVIII back to the throne in 1814, and his younger brother, Charles X, was on the throne between 1824 and 1830. The second revolution in France in 1830 introduced yet more political, social, and religious chaos and one can surmise that a work like *Robert le Diable* would be appreciated by its large audiences for an almost nostalgic glance back at a simpler, premodern, prerevolutionary era. In this work the evils of aristocrats are not really their fault because, after all, Robert's poor mother was seduced and impregnated by an agent of Satan so that his father literally is the devil. The Church in this work is similarly excused of its excesses, corruptions, and favoritism of the aristocracy, for it is presented as a literal bastion of the power of "good" to thwart the very real efforts of the devil to wreak havoc and misery on the lives of all, regardless of their class. Finally, this opera is reactionary in its celebration of the virginity of Isabelle, who is preserved on three different occasions through the literal power of divine intervention. Unlike Elvira and Antonia in Lewis's *Monk*, who are murdered and raped by their son and brother Ambrosio, Robert as son and brother honors his mother's will and resists the compulsion to rape Isabelle and dishonor his sister Alice. But this opera is not simply invested in chivalric, medieval postures, it also allows Robert and Isabelle the ideal of "human flourishing," a companionate marriage based on love, rather than a purely dynastic one of political alliances.

Meyerbeer also wrote *Les Huguenots* (1836, libretto by Émile Deschamps), an opera about a father who unwittingly kills his daughter during the St. Bartholomew massacre. The presentation of Catholicism in this work is altogether less benign. The swords used in the massacre are ritualistically blessed by the monks, while the last words of the opera are the screams of the mob: "God wants their blood" (Dieu veut leur sang). As Derek Hughes notes about a number of religious operas during this period, one of the most striking developments in the representation of sacrifice in romantic opera is that the practice is separated from religion: until late in the eighteenth century, "human sacrifice had principally been associated with religious barbarism, whether of paganism or of Christianity. With the weakening of Christianity, however, there is a sudden explosion and proliferation in the meanings attached to it" (146).

In addition to the theme of ritual sacrifice, other gothic operas attempted to explore regicide and the instability associated with the founding of the French republic. In particular, the recurrent imprisonment of women dramatized in different ways the efforts of the male population to restrain and contain women, especially those of lower social rank who had shown their energy and strength during the period of 1789–1792 by expressing their discontent with the misogynist, racist, and violent injustices of French patriarchal society. According to Charlton, the phases of the French Revolution produced opera's thematics in accord with the moment:

> The early years, 1789 to 1792, gave rise to works espousing hope in the equality of citizens, hope for constitutional monarchy, and for the self-determining unity of the French nation. The Terror years, 1793–94, produced intense didactic works about sacrifice and patriotism and works celebrating military victories. Then the fall of Robespierre (9 Thermidor II/27 July 1794) saw a resurgence of counter-revolutionary movements of all kinds; some contained old-fashioned royalists, others, constitutionalists; but they were all united against the memory of Robespierre and his "drinkers of blood." (2000, IX:57)

What we might recognize as gothic-melodramatic operas came to embody the desires and expectations of audiences that had been changed by the events of the revolutionary period. What Nodier called "the morality of the Revolution" included staged displays of pathos and presentations of virtue in distress, scenarios that enticed the audience, even if they did so with increasingly convoluted plots. Democratic in their appeal to a variety of spectators, these works advocated standing up to tyrants, traitors, or villains in order to find such secular values as individual as well as communal happiness and respect, domestic loyalty, the new work ethic, and the importance of social conformity.

III.

> The ideas of pain, and above all, of death, are so very affecting that whilst we remain in the presence of whatever is supposed to have the power of inflicting either, it is impossible to be perfectly free from terror.
> —Edmund Burke, "A Philosophical Inquiry into the Origin of Our Ideas of the Sublime and Beautiful" (1757)

Burke's aesthetic of the Sublime, with its recourse to pain, terror, and the fear of death, influenced the performative arts such as opera as well as the sentimental and gothic literary works of the period. Although this is a complex subject not wholly germane to my interests, it is important to note that the Burkean Sublime along with its association with Terror was considered to provide access to notions of the Divine and the expansive human soul. In their use of the acoustics of pain, imprisonment, and life-threatening events, rescue operas enacted in a grandiose manner their culture's political and religious upheavals. Their popularity before, during, and after the Revolution reveals a good deal about the vexed and ambivalent relationship between France, Germany, and England during this period. It is also important to recognize the gothic as an aesthetic mode that increased interaction between librettists, composers, and artists of the two countries who "borrowed" ideas, ideologies, acting styles, and even scripts and libretti from each other. Another crucial constituent of the genre's success was how audience dynamics had an impact on and reflected the popularity of the genre, together with the changing French public which started to resemble the more established British tradition of a diversified audience. With working citizens increasingly attending the theater and along with Shakespeare's growing popularity in France and Germany, spectators' tastes were altered and this called for a theatrical experience full of direct emotional appeal and involvement. This new audience was interested in action-packed scenarios (the three unities rule of classical theater forbidding actions on stage clearly did not apply to the new melodramatic plots), and rapidly developing intrigues rather than the slow building *tableaux* that had been popular in France earlier. Even though some theater critics considered the new theater to be a blatant pandering to the lowest elements, with its heavy reliance on grotesque prison scenes, dramatic escapes, wild crowd scenes, and the simplistic triumph of the just over the unjust, the public that sought entertainment rather than edification now expected to be able to witness recognizable personal experiences that could serve as a means to self-knowledge (Kennedy, 19–21).

Rescue operas developed along two somewhat different lines: "tyrant" operas or "humanitarian" operas within the general category of *opera semiseria*, or *opéra comique*. The first type corresponds to the loyalty gothic, with its focus on the trials and tribulations of the aristocracy, while the second type draws upon the virtue in distress or woman in jeopardy genre, with its focus on middle-class characters or women as the captured or besieged victims. The first category emphasized political injustice or abstract questions of law and embodied the threat of tyranny in an evil man who unjustly imprisons a noble character. Etienne Méhul's *Euphrosine ou le Tyran Corrige,* and H.-M. Berton's *Les rigueurs du cloître* (both 1790) are typical examples of this type. *Euphrosine,* for instance, concerns three sisters, Léonore, Louise, and Euphrosine, who seek the protection of the Count of Coradin after their father dies. Coradin's castle contains a young knight who is imprisoned in a tower, as well as Coradin's former fiancé, the Countess d'Arles, the villainess of the piece, who competes with Euphrosine for the love of the count and does so through all manner of convoluted stratagems involving the imprisoned knight. Only after Euphrosine pretends to swallow the poison sent to her by the confused Coradin, is the truth about the countess revealed and all can end happily. Part *Blue Beard, Lear,* and *Romeo and Juliet, Euphrosine* was an incredibly popular production and became famous for its vivid presentation of the emotions, particularly in the "jealousy" duet of the second act.

"Humanitarian" operas, on the other hand, do not depict a tyrant, but instead portray an individual—usually a woman or a worthy bourgeois—who sacrifices everything in order to correct an injustice or to obtain some person's freedom. Nicholas Dalayrac's *Raoul, Sire de Créqui* (1789) or J.-N. Bouilly and Luigi Cherubini's *Les deux journées* (1800) are examples, along with Sédaine's pre-1789 works. A very interesting rescue opera that actually combines both "tyrant" and "humanitarian" strains is *Ossian ou Les Bardes* by Jean-François Le Sueur, libretto by P. Dercy and Jean Marie Deschamps (1804). *Ossian* is based on the preromantic bard James Macpherson's *faux* Celtic ballads (*Fragments of Ancient Poetry, Collected in the High-*

lands of Scotland, and Translated from the Gallic or Erse Language, 1760; and *Fingal,* 1761), immensely popular in Britain, Germany, and France, and particularly beloved by Napoleon, who carried a copy of *Fingal* in his pocket and had a bust and painting of Ossian on display in Josephine's home, Malmaison (see Okun). In England the Ossian tradition made its way onto the stage at Drury Lane with the popular ballet-pantomime *Oscar and Malvina; or the Hall of Fingal* (1804). Whereas Germans saw in the Ossian legend a resurgence in Nordic mythology and translated all of Macpherson's works by 1769, the French saw instead a rival tradition, a Celtic spirit that vindicated their imperialistic and nationalistic ambitions. In fact, Napoleon claimed that the historical existence of an ancient Celtic tribe (the Gauls) actually provided his new French empire with an alternative pseudohistorical tradition that justified his overthrow of the effete Bourbons (see C. Smith, "Ossian"). The plot of *Ossian* is extended over five acts, but its events concern the usual fare of the rescue opera. Ossian's betrothed, Rozmala, has been captured by the savage Scandinavian Prince Duntalmo, who not only intends to force his son Mornal on her, but also to impose the worship of the alien god Odin on the Caledonians (the Celts). Ossian agrees to single combat with Mornal in order to reclaim the hand of Rozmala, but before such an event can occur, Ossian is lured onto a mountain bridge that is cut beneath him by the Scandinavians. Saved by his men, Ossian is captured and imprisoned in a vast cavern with Rozmala and her father, Rozmor, all three condemned to be burned at the stake as human sacrifices to Odin.

At this point in the opera, Act IV, Ossian falls asleep and has a long and elaborate dream about the afterlife that is staged through a series of vivid *tableaux.* This dream sequence was so visually spectacular on stage that it was the subject of a number of paintings by Jean-August-Dominique Ingres (1780–1867) that were immensely popular in both England and France. Although Ingres produced his masterpiece on the same subject in 1813, the earlier *tableaux* version designed for the operatic stage is reminiscent of the works of Raphael, an influence on both Ingres and William Blake, who also produced a number of engravings of the divinely inspired bard (see Mongan). Finally, at the moment before the sacrificial stakes are to be lit, the three prisoners are freed by the Caledonian warriors who have been led into battle by the chief Caledonian bard Hydala, and all ends happily for Ossian and Rozmala. What is most interesting about this opera, apart from the fact that it was commissioned by Napoleon, is its clear distinction between the rival Celtic and Norse heritages, the presentation of an alien and pagan religion associated with blood sacrifice, and the use of the bard as a political and military hero, as well as a culturally powerful figure. In suggesting that religions are tied to national identity and that clan membership requires the willingness to fight to the death to preserve one's borders, the *Ossian* myth activates and privileges an earlier, primitive worldview that, ironically, Napoleon the imperialist was keen to propagate.

In addition to the tyrant/humanitarian themes that we can see operating in a piece like *Ossian*, there were a number of *operas semiserias* that combined comic and horrible events with both aristocratic and lower-class characters, and were well suited to the sentimentality of the period. Ironically, in a manner reminiscent of Sade, these operas specialized in juxtaposing the pathetic with the appalling without having to carry through the action to a tragic conclusion. Ferdinando Paër is remembered today as one of the major practitioner of *opera semiseria*, and one of his most famous rescue operas was *Camilla, o sia Il sotterraneo* (Paris, 1790; Vienna, 1799; Haymarket 1806), whose plot bears a striking resemblance to the "Duchess C" episode of Genlis's *Adelaide and Theodore* (1783), as can be seen from the brief synopsis of the action, which virtually retells the same story (see Balthazar *NGD*, 816–18). This grand serio, comic opera makes heavy use of macabre settings, aberrant psychology, and jarring juxtapositions of the comic with the serious. The heroine Camilla has been imprisoned for seven years when the opera begins, forced to inhabit the underground vaults of a ruined castle in Naples owned by Duke Uberto, her husband by a secret marriage. The reason for Camilla's banishment is provided quickly: she has refused to reveal the identity of a man who once kidnapped and tried to seduce her, albeit unsuccessfully. After much confusion over false identities and forced confessions, Loredano and Cola, the duke's nephew and servant, rescue Camilla and her son Adolfo. Loredano is himself forced to confess that he was the abductor and he clears Camilla of suspicion of adultery so that she can be reconciled to her husband and son (Balthazar *NGD*, 1150).

Another example of an *opera semiseria* by Paër, *I Fuorusciti de Firenze* (1802), reveals yet another strain of the rescue opera, the exile or outlaw opera that would become particularly popular by 1830 (Balthazar *NGD*, 316). In this work, Princess Isabella of Florence has been kidnapped by Uberto's banditti and imprisoned in a ruined Tuscan castle. His inveterate enemy Edoardo de Liggozzi, Isabella's husband, had exiled Uberto himself from Florence twenty years earlier. In the disguise of a shepherd, Edoardo attempts to rescue his wife, but is captured and forced to reveal his true identity. Rather than kill the pair, Uberto suddenly reveals that twenty years earlier he had left an infant daughter in Florence when he was forced into exile: Isabella. As one might expect, a happy ending is provided amid much sudden light relief. A work such as *I Fuorusciti di Firenze* reveals how thoroughly the gothic had been sentimentalized or melodramatized by the turn of the century. By then, the use of the reconciliation or reunion between parent and child, a staple of stage melodramas such as Pixérécourt's *Coelina,* had infiltrated opera (Balthazar *NGD,* 1293–94).

It is also important to recognize the role that German composers played in the development of gothic opera, and here one could point to E. T. A. Hoffmann's "Zauberoper" (magical opera) *Undine* (1816), based on Friedrich de la Motte Fouqué's tale about a water spirit who disastrously trades her immortality in order to marry her human lover, Huldbrand. Also within the household is Bertalda, the beautiful daughter of a simple fisherman, who is tortured by visions of witches by Undine's evil uncle, Kühleborn, who is himself intent on keeping the marriage between Undine and Huldbrand intact. Hoffmann's operatic adaptation of the Motte Fouqué fairy tale was also a particularly important influence on Carl Maria von Weber (1786–1826), a Catholic and close friend of Meyerbeer. Weber's *Der Freischütz* (1821, libretto by Friedrich Kind) has been called by Linda Hutcheon "the most famous and influential of Romantic operas" (160). As she notes, Weber's opera "almost single-handedly created the German Romantic taste for gloomy forests, echoing hunters' horns, supernatural dangers, and young love threatened" (160). *Der Freichütz* (The Marksman) is based on a German folk legend about a young ranger named Max who needs to win a shooting contest in order to claim the right to marry his beloved, Agatha. Because he has missed his last several shots, he is vulnerable to the machinations of a fellow ranger, Kaspar, who has sold his soul to the devil and is hoping to find in the lovely Agatha a sacrificial substitute to offer to the devil in his place. A folk-version of the *Faust* tale, the similarity in plot to Maturin's *Melmoth the Wanderer* (1820) is also striking. Kaspar persuades Max to go with him to the ominous wolf's den at midnight in order to cast seven magic bullets that will have the power to kill anything the shooter wants.

Act II presents Agatha in a foreboding mood, recalling that a hermit in the forest had once warned her that if she should ever be menaced by some danger, she would be protected by wearing her bridal wreath, an obvious fetishization of virginity. The act concludes with the most gothic scene in the opera, the casting of the magic bullets in the dark and demonic wolf's gorge. As Max arrives, the ghost of his mother appears to him, warning him to leave. But Zamiel, the devil disguised as a "black" ranger, counters this by conjuring up the image of Agatha in the act of drowning herself in a watery grave should Max not win the shooting event (and the reference here to Hoffmann's *Undine* is obvious). Kaspar with the assistance of Zamiel supervises the creation of the bullets in the wolf's den amidst demoniacal screams. Act III begins again by emphasizing Agatha's victimization, showing her first in prayer and then suffering from an ominous and foreboding dream about the day's shooting match. As her cousin Ännchen delivers Agatha's bridal wreath, she opens the box only to discover instead a funeral wreath and Agatha again recalls the warning she had received from the hermit. At the match later that day, Max takes aim at a dove as his final shot, but Zamiel guides the bullet so that it hits Agatha (Finale: "See, oh see, he shoots his bride"). As foretold by the hermit who now stands by her side, the bridal wreath deflects the bullet and Agatha is saved. Zamiel grabs Kaspar in frustrated revenge and Kaspar dies with a curse for all on his lips. Duke Ottokar, the presiding justice, has Kaspar's body thrown into the wolf's gorge and allows Max to explain how he was tricked by Kaspar into casting the magic bullets. After a year's penance, Max and Agatha are allowed to marry with the duke's blessing.

Weber's opera is now considered the first German romantic opera, but is it also a gothic opera? Clearly, it uses gothic devices such as ghosts, ominous dreams, and demon possession, and it reworks a number of religious tropes in ways that are conservative and sympathetic to Catholicism. Richard Wagner (1813–1883) credited *Der Freischütz* as an early and important influence on his own *Der fliegende Holländer* (1843; The Flying Dutchman), writing "*Der Freischütz* in particular appealed very strongly to my imagination, mainly on account of its ghostly theme. The emotions of terror and dread of ghosts formed quite an important factor in the development of my mind. From my earliest childhood certain mysterious and uncanny things exercised an enormous influence over me" (qtd. Hutcheon, 160). The other major Germanic "Schaueroper" (horror operas) that were popular during this period were the two rival *Vampyr* operas that were produced in 1829, one by Peter Joseph von Lindpaintner and one by Heinrich August Marschner, and both based on the tale written by John Polidori (1819). *Der Vampyr* by Marschner was particularly influential on Wagner's depiction of the Dutchman, an undead spirit cursed by his immortality and forced to wander for eternity (much like the Wandering Jew).

To return, however, to the rescue opera as the quintessential embodiment of gothic opera, Beethoven's *Fidelio* (1805; 1814) is perhaps the most famous of all the so-called rescue operas, and considered by many to be the final flowering and only masterpiece of the genre. Beethoven's work was based on *Léonore ou l'amour conjugal* (Jean-Nicolas Bouilly's libretto and Pierre Gaveaux's score), an *opéra comique* that opened at the Théâtre Feydeau on February 19, 1798. Paër adapted the same opera as *Lenora, ossia l'Amore conjugale* (Dresden, 1804) and it was next adapted by Johann Simon Mayr as *L'Amour conjugal* (Padua, 1805). Each of these versions of the same story skillfully combines elements of both "tyrant" and "humanitarian" rescue-operas. Bouilly's *Léonore* drew on recent French innovations with the imprisonment *topos*, the female singer in the male role, and the use of the rescue plot. Performed in the former ultraroyalist but pro-Italian opera Théâtre de Monsieur, with its attendant social and political reputation, its composer played the role of Florestan in an intrigue that engaged "French history by dramatizing a political crime at a sensitive juncture in the Directoire (1795–99)." "[H]istorically self-referential," it showed with very slight disguise "events that had occurred in recent life." According to Charlton, the *Leonore* libretto belongs to the Thermidorean reaction period after the end of the monarchy and the beginning of the revolutionary dictatorship (2000, IX:57).

Beethoven's *Fidelio* was first performed in Vienna in 1805 as a three-act opera originally entitled *Leonore, oder der triumph der ehelichen liebe* (Leonore, of The Triumph of Married Love) as Napoleon invaded Austria. The 1814 definitive version bore the title of *Fidelio* instead, celebrated the triumph of liberty over tyranny, and clearly marked Napoleon as a tyrant in Beethoven's eyes. Indeed, *Fidelio* played over and over again during the Congress of Vienna in 1815. The extensive revisions of the 1814 opera most famously include a rewritten finale that occurs in the light of day rather than in the darkness of a prison cell, and Floristan's celebrated vision of Leonore in Act II in the form of an angel ("Und spur'ich nicht linde, sanftsauselnde Luft?"; "And do I not feel the balmy, gently rustling air?"). Originally set in Spain, the story concerns a young woman, Lenora, who has disguised herself as the boy Fidele in order to move into a jail that imprisons her husband Florestano. She apprentices herself to the jailer Rocco, hoping to be able to use her position to free Florestano, unjustly imprisoned for two years by the tyrant Pizzarro because Florestano had exposed the crimes of Pizzarro and thus made himself a victim of the unjust abuse of power. Pizzarro learns that his supervisor, Fernando, will arrive for a visit the next day, and he fears that his treachery will be discovered and punished. In desperation, he commands Rocco to prepare Florestan for assassination, to be performed by the masked Pizzarro, and witnessed by the devoted apprentice Fidele. But Fidele stalls long enough for Fernando to arrive and rescue her husband. Rocco is pardoned, and Pizzarro imprisoned. Even though Bouilly's politics bespoke liberalism, his *Léonore* avoided explicit political allegorizing. Structured around motive and incident, it nevertheless portrayed the villain Pizarro as a tyrannical monster. His cruelty, described by a chorus of prisoners in the dungeon, commented on the excesses of 1793–94 rather than made any commentary on the ancien régime, while the finale celebrated the return of justice and truth (Charlton 2000, IX:64–67).

Other works that anticipated *Fidelio* include Sédaine's *Comte d'Albert*, and his *Le déserteur*, which must have influenced Beethoven since it was "the most frequently performed stage work in Germany of any genre" (Charlton, IX:54–55). Dalayrac's *Raoul, Sire de Créqui* also prefigured *Fidelio* politically and dramatically and its English adaptation at the Theatre Royal, Drury Lane in 1792 includes the cross-dressing of two women as soldiers who seek to liberate the brother of one of them. A copy of Paër's score for *Lenora*, discovered among Beethoven's effects after his death, reveals that he had certainly studied and was influenced by Paër's version of the famous tale. In Beethoven's version, there are very few changes in the story. Again, Florestan is captured by the villainous Pizarro and held in a supposedly impregnable dungeon, while Florestan's wife Leonore disguises herself as a boy, as in the other versions, in order to rescue her husband.

Beethoven's musical genius elevates his version above the others, while the revised 1814 libretto by Georg Friedrich Treitschke emphasizes Leonore's status as "Retterin," or savior of her husband. The 1814 version most famously includes Leonore's aria, "Abscheulicher! Wo eilst du hin?" (Monster! Where are you hurrying?), in which she addresses the unjust tyranny of Pizzaro and declares her role as a divinely inspired wife, embodiment of feminine virtue, and heroic savior of the suffering victims of injustice:

> I follow an inner compulsion,
> I do not falter,
> Strengthened by the duty
> Of faithful married love!
> O you, for whom I bore everything,
> Could I but penetrate the place
> Where evil threw you in chains,
> And bring you sweet comfort! (II)

The *reconnaissance* or reconciliation scene between husband and wife in prison stands as the high point of the work, while the rescuing troops arrive in the nick of time so that the hero can be snatched from the jaws of death, rescued from autocratic tyranny, and welcomed into the brave new world of liberty, equality, and fraternity.

Clearly the rescue opera had become a popular genre throughout Europe by 1800 and Beethoven's *Fidelio* was embraced as a paean in praise of liberty and human dignity. But like gothic novels, rescue operas also played a particularly influential role in reforming notions of exactly what its genre should look and sound like. As Balthazar points out, such operas emphasized continuous action, formal complexity in structure, and a certain amount of dramatic and musical comedy (*NGD*, 1150). More importantly, however, they were one of the means by which the tropes of northern Romanticism, particularly the emphasis on individual responsibilities, Protestantism, and bourgeois morality and subjectivity, attempted to infiltrate southern Europe. This notion of rival northern/southern European traditions would be the basis of Germaine de Staël's historical paradigm in *De l'Allemagne* (1812), in which she argued that the sack of Rome by the northern barbarians had been providential because it allowed Europe to combine the best of both civilizations: the intellectual quickness of the Romans with the stern morality ("chivalry") and ponderous seriousness ("spirituality") of the Goths. For de Staël, the best literature is "gothic," that is, a mixture of chivalry and Christianity, preferably of the Protestant variety (Miles 2003). This mixing of northern European tropes with southern operatic styles produced a potent performative model that expressed serious religious, political, and social concerns at the same time it entertained the masses. And as I have argued, the agenda of gothic opera shifted, from an initial endorsement of the aristocracy to an increasingly liberal and secular investment in individual rights and the sanctity of the private conscience in union with its reformed public institutions.

Finally, what does it mean that European citizens flocked to a number of these rescue operas before, during, and after the French Revolution? What was at stake in staging and viewing the performances? The opera embodied a public space in which European citizens could vicariously experience the threats of violent political, social, and cultural revolutions. But ultimately, the rescue operas were secularizing productions that placed worthy bourgeois citizens in a variety of threatening but ultimately redeemed situations. The operas were also deeply nationalistic for each country, even though, ironically, they used the same tropes and told (and retold) the same narratives. Each country was trying to use the theater and the opera house to impose a form of secularized national identity on its emerging bourgeois populace. As Gerald Newman observes, Britain sought to see itself and its citizens in national and secular terms rather than in religious or tribal ones during the mid-eighteenth-century. This shift was made possible, according to Newman, because of cultural rather than political activity, with one of the central figures being the "artist-intellectual," an individual who "both creates and organizes nationalist ideology" (56). A composite figure begins to emerge here: the adaptation and use of Handel as the artist and Shakespeare as the intellectual, dual presences hovering as protectors over the secularizing landscape of European discourse. Benedict Anderson has also discussed the growth of secularism as allowing for a new sort of "imagined community," a country with a "national imagination" that would replace the religious construction of the medieval and renaissance communities (6, 36). But this notion has recently been challenged by Cohen and Dever, who argue that it is more accurate to see "transnational" and cosmopolitan forms of culture—like opera—created by "communities of sentiment" that exist in an imaginative space "in-between" nation-states, rather than "in" them (1–34). There is no question that the institutionalization of the popular, hybridized opera during the late eighteenth and early nineteenth centuries was a central development in the growth of the ideal of human flourishing.

Each of these countries evolved differently, with France undergoing a violent revolution that was distinctly different and yet uncannily similar in some ways to the earlier British revolution of the seventeenth century. At the conclusion of their brief experiment with a commonwealth, the British people welcomed back the king on their own terms, and the country has not seriously contemplated violent social or political reform since. France's prolonged sojourn in feudalism made for a combustible situation that ignited in 1789, and created an unstable and contested situation for most of the next century. Both countries staged dozens of rescue operas, read hundreds of gothic novels, and schooled themselves in the tenets of secularization, modernization, and nationalism. Taking their inspiration from northern European sources—Shakespeare, Ossian, and French and British history especially—these texts were written in the uncertainty that defines ambivalent secularization. Through the rescue trope, they romanced the past, lured in spectators with terrifying scenes and rhetorical turns, even as they hybridized genre and denounced the injustices and arbitrariness of the throne. So great was the appeal of the rescue opera that its descendant, the melodrama, remains with us to this day as the very embodiment of religious, political, and emotional hyperbole.

- CHAPTER 3 -

Ghostly Visitants

The Gothic Drama and the Coexistence of Immanence and Transcendence

I sing the Forms which magic Pow'rs impart,
The thin Creation of delusive Art,
And thro' the ambient Gloom bright Shapes display
Hid from the Sun, nor conscious of the Day.
Expand the sportive Scene, the Lantern show,
No gleam of Day must thro' the Darkness glow.
—Walter Titley, "The Magic Lantern" (1731)

I.

After something of an absence, ghosts began to rise up through trapdoors and onto theatrical stages throughout Europe during the eighteenth century, and the question is, why? The appearances of ghosts, particularly in the works of Shakespeare, had always produced an extremely popular dramatic effect, one that audiences anticipated and enjoyed. With the advent of sensibilities informed by the currents of rationalism and scientism, however, ghosts fell on hard times. As Keith Thomas notes, they had become socially irrelevant by the eighteenth century (1971, 606), so one of the central controversies during the development of gothic drama was what to do with the transcendent residue that was the ghost? How could a rational and reasonable European countenance the meddling of ghosts in the action of dramas? Or, as Henry Fielding put it in *Tom Jones,* ghosts "are indeed, like arsenic, and other dangerous drugs in physic, to be used with the utmost caution" (316). Although attempts were made to do away with ghosts and other supernatural paraphernalia, the gothic dramatist soon came to realize that banishing the supernatural altogether was not what the audience wanted. This chapter will trace the appearances of a variety of ghosts as lingering manifestations of what Taylor has defined as the "porous self." That is, by placing a ghost at the center of the dramatic action and forcing the protagonist to confront and sometimes speak to a ghost in order to solve the mystery, the gothic drama held up to its audiences a reanimated picture of the older transcendent belief system, suggesting that believing in such an option was still in fact imaginatively possible in a world in which one had many intellectual options for the pursuit of "human flourishing." By using Charles Taylor's theories, we can also claim that the ambivalent theatrical depictions of the ghost represent yet again the uncanny doubleness at the heart of ambivalent secularization. That is to say, gothic drama seeks to contain within itself the new secularization paradigm: both the old, premodern world view as well as the newer immanent perspective. At the conclusion of many of these dramas, a "buffered self" emerges and addresses the audience, but the focus and energy throughout the work has been on the trials and tribulations of the "porous self" who has been confronted with a ghost who represents the powers of the transcendent as well as the potency of the past. One could claim that in presenting both modes of consciousness on stage, the gothic drama attempted to have it both ways, preserving God, the devil, and the scientific agenda in one powerfully seductive imaginative construction. The gothic drama was immensely popular because it was invested in presenting for its audience a magical and imaginary space wherein the immanent and transcendent could coexist. Such a practice reveals that the rational and the supernatural were viewed as equal options for the audience to accept, with belief a question of the individual's own preference. As such, the reemergence of the ghost on the gothic stage represents yet another cultural practice that served to instantiate scenarios of ambivalent secularity.

It is necessary to begin, however, by sketching the broader conditions of the theatrical scene during this period. The growth of European theatrical entertainments in the late eighteenth and early nineteenth centuries was fairly sudden for a number of economic and social reasons. First, the sphere in which theaters competed with each other expanded as a robust economy produced an ever-increasing market of independent artisans and bourgeoisie with disposable income. Early nineteenth-century London also saw a dramatic increase in theatrical productions, largely resulting from the new and broader interpretations given to the Licensing Act of

1737. Originally, this act had created a theatrical monopoly for the two royal theaters (called patent theaters) in London—Drury Lane and Covent Garden—with a sort of loophole for the existence of the Haymarket, which was allowed to stage plays during the summer months. But in the early nineteenth century the theatrical legislation was reinterpreted to allow other and minor theaters to exist as long as they did not present dramas (which were defined as performances of spoken dialogue only). As Jane Moody notes in her study of "illegitimate" theater in London, it was the political culture of the 1790s, the fall of the Bastille, and England's war against Napoleon that "provided the iconographic catalyst for the rise of an illegitimate drama. This theatre of physical peril, visual spectacle, and ideological confrontation challenged both the generic premises and the cultural dominance of legitimate drama" (10). And very quickly technologies of visual spectacle developed to complement the "illegitimate" productions of melodrama, the gothic, pantomimes, burlettas, and various quadruped extravaganzas. The minor theaters for the most part confined themselves to melodramatic works, which by necessity included musical numbers, sung discourse (much in the tradition of operatic recitative), and military, nautical, and pantomimic fare. By 1843, with the revocation of the Licensing Act, there were twenty-one theaters in London alone, in addition to a number of optical entertainments such as panoramas carrying on the tradition of the Eidophusikon (Ziter, 20–21).

Theater managers who wanted to remain competitive in Paris or London had to keep pace in their use of pyrotechnics and other devices that would continue to enthrall their audiences. As Paula Backsheider has noted, the growth of the London minor theaters as a mass form of popular entertainment required "the bombardment of the senses and the use of techniques that fixed manipulative tableaux in the audiences' memories" (150). Intense activity on stage alternated with *tableaux vivants* and the designers of these extravaganzas intended to create what was known as *Stimmung,* "moments when a landscape seems charged with alien meaning, or what we would recognize as romantic epiphany" (169). As attendance at theaters increased throughout the nineteenth century, the technologies involved in stagecraft had to improve and advancements in lighting, stage machinery, setting, and sound effects were all of major importance in the spectacularization of theatrical fare. In 1815 Covent Garden opened for the first night of its new season, proudly announcing that "The Exterior, with the Grand Hall and Staircase will be illuminated by Gas." The Olympic Theater followed suit the next month, and in 1817 Drury Lane and the Lyceum both installed gas lighting (Rees, 9). It was not long before the gradual development of "gas tables" or "gas floats" allowed theatrical managers to control the intensity of light in separate areas of the stage during a performance.

Lighting effects were crucial to the development of gothic drama and, in particular, to depicting the supernatural on stage. Limelight was first used in 1837 at Covent Garden by heating a block of quicklime so that it would create a bright spotlight effect on the stage. Such developments extended the earlier work of Philippe Jacques de Loutherbourg (1740–1812), who had used colored lights for his Eidophusikon (1781), a miniature theater on Panton Street, off Leicester Square. As Paul Ranger notes, information no longer exists that would allow us to know exactly how he created his lighting effects, but we do have descriptions by his contemporary W. H. Pyne, who left a detailed record of one of the scenes at the Eidophusikon, of "dawn breaking over London." Serving as the design coordinator of Drury Lane between 1773 and 1781 under the management of David Garrick, Loutherbourg was responsible for, as he put it, "all which concerns the decorations and machines dependent upon them, the way of lighting them and their manipulation" (qtd. Ranger, 86). We also know that Loutherbourg mounted a batten of lamps above the proscenium that threw all their light on the scene while in front of them he placed stained glass chips of yellow, red, green, purple and blue, all of which rotated, changing and mixing as the altering atmospheric changes required (Altick, 123).

Loutherbourg also developed what Pyne has called "the picturesque of sound" to accompany his Eidophusikon. Lightning, thunder, rushing water waves, and the groans of devilish spirits trapped on the burning lake of hell were his particular specialties (qtd. Altick, 124), and we can see how lighting and optical effects were being combined when we look at the stage directions for an 1826 theatrical production of Henry M. Milner's *Alonzo the Brave, or The Spectre Bride*, itself an adaptation of Lewis's ballad "Alonzo the Brave and the Fair Imogene": "The figures cast back their mantles and display the forms of Skeletons! . . . [A] strong red light fills the back of the cavern" (qtd. Rees, 150). Such visual effects were extremely effective in conveying an atmosphere of the uncanny on stage and, as such, contributed to the popularity of gothic adaptations well into the midcentury. But it is also important to note that the gothic during this period was poised between two competing traditions: the older one was based on the appearance of mysterious, external, or supernatural forms of anxiety, such as those found in traditional religious beliefs (monks, nuns, witches, demons) during magic lantern shows; while the second and newer shape taken by the gothic was even more terrifying because it attempted to produce unstable, internalized hallucinations of monsters that emerged out of individual psyches through the power of the morbid and terrified imagination, for example, Joanna Baillie's *Orra* (see Hoeveler 2000). This second form is similar to the ethos captured in Goya's print of the monsters that are loosed during "the sleep of reason" (see fig. 1), and in many ways, attending the gothic theater during this period placed one into an uncanny space in which the immanent and the transcendent orders interacted with each, coexisted on the same plane, and reanimated the experience of the earlier "porous self" as it sought to protect itself against the realm of anima and magic.

II.

> The fleeting Forms abhor the envious Light,
> Love the brown Shade, and only live by Night.
> Darkling and silent in her lonely Cell,
> The Sorceress thus exerts her mystic Spell,
> Calls forth the Spectres, and unpeoples Hell;
> But when the Morn unfolds her purple Ray,
> Start the pale Ghosts, and fly approaching Day.
>
> —Walter Titley, "The Magic Lantern" (1731)

In December 1781, ten years after first arriving in London to work for David Garrick, Loutherbourg visited Fonthill Abbey, the estate of William Beckford, where he had been hired to transform the mansion into "a labyrinthine and necromantic environment for a three-day Christmas performance-masquerade" (Ziter, 19). This transformation was so effective and dramatic that Beckford himself described the event as "the realization of romance in all its fervours, in all its extravagance ... I wrote *Vathek* immediately upon my return to London at the close of this romantic villegiatura" (qtd. Altick, 122n). Although we have no detailed description of exactly how this "villegiatura" was constructed, we do have a few clues. Boyd Alexander, for instance, has proposed that Loutherbourg's chief contribution to the entertainments was taken from the Pandemonimum scene in his Eidophusikon program, described by viewers who saw it later in London:

> Here, in the fore-ground of a vista, stretching an immeasurable length between mountains, ignited from their bases to their lofty summits, with many-colored flame, a chaotic mass rose in dark majesty, which gradually assumed form until it stood, the interior of a vast temple of gorgeous architecture, bright as molten brass, seemingly composed of unconsuming and unquenchable fire. (83–84)

CHAPTER 3

This exteriorization of Miltonic tropes found its way into *Vathek* (1786) in perhaps no less dramatic ways, and if Loutherbourg inadvertently provided the visual stimulus for the creation of *Vathek,* he was also without doubt one of the most important pioneers in the development of optical entertainments, as his 1781 Eidophusikon produced a new and exciting visual experience for the London theater-going public. A miniaturized optical extravaganza, the Eidophusikon reproduced settings from the entire Mediterranean world that were then shown in conjunction with lighting effects that went from sunrise to moon glow to fire and storm. Using rear-lit transparencies, colored plates, a variety of fabrics, and panoramic dioramas, the Eidophusikon created in its viewers a new level of visual excitement and sophistication and established a new standard that the British theater-going public came to expect (Ziter, 19; also see McCalman).

Twenty years later, in 1801, the famous Belgian balloonist Étienne-Gaspard Robertson (1763–1837) arrived in Britain from France to present his "Gothic extravaganzas" for the public, and he was welcomed as a sensation but not a particularly new one. Robertson's originality as a stage-crafter was not in his conceptions, but in his more technically sophisticated use of mechanically projected images, set off one after another and accompanied by eerie music and lighting effects. Honing his skills in the deserted cloister of the Capuchins in Paris, Robertson had transformed the space into a "theater of the macabre" (Stafford, 301). Relying on sheets stretched from one end of the cloister to the other, Robertson mounted his "fantascope," a large magic lantern that was able to slide back and forth on a double track and project images on the screen from behind. These images could increase or decrease in size, but their subject matter was the major focus of the show: "looming ten-foot-high, bisexual, horned and web-footed devils," "the head of Medusa, a bloody nun, the tomb of the recently executed French king Louis XVI, . . . and the ghost of the Abbess Heloise" (Castle, 144–50). When he wasn't displaying the "Dance of the Witches" or "The Ballet of the Mummies," Robertson was creating other images that were then projected onto clouds of smoke and accompanied by eerie music played on a glass harmonica, said to have been invented by Benjamin Franklin (Stafford, 303).

As Simon During has noted, the art of projected images actually dates back to 1656, when a magic lantern show was first exhibited at the Hôtel de Liancourt in Paris. This performance was so spiritually unsettling that Jean Loret in the audience that night composed a verse about the spectacle: "Seeing this magic / Act with so much energy / I made certain / To cross myself / Over and over again" (qtd. During, 265). While the discovery of the microscope in almost the same year seemed to allow its viewers to behold the miracle of life, the use of the magic lantern reminded them of death, irrationality, and opaque and delusive thoughts. The next exhibition of the magic lantern show seems to have been in Leipzig during the 1760s, where the coffee-shop owner Johann Shröpfer converted a room in his shop into a séance chamber (Warner, 146; also see Myrone and Heard). Following that, the magician Paul Philipsthal (aka Paul Philidor) began perfecting his stage performances in Berlin (1790), Vienna (1791), Paris (1792–93), and London (1801).

But the magic lantern can be situated in other realms than the gothic, and Jonathan Crary places its origins in the discovery of the camera obscura in 1671 as developed by the Jesuit Athanasius Kircher (1601–1680). According to Crary, "Kircher devised techniques for flooding the inside of the camera with a visionary brilliance, using various artificial light sources, mirrors, projected images, and sometimes translucent gems in place of a lens to simulate divine illumination" (33). In this tradition, the magic lantern operates without the transparency to which truth aspires, while Kircher himself thought his experiment would allow people to communicate their "secret thoughts" across a distance (qtd. Crary, 39). Ironically, what began as a counter-reformation Roman Catholic demonstration of "divine illumination" became over time an emblem of the more interior, private, Protestant belief in a personal God or, barring that possibility, a visual descent into the realm of death.

The camera obscura's most dramatic use was its ability to produce flickering images within its narrow confines, for instance, either simulating branches moving in the wind or people walking along the street. As Crary notes, "movement and time could be seen and experienced, but never represented" (34), and hence the camera obscura "is inseparable from a certain metaphysic of interiority: it is a figure for both the observer who is nominally a free sovereign individual and a privatized subject confined in a quasi-domestic space, cut off from a public exterior world" (39). It is precisely the coexistence of the immanent and the transcendent as witnessed in the camera obscura/magic lantern show that will be examined in relation to the gothic drama. In the dialectical interplay between these two realms we can see how audience members are forced into the posture of "porous selves," are terrorized, and then gradually are directed to understanding the natural laws that explain the phenomena that they had just witnessed. In short, they moved from being porous to buffered in the act of viewing and de-mystifying the magic lantern show, a cultural performative technology that staged the very ambivalence at the heart of the secularization process itself.

CHAPTER 3

The "phantom" who appears most frequently in gothic dramas is a ghost who very literally stalks the stage and frequently speaks in order to warn the protagonist of impending danger. But such a material representation of a nonmaterial being was in itself an impossibility, as anyone who understood the world of the spiritual would have grasped. By reviving the ghost and presenting it as a gendered and material reality on the gothic stage, the dramatists of the period were participating in what Taylor has called a revival of the "porous self," a depiction of that earlier being who had little if any protection from the world of anima, magic, and random and chance disasters. Elite culture had made decisive moves to establish the "buffered self" as the ideal in its literary productions by presenting narratives that showed the triumphant operation of "disciplined, [and] instrumentally rational orders of mutual benefit" (295), and one can think here of the poetic works of Anna Letitia Barbauld as an example. But the popular gothic stage was another cultural sphere altogether. Here the "porous self" ran rampant and one suspects that the artisan and middle classes were much more comfortable in this ghost-haunted environment than in the chilly climes of Latitudinarian and Unitarian assurances against the existence of ghosts.

To return to the magic lantern, though, it is necessary to focus on its fairly crude subject matter: the series of shocking figures that it presented to viewers, derived from such stock gothic representations as the bleeding nun or ghost, adapted by Étienne-Gaspard Robertson in France during the Revolution, and then transported by him to London to wide acclaim. He advertised the first performance of his "Phantasmagorie" in the *Journal de Paris*, December 16, 1792. Draping the Capuchin convent walls in black and painting them with hieroglyphs, Robertson attempted to convey the atmosphere of a temple to Isis, while he began the performance with a speech: "It is a useful spectacle for a man to discover the bizarre effects of the imagination when it combines force and disorder; I wish to speak of the terror which shadows, symbols, spells, the occult works of magic inspire. I have promised that I will raise the dead and I will raise them" (qtd. Warner, 149). In a production that mocked the still-living revolutionaries Robespierre, Danton, and Marat—all of whom were depicted as having claws, horns, and tails—Robertson's performance was a daring and dangerous activity in the midst of politically uncertain times. In fact, as Marina Warner notes, the show was actually closed for a time because the police feared that it did actually possess the ability to bring King Louis XVI back to life (147).

But if the magic lantern show had a political context, it also had religious and scientific ones as well. Robertson's show displayed a series of ecumenical representations ranging from the shades of the dead in the underworld, Orpheus losing Eurydice, witches preparing for the Sabbath, and Banquo's ghost, to "Mahomet" displaying a sign that read "Pleasure is my Law" (Warner, 149). As Castle notes, Robertson and other producers of these early phantasmagorias frequently presented themselves as intent on serving the public interest by exposing religious frauds or charlatans who preyed on those easily duped into believing their own misguided senses: "Ancient superstition would be eradicated when everyone realized that so-called apparitions were in fact only optical illusions. The early magic-lantern shows developed as mock exercises in scientific demystification" (143). Walter Scott's friend David Brewster, inventor of the kaleidoscope (1819), also developed the double mirror trick that would later be called "Dr. Pepper's Ghost," a technique of angling panes of glass under and above the stage so that a ghost seemed to be hovering in the air before the audience's startled eyes, a device that suggests "the pervasive doubleness, the reflective and refractive nature of the pretend world of theatrical performance" (see Burwick 2009, 257). And as a historical contrast, we can recall that the infamous Count Cagliostro, the rumored Illuminati, had been traveling throughout Europe during the late 1780s staging his own fortune-telling extravaganzas designed to do just the opposite, to dupe his audiences into believing in the continued power of the supernatural and his control over those same forces.

In February 1802, Paul Philidor (the stage name for Paul Philipstal) presented his "phantasmagoria" in London at the Lyceum, and William Nicholson was in the audience to provide this eyewitness account:

> All the lights of the small theatre of the exhibition were removed, except one hanging lamp, which could be drawn up so that its flame should be perfectly enveloped in a cylindrical chimney, or opake [*sic*] shade. In this gloomy and wavering light the curtain was drawn up, and presented to the spectator a cave or place exhibiting skeletons, and other figures of terror, in relief, and painted on the sides or walls. After a short interval the lamp was drawn up, and the audience were in total darkness, succeeded by thunder and lightning; which last appearance was formed by the magic lanthorn upon a thin cloth or screen, let down after the disappearance of the light, and consequently unknown to most of the spectators. These appearances were followed by ghosts, skeletons, moving their eyes or mouths by the well-known contrivance of two or more sliders. (Nicholson, qtd. Rees, 81)

In a strange *hommage* to Ben Franklin, Philidor displayed the floating head of Franklin "being converted into a skull," and then followed this shocking sight with a display of "various terrific figures, which instead of seeming to recede and then vanish, were (by enlargement) made suddenly to advance; to the surprise and astonishment of the audience, and then disappear by seeming to sink into the ground." Other visual shocks included moving eyes and lips in floating specter faces, floating decapitated heads with teeth chattering, and dissolves that suggest a doubling of characters that may have influenced James Hogg, who attended Philidor's shows in Edinburgh (Warner, 153). The magic lantern show quickly became a staple of bourgeois entertainments, so popular in fact that magic lantern kits for middle-class children to build were sold all over England (Castle, 150, 154); however, the magic lantern was not used in legitimate theatrical productions until 1820, when Edmund Kean appeared as Lear at Drury Lane (Rees, 84). As Emma Clery has suggested, the magic lantern shows reveal how quickly the frightening can degenerate into parody given enough repetitions, which was exactly what occurred on the British stage (Clery, 146). There is no question that the gothic had become just this sort of parody very early in its history. But in its brief heyday, it was immensely popular and, as Backsheider has suggested, gothic drama is "the earliest example of what we call mass culture.... [A]n artistic configuration that becomes formulaic and has mass appeal, that engages the attention of a very large, very diverse audience, and that stands up to repetition, not only of new examples of the type but production of individual plays" (150).

Certainly, Lockean empiricism had frequently imaged the mind as dominated by the visual, with images and perceptions being passively recorded (like ghosts) on the mind's essentially blank slate, a representation that was contrasted to the romantic notion of the mind as active, with a shaping imagination. The contrast between these two positions led to M. H. Abrams's analysis of the well-known construction of the "mirror and lamp" epistemology. But more recently Gillen Wood has complicated Abrams's position, arguing that the real opposition between epistemologies was "between the lamp and the magic lantern": between romantic, expressive theories of imaginative production that privileged originality, genius, and the imagination and "a new visual-cultural industry of mass reproduction, spectacle, and simulation" (7). This new visual economy can be seen in phantasmagorias that "simulate the real and thus usurp the viewer's interpretive and imaginative powers" (Miles 2008, 69). The magic lantern was also associated in the public theatrical consciousness with superstition, and while claiming on the surface that the mind was a machine that could be controlled, the other message that was being conveyed sub rosa was that the mind was actually a "phantom-zone, given over, at least potentially, to spectral presences and haunting obsessions. A new kind of daemonic possession became possible" (Castle, 144). But how does this bifurcation of attitudes toward the mind explain the revival of the ghost on the gothic stage? Relying on Foucault, Crary charts the progression of the interiorization of perception from the discovery of the camera obscura to its use as a metaphor by Descartes, Locke, Kant, Condillac, and Goethe, and he cites Foucault on the camera obscura as "a form of representation which made knowledge in general possible":

> It was found that knowledge has anatomo-physiological conditions, that it is formed gradually within the structures of the body, that it may have a privileged place within it, but that its forms cannot be dissociated from its peculiar functioning; in short, that there is a nature of human knowledge that determines its forms and that at the same time can be manifest to it in its own empirical contents. (Foucault 1970, 319)

Foucault here locates the eye firmly in the body. Earlier, Goethe also believed that it was crucial to connect the subjective component of perception with the physiological, a position that was elaborated by the French philosopher Maine de Biran whose early nineteenth-century theory of the "sens intime" was an attempt to assert the primacy of interior experience (Crary, 72). For both Goethe and Maine de Biran, subjective observation cannot be understood as a theater of representations, but instead as a product of increasing exteriorization: "The viewing body and its objects begin to constitute a single field on which inside and outside are confounded; . . . the soul is necessarily incarnated [so] there is no psychology without biology" (Crary, 73).

This bifurcation between the mind and the body was the foundation for Charles Lamb's essay "On Garrick, and Acting; and the Plays of Shakespeare" (1812). Lamb here codifies the notion of "closet drama," the very antithesis of gothic drama in its interiorization of action. Lamb specifically condemns the theater of his day as an inferior venue because of its reliance on the purely visual: "What we see upon a stage is body and bodily action; what we are conscious of in reading is almost exclusively the mind, and its movements" (255). When he discusses the witches in *Macbeth,* Lamb notes that when we read the drama we experience them as "the principle of Evil" itself; we are "spellbound" by their horror. But when we see them made real on stage, they are just "so many old women" we are inclined to laugh at. For him, "this exposure of supernatural agents upon a stage is truly bringing in a candle to expose their delusiveness" (256). But the general population seems not to have reacted to the supernatural on stage in this same way. They did not laugh; they cowered.

It is also possible to see these changes in attitudes toward the primacy of the mind or the body as caused by the oscillating secularization process that I have been charting via Taylor. This ambivalence toward the spiritual—characterized by nostalgia as well as outright rejection—can be explained as part of the transformational process that occurred when numerous metaphysical choices were presented to a generally befuddled population. Long schooled in the tenets of supernaturalism and yet encouraged by the new sciences to reject such nonsense, the mass of European citizenry stood either paralyzed or partisan, but in either instance, they were aware that their religious choice of allegiance was just one of many, and that their friends and family members might and probably would be choosing differently, and that all of them would ultimately pursue what their culture most valued when all the debates were over: "human flourishing."

Although a ghost was briefly used in Harriet Lee's *The Mysterious Marriage* (1793), the ghost made its most spectacular return to the British stage in Matthew Lewis's *The Castle Spectre* (1797). The appearances of Lewis's female ghost were roundly criticized, particularly by the *Monthly Review* which condemned the play's use of "German spectres" as condoning "atheism" and irreligion (27 [1798], 66). Lewis's drama was in fact viewed as the epitome of Germanic (read: Jacobin) tastes and therefore was considered revolutionary and dangerous to the British public (*Monthly Mirror* 2 [1797], 355). Although the ghosts in Shakespeare's plays had been popular since 1700, the subject of supernatural revenants on stage assumed a new urgency in an era where religious debates were almost as contentious as political ones. James Boaden was actually the first gothic dramatist to use a male ghost dressed in armor and seen from behind a veil of gauze in his production of *The Fontainville Forest* (1794). In addition, bleeding nuns, a scythe-wielding Death, and a variety of "ambulant phantoms" were also stock figures in the gothic repertoire. *Raymond and Agnes, or The Castle of Lindenbergh* (Covent Garden, 1797) with "Music by Mr. Farley," was an early adaptation that advertised itself on the playbill as "founded chiefly on the Principal Episode in *The Monk*." Lewis himself adapted his own material in his gothic drama *Raymond and Agnes* (1809), and like the earlier versions, he focused his dramatic version on the legend of the bleeding nun, although it is necessary to point out that this legend was actually a transmogrification of the earlier Germanic demon lover ballad.

In Lewis's play Agnes is being held captive in Lindenburg Castle and, with the assistance of Raymond, makes her escape disguised as the Ghost of the Bleeding Nun, a legend that the family continued to evoke years after the original nun's death. The plot becomes complicated when the ghost herself actually does make appearances and the material realm uneasily coexists with the spiritual in an uncanny dance of the (un)dead with the living. In their presentations of actual ghosts onstage, both Lewis's play and Boaden's earlier *Fontainville Forest* relied on the same visual technique: a sheet of gauze producing a blue-grey haze and hanging between the audience and the ghost.[1] The ghostly effect was achieved by using the green halves of the shades of the Argand lamps that were placed in the wings of the stage (Warner, 148). So where there is a definite physical and material stratum to the gothic universe as depicted on stage, there was also a transcendent realm on display revealing that the spiritual could and perhaps always would coexist with the material real. Seeking to secularize and rationalize superstitions about ghosts and the afterlife, gothic dramas did not exorcise them, but actually gave them free rein. In other words, what the mind could no longer accept rationally now reappeared through the technologies of the magic lantern shows, the dramas, and the phantasmagoria so that audience members were once again forced to view their fellow citizens as "porous" in the presence of that which they had supposedly banished. What was once believed to be real—God, the realm of the spirit, the power of blood to ritually cleanse and purify—all of these manifestations of the supernatural now were revived and placed in equipoise with the physical. From Taylor's perspective, the ghost on display in gothic dramas represents the doubleness at the heart of secularization: that is to say, the possibility of living in an ambiguously tenuous balance between the immanent and the transcendent. By displaying a social imaginary in which audience members were encouraged to believe in a universe in which both the spiritual and material realms were equally possible and viable choices, then the phantasmagoria presents to its viewers the choice to endorse simultaneously the reality of both the supernatural and the rational. If ambivalent secularization is finally not a "subtraction story," but an expansion of imaginative possibilities, then the ghost story, the magic lantern shows, and the phantasmagoria are forms of the popular imaginary that say to their audiences that belief is a question of individual preference. As such, they represent a technologically based cultural practice that served to instantiate ambivalent secularity.

CHAPTER 3

III.

> All those large dreams by which men long live well
> Are magic-lanterned on the smoke of hell;
> This then is real, I have implied
> A painted, small, transparent slide.
>
> —Wiliam Empson, "This Last Pain"

How and why did the gothic drama ambivalently exploit the coexistence of the supernatural and the material, and how were those ambivalences—often excessive, hyperbolic, blatantly fantastical—manipulated so that the genre gained mass appeal? Eino Railo has listed four methods that gothic authors employed in dealing with the supernatural, and, more specifically, with ghosts as subject matter:

1. By dealing with supernatural events as such, that is, without argument or explanation.
2. By dealing with them in such a manner that they only appear to be supernatural and are capable of being satisfactorily explained.
3. By dealing with them in a manner that permits of "scientific" explanation.
4. By dealing realistically with horrors, of which the worst reach into abnormality. (324)

By putting a ghost on stage, gothic dramas fluctuated between strategy one (no explanation, as in *Fontainville Forest* or *The Castle Spectre*) or strategy four (consider the horrifying heart-eating scene in D'Arnaud's *Fayel* [1770], in which the heroine Madame de Coucy is forced by her husband to eat the heart of her lover, mercifully offstage. The theater management served cordials to revive spectators who passed out in the audience during this bizarre *coup de théâtre* [Frank 2002, 50]). Siddons's *Sicilian Romance* and Baillie's *Orra* employ the second strategy, and the dramatic adaptations based on *Frankenstein* are perhaps the best examples of the third strategy. The reason for the popularity of *The Castle Spectre* lies in its exploitative use of a visible ghost who presented the residue of the spiritual uncanny in a material and visually spectacular manner on stage. Implicit in the ghost's appearance, however, were the larger religious and metaphysical issues that the supernatural raised for this culture. The Burkean secular sublime, besides undergirding much of the gothic aesthetic, came to figure in gothic constructions of the divine. Founded on physiological responses to fear, the sublime, according to Burke, is also connected to religion and its ability to manipulate and assuage anxieties about death:

> Those despotic governments, which are founded on the passions of men, and principally upon the passion of fear, keep their chief as much as may be from the public eye. The policy has been the same in many cases of religion. Almost all the heathen temples were dark. Even in the barbarous temples of the Americans at this day, they keep their idol in a dark part of the hut, which is consecrated to his worship. For this purpose too the druids performed all their ceremonies in the bosom of the darkest woods, and in the shade of the oldest and most spreading oaks. (102–3)

For Burke, the "terrible" was located in "all that is dark, uncertain, confused, terrible, and sublime," while "terror," the divine's "inseparable companion," can only be found by tracing "power through its several gradations, into the highest of all, where our imagination is finally lost" (112). According to Burke, there was a clear link between the concept of infinity and the experience of terror, while infinity "has a tendency to fill the mind with that sort of delightful horror which is the most genuine, and truest test of the sublime" (112). In opposition to Locke's associationist theory about the cause of nighttime fears, Burke also comments on the original cause of the human fear of darkness, stating that "it is more natural to think, that darkness being originally an idea of terror, [it] was chosen as a fit scene for [ghosts and goblins], than that such representations have made darkness terrible" (IV:14). This position is remarkably similar to Rudolf Otto's claim that "in neither the sublime nor the magical, effective as they are, has art more than an indirect means of representing the numinous. Of direct methods, our Western art has only two, and they are in a noteworthy way *negative*, viz, *darkness* and *silence*" (68; his italics). Numerous discussions of the gothic sublime—included those influenced by Otto—foreground Burke's writing on terror, but it is perhaps most helpful to recognize that one of Burke's greatest contributions to aesthetic theory was his ability to secularize the supernatural and situate the divine as a confrontation with the stark inescapability of mortality and death.

This section examines the ghost's complicity in a variety of religious, social, and political ideologies that are explicit in the major gothic dramatic adaptations of the most popular gothic novels of the period: Matthew Lewis's *Castle Spectre,* arguably the most successful gothic drama produced during the period; James Boaden's *Fontainville Forest,* a gothic drama based on a vivid vignette drawn from a larger and unwieldy gothic novel, in this case Ann Radcliffe's popular gothic novel *The Romance of the Forest* (1791); and Boaden's politico-gothic *Cambro-Britons,* a drama that, like Wordsworth's *The Borderers* (1796; 1842), is complicit in constructing the new British nationalistic character that Burke was codifying in his prose. What is most curious about all of these works is their use of a ghost, in fact, a female ghost who in two of these works embodies both a socially conservative message and a direct political warning to the protagonists of the drama, and, by extension, to the audience.

Recall that in Ann Radcliffe's essay "The Supernatural in Poetry," she attempted to draw a clear distinction between terror and horror as aesthetic categories, "so far opposite, that the first expands the soul and awakens the faculties to a high degree of life; the other contracts, freezes and nearly annihilates them" (145). Presented as a dialogue between two men traveling to Kenilworth Castle, the essay defends Radcliffe's preference for terror and her use of obscurity rather than the heavy-handed use of terror that was increasingly popular with gothic writers such as Lewis. She also makes a very clear distinction between what she calls "the glooms of Superstition" (recourse to Catholic tropes) and the "glooms of Apprehension" (her skillful use of suspense in the technique of the explained supernatural). Interestingly, the debate takes place largely through recourse to a discussion of Shakespeare's ghosts, particularly Banquo and Hamlet's father. At one point the sympathetic Mr. Willoughton (Mr W——) describes the effect that seeing the ghost of Hamlet's father has had on him, and his friend Mr. Simpson (Mr S——) responds by saying:

> "Certainly you must be very superstitious . . . or such things could not interest you thus."
> "There are few people less so than I am," replied W——, "or I understand myself and the meaning of superstition very ill."
> "That is quite paradoxical."
> "It appears so, but so it is not. If I cannot explain this, take it as a mystery of the human mind." (145–52)

Walpole had tried to get at the nature of that "mystery of the human mind" in his only attempt at a gothic drama, *The Mysterious Mother* (1768), a play that is frequently discussed as the first gothic drama in England, but one that circulated only in manuscript form and was never publicly performed during Walpole's life. It is a very strange work in which the Countess of Narbonne, a grieving mother who has just lost her husband, decides to employ the medieval "bed-trick" and take the place of her son's mistress in his bed (and even more perversely, on the night that she learns of her husband's death in a hunting accident). She bears his child, a daughter named Adeliza, only to learn sixteen years later that the girl, living in the castle as her young "ward," has fallen in love with Edmund, her father/brother, and intends to marry him. The countess is forced to confess her crime immediately after learning of the marriage, and she and her family are destroyed as a result. Edmund rushes to death in battle, the daughter enters a convent, and the mother stabs herself while her estates appear to be confiscated by the monks Martin and Benedict, who have had their eyes on them for quite some time.

Cited by Radcliffe, Byron, and Melville in their own works, and reprinted by Walter Scott in 1811, the drama had a sort of cult status among gothicists and was recognized as "creating the paradigmatic Gothic drama of internecine family conflict and sexual depravity" by its modern editor Frederick Frank (26). In many ways the drama is best understood as a throwback to Sophocles' *Oedipus* or Euripides' *Hippolytus* or such Restoration tragedies as John Ford's *'Tis Pity She's a Whore* (1633) or John Dryden's *Don Sebastian* (1689). Walpole, in a Postscript written to accompany the play, claimed that the events depicted were based on two historical incidents, one in England and one in France, although he chose to present his play "at the dawn of the reformation; consequently the strength of mind in the Countess may be supposed to have borrowed aid from other sources, besides those she found in her own understanding" (252–53).

But the Countess of Narbonne's "strength of mind" is precisely what in question throughout the tragedy. When she is forced to explain herself to her son Edmund, she privileges both her body and her imagination as the reasons for her act of incest. Claiming that her husband had been "detain'd from my bed" for eighteen months, she asserts that when he finally was delivered, dead at her doorstep, "I rav'd—the storm of disappointed passions / Assail'd my reason, fever'd all my blood. . . . Guilt rush'd into my soul—my fancy saw thee / Thy father's image" (5:6, 43–63). This overlaying of her husband's face over the son's is a highly spectral way of recalling the uncanniness of the past and present, a technique that Walpole also used in *The Castle of Otranto*. This scene presents the female body as an unruly and irrational instrument at the mercy of the mind's fevered constructions, or is the mind at the mercy of the body? Is the countess a sexual deviant, a ravening, lustful aristocrat who would use her own son to sate her appetites (see Clery, 2001), or is she a manifestation of a failed buffered self, a modern subject who loses control of herself so thoroughly that she is powerless and forced to wreak havoc on her family and the larger society?

In fact, the drama can more accurately be seen as persistently misogynistic ("Artful woman!" says Benedict, "Thou subtle emblem of thy sex, compos'd / Of madness and deceit," 241) and blatantly anti-Catholic, with the monks Benedict and Martin using supernatural stories to terrify the secret sin out of the countess: "I nurse her in new horrors; from her tenants / To fancy visions, phantoms; and report them. / She mocks their fond credulity—but trust me, / Her memory retains their coloring" (184). But when he sees that he cannot use omens, signs, dreams, or superstitions to intimidate the countess to publicly confess her sin, Father Benedict begins to despair. Fearing that the countess is sympathetic to the cause of the Waldensian heretics, he determines to destroy her by exposing her secret sin. Later he praises those soldiers of the Church who have successfully burned the Waldensian heretics at the stake (222, 238–39). In his postscript to the drama, Walpole justifies his creation of the villainous Benedict, claiming that his purpose was "to divide the indignation of the audience, and, to intercept some of it from from the Countess. Nor will the blackness of his character appear extravagant, if we call to mind the crimes committed by catholic churchmen, when the reformation not only provoked their rage, but threatened them with total ruin" (254). In other words, Walpole's dramatic strategy was one of bifurcated demonization: both sexualized mothers and greedy Catholic monks are "othered" and condemned as monstrosities, both atavistic forms that the British Protestant imaginary has to reject and punish in order to move into a modern and secular nation free from such powerful threats.

Even more fraught with ideological baggage is another early gothic drama, this one based on a gothic novel. Henry Siddons's production of *The Sicilian Romance; or the Apparition of the Cliff* (Covent Garden, 1794) uses the device of a daughter saved by what appears to be her mother's ghost. This drama undercuts the supernatural element by revealing that the mother had been imprisoned by her evil husband so that he could bigamously marry a young and wealthy heiress. The mystery of her ghostly appearances at night, seen by many around the cliff where she is imprisoned, are resolved when the daughter Julia unbars a door and her mother magically emerges, as if from the dead. When the evil Ferrand discovers that the mother and daughter have reunited, he resolves to kill them both himself. As he rushes on them, the mother pulls a dagger and says, "'Advance not, on your life! / Spite of thy cruelty, I love thee still, / Still live in hopes to charm thy savage soul, / And melt it into tenderness and love'" (III.iv). This melting never occurs, and the father cannot be assimilated into the restored family that sings the praises of King George III in the closing scene. A drama that has presented the ruling patriarch of this tiny principality as a ravening, lustful madman concludes, then, by singing the praises of the mentally impaired George III, eliding in its public posture the irony of such a celebration.

Those involved in the construction of the gothic aesthetic, as Miles notes, embraced the hieratic function of keeping alive the sacred mementoes of the race (like the monarchy). But ideological conservatism intersected with the democratic nature of artistic production for the masses, creating what Foucault has called a site of "power/knowledge" axis at odds with itself. As a site of opposing strategies, the gothic drama became a "hazardous play of dominations" seeking to compose for itself a coherent position amid rapid social, historical, and cultural transformations (1993, 32). It is, for Miles, in the moments of slippage and discontinuity that the ideological business of the gothic aesthetic is most apparent. For him, the gothic aesthetic incorporates an idealized national identity with a myth of origins (50). This position is very close to the one put forward by James Watt, who claims that from the 1790s through the early 1800s, gothic works were written as reactions to Britain's defeat in America because they consistently portray a proud heritage of military victory played out within an unambiguous moral and political agenda. Setting their action around a real castle in Britain, these works present a stratified yet harmonious society, use real historical figures from the British military pantheon (Arthur or Alfred were particular favorites), and consistently depict the defeat of effeminate or foreign villains. Loyalist gothics are structurally bound to depict an act of usurpation that is always arighted, often through the supernatural agency of a ghost (7).

One example presented by Watt is William Godwin's early romance *Imogen* (1784), set in prehistoric Wales and idealizing a "pure, uncorrupted society in the mythical past as a bulwark against the hegemonic forces of English imperialism" (45). Unlike Gray's elegy, "The Bard," Godwin's novel hints that the act of trespass and usurpation made when Edward I conquered Wales could be reversed. The entity eventually known as "Great Britain" could only come into being through acts of usurpation of property and title condoned by the public, so these acts were played out in veiled form on the gothic stage, where women were usually depicted as powerless pawns of much more powerful and corrupt aristocrats. The act of forming itself into a secularized nation was, in effect, the most threatening trauma that was occurring in England and so it was enacted vicariously on the London stage for all to witness and finally accept.

The quest for an idealized national identity, however, needs to be set into the still larger historical context in which popular gothic dramas were produced. England and Scotland signed the Act of Union in 1707, finally ending hundreds of years of hostility and territorial skirmishing between the two countries. But this document was—as Tom Nairn has pointed out—a largely "patrician bargain" because the forgers were for the most part aristocrats (136). The task of the next hundred years was to imaginatively separate and differentiate England and Scotland in the popular consciousness, and that became largely the province of the gothic's cultural work. As Benedict Anderson has noted, one of the ways a country builds a sense of its own nationality is to imagine itself as antique (and thus we have a renewal of medievalism and gothicism in Keats, Coleridge, Shelley, Wordsworth, not to mention Walter Scott). But another equally effective way to build the consciousness of a nation-state is to construct a local adversary on a country's very borders in order, as Anderson points out, to create a clearly defined sense of space, a newly sacred territory enclosed and potentially threatened by lawless or crude infidels (xiv). Scotland, as well as its political and cultural doubles, Wales and Ireland, became for the English national consciousness just such border communities, the "others" that England had to separate from while at the same time master and suppress, dominate and oppress in order to forge its own sense of amalgamated nationhood.

There is no question that French gothic drama had established itself earlier than either British or German gothic drama, and that it influenced many British gothicists, particularly Lewis, who spent a fair amount of time attending theater productions in Paris and writing to his mother about their appeal. In a letter sent to his mother during the summer of 1791, Lewis notes that "*Les Victimes de Cloîtrées* is another [drama] which would undoubtedly succeed [in London]" (qtd. Railo, 85). Anticlericalism was perhaps the most dominant characteristic of early French gothic dramas and may be seen as originating in such works as Jean Baptiste de Boyer Argens's *Intrigues Monastiques ou l'amour encapuchonné*, published at The Hague in 1739. Olympe de Gouges authored *Le couvent, ou les voeux forcés* (*The Convent or The Forced Vows* [1790]), and Charles-Joseph Pougens wrote *Julie, ou la religieuse de Nîmes* (1792), in which the heroine is imprisoned in a convent much as was Suzanne in Diderot's *The Nun* (1759) or Agnes in Lewis's *Monk*. Another early work is Baculard D'Arnaud's anti-Catholic tragedy, *Coligny; ou La Saint Barthelemi* (1750), which depicted Catholic atrocities during the St. Bartholomew massacre and was a direct influence on Jacques-Marie Boutet de Monvel's gothic drama *Les Victimes de Cloîtrées* (1791) and later Elizabeth Inchbald's *The Massacre* (1792). Monvel's play concerns a noblewoman, Madame de Saint-Alban, who, intent on blocking the marriage of her daughter Eugenie to the honorable but poor Dorval, involves her confessor, Père Laurent, in an attempt to conceal the young woman in a convent. Thinking she is dead, Dorval enters the adjoining monastery and, unbeknownst to him, ends up in a cell next to his beloved. The drama was a source for both Radcliffe's *The Italian* and Lewis's *Monk*, but Lewis was so drawn to the material that he decided to make a direct adaptation of Monvel in his own drama *Venoni; or The Novice of St. Mark's*, with music by Michael Kelly

(Drury Lane, 1808). Baculard D'Arnaud's *Euphémie: ou, le triomphe de la réligion* (1768) was yet another early anti-Catholic dramatic monastic shocker (*drame monacal*), in which a young woman is forced into the convent after an unfortunate love affair only to die miserably there in the throes of spiritual dread and visions of hell (hence the ironic title "the triumph of religion"). Never performed, but avidly read by French as well as German and British gothicists, the drama anticipates modernist practices by presenting ghosts as the products of troubled or guilty imaginations, while religious belief is depicted as a pretext by which the powerful control the weak.

IV.

> Why need the ghost usurp the monarch's place
> To frighten children with his mealy face?
> The king alone should form the phantom there,
> And talk and tremble at a vacant chair.
>
> —Robert Lloyd, "The Actor" (1760)

When John Philip Kemble was invited to inaugurate the new Theatre Royal (Drury Lane) in 1794 with a production of *Macbeth*, he decided to make the ghost of Banquo a purely psychological manifestation of guilt in Macbeth's mind. His audience, however, was not particularly happy with this modernization in the production, although clearly the literary elite had decided that the appearance of ghosts on stage was an uncomfortable reminder of their Catholic past, with all its attendant superstitions. The presence of ghosts on the stage was indeed a controversial one, with critics arguing that such apparitions no longer could have any role in dramatic productions because no rational audience member could take them seriously any longer (Gamer, 134). In commenting on Boaden's *Fontainville Forest,* an anonymous reviewer for the *Monthly Review* (14 [1794]) noted, "He has introduced a ghost, a Being at present very improper for tragedy, for it is rather calculated to excite laughter and contempt than terror" (353).

Matthew Lewis's *The Castle Spectre* (Drury Lane, 1797) is generally considered the most popular gothic drama performed in England in the late 1790s and Lewis himself in his footnotes to the drama acknowledged that the "Dream of Francis in Schiller's *Robbers*" was an important influence on his play (Evans, 167). By my count, it was performed eighty-three times between December of 1797 and 1800, an incredible number for any stage play at the time, and it continued to be popular and produced until 1825.² Lewis began writing a prose romance shortly after he first read Walpole's *Castle of Otranto*, then he set the work aside, traveled throughout Germany, and spent 1792–93 in Weimar. After moving to Paris he regularly attended the opera, and read Radcliffe's *The Mysteries of Udolpho*, which he praised in a letter to his mother as "one of the most interesting Books that ever have been published" (qtd. Peck, 208). When he sat down to finish the prose romance he had begun almost two years earlier, it became *The Castle Spectre*, a drama written under the influence of an amalgam of gothic texts. As an anonymous reviewer in Walker's *Hibernian Magazine* observed:

> Mr. Lewis's intimacy with German literature is strongly proclaimed through the whole of the *Castle Spectre*. The *dream of Osmond*, his *Atheism*, Reginald's sixteen years immurement, (derived, probably from the Robbers) and the frequent appeals to Heaven, with a levity unusual to our stage, are all *German*. The licenser, if he had known the intention of his office, would have *struck his pen* across such expressions as "*Saviours of the world*," "God of Heaven," etc. (his italics; qtd. Parreaux, 150)

What is most significant for my purposes is Lewis's use of the unexplained supernatural and the intervention of a ghost in ways that certainly Radcliffe eschewed. In his own defense, Lewis noted in an appendix to the second edition of the play, "The Friends to whom I read my Drama, the Managers to whom I presented it, the Actors who were to perform it—all combined to persecute my Spectre, and requested me to confine my Ghost to the Green-Room" (224).

Lewis sets his drama's action in a contested castle on the border of Wales and England during the tenth century, and this shift is surely significant in both localizing the place and in making the gothic more clearly a British phenomenon, a move that allowed the drama to explore British anxieties about nationhood, borders, and outsiders—women and Africans—clamoring to breach the moats that an aristocratic and male-dominated culture had so carefully constructed for itself. Angela, the besieged gothic heroine in this drama, is aided in her struggle against her evil uncle Osmond by a group of social outcasts: a fool, a gluttonous friar, servants, and finally, the ultimate outsider, her murdered mother's ghost. We learn that sixteen years earlier, Osmond had devised a plan that he thought would allow him to marry his sister-in-law Evelina. Thinking that he could ambush and kill his elder brother and Evelina's husband, Reginald, Osmond and his four African henchmen botched the job and instead Osmond accidently murdered Evelina who died by throwing herself between the two brothers, thereby saving the life of her husband. While Osmond thinks his brother has perished, Kenric, one of Osmond's servants, discovers that Reginald survived the attack and he decides to hide him in Castle Conway, which now is the property of Osmond, Reginald's usurping brother. In the meantime, Angela, the daughter of Reginald and Evelina and unaware of her true identity, has been raised as a peasant by foster-parents. Osmond decides to reclaim his niece upon her sixteenth birthday and promptly lusts after her, particularly given her resemblance to her dead mother. When confronted with the incestuous overtones of the marriage that he desires with her, Osmond replies nonchalantly, "I have influence at Rome—The obstacle will be none to me" (217). The charge of hypocrisy against the Catholic Church in matters of marriage would not have been lost on the audience here, particularly given the legacy of dynastic chaos that erupted when King Henry VIII sought to have his marriage to Catherine of Aragon annulled by Rome, 1525–33. In addition to this reference, Lewis introduces an absurdly comic and superstitious priest, Father Philip, a bumbling, greedy, lecherous, and buffoonish man who functions throughout the play as a caricature of the ineffectual and flawed Catholic clergy.

The "ghost scene," famously set to music by Michael Kelly and employing special lighting effects, occurs at the conclusion of Act IV as a salvific haunting of the beleaguered daughter by the spirit of her protective, angelic mother. Clutching for protection the same blood-stained poignard that Osmond had used to kill her mother years earlier, Angela fends off Osmond's incestuous advances and kneels before the portrait of her dead mother, praying, "Mother! Blessed Mother! If indeed thy spirit still lingers amidst these scenes of sorrow, look on my despair with pity! Fly to my aid! Oh! Fly and save my father!" (205). Believed to inhabit the castle's "Oratory," the ghost appears dressed to resemble the Bleeding Nun from *The Monk*, while stage directions make the uncanny aspects of her appearance very clear:

> The folding-doors unclose, and the Oratory is seen illuminated. In its centre stands a tall female figure, her white and flowing garments spotted with blood: her veil is thrown back, and discovers a pale and melancholy countenance; her eyes are lifted upwards; her arms extended towards heaven, and a large wound appears upon her bosom. Angela sinks upon her knees, with her eyes riveted upon the figure, which for some moments remains motionless. At length the Spectre advances slowly, to a soft and plaintive strain; she stops opposite to Reginald's picture, and gazes upon it in silence. She then turns, approaches Angela, seems to invoke a blessing upon her, points to the picture, and retires to the Oratory. The music ceases. Angela

rises with a wild look, and follows the vision, extending her arms towards it. . . . The Spectre waves her hand, as bidding her farewell. Instantly the organ's swell is heard; a full chorus of female voices chaunt "Jubilate!"—a blaze of light flashes through the Oratory, and the folding-doors close with a loud noise. (III.ii.206)

The audiences who witnessed this scene were enthralled, and the musical accompaniment was considered to be particularly effective in staging the power of the scene. Boaden in his *Life of Kemble* noted that "Jomelli's *Chaconne,* in his celebrated overture in three flats" (II:206), was adapted by Kelly, who himself said that the music "was thought an odd choice of mine for so solemn a scene; but the effect which it produced, warranted the experiment" (I:227). As Garlington observes, it is somewhat ironic that the music Kelly chose in order to convey the "ghostly" mother was written by an Italian composer during his German sojourn, an apt illustration of a British composer importing the foreign to convey the eruption of the transcendent gothic on the stage (56–58). But apart from the resemblance of the ghost to the Bleeding Nun, there is little question that the female presence being invoked here makes reference to the Virgin Mary, a Catholic specter who I would claim continued to hold uncanny power over the British imaginary. Appearing as a visual spectacle, the maternal ministrations of the ghost of Evelina is the high point of this gothic drama and a moment so culturally significant that it would continue to be replayed in gothic chapbooks for the next twenty years (see chapter 6). The fact that the scene was understood as religious can also be seen by the censorship of its language. As Jeffrey Cox points out, the Larpent version of the play has "Hallelujah" rather than "Jubilate," but this is crossed out, suggesting the continuing concern about the use of religious language on stage during the period (206n133).

This second appearance of Evelina, to protect her husband Reginald against the attack of Osmond, so startles Osmond that he drops his sword and Angela "suddenly springs forward and plunges her dagger into Osmond's bosom" (219). It is Angela who calmly steps forward and gives instructions for the care of her wounded uncle, hoping that he will "gain time to repent his crime and errors!" (219). For all his sufferings, Reginald is also quick to forgive his brother: "Let me hasten to my expiring brother, and soften with forgiveness the pangs of death!" (219). With an almost medieval tenor to the finale, Reginald announces that "'I knew that I was guiltless—knew that, though I suffer'd in this world, my lot would be happy in that to come!'":

And, Oh thou wretch [Osmond]! Whom hopeless woes oppress,
Whose day no joys, whose night no slumbers bless!
When pale Despair alarms thy phrensied eye,
Screams in thine ear, and bids thee Heaven deny,
Court thou Religion! Strive thy faith to save!
Bend thy fixed glance on bliss beyond the grave!
Hush guilty murmurs! Banish dark mistrust!
Think there's a Power above! Nor doubt that Power is just! (220)

In an earlier version of the play, the final line read "And think there is a God! That God is just!" (220n149), but it was changed in a manner that secularizes the supreme power while at the same time leaving no doubt that a conservative religious ideology is being invoked.

Lewis's drama was popular because of its use of the unexplained supernatural, and Lewis defended his use of the ghost, arguing in his appendix to the drama that ghosts could now safely be presented on stage

> because the belief in Ghosts no longer exists! In my opinion, that is the very reason she may be produced without danger; for there is now no fear of increasing the influence of superstition, or strengthening the prejudices of the weak-minded. I confess I cannot see any reason why Apparitions may not be as well permitted to stalk in a tragedy, as Fairies be suffered to fly in a pantomime, or Heathen Gods and Goddesses to cut capers in a grand ballet; and I should rather imagine that *Oberon* and *Bacchus* now find as little credit to the full as the *Cock-lane Ghost,* or the Spectre of *Mrs. Veal.* (223; emphasis in original)

But a writer for the *Analytical Review* did not agree, arguing that "[t]he belief in the occasional disclosure of the world of departed souls is nearly coeval . . . with the existence of man, and will probably continue till the dissolution of the present system. [Nearly everyone has] experienced the thrilling of fears, which the most enlightened reason, unwilling to approve, has been unable to counteract or refute" (28 [1798], 184). A statement such as this reveals that bourgeois literary and cultural critics recognized all too well the seductive and lingering lure of the supernatural over the human imagination, and they sought to control its use by limiting the appearance of ghosts on stage.

Critics were also quick to point out that the ghost of the mother, Evelina, was gratuitous because she contributes nothing to the action of the drama; according to one reviewer for the *Analytical Review,* she "makes no discovery and promotes in no degree the progress of the drama." In Act IV she "divulges no secret" that Angela has not already been told by Kendric, and in Act V she does not act to do anything that could not have been done "by a less insubstantial agent" (28 [1798], 184–85). As late as 1832, John Genest wrote about the popularity of *Castle Spectre:* "The great run which this piece had is a striking proof that success is a very uncertain criterion of merit—the plot is rendered contemptible by the introduction of the Ghost" (III:332–33). As Reno points out, these objections remain "oddly rationalistic by continuing to deny a symbolic or psychological acceptance of the supernatural" (103).

The ghost of the sacrificial mother here suggests not simply a return of the Catholic uncanny, but also a manifestation of the transcendent within the immanent order. She allows a contemporary audience member to entertain the possibility that yes, perhaps the spiritual realm does continue to exist and therefore a ghost could appear to right a wrong that was perpetuated long ago. This reanimation of Angela as the "porous self" who inhabits both worlds simultaneously, the world of her dead mother and the realm of the material "real," vicariously permits the audience to participate in just such a dramatic universe as well. The ghost of Evelina can also be read as an example of the unexplained supernatural that contributed to the popularity of so many gothic novels. James Norris Brewer, in his four-volume gothic novel *A Winter's Tale* (1799), observed about his own use of a real ghost: "[T]he times of which I write . . . must be considered. Prejudice was then nearly in its zenith. Visitations, omens, and warnings of death were implicity believed to exist by almost all ranks of people; and a story of those days, which failed to talk of ghosts, and strange and foreboding noises, would want the characteristic of its class" (I:vii). Whereas critics have been quick to claim that there are very few "real" ghosts in gothic texts, Tarr has identified the use of ten in the sampling of gothic works she examined, and that number could be increased well into the hundreds were one to include the "real" ghosts that appear throughout the gothic chapbooks (see chapter 6).

But just as the ghost was a controversial figure in the drama, so were the "Negroes" who functioned as Osmond's servants. The character of Hassan is, by Lewis's own account, "misanthropic" because "he has lost every thing, even hope; he has no single object against which he can direct his vengeance, and he directs it at large against mankind" (222). It is, as Lewis recognizes, an "anachronism" to have Osmond "attended by *Negroes*" (223; emphasis in original), but Lewis makes no apologies: "I thought it would give a pleasing variety to the characters and dresses, if I made my servants black; and could

I have produced the same effect by making my heroine blue, blue I should have made her" (223). This is a flippant and curious remark given Lewis's own status as a slave holder in Jamaica, but it reveals some of the spectacularizing contortions that Lewis was willing to take in order to animate his work. It also works to equate women and blacks in ways that suggest their use as visual props in the gothic imaginary. Both are strangely presented as pure surfaces of color, and both are in some ways "anachronisms"; in other words, they are premature presences who should not be functioning in the supposedly historically real world that the dramatist has created.

In contrast to *A Sicilian Romance,* the ghostless version of Radcliffe's novel penned by Henry Siddons, *Fontainville Forest* by James Boaden (1762–1839) was based on Radcliffe's *Romance of the Forest* and makes use of a ghost who is clearly intended to represent the heroine Adeline's murdered father.[3] Boaden himself justified the use of the supernatural in the drama by writing that the action was set at "the beginning of the fifteenth century," and therefore permissible because its actions are "selected from the olden time" (*The Life of Kemble* II:97). Well aware of the critical injunction against silent apparitions, Boaden had his phantom repeat three times the phrase, "'Perish'd here!'" in reference to his place of murder. A writer for the *Monthly Review* was so outraged by the ghost in *Fontainville Forest* that he observed, "We should ourselves be guilty were we not to pronounce this to be the most pernicious doctrine; the offspring of barbarous ages, which every writer, especially a christian writer, should make it his duty to detect and expose" (14 [1794], 352).

Fontainville Forest (Covent Garden, 1794) is prefaced in its printed text with an epigraph from *Macbeth:* "It will have blood, they say, blood will have blood. / Stones have been known to move, and trees to speak," a passage that clearly positions the drama in the tradition of Shakespearean supernaturalism that was popularized by David Garrick's productions of *Macbeth, Hamlet,* and *Richard III,* all of which employed ghosts. As Emma Clery has noted, earlier critics such as Addison, Dryden, and John Dennis had attempted to resuscitate the use of ghosts on the British stage, and Dennis in particular framed his defense in religious terms. For him, ghosts should be welcomed on stage because they "produc[ed] enthusiastic Terror," and such "enthusiasm" for Dennis was defined as "a god-inspired zeal," thereby linking terror to its religious function (qtd. Clery, 35). The production of terror or fear, as we have seen, became crucial components in the quest for the Burkean sublime, with the appearance of a ghost on stage becoming an important part of this larger aesthetic debate. But it has been typical to overlook the broader cultural and religious issues, in particular the secularizing impulse at stake in many of these discussions of the evolving sublime aesthetic.[4]

Boaden's *Fontainville Forest* makes no attempt to enunciate a new approach to the delineation of the sublime or to theories of a new aesthetic. It intends only to be well-received and to exploit the popularity of Radcliffe's novel. To do so, it presents a mysterious ghost, simply called a "phantom," who speaks three times to the heroine Adeline at the conclusion of Act III in the "secret Apartment" where Adeline has found an old manuscript that relates the history of her father's imprisonment and murder. As she reads her dead father's journal, Adeline hears the phantom speak on three different occasions to confirm her worst fears, that, yes, her uncle was the usurping murderer of his own brother and now, incestuously, pursues her, his niece. The phantom, dressed in armor and seen from behind a sheet of gauze, "glides across the dark part of the Chamber" (40) and disappears, but he is clearly meant to represent the heroine's dead father, so that the crime here is not matricide, as it becomes in Lewis, but fratricide. In fact, the play makes this explicit when the evil Marquis has a guilt-induced vision of the phantom and exclaims: "See, he unclasps his mangled breast, and points / The deadly dagger" (41). Later, as the evil Marquis grasps the struggling Adeline, he marvels, "In vain this struggle! / How lovely is this terror!" (50). But very quickly the discussion between victim and victimizer turns theological, and both of them begin talking about fate and God as retributive forces.

The mother's miniature portrait that Adeline wears around her neck serves as the identificatory talisman that allows the Marquis to realize that he is pursuing his own niece, and that an inexorable fate ("Dreadful certainty") has brought them together. He asks her, "is there yet some living instrument / To punish fratricide?", while she responds in prayer: "Amazement wraps my senses! Gracious God, / In awful sorrow I adore thy justice! / Protector of the Orphan, O direct me! / And lead the Child, miraculously sav'd / To pull down vengeance on her father's murd'rer" (51). After a series of misadventures that eventually unmask his identity and crimes, the Marquis stabs himself rather than face the scaffold and the onlookers praise the "secret Providence" that has revealed the truth and returned Adeline to her name and properties (67). Adeline, for her part, salutes "the great Avenger of perverted nature / [Who] Before us has display'd a solemn lesson, / How he dispels the cloud of mystery, / With which the sinful man surrounds his crimes; / It calls us to adore in awful wonder, / And recommend ourselves by humble virtue" (68).

This final speech aims to produce something like the effect of an antiquated medieval religious posture as well as an antisublime. The "solemn lesson" that the godhead teaches can only be learned once the mystifications of error and sin are removed and humans return to a humble posture of virtue and adoration. The use of a ghost is congruent with this worldview, and Boaden has Mrs. Pope (in the character of Adeline) defend the appearance of the ghost in the epilogue that concludes the play. In a mocking tone, she asks: "Think you, our friends, one modern ghost will see, / Unless, indeed, of Hamlet's pedigree: / Know you not, Shakspeare's petrifying pow'r / Commands alone the horror-giving hour?" (69). Invoking the spirit of Shakespeare to sanction the phantom of this play, Adeline speaks on behalf of the condemned playwright who has been pressured to eliminate the ghost: "I come his advocate, if there be need, / And give him *absolution* for the deed. / You'll not deny my spiritual power, / But let me rule at least one little hour!" (70; emphasis in original). Again, the use of religious language suggests that the appearance of the unexplained supernatural on the gothic stage was a way of reviving traditional religious symbols and tropes, even if they were just being invoked as performances, one choice among many belief systems, rather than a shared or universal dogma.

The reanimated ghost, dynastic intrigue, warring brothers, and the eroticized daughter-figure were all stock gothic devices by this time, cultural practices that attempted to alter the "background" of the European social imaginary. Their very persistence as tropes, however, causes us to ask: what is the cultural work being performed? Why would ghosts appear on stage to direct the action of the living? Saggini has seen the ghost as a "hieratic figure" representing Adeline's fears, passion, and terror (201), while Reno has noted that the use of onstage ghosts at this time had nothing to do with the contemporary elite disbelief in supernatural apparitions. But these positions are not, as I have suggested, the issue. The fact is that there was during this period an ambivalent and uncanny "doubleness" in the secularized consciousness that demanded the coexistence of the supernatural and the natural on stage in order for the audience to see dramatized the coexistence of both of its intellectual and spiritual choices. When Boaden tried to revise the play in order to remove the ghost, the audience's disapproval and disappointment were strongly expressed and therefore he reinstated the phantom. But why does a male ghost—the dead father—haunt this play rather than the dead mother? Is it fair to conclude that the state as well as the family are under social and political siege? Rapid transformations in the family structure had caused even the patriarch, it would appear, to tremble in his own domicile.

Boaden spent his career associated with the London Theatres Royal in his dual role as reviewer and author of eight dramatic productions during his lifetime, but he is perhaps best known for his five theatrical biographies, most notably the *Life of John Philip Kemble* (1809), still used today as a primary source for information on the late eighteenth- and early nineteenth-century theater. Following his successful adaptations of Radcliffe's novels, Boaden wrote a politico-gothic drama *Cambro-Britons,* in the style of Shakespeare, first performed on July 21, 1798, at the Haymarket, and generally regarded as his unsuccessful bid to be taken seriously as a dramatist in the manner of Shakespeare.[5] A play that depicts the conquest of Wales by England in the thirteenth century, the drama was actually composed with France in mind. As Boaden noted in his *Life of Kemble,* he intended the play to meet "the menaces of foreign invasion, in the year 1798, with patriot sentiment." But as Cohan has observed, the play was written at the height of invasion fever, with the public firmly convinced that France would invade the mainland of England through Ireland. A disastrous attempt by France to invade actually did take place a month after the play's opening (xxvi). In the same biography Boaden went on to explain that dramas should not be the venue for party politics, and that the theater would be "deficient in its noblest duty, when it inspires no ardour against an invading enemy" (preface to *Cambro-Britons*). Further, Boaden thought that the play would inspire everyone in the audience to "thank" him for "seeking to sustain the independence of his country" (qtd. Cohan, xxvii). But what Boaden failed to understand, as Cohan rightly observes, was that the audience's sympathies would be with the Welsh, who were struggling to maintain their independence against the oppressive and corrupt English, led by King Edward in 1282. The drama's analogy actually works against England, aligning the 1798 England with France, an unlawful and greedy usurper of land not its own. Like Lewis's depiction of the African slave Hassan, the gothic seems to be particularly prone to being historically fissured, its exterior working against and undercutting the interior of the argument that the drama actually makes through both its action and its resolution.

In addition to its confusing and ultimately contradictory political allegory, Boaden uses a female ghost, as Lewis did in *Castle Spectre*. In Boaden's drama the dead mother of Prince Llewellyn and his traitorous brother David appears on the altar of a church, urging her two warring sons to reconcile and join together to fight their common English enemy. This ghost garnered the most attention for the play and manifested how far the illegitimate dramatic forms had gone in privileging spectacularism and supernaturalism. In fact, the appearance of the ghost actually caused a number of critics to accuse Boaden of plagiarizing Lewis's *Castle Spectre,* which Boaden hotly disputed. In defense of himself, Boaden pointed out that if anyone was the plagiarist, it was Lewis, whom he accused of stealing the idea for a ghost from Boaden's own earlier ghost in *The Fontainville Forest* (see his preface to *Cambro-Britons*).

Boaden's play begins with an atmosphere of suspicion and paranoia, as every soldier, including Llewellyn's own brother, is suspected of disloyalty to the preservation of Welsh independence. As one Welsh soldier remarks after accepting a bribe to change allegiance, "We have now no safety but in the conqueror's mercy" (I.i.8). Interestingly, one of the first figures to speak in the drama is the Irish minstrel O'Turloch, who functions as a bard and entertains the Welsh royalty with a song about King Arthur, said to have been imported by Scottish minstrels. The song concerns a woman who pleads with Arthur to avenge her against a knight who has raped her, a situation that parallels Llewellyn's wife who has been pursued aggressively and incestuously by David, his twin brother. The presence of Arthur, the last Celtic king, became a stock device in a number of loyalist gothic texts that were trying to recall an idealized Celtic golden age, pre-Norman, pre-aristocratic, and pre-Hanoverian. But the presence of the bard in this work also recalls Katie Trumpener's thesis in *Bardic Nationalism*:

> For nationalist antiquaries, the bard is the mouthpiece for a whole society, articulating its values, chronicling its history, and mourning the inconsolable tragedy of its collapse. English poets, in contrast, imagine the bard (and the minstrel after him) as an inspired, isolated, and peripatetic figure. Nationalist antiquaries read bardic poetry for its content and its historical information; their analyses help to crystallize a new nationalist model of literary history. The English poets are primarily interested in the bard himself, for he represents poetry as a dislocated art, standing apart from and transcending its particular time and place. (6)

For Trumpener, the contrast here points to the collapse of Celtic clan culture (in Ireland, Wales, and Scotland) and the rise of a new form of individualism and literary commodification in England that eventually triumphed over the earlier oral-based culture.

The high point of the drama occurs not on a battlefield, as one might expect, but in a gothic chapel where a shrine to the mother, Lady Griffyth, is located. Informed by his wife, Elinor, that his brother stills pursues her and has traitorously thrown in with the English invader, the "haughty Edward," Llewellyn confronts his brother before their mother's tomb. As they each draw swords to settle their longstanding rivalry, the ghost of their mother suddenly appears and speaks: "'Forbear!'" As the swords magically fly out of the brothers' hands, their ghostly mother goes on to pronounce: "'Have I not loved you?—Be peace between you! / Confirm it at the altar!'" After the two men kneel and embrace, their mother gives her blessing and the chorus of spirits declares: "Grateful the voice that bids your hatred cease, / A mother's mandate of fraternal peace." In the elaborate stage directions that accompany the scene, we are informed that the funereal dress falls off the mother and "her figure seems glorified; and through the opening window she is drawn, as it were, into the air, while music, as of immortal spirits, attends her progress. The brothers gaze silently after the vision" (II.v.58). This miraculous disrobing and ascent would appear to replay aspects of the bleeding nun legend in which a murdered woman can have no eternal peace until she is avenged and buried in hallowed ground, but it also recalls the Catholic belief in the miracle of the Virgin Mary's bodily assumption after her death. Boaden's adaptation of the legend on the simple plot level suggests that the mother cannot ascend to Heaven until her two sons are reconciled, but as a political allegory, the image is loaded with contradictory freight. Reconciled, the brothers fight the tyrant Edward to a standoff. After much singing, Edward recognizes Llewellyn as the Prince of Wales, and declares to him, "'Be my friend—/ My nearest, best ally; and, in her perils, / Let England ever find her warmest champion, / Her grace, her glory, in the prince of Wales!'" (III.iv.88).

The political agenda motivating this drama would appear to be a belief in a fictitious reconciliation of all rival claims to land through the appearance of a beneficent maternal presence, ghostly but powerful, absent but present. The dead mother, rising from her grave to demand cooperation from the warring and rival brothers, suggests, in addition to gothic and religious representations, at least the avatar of Elizabeth I, the dead but undead political and Protestant mother, wise, skillful, and infinitely diplomatic in the ways of avoiding direct conflict and open warfare. Is it possible that, in addition to displaying religious ambivalence about the supernatural and rival Christian traditions, the dynastic emphasis in so many gothic dramas was the result of anxieties about the condition and suitability of the heir to George III's throne? Rather than simply nationalistic debates or French invasions, another anxiety motivating much of British gothic dramas was the very tangible fear that the Protestant House of Hanover had come to an inglorious end in all but name. The baby daughter of George IV, Princess Charlotte (b. 1796), appeared to many to be a tenuous hope for the British monarchy, and in order to buttress her potential monarchical status the specter of the last great female queen begins to appear, disguised as a female ghost haunting the disputed borders of Wales and England, Scotland and England, England and its own colonies abroad. The intense mourning that gripped England when Charlotte died in childbirth a mere twenty-one years later found expression in, as Stephen Behrendt documents, a huge "Charlotte industry," poems, broadsides, and souvenir trinkets (122). If her death caused such intense, hyperbolic, and theatrical displays of mourning, might it not be conjectured that her birth—rather than the birth of a son—was also the subject of a certain amount of anxiety?

The female ghost who appears in these dramas also suggests an intense uneasiness about the role and nature of women in the coming century. The fact that these ghosts are mothers—murdered, displaced, separated from their children—also suggests a deeply conservative agenda. Women, it would seem, are being properly positioned on the stage in their maternal roles, because the gothic aesthetics of the visual presupposes a masculine subject dazzled not simply by an eroticization of the female body but also by her maternal function. In addition, the aesthetics of the sublime presupposes a female subject-position disciplined through the presence of the male gaze—or what I would call the bourgeois social imaginary. The mass audiences that flocked to the gothic dramas remembered the ghost scenes because those were the most dramatic, most frightening, most uncanny appearances of either dead mothers or dead fathers on the stage. In a nation struggling to consolidate land it had only recently claimed, as well as land it was claiming abroad on a tenuous basis at best, the spiritual ambivalence, political guilt, and social anxiety must have been intense. At the same time that the national borders were viewed as precarious and diffuse, so were the psychic ones. The ghosts haunting the gothic stage can perhaps be seen as the ghosts of empires lost and found, mothers and fathers displaced and replaced, and children, black as well as white, used and abused. But these ghosts also represent the depiction on the stage of an ambivalent secularizing process that encouraged its audiences to examine the claims of both the past and the present, the transcendent and the immanent, and, in doing so, to present these positions as options, choices that they would have to make as they determined the balance that the spiritual and the material would have in their own social imaginaries.

- CHAPTER 4 -

Entr'acte. Melodramatizing the Gothic

The Case of Thomas Holcroft

The theatre, however it may be debased by the nightly intrusion of unhappy and improper persons, has a most powerful and good influence on morals, which increases with industry, and as the means of gaining admission among the lower-class increase. Much time is there spent to the best, the noblest, of purposes; the body's fatigues are forgotten, the mind is beguiled of its cares, the sad heart is made merry, fictitious sorrow obliterates real, and the soul, imbibing virtuous and heroic principles, is roused and impelled to actions that honour not only individuals but nations, and give a dignity to human nature.

—Thomas Holcroft, Preface to *Seduction* (1787)

I.

When Thomas Holcroft (1745–1809) wrote the *Preface* above he was articulating to the London literary establishment one of the first class-based defenses for a rapidly changing theatrical scene in Europe.[1] For the autodidact Holcroft, it was necessary that London critics recognize that the theater was not only increasingly serving as a locus of secularized religion, but also as a place where the lower classes could be educated in the behaviors and attitudes that would allow them to function usefully in a rapidly changing society. In addition to serving a "civilizing process" (in Norbert Elias's sense of the term), the contemporary theater also had a political role, its aim being to "rouse" and "impel" the lower-class audience to "actions" that could be considered "heroic" (P. Cox, vii–viii). Holcroft's early plays, like *The Road to Ruin* (1792) or *The Deserted Daughter* (1795), are largely comedic imitations of Molière or Oliver Goldsmith's works, while his most important plays are those that imported the techniques of the French *mélo-drame*. In bringing the French tradition onto the British stage, he secularized the gothic ethos, creating a form of gothic melodrama that has persisted in popularity to this day.[2] Whereas the gothic adaptations of Boaden, Siddons, and Lewis had a fairly limited vogue on the stage, the gothic melodrama has had real staying power as a popular dramatic form with the lower and middle classes, and the question is why? And how does the gothic melodrama differ from the slightly earlier works of gothic drama? These answers can only be discerned by returning to its origins and examining two of Holcroft's best-known adaptations from the French, *Deaf and Dumb: or, The Orphan Protected* (1801) and *A Tale of Mystery, A Melo-Drame* (1802).[3]

In Paris, September 1800, at the apex of Napoleon's reign, a displaced aristocrat named René Charles Guilbert de Pixérécourt (1773–1844) perfected a new dramatic form—the melodrama—by building on the earlier work of J. N. Bouilly (1763–1842) and François Thomas Marie de Baculard d'Arnaud (1718–1805). Pixérécourt had managed to survive the worst of the French Revolution by hiding in a Parisian attic, and although one would think he might have been somewhat distracted, he managed to cobble together this new hybrid genre, which in turn would prove to be one of the most lasting artistic legacies of the Revolution. His *Coelina ou l'Enfant du mystère,* originally performed in 1800 at the Ambigu Comique in Paris, became the first full-fledged example of a melodrama as we understand the genre today (although some critics have assigned this honor to his slightly earlier *Victor, ou l'enfant de la forêt,* also performed at the Ambigu Comique in Paris, 1798). But also roaming around Paris during that 1800 theater season was Thomas Holcroft, a British Jacobin who was searching for theatrical and novelistic ideas to bring back with him to an England that he hoped had become more sympathetic to the Revolutionary cause. Holcroft noted later that he saw advertisements for eighteen different theaters in Paris that season, but there were actually twenty-three in 1789 and thirty-two by 1807 (Rahill, 41). Holcroft is primarily remembered today as a writer of Jacobin novels, a compatriot of Wollstonecraft, Inchbald, Godwin, and Helen Maria Williams. But it would appear that it is more accurate to see Holcroft as the man who wrote—or more accurately stole—the first British melodramas from France. J. N. Bouilly's *L'Abbé de l'Epée* (1800) became Holcroft's *Deaf and*

CHAPTER 4

Dumb, or the Orphan Protected (Drury Lane, 1801), while Pixérécourt's *Coelina* became in Holcroft's hands *A Tale of Mystery* (Covent Garden, 1802). But as Holcroft's adaptations of both works are virtual translations (or in the case of *A Tale of Mystery*, practically a pantomimed version) of its source, their analysis has to begin with the French origins of melodrama (see Marcoux).

It is necessary first to sketch Holcroft's background in order to understand the role he played in transporting melodrama from France to England. In the first chapters of his *Life*, which he himself composed (the remainder was completed by Hazlitt after his death), Holcroft tells us that both his parents were peddlers and that he spent his early years following them from town to town, sometimes working as a stableboy or a shoemaker, eating so little that his growth was permanently stunted. In 1770, at the age of twenty-five, he joined a troupe of traveling actors, primarily playing roles in comedies. Marrying for the first time at an early age, he found himself in need of money as his family increased. It was then that he turned to writing for the stage, as well as writing novels and translating the works of Madame de Genlis, Johann Caspar Lavater, Frederick II, Baron Trenck, and Goethe from the French and German (Gregory, 53). His first trip to France was in 1783 as a foreign correspondent for the *Morning Herald*, but he returned the next year with the intention of watching enough performances of Beaumarchais' thrashing of the aristocracy in *Le Mariage de Figaro* to present his own English version on the London stage. His 1784 adaptation, *The Follies of a Night*, proved unsuccessful, but the strategy of adapting a liberal French play for British audiences henceforth became one of Holcroft's primary means of support. Holcroft's political sympathies were liberal long before the French Revolution gave a focus and impetus to his beliefs. In 1783 he published a theatrical review that made explicit his position that the theater should be institutionalized by the state in order to serve as a force to liberalize and educate the populace as a whole:

> The Theatre is as well worthy the contemplation of the Philosopher and the Legislator, as the Man of Taste. We are persuaded it contributes, in its present state, to humanize the heart, and correct the manners.... If it is not uniform in the tendency of its effects, it is because Legislators have never yet been sufficiently convinced of the power of the Drama, to incorporate it with the constitution, and make it a legal and necessary establishment; or rather, perhaps, because some men were fearful, lest while they were erecting the temple of morality, they should erase the tottering structure of superstition, in the preservation of which themselves, their children, or their dependents were materially interested. (qtd. Bolton, 17)

Positioning "morality" against "superstition," Holcroft became a major voice in the secularization process that was occurring during this period. As Betsy Bolton observes, Holcroft's theories "link the civilizing force of the drama to a leveling of social classes" (17), while other London critics of the period feared that the theater actually encouraged class warfare in its pitting of the audience against the theater managers (witness the Old Price Riot in 1809). Clearly, the theater has functioned as one of society's most publicly contested spaces, a ritualistic arena where social, cultural, sexual, and religious ideologies converge in staged combat, poised to compete for the hearts and minds of the audience. In late eighteenth- and early nineteenth-century British culture, however, the public-private debate took on a new urgency and the stakes were indeed high. A corrupt aristocracy sought to stave off the sort of political unrest that would shortly engulf France, and the theater was very obviously a potent weapon in either calming the populace or enflaming it. In a blatant bid to shore up British nationalism and patriotism, revivals of Shakespeare and classical works dominated the early eighteenth-century theater, but increasingly the public was attracted to works that dealt with contemporary social and political issues. Once the theater was recognized as one of the spaces where public instruction in manners, civility, and proper class-based conduct could occur, the struggle was on for control of the stage. As Bolton argues, "Romantic nationalism relied on spectacle both in appealing to the public's patriotic sentiments *and* in projecting a sentimental code of honor: benevolent mastery of domestic and international affairs" (21; emphasis in original).

But where does this place Holcroft as a melodramatist with a liberal (nay, radical) agenda? Writing in a culture where the patriarchy was both under siege and vigorously buttressed, Holcroft imported the melodrama, a mixed genre that embodied ambiguity and moral oscillation in its very nature.[4] Unable to outright condemn the corrupt king-father, Holcroft instead presented morally flawed fathers or sinful patriarchs who are admonished by the female and bourgeois voice of common sense in the conclusion of his plays. Such admonishment has led at least one critic to argue that *A Tale of Mystery* is a radical, avant-garde production, in line with Holcroft's political sympathies (Shepherd, 507). And certainly there is no question about Holcroft's atheism or his Jacobin allegiances, for, in addition to his work as a dramatist, Holcroft was also a private secretary to the abolitionist Granville Sharpe, and a member of the London Corresponding Society, a group that advocated constitutional reform and that explicitly encouraged public debates. He was also part of the Hardy, Tooke, and Thelwall "conspiracy" of "constructive treason" against the crown in

1794. Although he was briefly held in custody, Holcroft was never tried for supposedly "imagining the King's death," but he did spend the rest of his life labeled as "an acquitted felon," and hence found attendance at his plays and purchases of his novels decline (Barrell, 411–14). In fact, his reputation had fallen so low by 1795 that he had to submit his comedy *The Deserted Daughter* for production under the name of his friend Elizabeth Inchbald (P. Cox, xxiii).

After the failure of his 1798 play *Knave, or Not?* Holcroft concluded that he might be better off financially if he emigrated, leaving first for Hamburg and later moving to Paris where he lived from 1800 to 1802. Gary Kelly characterizes him as an advocate of "a kind of English Jacobin theology," a believer in condemning "pride, avarice, lust, wrath, gluttony, envy, and sloth" not so much as sins but as "bad habits [that] are best laughed at rather than hated" (139–40). By examining Holcroft's *Deaf and Dumb* and *A Tale of Mystery*, we can understand how gothicism merged with melodrama as the latter made its way from France to Britain. During the eighteenth century the British stage was flooded with works that employed sentimental categories clearly derived from Samuel Richardson, but after the importation and adaptation of *Coelina* onto the London stage, British drama veers off to become a distinctly hybrid genre, one that merges tragedy and comedy into something that we would recognize today as tragicomedy, an amalgam of "tears and smiles," an uncomfortable mixture of bathos and pathos, snickers and sneers (see Ellis; Sherbo). As always, the most interesting question for the literary historian is: why? Why would a culture want to place extreme, hyperbolic—one might say absurd—emotions on public display? And why would dramatists create the most untenable plot situations—most of which we would be charitable to recognize as unrealistic? And even more puzzling, why would lower- and middle-class audiences flock to these productions, knowing before the play began that they were soon to witness yet another variation on a few simple themes: the beautiful orphan in distress, the machinations of the unmasked greedy villain, the exaltation of the virtuous mother or chastised father, and the eventual triumph and restoration of the patriarchal family? The answers to these questions can only be discerned by starting at the beginning.

The term *melodrama* is itself subject to a fair amount of debate (see Shepherd and Womack). Some critics have claimed that the term is derived from the Greek word *melos* (music), because melo-drama originated in the mingling of music with action and spoken dialogue on stage. *The Oxford Companion to Music* now defines "melodrama" as "a play or passage in a play, or a poem, in which the spoken voice is used against a musical background." Theater historians, however, have suggested that the French verb *mêler* (to mix) is actually the origin for the term. Contrast these positions to one provided by the *Oxford English Dictionary:* "a dramatic piece characterized by sensational incident and violent appeals to the emotions, but with a happy ending" (Scholes, 624), and one can see that both literary critics and musicologists have attempted to lay exclusive claim to the genre. It is clear, however, that melodrama's origins are most accurately understood as a mixture of words and music, and that the genre has to be approached through both mediums in order to be fully appreciated as well as understood. As music (and ballet) faded from the repertoire of the romantic melodrama, something had to be inserted in order to sustain the same level of audience involvement. Enter "tragedy," that is, the mute character who acts out his buried and abusive history through the dumb show that explains his extended stay in a prison, a hospital, or a pirate ship.

Musicologists as well as theater historians locate the origin of melodrama in Jean Jacques Rousseau's *Pygmalion* (Lyons 1770; Weimar 1772; Paris 1775), a short *scène lyrique* with libretto composed by Rousseau. Although he acknowledged that he was borrowing from the Italians, Rousseau was the first to use the term "Mélo-drame" in 1766 to describe his *Pygmalion,* explaining that he was using music to express emotions in a particular situation, while another actor used pantomime to act out the same scene. Only when the music concludes does the actor speak, expressing verbally what had just been communicated through gestures and accompaniment. Certainly the development of such a style suggests the continuing power of an oral-based culture. The next influences on the evolution of melodrama were the theatrical antics perfected at the Jacobin Boulevard du Temple, where all manner of jugglers, pantomimes, and freaks performed, juxtaposed with outlandish adaptations of fairy tales taken from Perrault. The crucial element in this strain of melodrama is its use of pantomimes, set to music, and based on mythic, historical, or moral topics. Large word boards were used to help the audience understand the action, much like the use of print in early silent films. *Pantomime Dialoguée* seems to have fully evolved by 1785, characterized by fragments of spoken dialogue, stolen operatic arias, and a mixture of broad pantomimic actions (see J. Smith; Bentley).

British dramas were highly dependent not just on French models, but also on German works like *Die Räuber,* as well as the sentimental dramas of August von Kotzebue (1761–1819), which were adapted for performance quickly in both England and France. For instance, Bouilly's *L'Abée de l'Epée* was not simply adapted by Holcroft, but also by Kotzebue, who staged a production in Germany as early as 1803.[5] The success of these melodramas across Europe illustrates what Charles Taylor (using Max Weber) has called the reanimation of the "enchanted world [where] the line between personal agency and impersonal force was not at all clearly drawn" (32). In the enchanted world of melodrama, a "whole gamut of forces" ranging from Satan to minor demons (like the melodramatic villain) inhabit a world where there is "a perplexing absence of certain boundaries which seem essential to us" (33), like the boundary around the mind that had been "constitutionally porous" during the premodern period (40). Without these boundaries, meanings exist outside of human beings, prior to contact with us, and as such, they have the power to take possession of us from the outside; they can take up residence not only in the minds of characters, but also in things that are external to us, what Taylor calls "charged objects" (34–35). Along with our vulnerability to being attacked by evil things that exist outside of us, the enchanted worldview presents a universe in which we are forced to continually propitiate these forces through staged demonstrations of guilt and punishment (37), and hence we can see how the plotlines of melodrama evolved as enactments of propitiation. Because there is no clear distinction between the mind and body in the enchanted worldview, the "porous self" can never effectively disengage from either the internal or the external realms. Melodrama stages this immersion into the psychic and physical vulnerability of the enchanted world over and over again, and in its use of the large identificatory portrait or the scar on the arm, melodramas present us with "charged objects" that are almost magical in their ability to either protect or harm their heroes and villains.

As melodrama developed, it increasingly invested in attempting to present the development of the modern "buffered self," a being who claimed that he could avoid distressing or tempting experiences because he could disengage from everything outside of his own mind (Taylor, 38). This hero became modern by possessing the ability to distance himself from both his emotions and from "charged" external objects that no longer held power over him. Taylor notes that "as the creation of a thick emotional boundary between us and the cosmos" developed, we increasingly tried nostalgically "to recover some measure of this lost feeling. So people go to movies about the uncanny in order to experience a frisson. Our peasant ancestors would have thought us insane. You can't get a frisson from what is really in fact terrifying you" (38).

Melodrama is also a cultural practice that stages depictions of the family as the acme of human flourishing. It is a textual practice that stages the triumph of the bourgeois system of morality by claiming that the fate of an entire class of people could be represented by the actions of one family, for the private and interior spheres come to ensure order, social protection, and the powers of redemption. In this final phase of melodramatic consciousness, God is banished in favor of a worldview dominated by the notion that "buffered selves" live in a society that they are increasingly able to control and dominate without recourse to external or supernatural aids. The earlier melodramatic, however, would appear to be a genre caught between the premodern, traditional worldview of tragedy and the new consciousness of the bourgeois individual triumphing over all social constraints in a bold act of self-assertion and self-possession.

As we have also seen, the gothic dramatic aesthetic, with its celebration of a loyalist, chivalric code of ethics, infiltrated the stage in response to an audience that had come to expect sightings of ghosts, supernatural events, and a Manichean system of justice. Paula Backscheider argues, in fact, that melodrama is a continuation of the gothic (174). Further, she claims that gothic narratives all display the same structure of feeling, stock characters, codified settings, and highly stylized plots (155–56). Certainly one can see that Lewis's *Castle Spectre* contains a number of incipient melodramatic elements and characters, including the supposedly orphaned heroine, the evil uncle, and the hero disguised as a peasant. And one can also see incipient melodramatic aspects in James Boaden's adaptations of Radcliffe's novels (see chapter 3). But it seems necessary to distinguish between gothic drama as a unique genre separate from although related to melodrama. Gothic dramas contain historical and nationalistic elements that melodramas do not. Indeed, we could claim that the two genres—like bookends—reveal the public and historical (gothic) and private and domestic (melodrama) faces of the culture. The conventions of melodrama are a curious mixture, then, of musical forms, literary genres, and conservative political and social sympathies all bound up in a strikingly visual manner, suggesting the pantomimic background of the genre, with the broad gesture and the silent, mute wound at the core of the tale. Consider the prevalence of the telltale scar (originating, as Erich Auerbach has noted, most likely from the scene where Eurycleia recognizes Odysseus by the scar of the boar hunt on his leg), or the prominence of the portrait of the dead parent in melodramas and gothic fictions, the theme of secret marriages or disputed inheritances in both, the letter that is either indecipherable or deceptive, the arrival of the supposedly orphaned child or parent long believed to be dead, and finally, most melodramatic of all, the conspiracy of the powerful against the innocent or the foiled in the nick of time seduction or murder plot.

CHAPTER 4

II.

Why was a voice denied to [a] sensibility so eloquent!
—*Deaf and Dumb*, I.ii.34

J. N. (Jean-Nicolas) Bouilly is remembered today, not as the author of *L'Abbé de l'Epée*, one of the close to a dozen minor plays he wrote, but as the writer of *Léonore, ou l'Amour conjugal* (1798), which formed the basis of the libretto for Ludwig van Beethoven's *Fidelio* (1814; see chapter 2). Originally trained as a lawyer, his numerous works include operas, plays, stories, and a memoir, and it is interesting that, unlike Pixérécourt, he did not spend the height of the revolution in hiding, but rather as the head of the Military Commission in Tours. His interest in the Institution for the Instruction of the Deaf and Dumb in Paris was inspired by firsthand experience and observation during the years he spent working in Paris for the Committee of Public Instruction (1795–98). Based on the historical character of Charles-Michel de L'Épée (1712–1789), the play acquaints its audience with the use of the gestural alphabet for the deaf (sign language), and educates them about the basic human rights due to the disabled, as well as the fact that deaf and dumb people are capable of having feelings and thoughts, as well as inheritances and rights. The use in this play of a deaf and dumb hero allegorizes the struggles faced by the rise of the lower class and the dispossessed, or, as Jane Moody has noted about the play, the subject of muteness "is endowed with a powerful political subtext. . . . [M]uteness becomes a political as much as a semiotic condition." For Moody, the slight adaptations that Holcroft made in his source material "suggest that muteness constitutes a political experience as much as a physical disability. Indeed, Holcroft was no doubt attracted to this play precisely because it offered an idealistic counterpoint to that suppression of political opposition taking place in Britain" (89–90).

Holcroft's *Deaf and Dumb* is reminiscent of a number of earlier gothic dramas, complete with an orphaned hero, Julio, the Count of Harancourt/ aka Theodore; Darlemont, a greedy uncle who usurps the deaf and dumb boy's estate; the Abbé, a virtuous holy man who seeks to restore the boy to his rightful inheritance and identity; and Dupré, a conscience-stricken accomplice/servant to Darlemont. The gothic tropes continue in the "charged objects" or identificatory tags that figure throughout the play, all of which would have been familiar to audiences since the genre's early days. In particular, the use of a "whole length portrait" of Julio is reminiscent of the walking and breathing life-size portrait that begins Walpole's *Castle of Otranto*, as well as the oval portrait lockets that had functioned so prominently in Reeve, Radcliffe, and Lewis. Rather than use a miniature portrait that would not visually signify on the stage, *Deaf and Dumb* employs a life-size portrait of the missing and supposedly dead heir, commissioned by Darlemont when he was informed that Julio died in Paris. In truth, eight years earlier Darlemont and Dupré had taken the boy Julio to Paris, dressed him in rags, and then abandoned him to die in the Parisian streets, thinking that a deaf and dumb boy with no resources would not be able to survive. In addition to his distinctive disability, however, Julio carries the ultimate gothic identificatory tag on his arm, a wolf bite that the boy suffered when he saved his cousin St. Alme's life. As this cousin is also the son and heir of Darlemont, all of the elements of the gothic plot of restored inheritance and the punishment of the usurper are in place.

Deaf and Dumb begins with three standard gothic moves, the haunted portrait, the ominous dream, and the guilty conscience. In the very first scene Dupré confesses to his fellow servant Pierre that he can no longer bring himself to look at the full-length portrait of Julio prominently displayed in the central room of the palace because he has seen "him start from his frame, and stand before me. . . . I believe, it was only a dream.— Perhaps, he lives" (I:i). This recourse to a device used in Walpole's *Castle of Otranto* suggests not simply the gothicness of the drama, but also its employment of the uncanny, the doubling of the rightful heir with his simulacra or counterfeit, the painting that can walk and exact vengeance on the guilty Dupré much as the ghost of the portrait of Prince Manfred's grandfather does in *Otranto*. As Hogle, using Baudrillard has noted, the "ghost of the counterfeit" refers to both fakes and to a nostalgia for a time when images referred to embodied people who were firmly "ensconced in a class and role [that was] predetermined and immutable" (2008, 216). Ghosts look, like counterfeits, "both back towards a more grounded condition (as an object of desire) and away from such foundations to a conflict among ideologies about ghosts that exacerbates, even as it also stems from, the breach between sign and substance in the counterfeit that also longs for no breach at all" (2008, 217).

We can see this ghosting of the counterfeit when, confessing to Darlemont that he feels "haunted" by the presence of the painting, Dupré is quickly reminded by Darlemont that he is "a slave" to his master, to which Dupré responds, "I remember too that you are mine: accomplices in guilt are of necessity the slaves of each other" (I:i). This master/slave dialectic ironically functions to inform the class relationship in this drama, as Darlemont holds his inheritance only as long as the servant Dupré continues to swear that he did indeed see Julio's dead body and has signed a legal document to that effect. This melodramatic spin on class status suggests that the aristocracy holds its power only so long as the lower class allows it to possess what is not rightfully theirs to hold. As Gabrielle Hyslop has noted about those who defended the melodrama, the genre did "provide a much needed form of social control for the potentially dangerous subordinate classes at a crucial stage in French [and British, I would add] political history," and certainly it is possible that "individual spectators found within the plays themselves representations of class conflict in which oppressed members of the subordinate classes triumphantly overthrew their ruling-class tormentors" (65–66). The revolutionary implications of *Deaf and Dumb* are only too clear, and yet the Jacobin flavor of the work is undercut by the fact that Julio is himself an aristocrat who has been disinherited by his scheming maternal uncle, described as "but a petty merchant" before he maneuvered himself into his young nephew's title and estate (I.i.345). Like so many literary works of this period, it is certainly possible to read *Deaf and Dumb* as a loyalist drama that privileges the "true" aristocracy of direct blood descent over the collateral (maternal) branches of a family. It also speaks quite negatively about the tainted natures of those who have compromised their character by bourgeois employment.

Not content simply to usurp his nephew's estate, Darlemont seeks to cement his newly gained class status by marrying his son St. Alme to the president's daughter. This would not be a melodrama without a romantic complication, and St. Alme provides one when he tells Pierre that he is determined to marry his true love, Marianne, the daughter of Franval, "the most renowned advocate of Toulouse" (I.i.345). It is no coincidence that a lawyer is introduced into the dramatic proceedings, because melodrama frequently has recourse to the law to resolve its central issues: inheritances, identities, and marriages. The Franval family has recently fallen on hard times, as Madame Franval explains when she complains that her husband once held the "office of Sénéchal [governor]," but that she was compelled to sell it at his death "and the degradation cuts me to the soul" (II.i.356). This upper-class family has been reduced to having to work for its survival, rather than to "govern" from a position of inherited privilege. As the lawyer-son Franval explains to his mother, "[T]his circumstance [the family's loss of status] has stimulated me to attain by my own talents that consideration in the world, for which I should otherwise, in all probability, have stood indebted merely to accident and prejudice" (II.i.356). Madame Franval can only consider St. Alme and his father as a "mushroom family," sprung up only "yesterday" from their earlier status as "petty traders." "What," she asks, "have his riches made him forget the disparity of our births?" (II.i.357). Clearly, the eventual marriage of St. Alme and Marianne is meant to suggest the construction of a new and improved class, one tempered and chastened by their loss of the inherited privileges that they did not deserve to possess without their own personal struggle and effort.

Holcroft, following his source, has presented a series of class conflicts that are all too familiar on the gothic stage. He also presents a religious ideology that bears scrutiny. In the last scene of Act One, the Abbé and the deaf and dumb Theodore are introduced as traveling throughout France in an effort to help Theodore discover his native home and identity. As Theodore signs to the Abbé that he recognizes the Palace of Harancourt in the city of Toulouse, the Abbé bows his head and prays, "O, thou, who guidest at thy will, the thoughts of / men,—thou, by whom I was inspired to this great undertaking,—O, power omnipotent!—deign to accept the grateful adoration of thy servant, whom thou hast still protected—and of this speechless orphan to whom thou hast made me a second father!" (I.i.350). Later, he remarks to Theodore that he suspects Theodore has been "the victim of unnatural foul-play," and he prays again to "Providence" for the ability to "unmask and confound it! So men shall have another proof, that every fraud will soon or late be detected, and that no crime escapes eternal justice" (I.i.351). Finally, the Abbé lectures Darlemont when he tells the villain that "chance, or rather the good Power that governs chance and the destiny of man" saved his nephew from death (V.ii.387). The god who is invoked here suggests how much in flux the melodramatic cosmos was, for initially this god is presented as an "omnipotent power," a sort of providentially deistical presence, and then as a manifestation of the long arm of the law, and finally as a fatalistic form of chance.

Legal complications occur when Franval is presented with incontrovertible proof that Theodore is in fact the supposedly dead Julio, and that Darlemont has been the mastermind of the scheme to eliminate Julio so that he can usurp the Harancourt estate. Franval is motivated to handle the matter with the utmost of discretion because he wants to protect St. Alme's reputation as the future husband of his sister. As he argues to his mother, "'Ought we to make him responsible for his father's faults?'" (III.ii.367). He goes on to explain, "'[S]uch are the prejudices of the world, that I cannot publish the guilt of the parent, without reflecting the disgrace of his actions on his blameless son'" (III.ii.367). What is interesting in the melodrama is the persistent privileging of this premodern web of familial alliances, this anti-individualist notion that all people are inextricably connected to their families and that the actions of one family member bear on the character of all other members of that family. Such a belief is very close to the world depicted in the Brueghel painting (cover), and it stands in sharp contrast to the social realities that had been evolving in Europe for the past century. Melodrama appears to depict this earlier, lost world of tight family clans

CHAPTER 4

that by the early nineteenth century had been replaced by a new political state and capitalist system that had the power to define each individual's status and worth.

The secularization process also reveals itself in this work through its endorsement of the bourgeois premium placed on literacy. Strangely, in a genre so given to the unspoken or pantomimic, literacy emerges in the melodrama as central to its depiction of the modern subjectivity of "buffered selves." As Stone has shown, popular literacy had been steadily but slowly increasing in England and by the end of the seventeenth century 40 percent of the adult male population was able to read, while by 1800, 60 percent of men and 40 percent of women could read in Britain (1969, 109, 125). In addition, literacy was seen by religious reformers as allowing Christians to read and interpret scriptures for themselves, thereby freeing them from the domination of a self-serving clergy. Papists were accused of discouraging literacy, and a prejudice against illiterates became one of the central tenets of anti-Catholic polemic (Shell 2007, 14). It is perhaps no coincidence that so many melodramatic heroes are mute, for it forces them to pick up the pen in order to communicate, and in this act we can see the importance of literacy and public education reified on the stage. It is also clear that literacy is the crucial tool that enables so many happy endings in the melodramas that were patronized by the lower class and bourgeoisie. The Abbé publicly proves Theodore's worth and identity as an aristocrat by demonstrating his "feeling heart" and "enlightened mind" when he arranges a public test of Theodore's writing and cognitive skills. He asks Marianne to address any question to Theodore, and she asks him to identify the greatest genius that France has ever produced. Theodore's written answer: "Science would decide for D'Alembert, and Nature say, Buffon; Wit and Taste present Voltaire; and Sentiment pleads for Rousseau; but Genius and Humanity cry out for De l'Epée; and him I call the best and greatest of all human creatures" (III.ii.369–70).

Aside from the nationalistic tenor of the question and answer, this response displays the superiority of an evolving public educational system and the Abbé's efforts as a teacher of literacy. As the Abbé himself states about his educational mission, "'[J]udge what are my sensations, when, surrounded by my pupils, I watch them gradually emerging from the night that overshadows them, and see them dazzled at the widening dawn of opening Deity, 'till the full blaze of perfect intellect informs their souls to hope and adoration. This is to new-create our brethren. What transport to bring man acquainted with himself!'" (III.ii.370). The celebration of literacy is connected here with religious and spiritual significance, so that to read is to know the deity, to write is divine. But there is also something of the magical about this scene. Someone who should not be able to communicate is suddenly able to conduct a philosophically sophisticated "conversation" with his auditors, and perhaps the most pertinent question is: how would this scene have been understood by the theatrical audience of 1800? The advances of science are clearly being privileged in ways that present the secularization process here as a species of magic, allowing the dumb to speak and the deaf to hear, much as Jesus did in the miracles attributed to him in the New Testament. In other words, science is not an alien force to be feared by the Abbé and his traditionally spiritual followers, but in fact the fulfillment of scripture.

Theodore's restoration to his name and inheritance is dependent on a number of other more prosaic factors, not the least of which is the machinations of the female servants in the household, Dominique and the nurse of his infancy, Claudine, who identify him as the long-lost Julio. The importance of lower-class female servants will be developed further by Holcroft in the later *A Tale of Mystery*. A full confession from the remorseful Dupré is also necessary, and the final identificatory tag emerges in all its prominence when Theodore confronts his cousin. The skeptical St. Alme is convinced that the dead indeed can return only when Theodore "bares his right arm, and points to the scar upon it" (IV. ii.379). With his identity confirmed, Theodore now becomes Julio, the rightful Count of Harancourt, except that his uncle continues to hold that position and will not relinquish it short of the embarrassment of a public trial. The rest of the drama works to prevent that very public shaming of the family unit, with all participants convinced that such an exposure would equally condemn all members, even the innocent, to infamy and disgrace. All of the principals now descend on Darlemont, who has come to represent tyranny (read: the aristocracy) and the abuse of power over the deserving weak (read: the lower class and bourgeoisie). According to the Abbé, the muteness of Theodore "'left [him] destitute of that distinctive prerogative of man, the power of appealing against injustice and oppression!'" (V.ii.387), and this statement is the closest the work comes to making explicit its political agenda. That is, if we read this melodrama allegorically, we realize that the play is a fantasy rewrite of the Revolution, whereby the Church speaks for the dispossessed lower class, and the Revolution itself is given divine sanction. We know that the clergy were in fact one of the first targets of the Revolution for their long-standing complicity with the aristocracy, so the ideological work of *Deaf and Dumb* actually allows the supporters of the Revolution (Bouilly as well as Holcroft) the chance to rewrite history and align themselves with an idealized clergyman and his more palatable and liberal divinity.

The power of the legal system is the final ambivalently presented institution in the drama, with the lawyer Franval operating as something of a *deus ex machina,* holding over Darlemont the threat that he will subject him to a public exposure of his crimes if he does not renounce his claims to Julio's title. Darlemont, for his part, continues to cling to the letter of the law, claiming that Julio's death has been established through "a formal register of death," a piece of paper signed by Dupré as (false) witness (V.ii.388). Only after St. Alme tells his father that he will kill himself before his very eyes, "the dread of indelible disgrace—the cry of my despair—the horror of my death prevail'd—nature triumph'd—my father relented" (V.ii.391). The recourse here to "nature" suggests that the final arbiter for the melodramatic conscience is the appeal to blood ties. Darlemont may be a monstrous usurper, but finally he is a father and he was motivated by the very human (or "natural") feelings of a father who desired not simply to be rich for himself but to advance the standing of his son. Melodrama cannot bring itself to recognize irredeemable evil in the world, and so it obfuscates and presents endings that undo much of the dramatic action that has occurred. When Theodore becomes Julio, he promptly writes a letter in which he bequeaths half of his fortune to St. Alme, declaring, "'From our cradles we were accustomed to share every good, like brothers—and I can never be happy at the expense of my friend'" (V.ii.392). Closing the play are the words of the Abbé, who pronounces that he hopes "the example of this protected orphan, may terrify the unjust man from the abuse of trust, and confirm the benevolent in the discharge of all the gentle duties of humanity" (V.ii.392). Notice that the melodrama concludes, not by invoking a divinity, but only by appealing to a secularized system of justice predicated on a sentimentalized vision of human nature.

Holcroft's melodrama was so popular that it was quickly transformed into a chapbook, *Julius, or the Deaf and Dumb Orphan,* a tale intended "for the youth of both sexes" (1806). This anonymous pamphlet went through three editions in one year and faithfully translated the ideologies of Holcroft's drama to children. Here the Abbé prays to a "providence whose sovereign will directs both fate and fortune," while the greatest "happiness" in life "springs from the powers of reflection, and the communication of ideas" (48; 78). So there is no luck or chance in life, only effort and the attainment of useful skills. The bourgeois agenda could not be stated more clearly.

III.

> Fiametta: He can't speak.
> Bonamo: But he can write.
> Fiametta: I warrant *him*. *I'm sure he's [a] gentleman*.
> —*A Tale of Mystery*, I:402

Following the tradition that had been established by Bouilly, Pixérécourt understood the melodrama as asserting "religious and providential ideals" (4:498), while Charles Nodier in his Preface to Pixérécourt's collected plays observed that they conclude by asserting that the "old order was right" and "that moral stability wins out over political innovation" (I:vii–viii). As the "father of melodrama," Pixérécourt further developed the genre by using all of the devices that the British gothic had contributed to the French stage, and, for good measure, he introduced a hero whose tongue had been cut out, thus ensuring the pantomimic nature of much of the stage action of his *Coelina*. Translated into Dutch, German, and English, *Coelina* was so popular that it ran for 387 performances on the Boulevard du Temple (J. Smith, 6). As was typical of the time, *Coelina* the melodrama was adapted from another source, *Coelina, ou l'enfant du mystère* (Paris, 1799), a six-volume *roman noir* written by François-Guillaume Ducray-Duminil, who, along with Baculard d'Arnaud, was the most important author of French gothic novels (*roman noir*) during this period. Ducray-Duminil's earlier novel, *Alexis; ou La Maisonnette dans les bois* (1780) was the source for much of Radcliffe's *The Romance of the Forest* (1791), while his *Victor, ou l'enfant de la fôret* was translated into English and published by the Minerva Press in four volumes in 1802 (Mayo 1941). Exploiting the success of Holcroft's play, *Coelina* was translated into English as a four-volume novel entitled *A Tale of Mystery, or Celina* by the British gothic novelist Mary Meeke (Minerva, 1803). All of Ducray-Duminil's works are concerned with the quest for truth and identity, and the importance of reestablishing domestic and social order. Often set in prison cells amidst underground passages, Ducray-Duminil's novels move from uncanny spaces to the familiar, reassuring his lower-class readers that the threats assailing them will be resolved in fairly short order either by the king (as in his early 1789 *Alexis*) or through the good offices of the family (as in the postrevolutionary *Coelina*).

Like Ducray-Duminil, Pixérécourt was able to change his political colors to suit the mood of the times, and therefore his *Coelina* simplified Ducray-Dumenil's *roman noir* to cohere to the about-face of the Napoleonic era. By transforming Ducray-Dumenil's emphasis on fate and the superior power of Nature (the storm) that resolves the destinies of the characters and exposes the villain, Pixérécourt's use of the "archers" and the powers of the new military state illustrate perfectly the new Napoleonic Civil Code (see Martin). In Pixérécourt's melodrama, the heroine Coelina is an orphan living with her uncle Dufour and courted by her wealthy neighbor Trugelin, although Coelina herself loves and is loved by the uncle's son, Stéphany, her cousin. The villain-suitor is motivated by the promise of a large dowry and the adjoining estates that Coelina will bring to the marriage, all of which he reveals to the audience in a series of soliloquies that conceal none of his greed or villainy. Also living in the household of Dufour is a mysterious and mutilated stranger named Françisque Humbert, a man who cannot speak but who conveys through pantomimic gestures his history to his adoptive family: he was betrayed, sold into slavery on a pirate ship, and had his tongue cut out. Once returned to land, he was attacked in a wild mountainous region and left for dead. Coelina is strangely drawn to the old man, as he is to her. Such a device, called the "voice of the blood," was a standard recognition technique also used in such gothic works as Radcliffe's *The Italian,* among others. But if the displaced hero cannot help being recognized, neither can the villain. When Trugelin confides to his thuggish assistant Germain that he had attacked Françisque years ago and now intends to kill him that night, his confession is overheard by Coelina, hidden nearby. His plot backfires and Trugelin himself is revealed as the villain, so he resorts not simply to absconding but to delivering more threats: "'If I do not receive your consent [to the marriage] by ten o'clock tomorrow, tremble! A single word will break off the nuptials you plan [with Stéphany] and that word I shall utter.'"

All of this action occurs in the first act, while the second act begins with preparations for the immediate marriage of the hero and heroine, neither of whom appears to take Trugelin's threats seriously enough to find out what it is he has to say. Following a comic interlude between two country bumpkins, the villagers gather for the wedding, and at this point a formal ballet occurs, again revealing the residue in early melodrama of the carnival and festival, as well as music and dance as crucial pantomimic elements of an essentially oral culture. This pastoral vignette is rudely interrupted by the arrival of Trugelin, who appears amid a flourish of "charged objects," the supposedly legal documents that assert that Coelina is not the daughter of Dufour's dead brother, but instead the illegitimate child of Françisque (the mute) and Trugelin's adulterous sister. The recognition scene between father and daughter—so central to sentimental, gothic, and melodramatic cultural practices—occurs, but the happiness of this pair is marred by the accusations of illegitimacy and the mother's adultery, not stains that can be easily dismissed in the melodramatic universe. In accordance with the dictates of melodramatic characterization, the once amiable Dufour suddenly is transformed into an evil uncle, compelled to banish both father and daughter for their sins against the honor of the family. Dufour quickly regrets his action when he learns that it was Trugelin who had assaulted Françisque so many years ago. Exposed by the local doctor as the villain he is, Trugelin flees to the same woods where he had earlier attacked Françisque—scene of act three's most spectacular action as well as scenery, the wild mountainous pass in Savoy where all the principals meet to resolve their melodramatic fates.

Act three is announced by claps of thunder and the fleeing figure of Trugelin, now disguised as a peasant. In the melodramatic logic of repetition and reversal, the same man who had assisted Françisque eight years earlier at the time of the initial assault on his person by Trugelin, now appears to assist Trugelin in his desperate bid to escape the forces of the law closing in on him. As he tells his version of the events to Trugelin, the miller shakes the villain's hand and notices a large scar on it. Only later, when it is too late to easily capture him, does the miller realize who the supposed peasant was. By that time, however, father and daughter have arrived, seeking shelter. Almost immediately, Trugelin engages once again in a struggle with Françisque and tries to kill him, stopped only when Coelina throws herself across the body of her father (recalling Lewis's *Castle Spectre*). When the archers finally capture the villain, peasants descend, wanting to kill the man on the spot. Dufour suddenly appears—*deus ex machina*—and pronounces, "'Leave him to the law,'" a statement that reveals how thoroughly trusted Napoleon's new Civil Code had become. In other words, in lieu of the caprices of a king, now there is a system of law administered by a tribunal of citizens, presided over by a secularized and omnipotent warrior-emperor. All that is left is the redemption of Coelina, and this Françisque supplies by informing the assembled that he was actually married to Isoline, whose later marriage to Dufour's brother was a bigamous one, forced upon her by the threats of her evil brother Trugelin. After a quick marriage ceremony, the action concludes with a ballad and dance signifying the closing and healing of the social and familial units.

Pixérécourt's *Coelina* has been called "the prime example of the essentially reactionary drama engendered by the Revolution," a work that "restrained, even defused, the radical impetus for change" (G. Taylor, 203), while Jeffrey Cox sees Holcroft's version of the play as the very embodiment of "transnational literary Europe," a work that expresses the spirit of the Treaty of Amiens, signed by England and France on March 25, 1802

(2007, 122). With a run of thirty-seven performances, Holcroft's version, *A Tale of Mystery,* is a very close translation, in two acts, with only one scene and the ending slightly changed (more on both anon). The interesting question, however, is what does Holcroft's use of Pixérécourt reveal about the evolution of gothicized melodrama in Britain and its role in the secularization process? As Moody has noted, Holcroft "expunges much of the play's original dialogue, and substitutes the silent dramaturgy of pantomime. . . . [A]s Holcroft pared away the language of *Coelina,* the moral, legal, and hereditary order of Pixérécourt's play began to disintegrate" (90). Further, she observes that one of the most important subjects dramatized by illegitimate theater is "the questionable authority of the law, and, more generally, of the state. Mute characters often embody the failure of law to prevent the tyranny of the powerful over the powerless; false accusation is another important trope in these plays" (91). The use of mute characters like Julio/Theodore in *Deaf and Dumb* as well as Françisque/Francisco in *A Tale of Mystery* "enable Holcroft to create what is in fact a political drama about the possession and the loss (or censorship) of speech" (91).

Holcroft's *Deaf and Dumb* as well as his *A Tale of Mystery* represent, as several theater historians have noted, the birth of a new genre in Britain, the melodrama. But where exactly is the distinction between the slightly earlier sentimental works (like *Nina,* chapter one) and the newer melodrama? I would claim that sentimentality attempts to read human character through the theories of Rousseau or Shaftesbury, believing in either an innate human goodness or the potential for human perfectibility. In contrast, Holcroft's works privilege the theories of Johann Caspar Lavater (1741–1801) and Thomas Hobbes (1588–1679) in their construction of a static and less sympathetic human character. In fact, Holcroft's melodramas focus on trying to understand people's characters and motivations through reading their eyes or the slant of their facial features. When Stephano and Selina approvingly discuss the mysterious stranger Francisco, Selina notes, "'I am interested in his favour. His manners are so mild!'" To which Stephano replies, "'His eye so expressive'" (I:401). As Philip Cox has noted, the theories of Lavater "go against a Godwinian notion of human perfectibility, for, in Lavater's view, each individual 'can be but what he can, is but what he is. He may arrive at, but cannot exceed, a certain degree of perfection, which scourging, even to death itself, cannot make him surpass'" (*Essays on Physiognomy,* trans. Holcroft [1789]; qtd. Cox, xv). In other words, for Lavater character is fixed, not subject to reform, and as such, his view of character is premodern in its static quality. It is important to appreciate that Holcroft translated Lavater's *Essays on Physiognomy* (1789) and went on in a review published in the *Monthly Review* (1793) to defend

Lavater, who was being satirized as "Lord Visage" in the contemporary farce *False Colours* (1783):

> Lord Visage, we think particularly objectionable. He is a physiognomist, and in his character Lavater is satirized, or, to speak more accurately, burlesqued. A poet, who does not consider the moral effects of his satire, is, in our opinion, highly culpable. Any attempt to make men believe that the countenance of man does not bear visible signs of individual propensities, and of vicious or of virtuous habits, is immoral, because it is false. (qtd. J. Graham, 569)

Holcroft was, in other words, a true believer, and his melodramas are full of attempts by characters to read the faces of others as if they were books that were available for scrutiny. Lavater's *Essays on Physiognomy* (1772) was so popular that it went through nine printings in Germany by the 1780s, twelve versions in England by the 1790s, and eleven different translations in France by 1800. Matthew Lewis is listed as a subscriber to the ornately illustrated version of Lavater translated from French into English by Henry Hunter (1789–1798) and illustrated by William Blake (Graham, 567). By 1810 there were fifty-five different versions of the work, including Dutch and Italian ones (Graham, 562). As Graham notes, Lavater managed to "fuse science and religion through a personal enthusiasm and sensibility that satisfied an age in which emotional response and almost occult perception were to become the criteria of the new 'ideal' man" (563). It was not for nothing that William Godwin called in a physiognomist to produce a lengthy report on the facial features of the infant Mary Wollstonecraft Godwin. Like Holcroft, Godwin was also a true believer, declaring, "[N]othing can be more certain than that there is a science of physiognomy" (qtd. Graham, 568). But the theories of Lavater were not universally accepted; indeed, Hannah More and Maria Edgeworth both criticized him as a "mountebank" and a fraud, as someone who might as well be using a "divining rod" in his so-called studies (Graham, 566–67).

What I am calling a premodern and static quality to the characters in melodrama needs to be supplemented by the theories of Hobbes. As a secularist, Hobbes was intent on nothing less than, as Mark Lilla has phrased it, "the dismantling of Christendom's theological-political complex" (75). In his *Leviathan* (1651), Hobbes set out to use physiology, specifically the analysis of the human eye, in order to understand religion and politics. For him, the basic realities of human existence could be understood, not through metaphysics, but by coming to terms with the fact that we are all "bodies alone in the world" (Lilla, 76). The push-pull that sense impressions, memories, and imagination have on human subjects causes them to imagine that they have a "soul," something inside their essentially hollow bodies and minds. To Hobbes, what we have is nothing more than "matter driven from within by nothing but the basic passions of appetite and aversion. Henceforth we shall not speak of the soul; we shall speak only of human striving" (qtd. Lilla, 77). In the Hobbesian worldview, human beings are much like puppets whose strings are pulled, not by the sort of ideals that operate in the sentimental universe, but by their own crudest appetites or basic needs, and such a vision is not far from the characters we actually do see in the world of melodrama.

The logic of the melodramatic worldview works in a very similar manner, moving toward confrontation with the mysterious, unknowable, and hidden until there is a veritable public and private explosion and the truth is revealed in the most painful and humiliating way possible. In the conclusion, all the characters sort themselves out by realigning into tighter and closed clan or tribal units that vindicate the value of maintaining a rigid class system. But there is always a residue left from the melodramatic conflict and that trace is the recurring theme of the survival of the fittest. A secularized moral tenor pervades melodrama, but the voice of morality is not exclusively male, nor is it aristocratic, nor is it transcendent, although all of these characters still do occasionally raise their heads in these works. The melodramatic evolved in England as a vehicle by which the audience was again schooled in the importance of literacy (note that Francisco tells his tale through the act of writing), while women, specifically lower-class women, are given the final word, and that word is the voice of simple common sense.

We can see some of these shifts in emphasis by looking at the changes that Holcroft made as he adapted Pixérécourt for the British stage. The longest speeches in the melodrama now belong to the maid Fiametta, and it is she who narrates the attack on Francisco as an eyewitness:

> It is now seven or eight years ago, when, you having sent me to Chambery, I was coming home. It was almost dark; every thing was still; I was winding along the dale, and the rocks were all as it were turning black. Of a sudden, I heard cries! A man was murdering! I shook from head to foot! Presently, the cries died away, and I beheld two bloody men, with their daggers in their hands, stealing off under / the crags at the foot of the mill. I stood like a stone: for I was frightened out of my wits! So I thought I heard groans; and *afeared* as I was, I had the sense to think they must come from the poor murdered creature. So I listened, and followed my ears, and presently I saw this very man. (I:401; emphasis in original)

This very gothic scene is conveyed in language that is virtually telegraphic, while music becomes an invisible character, used "to express pain and disorder" (I:403), "doubt and terror" (I:407), "pain and alarm" (I:408). As Pixérécourt himself observed, "[A] melodrama is nothing but the *drame lyrique,* where the music is performed by the orchestra instead of being sung."[6]

When Francisco writes his responses to a series of questions delivered by Fiametta and Bonamo (the Ducour figure), he recalls Julio/Theodore in *Deaf and Dumb,* a dispossessed victim of tyranny and greed who nonetheless is constrained by familial ties that prevent him from openly identifying or condemning his oppressor. Francisco makes it clear that he knows who attacked him and sold him to "the Algerines" as a slave, but he refuses to name this person because, as he writes, his attacker is "Rich and powerful" (I:403). This particular scene was in fact one of the most frequently reproduced from the melodrama, and the subject of a popular painting by Samuel de Wilde depicting Francisco posed as if in a *tableau vivant* and delivering his handwritten explanation. The theme of unjust class oppression emerges in both melodramas, suggesting one of the ways that they directly appealed to the growing lower-class and bourgeois audiences in attendance at these productions.

In Holcroft's adaptation, Bonamo refuses to consent to the marriage between his niece and ward Selina and Stephano, his son, stating that he would instead defer to her free choice of a spouse "lest marriage become a farce, libertinism a thing to laugh at, and adultery itself a finable offence!" (I:404). The ideological agenda motivating much of the action concerns the validation of companionate marriage against dynastic or arranged marriages for the purpose of acquiring property. Holcroft's liberal agenda is actually undercut by the fact that the play ends with the promised marriage of Bonamo's son Sephano to his cousin Selina, thereby creating an even tighter familial clan and hold on property. But before that happy ending can occur, the crisis of the work centers on Bonamo's refusal of this love match once he learns that Selina is illegitimate. Despite the pleadings of his son, Bonamo threatens to disinherit and curse him should he marry Selina without his father's consent. This impasse is quickly resolved when the servant Fiametta enters to tell her employer exactly what she thinks of his decision: "'I don't care for you. I loved you this morning; I would have lost my life for you; but you are grown wicked'" (II:415). When Bonamo tries to silence her, she continues to speak in a manner that very few female servants had used before on stage: "'I know the worst: I have worked for you all the prime of my youth; and now you'll serve me as you have served the innocent wretched Selina; you'll turn me out of doors. Do it! But I'll not go till I've said out my say: so, I tell you again, you are a hard hearted uncle, an unfeeling father, and an unjust master! Every body will shun you! You will dwindle out a life of misery, and no body will pity you; because you don't deserve pity'" (II:416). Sounding very much like a curse, this speech enacts the same sort of revolutionary ideological work that was accomplished when L'Abeé de l'Epée confronted Darlemont with his crimes in *Deaf and Dumb*. In fact, in examining Fiametta as well as Pierre in *Deaf and Dumb*, one is reminded of Bruce Robbins's observation about the literary portrayal of servants during this period, "[T]here was in fact a sudden and well-documented new anxiety on the part of masters and mistresses about the damage that servant spies and informants could do" (108).

But what is most important in Holcroft's revision of *Coelina* is that he removes the villain's prayers to God after his capture and instead inserts an earlier scene in which Fiametta, the maid, essentially takes the place of God. Shepherd argues that Holcroft's revisions of his French source reveal a new subjectivity, an anarchistic posture toward the state and the family, a condemnation of marriage, and a much more complicated position toward justice, law, class structure, and family (510–11). One way in which this anarchy can be seen is in Fiametta's outburst, for here she issues orders and offers condemnations and curses to her aristocratic employer; it is she—not the clergy or the aristocracy—who has assumed the voice of moral authority in the play. It is she who will forgive or not and allow the master to continue in society, not God or anyone else. As Shephard notes, early bourgeois British dramas were predicated on the exclusion, marginalization, and victimization of female characters, all of which served the "male-centeredness" of the stage's actions and the audience's expectations. Lower-class-artisan culture was itself the product of working practices that ensured a "closed shop," a union that excluded women as workers (514). Such a culture expected to see men at the center of the stage, not women, and hence the gothic—with its victimized and orphaned heroine in need of male protection and intervention—very much suited its tastes. What is most revolutionary about Holcroft's *Tale of Mystery* is the positioning of the woman—and a maid—at the center of the stage and as the voice of moral and social authority.

In *A Tale of Mystery*, the heroine Selina sleuths, uncovers a murder plot, aligns herself with her disgraced father, and then in the final scene she pleads for her evil uncle's forgiveness as the soldiers close in on him in order to kill him. We do not see her aligned with her fiancé Stephano in Holcroft's version, although clearly a marriage is promised. Instead, we see her standing between father and uncle, the feminine mediator in

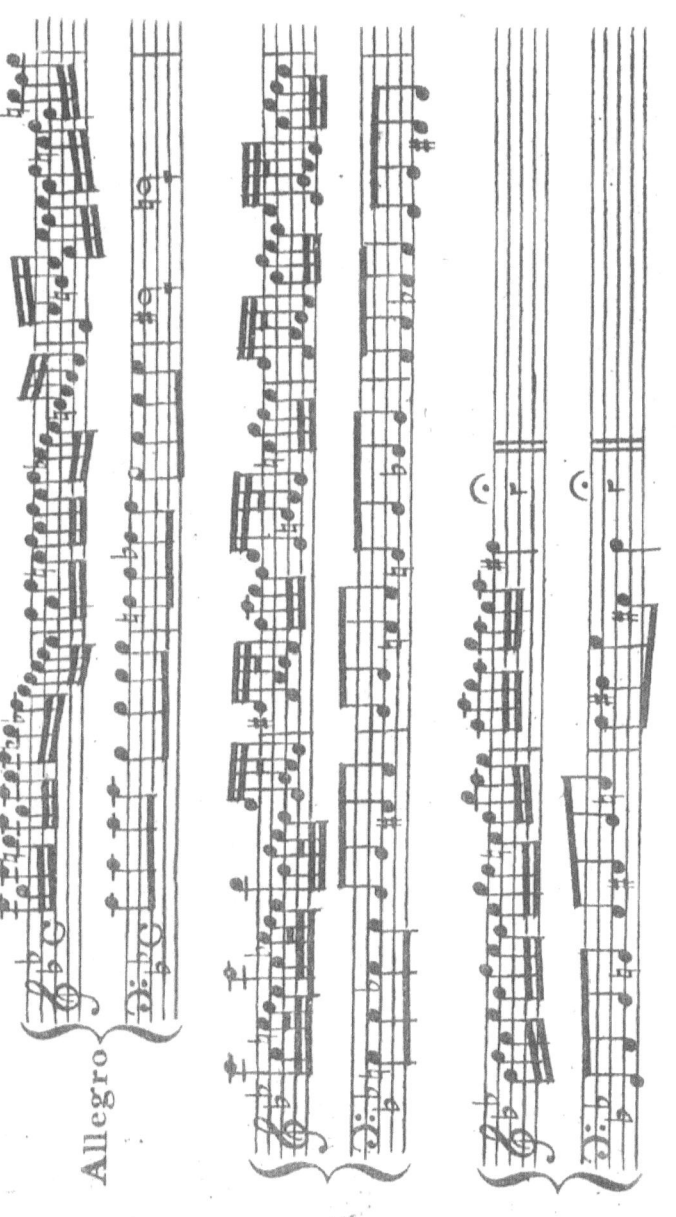

FIGURE 6: Musical score by Thomas Busby for last act of *A Tale of Mystery*

a system of masculine dyadic dysfunction. The crucial recognition scene occurs when Michelli, the miller, "makes the sign of biting his right hand" to Francisco so that Francisco can verify to him that Romaldi indeed was his assailant. As Romaldi flees the miller's house with his pistol, Francisco "opens his breast for him to shoot, if he please. Selina falls between them. The whole scene passes in a mysterious and rapid manner. Music suddenly stops" (II:422). As Hibberd and Nielsen have observed, the music in *A Tale of Mystery* is simple because the moral aspects of melodrama are "unambiguous" and the emotions depicted are connected with moral issues: "the music is implicated at a fundamental level because of its explicit as well as its non-specific language and its ability to heighten emotional extremes." The intensity, indeed fury, of the music can be suggested by the excerpt below, which accompanies the climactic confrontation scene between the two brothers and Selina, who attempts to figure as a mediator (see fig. 6).

The pantomimic quality here is reinforced by a very primitive recourse to blood ritual and sacrifice. Romaldi refuses to shoot his brother, shouting, "'No! Too much of your blood is upon my head! Be justly revenged: take mine!'" (II:423). As the peasants supplemented by the Archers prepare to kill Romaldi, again "Francisco and Selina, in the greatest agitation, several times throw themselves between the assailants and Romaldi." In the final lines of the work, Selina screams, "'Oh, forbear! Let my father's virtues plead for my uncle's errors!'" while Bonamo sounds the quasi-religious reconciliatory note by stating, "'We all will intreat for mercy; since of mercy we all have need: for his sake, and for our own, may it be freely granted!'" (II:423).

The Christian tone to this conclusion is both significant and paradoxical. The appeal to "his sake" echoes a traditional Christian prayer requesting the intercession of Jesus Christ, "in whose name we ask forgiveness." Instead, in this passage Bonamo (the "good" secularized father) asks that the forces of the state and the laws "freely grant" forgiveness and mercy to Romaldi, a man who has destroyed the life of his brother, his brother's wife, and orphaned their daughter. Also odd is the positioning of Selina as very much in the center of the action. Selina is more than a daughter functioning to prop up a tottering and corrupt patriarchal system. She is a social arbiter, a political advocate who cautions against rash revenge and instead pleads for forgiveness and acceptance of those who have committed even the most heinous crimes against their fellows. In short, the evolution of melodrama is predicated on the emergence of women as forces to be reckoned with in an increasingly secularized society. God is replaced in the melodramatic universe with wise women who do not hesitate to speak truth to power.

So if *speaking* is the issue, why is the hero mute? When Shepherd attempts to answer this question he observes:

> The emotion of the moment of speaking out is something very different from the frustration experienced when the dumb man cannot speak to clear himself. Being able to acclaim the truth is the opposite of being trapped into a false truth. Melodrama may be said to construct excitement out of the possible alternation between being trapped in circumstances and being able to change them. (201)

For Shepherd, the rhetoric of false virtue and self-serving hypocrisy can finally be defeated only by the ontological reality of truth which does not speak; it simply is. Whereas Shepherd wants to argue that melodrama serves a liberal agenda, George Taylor insists that melodrama is inherently conservative, invested in depicting "tradition as innocent and change as evil" (205). Brooks, on the other hand, points out the highly metaphorical aspect of muteness, arguing that the mute gesture is "a displacement of meaning . . . whose tenor is vaguely defined by grandiose emotional or spiritual forces and gestures that seek to make present without directly naming it, [and instead] by pointing at it" (72).

We might also recall that Burke in his essay on the sublime had listed a number of "general privations" that he considered "great, because they are all terrible; *Vacuity, Darkness, Solitude,* and *Silence*" (II.v.115–16; his emphasis). In some ways, the deaf and dumb heroes of Holcroft's melodramas inhabit a silent world in which their inability to communicate places them in terrifyingly vulnerable positions. But what exactly does the mute hero point to but his own maiming at the hands of a patriarchy in which he himself was/is complicit? The rhetoric of the melodrama swerves violently between hyperbole to mute silence, enacting cultural anxieties that are caused by a moral code that is allied with a conservative political agenda. Such a strategy served to defuse free-floating cultural anxiety by first enacting the worst that could happen and then containing that performance in fantasies of resolution on the stage. This technique reassured its audience that evil would be recognized and punished, good would be restored and vindicated, and stability and harmony would triumph over the capricious or chaotic. Melodramas, in short, are about the struggle to remain a believer in a world that no longer sanctioned such premodern belief systems.[7] God is absent, but his presence is mourned and nostalgically remembered in the melodramatic universe. The god that failed in melodrama is embodied in the evil uncle, the corrupt father, the patriarch who oppresses and seduces, while the savior is the daughter/mother figure, a class indeterminate woman who reminds her culture that life has value in and of itself and that familial codes of appropriate conduct must function in lieu of abstract and outmoded religious principles. The melodrama works to make social and class relations feel like familial structures, the public becomes privatized, or as Shepherd observes, the melodrama "makes [the] forms and structures of society feel like private relations, elements of the inner person" (508). In short, the melodrama dramatizes the challenges faced by the older "porous self" as it finds itself confronted with a variety of changes that a modern epistemology has created.

How ironic that a committed political radical should be credited with importing melodrama, a genre that George Taylor has termed "the classic reactionary genre" (199), into Britain. And how revealing that the changes Holcroft made in his French sources caused melodrama to swerve toward the increased power and prominence of lower- and middle-class women as social arbiters in this new bourgeois nation. In fact, this trend had been recognized by Hegel in his discussion of Kotzebuean melodrama when he noted that these works tended to extol an "ordinary morality" (92).[8] One of the legacies of Holcroft's swerve can be seen in later gothic works like *Jane Eyre* or *Wuthering Heights*, where servants frequently chastise aristocrats for their excesses and follies. Holcroft revealed the moral vacuity at the social core that aristocratic Britain had constructed for itself, while his "temple of morality" became the nascent Jacobin stage presided over by a sharp-tongued maid who was morally centered enough to understand that society could not be based on outmoded codes of rank and privilege, but on forgiveness, generosity, and human decency.

- CHAPTER 5 -

The Gothic Ballad and Blood Sacrifice
From Bürger to Wordsworth

> The history of mankind is a romance, a mask, a tragedy, constructed upon the principles of poetical justice. . . . We may depend upon it that what men delight to read in books, they will put in practice in reality.
> —William Hazlitt, *Characters of Shakespear's Plays* (1817)

I.

Gothic ballads, with their dead babies, seduced nuns, abandoned mermaids, undead knights, and malicious monks, enjoyed a heyday in Germany and England from the late eighteenth through the early nineteenth centuries. Steeped in folk and oral traditions, these neoprimitivist ballads were a transitional genre—part oral, part written—and as such they mediated in their very existence a culture in rapid flux, partly singing and partly writing its way into modernity. If genre is, as Ralph Cohen has observed, a "structure that always includes features that have continuity with the past . . . [then it also has] features that are innovative. Genre by this definition is constituted by linguistic codes that are inconsistent in their implications" (11–12). The ballad is perhaps one of the most "inconsistent" genres in its implications, highly traditional and providential, while its later manifestations appear to advocate the need to renounce superstitions in favor of the emerging rationalistic code of conduct that

CHAPTER 5

bourgeois Europe was tentatively embracing.[1] Clifford Siskin has noted about genre in the romantic period that its history actually reveals how "man reconstituted himself as the modern psychologized subject: a mind, capable of limitless growth, that takes itself to be the primary object of its own inquiries" (1998, 212–13). And Siskin's recourse to Bishop Thomas Percy's "Appendix II: On the Ancient Metrical Romances" attached to his *Reliques of Ancient English Poetry* (1765) is telling in regard to the presence of ballads within the larger gothic imaginary. Percy's need to construct a dark northern origin for Britain, shrouded in mists of obscurity, suggests for Siskin "a mysteriously romantic time that gave way to an enlightened present; it also includes our ongoing fascination with what Gothicism—with its strange mix of chivalry haunted by trips to Catholic countries and hints of the forbidden East—was and, to a large extent, still is . . . a site for the symbolic violence of selective forgetting and remembering" (1988, 11). We will be able to detect all three of these phenomena—violence, forgetting, and anxious remembering—in an examination of the secularizing trend in a few representative gothic ballads by William Wordsworth (1770–1850).

The late eighteenth-century European ballad craze originated in the publication of Percy's *Reliques,* which was enthusiastically received in Germany and then made its way back to England, exerting a powerful influence on Wordsworth, Coleridge, Southey, Lewis, and Scott. Frank Sayers's *Dramatic Sketches of the Ancient Northern Mythology* (1790) was also popular in both England and Germany and seemed to promise the rise of a new type of literature steeped in Anglo-German romantic sensibilities (see Chandler). But even more gothically potent, the supernatural poetic tales of Gottfried August Bürger (1748–1794) were translated from German into English by the early 1790s, circulated widely in manuscript form, and were finally published in the *Monthly Magazine* in 1796. Widely hailed as inaugurating a new and vigorous literary style, Bürger himself admitted that he had been initially influenced by the traditional English ballad "Sweet William's Ghost" (Conger, 136). Walter Scott began his literary career by translating Bürger's "Lenora" as "William and Helen" in 1796, remembering years later how the "fanciful wildness" of "Lenora" as read by Anna Barbauld to an Edinburgh literary society "electrified" the reading public and inaugurating a new era in poetic sensibilities ("Minstrelsy," IV:37–38). In concert with the young Scott and his less than enthusiastic collaborator Robert Southey, Lewis attempted to exploit the Bürger craze by publishing sixty ballads in his *Tales of Wonder* (1801), a two-volume assortment of both original compositions (mainly in volume one) and adaptations or translations taken from the German as well as earlier British ballads by Jonson, Dryden, Gray, Burns, Percy and others (volume two). In a 1799 letter to Scott, Lewis wrote that his collection would feature "a Ghost or a Witch [as the] sine-qua-non ingredient in all the dishes, of which I mean to compose my hobgoblin repast" (Lewis 2009, 17). By translating *volk* ballads such as Herder's "The Erl-King's Daughter," and "Elver's Hoh," Bürger's "Der Wilde Jäger" and Goethe's "The Erl-King," and positioning them alongside earlier British works such as Jonson's "The Witches' Song" or Gray's "The Fatal Sisters," Lewis attempted to forge nothing less than an alternative supernatural literary genealogy for British poetry, one that seamlessly incorporated the Germanic as part of its heritage, rather than as a "foreign importation" (see Mortensen, 82; Wilson). Indeed, he was so successful in this attempt that in 1851 David Moir suggested that writers such as Lewis, Radcliffe, Leyden, Bannerman, Scott, and Coleridge should be grouped together and appreciated as "the supernatural school" of British literature (qtd. Craciun, 180).

In addition to the enthusiastic support that ballads received from Lewis and Scott, Southey also contributed eight ballads to *Tales of Wonder* and published additional gothic ballads in the *New Monthly Magazine* (1796–99), notably "Donica," "Rudiger," and "Jasper." His most successful attempt at a gothic ballad inspired by Bürger's "Lenora" was, in his own opinion, "The Old Woman of Berkeley" (1802), composed as a deliberate attempt "to restore the pure stream of 'German sublimity'" to the problems that he had denounced in Coleridge's "Ancient Mariner" (see Chandler). In this ballad, a dying witch pays a priest to use every superstitious device allowed by the Catholic Church (chains around her coffin, burning candles, rosaries, and novenas) in order to protect her dead body from demon possession; however, the devil still enters the church to claim her body and soul: "She rose on her feet in her winding sheet, / Her dead flesh quiver'd with fear, / And a groan like that which the Old Woman gave / Never did mortal hear . . . The Devil he flung her on the horse, / And he leapt up before, / And away like the lightning's speed they went, / And she was seen no more" (167). Southey's ballad presents us with a vision of the premodern past, the "porous self" trapped in the inescapable world of anima, and as such it is much more in tune with a Germanic ballad sensibility rather than the more self-conscious, distancing British productions that query or interrogate such a perspective.

Wordsworth and Coleridge during this time also began their own approach-avoidance dance with the gothic ballad, and certainly both were, to some extent, caught up in the "Bürger craze" that swept England and reached the height of its popularity in 1796, when his "Lenora" was illustrated by William Blake and translated by six different poets and antiquarians in one year, most notably William Taylor of Norwich (1765–1836), who published his version in the *Monthly Magazine* (March 1796). As Maureen McLane has noted, there is a certain irony in the use of ballads as the genre most "implicated in the romantic exploration of primitivity, modernity, and historicity" (2001, 424). Standing as literary "relics" to a distant historical past, ballads were considered to be the narratives that were left behind like so much residue in the manic quest to achieve modernity and a desacralized sense of the past. These *faux*-medieval poems represent, as Susan Stewart has observed, one of several "distressed genres," like the epic, the fable, and the proverb, that declare their antiquity like a valuable patina (69–93). But the major component of this patina was its revival of a number of premodern superstitions like demon-possession and the material reality of ghosts that an ambivalently mixed secularizing agenda aimed to reanimate and at the same time needed to contain. The irony implicit in this contradictory ideology was certainly recognized at the time. In 1799 the Irishman Samuel Whyte offered a warning about the dangers of "Lenora," stating that the ballad perpetuated superstitions and "seemed calculated to keep alive and propagate the exploded notions of ghosts and hobgoblins [as] the great annoyance of poor children, whose ductile minds are liable to fearful impressions, which by the strongest exertion to reason and good sense are scarcely ever afterwards to be wholly obliterated" (qtd. Mortensen 2004, 212n10). Even one of the translators of "Lenora," Henry James Pye, remarked about it: "This little poem, from the singularity of the incidents, and the wild horror of the images, is certainly an object of curiosity, but is by no means held up as a pattern for imitation" ("Advertisement," 2). In a very similar vein, the anti-Jacobin T. J. Mathias observed: "No German nonsense sways my English heart, / Unus'd at ghosts and rattling bones to start /.... Say, are the days of blest delusion fled? / Must fiction rear no more her languid head?" (qtd. Spacks, 105).

Bürger's most famous ballad "Lenora" is set in Germany at the conclusion of the Seven Years' War (1756–63) and tells a now-familiar tale of demon-possession: a young woman's beloved, Wilhelm, does not return from war and is presumed to be dead. The woman curses God and, in her inconsolable grief, wishes herself dead. Although her mother begs her to take back the sacrilegious curse, Lenora goes to bed unrepentant and defiant. That night her lover appears at her door on horseback and begs her to elope with him, to which she agrees. Their ride is filled with imagery of the dead—ghosts, specters, goblins—and ends at a graveyard where the lover lifts his visor just long enough to reveal that he is a skeleton and with that he promptly takes his beloved with him into a single grave. This particular scene, the wild backward ride of Lenora on a horse ridden by the devil, became one of the stock gothic visuals of the era, spawning innumerable paintings and engravings throughout Europe. Ironically, Lenora has had her wish; her curse has been fulfilled in her own death. The ballad concludes with a pious and traditional Christian admonition, warning readers to have "Geduld" (patience), for it is folly to quarrel with "Mit Gottes Allmacht hadre nicht!" (God's omnipotence). Filled with primitive tropes of fiendish ghouls who have the power to enact God's punishment on anyone foolish enough to wish herself dead, the ballad also presents the power of animism and magical thinking, and resurrects the feudal world of primitive Christianity, where orality has the power to cause events and a wish is fulfilled through the intervention of supernatural powers. A contemporary critic at the time, William Preston, condemned it for "irreligion and profanation" and declared it a "blasphemous exclamation against Providence." Its convoluted attitude toward what appears to be a despotic and tyrannical Providence can best be seen when we consider that this God has interfered in the life of a suffering woman, going so far as to use demons to enact vengeance on a grieving girl. Others have noted that as a clergyman's son, Bürger became increasingly skeptical about God and eventually left the Lutheran Church altogether (Mortensen 2004, 49), but not before he delivered this stinging assault on God as operating in league with the devil.

After reading the ballad in German, Wordsworth wrote to Coleridge: "Dorothy and I have read *Lenore* and a few little things of Bürger; but upon the whole we were disappointed, particularly in *Lenore* which we thought in several passages inferior to the English translation by William Taylor" (*Letters*, 233). Wordsworth's German, as we know, was not strong, so it is perhaps a defensive gesture as well as a nationalistic one that he should prefer the translation. And again, after reading Bürger's "Der Wilde Jager" ("The Wild Huntsman") in late 1798, Wordsworth wrote to Coleridge:

> In poems[,] description of human nature [. . .] and character is absolutely necessary, &c: incidents are among the lowest allurements of poetry. Take from Bürger's poems the *incidents,* which are seldom or ever of his own invention, and still much will remain; there will remain a manner of relating which is almost always spirited and lively, and stamped and peculiarized with genius. Still I do not find those higher beauties which can entitle him to the name of a *great* poet. (*Letters,* 234; his emphasis)

There is evidence here of a condescending attitude to the jaded tastes of the masses, a distinction being drawn between poetry as an exploration of emotions and ideas and poetry as a crude novelizing recitation of events.[2] Wordsworth also appears to be congratulating himself, as he did think that he at least had begun to write poetry that embodied those "higher beauties" that could be located in something other than "incident," and it is in defining those "higher beauties" that the essence of his adaptations, experimentations, and tentative attempts at modernization and secularization can be found.

Although Wordsworth continued to claim throughout his life that his *Lyrical Ballads* were best understood as purely British products and that they should be read as operating in a direct line of descent from Bishop Percy's *Reliques* (1765), as well as the poems of Robert Burns and William Cowper, this claim is more than a bit disingenuous. Literary historians such as Friedman, Laws, Jacobus, Gamer, and Mortensen have all noted that Wordsworth and Coleridge were clearly indebted to Bürger's ballads, but by the time Wordsworth wrote the revised *Preface* to the second edition of the *Lyrical Ballads* (1800), he was compelled to condemn "frantic novels [and] sickly and stupid German tragedies," and to distinguish his and Coleridge's poems from the popular, Jacobin-inflected gothic tradition that had fallen out of favor rather quickly (which is why "Christabel" had to be suppressed and the 1798 "Rime of the Ancyent Marinere" had to be radically revised). Certainly both poets were familiar from earliest youth with Britain's homegrown ballad tradition as presented by Percy, Burns, Cowper, and Macpherson and, as Mayo and Fowler have both shown, they were well aware of the magazine poetry and the broadside ballad traditions that were widespread throughout urban and rural Britain during the eighteenth and early nineteenth centuries.

Despite the evidence that Wordsworth and Coleridge were motivated to compose a volume of ballads that would appeal to the reading public's taste and exploit the techniques of gothic ballads with all their supernatural trappings, there has been a persistent critical effort to depict these early works as "challenges" to the prevailing public taste in ghosts and demons. As Siskin observes, Mayo was complicit in the attempt to shore up Wordsworth's own claims to originality, even though Mayo's own research into the magazine ballads of the day proved otherwise. Claiming that a "careful reading" of the *Lyrical Ballads* reveals "a tremendous impression of clarity, freshness, and depth," Mayo goes on to see Wordsworth's "true genius" operating in another "dimension" than the historical, that is, in the transcendent lyric realm (1988, 19). But Wordsworth's "transcendent lyricism" was not readily on display at the time he was first publishing in 1798, and, indeed, is only visible after close to fifty years of revisions on *The Prelude*. As for the earlier ballads, as Marilyn Butler has observed about the *Lyrical Ballads* in its historical context: "Of course it is an irony that later critics have persisted in seeing [them] as heralding a new kind of poetry—when the abler contemporary critics saw them as the epitome of an older, if recent and short-lived kind, which became unacceptable once England's destiny was to champion the counter-revolution" (64). And so on one hand this other poetry, the Germanic gothic ballad, was, from its introduction into Britain, associated with freethinking, political sedition, and threateningly new forms of social and religious reforms. On the other hand, the ballad was associated with lower-class, plebian literary forms, the literature of the *volk*, and it is useful here to consider the similarity of the volume to what were called "garlands" during the period, collections of ballads in eight-page pamphlets similar in size and formatting to the chapbooks of the day. Obviously, *Lyrical Ballads* is a much more ambitious and elite production, but it would have been recognizable to its contemporary audience as a collection of traditional ballads that sounded very much like the popular gothic ballads that were currently being imported from Germany (see Leask).

There has been no shortage of opinions on how much Wordsworth was influenced by the gothic and exactly when he renounced its influence on his writings altogether. There appear to be, according to Irving Buchen, two distinct phases to Wordsworth's flirtation with the gothic. The first period, running from 1787-1797, produced "The Vale of Esthwaite" (1787), "Fragments of a Gothic Tale" (1791), "Guilt and Sorrow" (1793-94), "Incipient Madness" (1795), *The Borderers* (1795), and "The Three Graves" (1797; coauthored with Coleridge). These works are characterized by a number of familiar gothic tropes, namely the fear of madness, the landscape of nightmare, and what we can recognize as an attempt to tap into the aesthetics of the Burkean sublime. According to Burke, "[W]hatever is fitted in any sort to excite the ideas of pain and danger, that is to say, whatever is in any sort terrible, or is conversant about terrible objects, or operates in a manner analogous to terror, is a source of the sublime, that is, it is productive of the strongest emotion which the mind is capable of feeling" (105). We can see Wordsworth (rather crudely) trying to employ the Burkean sublime in a number of his early poetic efforts. In "The Vale of Esthwaite," for instance, the poet retreats to "gloomy glades, / Religious woods and midnight shades, / Where brooding Superstition frowned, / A cold and awful horror round" (I:25–28). Amidst references to "druid sons" and "black damp dungeon[s] underground," he asks, "Why roll on me your glaring eyes? / Why fix on me for sacrifice?" (I:32–40). Amidst this atmosphere of religious paranoia and guilt, the poet stumbles into a "Gothic mansion" (I:47) inhabited by "spirits yelling from their pains" (53) and a temptress with "dark cheek all ghastly bright" who leads the hero to a hideous chasm (I:287). This wintry and nightmarish landscape is also dominated by a specter whose eyes are like "two wan withered leaves" and whose "bones look'd sable through his skin" (I:337–39), and we can recall here Coleridge's own use of "black bones" in the deleted stanza from "Rime of the Ancyent Marinere" (see below). Almost like a checklist that he is trying to employ, Wordsworth's use of "darkness," "vacuity," and "power" seems to have been informed by his adherence to a fashionable Burkean aesthetic practice.

Similarly, "Fragments of a Gothic Tale" concerns a young man who decides to murder a blind old sailor for no apparent reason. Just as he is about to commit the deed, lightning crashes and the youth's hand is stayed: "And all which he, that night, had seen or felt / Showed like the shapes delusion loves to deem / Sights that obey the dead or phantoms of a dream" (219–21). Even for the early Wordsworth, the gothic begins in a transcendent supernatural realm but moves fairly quickly to the immanent secular city. Gothic crimes in Wordsworth are also situated in all too familiar public as well as personal sins, betrayal and desertion, but in every instance the focus is on individual spiritual failings, challenges encountered, or finally on the inability of his poetic subjects to understand their emotions so that they are unable to form a coherent sense of selfhood in the face of challenge and threat.

The second phase of Wordsworth's gothic experiments is much more limited and coincides with the period of his greatest creativity, 1798–1800. The major gothic works here include "Goody Blake and Harry Gill," "The Idiot Boy," "The Thorn," "Peter Bell," the Lucy poems, "Ruth," "Her Eyes Are Wild," and "Hart-Leap Well." Alienated solitaries redeemed by the humanizing imagination or abandoned and mad women (as in "Her Eyes Are Wild"), these are typical gothic tropes, but the use of gothic machinery is clearly decreasing in these works. One is tempted to observe that in fact Wordsworth is not writing gothic works any longer per se because his society, the generally paranoid political period of the Revolutionary and Napoleonic wars, had actually become closer to the gothic landscape that had only been imagined a few years earlier. For instance, in looking at Wordsworth's depictions of mad women, women who kill their infants, or women who kill themselves out of desperation, it is useful to recall that not so very much earlier there had been a very strong belief in witches, fairies, and ghosts. As Joseph Addison observed in his *Spectator* essay on *The Pleasures of the Imagination* (1712):

> Our Forefathers looked upon Nature with more Reverence and Horrour, before the World was enlightened by Learning and Philosophy, and loved to astonish themselves with the Apprehensions of Witchcraft, Prodigies, Charms, and Enchantments. There was not a Village in England that had not a Ghost in it, the Church-yards were all haunted [recall "We Are Seven"], every large Common had a Circle of Fairies belonging to it, and there was scarce a Shepherd to be met with who had not seen a Spirit. (3.572)

As McWhir points out, the Witchcraft Act was not repealed in England until 1736 and the popular belief in ghosts, witches, and magic continued for many years (29), indeed one is tempted to observe that it still exists today in certain quarters. A witch was lynched in Herefordshire as late as 1751, while the Cock-Lane Ghost was believed by many to be haunting London in 1762. This mixture of the supernatural and its opposite is, as we have noted throughout, yet another manifestation of the coexistence of transcendent and immanent beliefs that characterizes so much of the content of the gothic ballad, a literary technology that embodied within itself the ambivalent secularizing impulse.

A major part of Wordsworth's interest in subjective experiences lies in his presentation of human suffering, while scenarios of almost sadomasochistic suffering dominate the gothic and sentimental aesthetic and can be understood in two ways: first, as attempts to appropriate and secularize Christian iconography, and secondly, as stylized responses to rapid cultural and religious changes. Wordsworth observed in his only attempt at a gothic drama, *The Borderers* (comp. 1796–97), that "action is transitory, a step, a blow—," while "Suffering is permanent, obscure and dark, / And has the nature of infinity" in it (III.v.60–65). When Wordsworth attempted to rewrite the ballads of Bürger in a number of the poems he contributed to the *Lyrical Ballads*, he minimized the incidents and increased the suffering, thereby creating something like a substitutive religious ethos: individualized and particularized rather than universalized, secularist rather than theistic, dark and obscure because all of us are capable only of viewing like voyeurs the opaque surfaces of our fellows, and thereby never truly appreciating or truly feeling the suffering of others. We can, of course, exquisitely experience our own sufferings, but the sensibility that Wordsworth creates for Martha Ray (in "The Thorn"), for instance, is transferable and understandable only in the abstract. Her suffering can only be mediated by a third party, an obtuse narrator, who uses qualified language that further distances us as readers from the immediacy of the incident and her emotions. As a number of recent theorists have noted, the divide between

CHAPTER 5

modern and premodern, self and other, private and public, visual and sublime is in fact the root of the distinction between the romantic and the gothic.³

II.

> Let ghastliest forms, pale ghosts, and goblins grim,
> Form of your verse the terrible sublime!
> Paint the dire skeleton, uncloth'd with skin,
> With grave-worms crawling out and crawling in,
> All hell's red torches in the numbers shine,
> And fiends on horseback gallop through the line.
>
> —Joseph Fawcett, *The Art of Poetry* (1798)

How exactly did the gothic ballad, with its heavy emphasis on the supernatural, the aristocratic, and the uncanny, transmute into the poems that became, after much fussing and feuding, the *Lyrical Ballads?* This section will examine some of the gothic ballads of Bürger as sources for not simply some of the *Lyrical Ballads*, but for the conception and ambience of the volume as a whole. Wordsworth and Coleridge were not trying simply to "speak to common men in the language of everyday life" in the *Lyrical Ballads*, they were instead appropriating and at the same time revising, nationalizing, and secularizing a Germanic sensibility for the British audience that they wanted to claim as theirs, seeking in such an act to align themselves with the cultural ethos of northern Europe in opposition to the southern and Catholic areas of Europe. For all their claims to the contrary, the gothic ballad in Wordsworth and Coleridge's hands became a nationalistic and secularist discourse designed to position Britain alongside its Norse, Anglo-Saxon, and Germanic neighbors, in opposition to French, Italian, and Catholic traditions that were viewed as increasingly dangerous to the interests of Great Britain (see Oergel). And through their acts of appropriation they were not simply domesticating, nationalizing, and naturalizing a discourse that had used the supernatural for effect, they were modernizing and secularizing British subjectivity and poetic traditions.

One approaches the *Lyrical Ballads* with more than a little trepidation, as the volume has assumed the status of something like the holy grail of canonical romantic studies. But as we know from a number of statements made later by both Wordsworth and Coleridge, to some extent the entire volume was predicated on an attempt to explore the supernatural and its opposite: the "natural." In his *Biographia Literaria*, Coleridge describes the evolution of the *Lyrical Ballads:*

> The thought suggested itself (to which of us I do not recollect) that a series of poems might be composed of two sorts. In the one, the incidents and agents were to be, in part at least, supernatural; and the excellence aimed at was to consist in the interesting of the affections by the dramatic truth of such emotions, as would naturally accompany such situations, supposing them real. And real in *this* sense they have been to every human being who, from whatever source of delusion, has at any time believed himself under supernatural agency. (*BL* II:1–2)

Coleridge does not expand on the most interesting part of the statement here, that there is a "dramatic truth" in "emotions" created by exposure to "supernatural agency," but he does go on to note that it was his assignment to compose the supernatural ballads "so as to transfer from our inward nature a human interest and a semblance of truth sufficient to procure for these shadows of the imagination that willing suspension of disbelief for the moment, which constitutes poetic faith" (II:2). This definition of the imagination has assumed a canonical status that rivals Wordsworth's own definition of poetry as "the spontaneous overflow of powerful feelings from emotions recollected in tranquility." But these two rival approaches arise, I would argue, out of the initially opposed postures taken by Coleridge and Wordsworth toward the supernatural, for in their different "assignments" we can see that both were already committed to trying to find a way to resuscitate or secularize in their ballads the uncanny residue of the spiritual and transcendent.

But Coleridge was not an altogether enthusiastic advocate for the supernatural gothic and, in fact, this may be one of the primary reasons he was unable to ever complete "Christabel" (see Hoeveler 1990, 169–88). He seems to have taken something of the same skeptical position toward the gothic that Wordsworth did. In his review of Lewis's novel *The Monk,* for instance, Coleridge claimed that "tales of enchantments and witchcraft can never be *useful*: our author has contrived to make them *pernicious,* by blending . . . all that is most awfully true in religion with all that is most ridiculously absurd in superstition" (*Critical Review* 19 [1797], 197; emphasis in original). This attempt to condemn the gothic for its trafficking in "absurd" superstitions actually obscures the animus that motivated a good deal of Wordsworth and Coleridge's resentment of the gothic's popularity: its marketability and the financial success of writers like Lewis and Radcliffe (the highest paid novelist in England at the time). There can be no denying the fact that in their first 1798 volume, Coleridge and Wordsworth did attempt to capitalize on the gothic's market share, and we can see this most clearly in the first version of the "Rime of the Ancyent Marinere," complete with a hero who commits a senseless crime, sucks his own blood, is haunted by disembodied voices and spectral persecutory figures, is condemned to an eternal life-in-death, is transported by a crew of the living dead, and is magically saved by the ability to pray. Extremely controversial and viewed by critics as both gothic and anti-gothic, the "Rime" employs sacramental and Christian imagery only to suggest that such readings are inadequate and simplistic in light of the horror and terror implicit in life's choices. But clearly the ballad uses supernatural effects throughout, and perhaps in no place is this attempt to reanimate the supernatural more evident than in the "gothic stanza" that Coleridge included in his first published version of "Rime of the Ancyent Marinere":

> *His* bones were black with many a crack,
> All black and bare, I ween;
> Jet-black and bare, save where with rust
> Of mouldy damps and charnel crust
> They're patch'd with purple and green. (1798, 18; his emphasis)

This lurid depiction of one of the dicing pair recalls not simply Burke's association of the sublime with "black," but also places Coleridge's ballad within the more extreme contemporary terrain of Matthew Lewis and the Germanic gothics. In agreeing with Wordsworth's requests to revise the ballad and add the explanatory gloss, Coleridge was attempting to naturalize the supernaturalism that he had initially agreed to create. Although deeply offended by Wordsworth's demand that he revise the ballad by removing all of the clichés and codes of the gothic, Coleridge actually made his ballad more psychologically plausible, brought it in line with the spiritual angst of the period, and hence his audience was all the more terrified when they found themselves sitting in a dinghy with the mariner and a particularly ineffectual trinity.

The status of the *Lyrical Ballads* rests not simply on the theoretical intentions of the poets as defined after the fact, or the quality of so many of its poems, but on the scaffolding that Wordsworth's new *Preface* provided for the 1800 volume (and expanded in 1815). It is in this document that he makes the boldest claims for the volume's poetic originality, all of which are too well known to be extensively rehearsed here. But for a reader of the gothic ballad and certainly for a contemporary reader such as Robert Southey, many of the poems sounded very familiar because they were steeped in the literary ambience of the late eighteenth century and were, in fact, not as original as Wordsworth would have liked his audience to believe.[4] Gamer has argued that Wordsworth was motivated to purge the most blatantly gothic elements from the first edition of *Lyrical Ballads* because of the critical responses of Southey, who famously condemned "The Rime of the Ancyent Marinere" as a "Dutch attempt at German sublimity. Genius has here been employed in producing a poem of little merit" (qtd. J. Jackson, 53). Charles Lamb, in Coleridge's defense, less famously defended the ballad as "a right English attempt . . . to dethrone German sublimity" (I:142). But Gamer sees Wordsworth's "defensive" 1800 *Preface* as a response to the negative review of the first edition that Southey published in the *Critical Review* in October 1798 (117–18). Certainly Gamer's argument is much more complicated than this, but he as well as Parrish, Bewell, and Swann (to cite only a few critics) have all attempted to analyze how Wordsworth's ballads negotiated and then renegotiated a complex relationship to their own gothicism. Different critical approaches to the ballads have focused on examining them as miniature dramas, as manifestations of the rise of scientific and medical discourses, as examples of the tradition of romantic orality, as a feminizing of the emotions, and as one means by which we can recognize the history of psychology and hysteria. It is also important to recall that by 1799 the gothic was being depicted in the popular British press as a frivolous genre that served no serious cultural purpose, while at its worst it was depicted conversely as both "Jacobin" and politically reactionary in its "antiquarian fondness for medieval" tropes, its chivalric social structure, and its antiscientific worldview (Gamer, 103). In short, the ballad, like the gothic, was already fissured in its meanings, as a discourse system it was split between looking backward to a belief system steeped in transcendence while at the same (confusing) time it presented a worldview informed by immanence and materialism. By combining both "ballad" and "gothic," Wordsworth and Coleridge were participating in a culturally, politically, and religiously fraught enterprise, one doomed it seems to provoke confusion and bitterness between themselves and with their sternest critics.

We know that Wordsworth initially composed "The Thorn" shortly after he finished MS. B of *The Ruined Cottage* (Averill, 172). But by the time he was preparing the second edition of the *Lyrical Ballads,* he decided to add a rather extensive note indicating that "The Thorn" needed to be preceded by "an introductory poem" in which the narrator would be more fully identified as a retired sailor living in a small town whose ways and customs he did not understand. Such men, "having little to do, become credulous and talkative from indolence, . . . they are prone to superstition." Presumably, he claims by way of this description, that superstition is the motivating factor that has influenced the narrator to tell his version of events in the way he does:

> Superstitious men are almost always men of slow faculties and deep feelings; their minds are not loose, but adhesive; they have a reasonable share of imagination, by which word I mean the faculty which produces impressive effects out of simple elements; but they are utterly destitute of fancy, the power by which pleasure and surprise are excited by sudden varieties of situation and by accumulated imagery. (*LB*, 288)

But, in fact, superstitious is exactly what the narrator of "The Thorn" is not. He is a man of science who resorts to using a telescope and a measuring stick to analyze his surroundings. The clue to Wordsworth's method is something more obscure, and it can be explained by analyzing the word "tautology" as Wordsworth uses it in his note to the poem:

> There is a numerous class of readers who imagine that the same words cannot be repeated without tautology: this is a great error; virtual tautology is much oftener produced by using different words when the meaning is exactly the same. Words, a poet's words more particularly, ought to be weighed in the balance of feeling, and not measured by the space which they occupy upon paper. For the reader cannot be too often reminded that poetry is passion: it is the history or science of feelings. (*LB*, 288–89)

Tautology, or the complex interplay of repetition, substitution, and difference, is not particularly the strongest rhetorical device at a poet's command, despite Wordsworth's claims to the contrary. It is prone to redundancy, hesitation, and deviation, and it tends to rely on two principles: equivalence and similitude, lending itself to circularity in argument. Wordsworth ignores this problem and goes on in his note to point out that "there are various other reasons why repetition and apparent tautology are frequently beauties of the highest kind. Among the chief of these reasons is the interest which the mind attaches to words, not only as symbols of the passion, but as *things,* active and efficient, which are of themselves part of the passion" (*LB*, 289; emphasis in original).

Tautology is an interesting concept for Wordsworth to use here, for it has two meanings: first, it is a rhetorical term describing the use of redundant language that adds no real information to an argument; and second, it is a statement of prepositional logic that is true by virtue of its logical form. To be more specific, prepositional logic may consist of "a set of axioms that may be empty, a nonempty finite set, a countably infinite set, or be given by axiom schemata. A formal grammar recursively defines the expressions and well-formed formulas of the language." In addition, tautology may be understood as a semantics that defines truth and valuations (or interpretations). The language of a propositional calculus consists of (1) a set of primitive symbols, variously referred to as atomic formulas, placeholders, proposition letters, *or* variables, and (2) a set of operator symbols, variously interpreted as logical operators or logical connectives. A well-formed formula (wff) is any formula that can be built up from atomic formulae by means of operator symbols according to the rules of the grammar.[5]

With this linguistic definition in mind, it is possible to ask if Wordsworth wants his readers to focus on the need to find meaning and "passion" within "primitive symbols" like the thorn, the pond, and the woman, or is he in some ways comparing the tautologies in his ballad to earlier discourses like the sermon (with its highly stylized and repetitious refrains) or the even earlier method of "preaching" the gospel through the visual symbols of the stained glass window. In a preliterate culture, the Church relied on telling its central narrative—the tale of suffering and redemption—through depicting aspects of the lives of exemplary beings writ large along the walls of its cathedrals. The episodic and repetitious style of these windows, their use of telegraphed images, and abbreviated scenes of intensity that carry the story line, all of this is very much a part of the oral ballad tradition and the tautologies that Wordsworth is discussing in his note to the poem.

Wordsworth's use of tautology also can be read in concert with the theories of Jürgen Habermas, in particular the notion of "placeholders" and communicative action. All of this suggests that the specific focus on particular symbols during the period facilitated the move to modernization and secularization that Habermas and others have charted in the long eighteenth century. Habermas's emphasis on the growth of a print culture, the evolution of a public sphere, and concomitant counter–public spheres, all of these issues are certainly part of a larger social and historical trajectory that occurred at the time, but another development was taking place as well, and this development was largely one of interiority. The poetry of the ballad, both in its traditional oral manifestations and in its later written forms as they appear in Wordsworth, Coleridge, and Scott, went a long way toward soothing the rough edges of history's progress. If the modern era can be imagined as singing its way into existence, then the ballad was one of the major musico-literary genres in that repertoire.

Habermas claims in his major works that there is a profound connection between human language and values like justice and empiricism that are implicit in the modernization project. What he calls "communicative action" is actually a type of social reform, a means by which individuals form new systems of understanding. As a sociologist, Habermas relies on the findings of Emile Durkheim, particularly his analysis of the "sacred" and the process by which religion is secularized. Habermas (1981; 1992) sees the "language—communication" framework as a new way of reaffirming the project of modernity and, in fact, he wants to show how the transformation from a traditional society to modernity involved a progressive secularization of normative behaviors reconstructed through communicative actions. Drawing on his assessment of the communicative competence of what he calls "social actors," Habermas (1981) distinguishes between "action oriented to success" and "action oriented to understanding" and also between the social and nonsocial contexts of action. Action oriented to success is measured by rules of rational choice, while action oriented to understanding takes place through "communicative actions." This manifestation of communicative action materializes by mutual and cooperative understanding among its collective participants.

Although I am aware that Habermas is controversial among postmodern theorists, I would like to apply his broad schema to *Lyrical Ballads* by claiming that Wordsworth's motivation in seeking to dissociate himself from Bürger and the gothic was in fact a species of "communicative action." Seen in this light, *Lyrical Ballads* was part of a larger project of modernity that sought to secularize culture through fostering "action oriented to understanding." In Wordsworth's case, he gradually came to see his role as a poet in terms of becoming a "social actor" in the great scheme of nationalization and modernization through purposefully nostalgic language acts (i.e., poems connected to their oral traditions and yet written in everyday language about quotidian social activities). The construction of romanticism as a discourse system that would displace gothicism had to occur if Britain was to move past the factionalism and parochialism, the medieval feudal class system, and its historical ties to the Catholicism of Southern Europe. Part of this role of being a "social actor" required that Wordsworth locate substitutive powers for the ones he was debunking, and we can only surmise that it would be a difficult act to try to replace one long-standing discourse system with another. For Wordsworth, "imagination" became the primary code word for human power in his new ideological system of belief. If the gothic clung to such outmoded codes as the supernatural, the moral, God and the devil, wandering Jews, and inquisitions, then the romantic would sweep the deck clear and replace all such mummery with the power of the imagination to create an authentic external world as a projection of the workings of its own quasi-divine mind.

In a letter to Southey (April 7, 1819) revealing his secularist intentions,

Wordsworth noted that his *Peter Bell* was

> composed under a belief that the imagination not only does not require for its exercise the intervention of supernatural agency, but that though such agency be excluded, the faculty may be called for as imperiously, and for kindred results of pleasure, by incidents within the compass of poetic probability in the humblest departments of daily life. Let this acknowledgement make my peace with the lovers of the supernatural. (*Prose Works*, 331)

There is one side of Wordsworth that intended to mock the supernatural, and we can see this perhaps most clearly in his "The Idiot Boy," where he famously rewrites Bürger's "Lenora" in a lampooning manner (see Gonslaves). Wordsworth's ballad makes a mockery of the outlandish incidents in the gothic ballad, replacing them with the stuff of everyday plebian life, the demon lover transformed into only a worried mother, concerned about her missing and half-witted son who has been spirited away by nothing more than his own befuddlement. In one of his most well-known instances of displacement, Wordsworth depicts this "idiot boy" racing around backwards on his horse all night long, lost in his confused attempt to find a doctor for a neighboring friend of his mother's. In writing "The Idiot Boy" Wordsworth effaces "Lenora" and her midnight ride with her visored, demon lover, a figure that, as Nicolas Kiessling has shown, emerges out of three separate traditions—the Judeo-Christian, Early Germanic, and Celtic—each with their own contradictory associations (22). Whereas Bürger's ballad recalls the fertility rites of ancient societies that offered virgins for sacrifice so that crops would grow (recall Persephone and Demeter's struggle with Hades, god of the underworld), as well as the world of the transcendent and the superstitious, Wordsworth's poem is almost postmodern in its play, suggesting a growing climate of immanence, professionalization, and the recognition even among peasants of the need to use educated doctors to cure illnesses.

III.

> The wildness, the mysterious horror of many situations and events in Mrs. Radcliffe are rather German than English: they partake of Lenora's spirit: they freeze, they 'curdle up the blood.' They are always incredible: they are, apparently, supernatural.
> —*Anti-Jacobin Review and Magazine* 7 (1801), 30

As the above passage indicates, "Lenora" had become a code word by 1801 for the supernatural, and not in any positive manner. The demonization of "German" Jacobinism and the German horror-ballad was complete by the time Wordsworth published his revised second edition of *Lyrical Ballads*, and what was earlier an international flirtation with the Germanic ballad tradition, was by this date something that needed to be suppressed, hence the revision of Coleridge's "The Ancyent Marinere," the limbo status of "Christabel," and Wordsworth's own decisive turn away from the gothic. It is possible to examine some of these issues by constructing something like a case study by looking more extensively at one poem, Wordsworth's "The Thorn" (1798) and its source material in Bürger: his ballad "Des Pfarrers Tochter von Taubenhain" translated as either "The Lass of Fair Wone" by Taylor (published in the *Monthly Magazine* in April 1796) or later by Charlotte Dacre (published in her *Hours of Solitude* in 1805; see appendix to this chapter for a side-by-side comparison of the two translations). Duncan Wu has traced Wordsworth's reading of the ballad to Bürger's *Gedichte* in late March 1797, while he was in Hamburg, while Coleridge probably read it as early as July of 1796 (1993, 21). Focusing on this one ballad and its source material allows us to examine Wordsworth's complex approach-avoidance dance with gothicism, because "The Thorn" is usually discussed as an "anti-gothic" poem which is in my opinion a bit too simplistic. In fact, it might be more accurate to see "The Thorn" as a parodic gothic ballad, for, as Graeme Stones notes about romantic parody, it exhibits a "simultaneous commitment to exalted visions and to a renegade impulse which mockingly dissolves them" (I:xxi). In much the same way, "The Thorn" plays with its reader, toys with us in presenting both an absolute gothic horror (a mother murdering her baby and that baby's dead face staring back at you the reader) and a conventional absurdity (a mound of earth shaking in protest) so that finally we inhabit a poetic realm that is a truly uncomfortable and ambiguous emotional space.

By way of historical antecedents, I might mention an earlier and well-known ballad "A Pitilesse Mother" (1616), in which a Catholic woman who has married a Protestant decides to murder her children so that they will not be raised as heretics (Travitsky, 55). Another potential source is Goethe's ballad "Die Braut von Korinth" ("The Bride of Corinth," 1797), translated by Matthew Lewis. This work, like "A Pitilesse Mother," merges sexuality and ritual sacrifice in yet another way. Goethe's ballad concerns a young Athenian pagan who travels to Corinth to marry the woman to whom he has been betrothed since youth. But Corinth has recently become Christian, and the night before the wedding ceremony the youth is visited by a mysterious white maiden who tells him that the cult of Christianity has triumphed over the old ways of Corinth: "victims are sacrificed here:

neither lamb nor bullock, but human sacrifice on a huge scale" ("Opfer fallen hier, / Weder Lamm noch Stier, / Aber Menschenopfer unerhört"). Stating that they had been promised to each other in a binding oral bond by their fathers, the maiden complains that now he is intended to wed her sister. What she fails to tell him is that she is, in fact, dead. They exchange tokens, she drinks blood-red wine, refuses bread, and they make love. Declaring that nothing can break the oaths sworn in the temple of Venus, she sucks his blood like a vampire and tells him that he will soon be joining her in the afterlife, where they will meet the old gods (Hughes, 131–32). Ritual sacrifice as well as the trope of the interrupted wedding had by now become integral components of the gothic aesthetic, and in the ballad form itself we can see a debate played out between the residual claims of the primitive, blood culture, and the new, enlightened forces of rationality for control of the individualized and modern subject. By the time Wordsworth was composing his ballad, the subject of infanticide had long been connected with anti-Catholic and religious traditions.

In addition to these works, there were a number of German ballads published in the 1770s and 1780s that reveal a cultural obsession with infanticide or what Nicola Trott labels as the "community's pet fantasy" (55), the crime of child murder and ambivalent sympathy for the desperate, murderous mother: Friedrich Schiller's ballad "Die Kinsmörderin" ("The Infanticide"), Karl Staudlin's fragment "Seltha, die Kindermörderin," and literally dozens of others, any number of which Wordsworth could have read during his own German sojourn.[6] More locally, Southey's ballads were also important sources for Wordsworth's "Thorn" (see C. Smith). His "Poor Mary, the Maid of the Inn" (1797), "Hannah" (1797), and "The Circumstance on which the following ballad is founded, happened not many years ago in Bristol" (1799) focused on "vagrant" women, one of whom was discovered burning her stillborn baby in Bristol. Two well-known Scottish broadside ballads that date back to the seventeenth century, "The Cruel Mother" (Child ballad #20) and "The Duke's Daughter's Cruelty: Or the Wonderful Apparition of two Infants whom she Murther'd and Buried in a Forrest, for to hide her Shame," both deal with infanticide and were republished in David Herd's *Ancient and Modern Scottish Songs* (1776). The latter ballad reads:

> And there she's lean'd her back to a thorn
> Oh! And alas—a day oh, (etc.)
> And there she has her baby born
> Ten thousand times good night and be wi' thee,
> She has honked a grave ayont the sun.

CHAPTER 5

Oh! (etc.)
And there she has buried the sweet babe in.

Wordsworth copied these exact lines into his *Commonplace Book of Extracts*, with the words "Wm. Wordsworth Grasmere, Jan. 1800" on the title page (*Poetical Works*, 513–14), so we know he was familiar with this ballad by 1800 if not earlier. Although Wordsworth was increasingly embarrassed by his youthful gothic interests and the sensationalistic content of some of the *Lyrical Ballads*, we know that he was certainly no stranger to their delights. Bürger's ballad and the many popular works that we know he read on infanticide, as well as his own "The Thorn," all rely on similar tropes: the seduced and abandoned maiden, the murdered or mysteriously disappeared baby, the mound of earth that is haunted by the mother and baby, uncannily shaping itself into the form of a baby's face, and is marked by a blue light or a misshapen thorn.

The Taylor version of Bürger (appendix) makes much of the class differences between the aristocratic seducer and his victim, "a peasant maid," while emphasis is also placed on his cruelty, his beating of her to the point of drawing her blood, and his deceit and selfishness as he boasts that he will marry a woman from his own class. In this version, the desperate young woman stabs her newborn son and then is lynched by her community, her decomposing body left hanging by a gibbet over the baby's grave. The mother and child are essentially communal and blood sacrifices, while the baby's burial mound is depicted as haunted by the hovering ghost of the mother. In the Dacre translation of the Bürger ballad, the young woman kills herself next to her baby's burial mound, and then casts her body on the grave so that it will rot in full view of the community on that very same spot (see Jacobus 1976). And like the Taylor version, the mother's hand continues to hover over the tomb, haunting it with a supernatural presence. In both versions of the ballad, the woman is replicated in the only roles permitted to her by her society: either as a sacrificial victim or a destroyer of her own child.

Wordsworth's much more complex version of this old story of seduction, betrayal, and infanticide/suicide is told in flashback by a "loquacious" narrator (this is Southey's word) who is himself totally uncertain of the events that he relates second- and even thirdhand. Twenty years have passed since the disastrous event, and yet the residue of suffering still marks the landscape in the haunting of the red cloaked mother at her baby's grave, a blatant gothic touch. The story of Martha Ray was presumably based on the scandalous history of the mother of his friend Basil Montagu (see Miles 2008, 82), but in Wordsworth's ballad (unlike Bürger's) she is individually named, as is her seducer, Stephen Hill, who marries another woman and leaves the three months pregnant Martha to her fate. The baby is never seen by anyone and "some will say / She hanged her baby on the tree; / Some say she drowned it in the pond" (ll. 203–5). The ballad reaches the first height of its supernaturalism when the skeptical narrator reports that "For many a time and oft were heard / Cries coming from the mountain head; / Some plainly living voices were, / And others, I've heard many swear, Were voices of the dead: / I cannot think, whate'er they say, / They had to do with Martha Ray" (ll. 159–65). But this statement appears to be presented as a case of the narrator refusing to countenance the presence of the spiritual and the supernatural in a world that he wants to believe is material and rational. This layering of different voices and of past events on the present moment of explanation recalls not simply Bakhtin's theory of heteroglossia, the play of social languages within the same text, but his colleague V. N. Voloshinov's description of "reported speech" or the "way one social language cites and represents another [so as to] crucially recognize relationships of priority, power, engagement, and disengagement with discourse. . . . Voloshinov's direct, indirect, and quasi-direct modes of 'reported speech' represent not only another's speech, but another's relation to his audience as that speech enacts it" (qtd. Klancher, 11).

The narrator's voice, in other words, is layered over Martha's purported history so that what we have in the poem is a series of power-invested masculine voices (the narrator, the community) that effectively silence or obscure the "voice" of Martha as gothic and sacrificial victim: "I've heard, the moss is spotted red / With drops of that poor infant's blood / But kill a new-born infant thus, / I do not think she could!" (ll. 210–13). This rumor of blood recalls the gothic trope of the bloody trail that leads back to the murderer and the scene of the crime. What puzzles the community here is the absence of the baby given the fact that all were witnesses to Martha's expanding belly. The horror of the crime, so commonplace a subject in "sensational" ballads of the day, is finally spiritual: how can a society continue to function when mothers are capable of killing their own babies? What values and beliefs will ground a culture when the community cannot even trust maternal instinct?

The narrator is also our source of information for the second and most gothic moment in the text: a description of the time when some of the villagers tried to excavate the baby's corpse, and the hill of moss over it shook in protest for fifty yards around:

> And some had sworn an oath that she
> Should be to public justice brought;

> And for the little infant's bones
> With spades they would have sought.
> But instantly the hill of moss
> Before their eyes began to stir!
> And, for full fifty yards around,
> The grass—it shook upon the ground!
> Yet all do still aver
> The little Babe lies buried there,
> Beneath that hill of moss so fair. (ll. 221–31)

What we have here is a familiar triangular linguistic configuration whereby two people (the community and the narrator) conspire to get rid of, contain, or commodify the third party (Martha Ray's "baby"). This mound of perhaps moldering baby bones represents the gothic core of the ballad and, in some ways, mirrors Wordsworth's own immersion in the gothic landscape of stone, rock, and the geological record of human and natural history poised against the inherently false and supernatural record that the human imagination has attempted to create in opposition to it. In presenting the possibility that Martha has disposed of the baby in a ritualistic act of sacrifice, the ballad returns to its origins in the world of the immanent, matter, and fossil records. But the thorn that marks the supposed grave of the sacrificed child functions as something of a secular reliquary for the baby's bones. The gothic, as Punter and Bronfen have argued, "recognizes that in fact wherever one digs one will come across the bones of the dead—hence the functional prolixity of the Gothic—and that instead of such excavations providing a new historical security, a new sense of order and origin, they will merely produce an 'overhang,' an increasingly unstable superstructure as the foundations are progressively exposed" (16).

In addition to the repeated recourse to the thorn, we are also directed to the pond, "three feet long and two feet wide," the apparent scene of the crime because the narrator tells us that he has "measured it from side to side" (ll. 32–33):

> Some say, if to the point you go,
> And fix on it a steady view,
> The shadow of a babe you trace,
> A baby and a baby's face,
> And that it looks on you;
> Whene'er you look on it, 'tis plain
> The baby looks at you again. (ll. 225–31)

This investigation of the crime scene seems to suggest that the community has the need to haunt itself, to stare at the site so long that they convince themselves that they can see the baby, that its face is not simply an optical illusion that proper measurement will produce, but the real thing, watching you with its own accusing eyes. But in participating in such an act, is not the community reproducing their own guilty reflection in the baby's face, seeing in the pool as in a mirror an uncanny manifestation of not simply death, but its own act of betrayal for deserting Martha Ray?[7]

Again, though, all this may be presented as just so much superstition by the narrator who protests just too much to be convincing even to himself. He concludes the poem by noting:

> I cannot tell how this may be
> But plain it is the Thorn is bound
> With heavy tufts of moss that strive
> To drag it to the ground;
> And this I know, full many a time,
> When she was on the mountain high,
> By day, and in the silent night,
> When all the stars shone clear and bright,
> That I have heard her cry,
> "Oh Misery! Oh Misery!
> Oh woe is me! Oh Misery!" (ll. 232–42)

The tautology, the incremental repetition here of the "misery" refrain, its fifth appearance in the ballad, suggests the traces of orality that would have been employed in the earlier broadside ballads that we know Wordsworth was familiar with from his earliest youth. It is also possible, though, to interpret Martha's ability to speak only those words, "Oh misery! Oh woe is me," like a ventriloquizing parrot, as suggesting her otherness, her dehumanization, and her use as an object ready-made for construction and commodification by the superior male consciousness of the ballad. Averill has suggested that these words are "the hard core of language to which the narrator's mind returns and from which he recoils as from an impenetrable mystery" (176), the persistence of human suffering. And Steve Newman has observed that there is a "perverse erotics [in] the supernatural ballad," that it is in this spectralization of Martha's suffering that we witness the voyeuristic participation that the audience would have wanted to vicariously experience in her and her body's sacrifice (166). There is also in her repeated refrain something like a ritual of grief and expiation, a confession of her sins in a quasi-public space, the scene of the crime. All of this also recalls Wordsworth's "The Reverie of Poor Susan" (indebted to Bürger's ballad "Des Armen Suschens Traum"), and written for the 1800 volume. By placing those two ballads against one another, we can see that in fact Bürger has allowed the woman to speak in her voice and to tell her own tale, while in Wordsworth's adaptation it is the male narrator who mediates the suffering of the woman, thereby commodifying her voice and suffering and putting them up for sale so to speak.

As in "The Idiot Boy," Wordsworth clearly focuses in "The Thorn" on the human rather than the supernatural, but by using the very well-known ballad by Bürger as his primary source material, isn't he having it both ways? Isn't this poem, like so many in *Lyrical Ballads,* a transitional text that straddles worldviews or what Habermas calls *Lebenswelt* or "lifeworlds," that posits a modern sensibility, all the while trafficking nostalgically in the dead but not yet buried world of superstition and the transcendent? Wordsworth's initial intention seems to be the desire to replace and debunk a providential worldview that kept alive the supernatural, with all of its strict codes of morality and its belief in hell, the devil, and an omnipotent God who hears and answers the prayers as well as the curses of his believers. But to construct a scientific, rationalistic, and materialist worldview with no code apart from the survival of the fittest, was not so easily accomplished. Such a task would be difficult for any poet, let alone one as ambivalent about his sources and intentions as was Wordsworth. In his case, he clung to the vestiges of whatever immortality could be found in the human imagination, for him a supernatural capacity that could both humanize modernism and preserve the old and primitive religions of blood, sacrifice, and violence. As he stated in his *Preface* to *Lyrical Ballads,* he was appealing to the "discriminating powers of the Mind" in which "the understanding of the Reader must necessarily be in some degree enlightened, his taste exalted, and his affections ameliorated" (*Prose Works,* I:126). Further, he noted that "it is desirable that such readers, for their own sakes, should not suffer the solitary word Poetry, a word of very disputed meaning, to stand in the way of their gratifications; but that, while they are perusing this book, they should ask themselves if it contains a natural delineation of human passions, human characters, and human incidents" (*Prose Works,* I:383). The question being begged here is what and who is "human"? Martha Ray is certainly less human than the narrator with his command of a telescope to accomplish his rather aggressive surveying of his surroundings, while certainly females are objectified throughout the *Lyrical Ballads* in much the same way that they are commodified and scapegoated in the gothic. Neither discourse system had resolved the problem of the female, who continues to be ravaged, murdered, or disappeared in ways that recall Persephone, Demeter, and Lucy Gray.

Somewhat incongruously, there is no question that when Wordsworth condemns "frantic novels, sickly and stupid German Tragedies, and deluges of idle and extravagant stories in verse" he is attempting to appeal to the tastes of an elite, modern audience, and, should one not quite exist, Wordsworth is only too willing to assist in the process of constructing one. This elite reading audience is characterized by its ability to exert control over its emotions and to rationalize its responses to the hyperbolic theatrical and literary productions that were being offered on a daily basis on the gothic stage. As Elizabeth Fay has pointed out, the audience Wordsworth constructs throughout his *Preface* is a decidedly male audience ambivalently imbued with both notions of bourgeois control and medieval chivalry toward weak and hyperemotional women. This ambivalence toward the gothic (not to mention femininity) is precisely the sort of phenomenon that Habermas has defined as a "communicative action" that constitutes modernity. The gothic for Wordsworth is not simply "sickly" and "stupid," and "German," it is also "idle" and "extravagant," meaning that it produced no usable emotions in its auditors (recall Coleridge's condemnation of the emotions provoked by Lewis's *Monk* as not "useful"). But what exactly would usable emotions enable people to do? Would they face tragedy and death, not to mention struggle and suffering, more effectively? Does Wordsworth claim to reject the gothic because it places him and his readers in feminized postures, weak and superstitious, cowering before the slings and arrows that fate has in store for them? The challenge he faced in "The Thorn" was how to write himself into this new discourse system while at the same time distancing himself from the embarrassment of its emotional excesses and vulnerabilities.

But also at the root of the misery in "The Thorn" is both the heritage and evolving nature of Protestantism. It is interesting to note that Wordsworth was identified by the *Anti-Jacobin* as a potential "modern-day [Alexander] Pope," a fact that has caused Kenneth R. Johnston to observe that Wordsworth's early poetry can be read as a response to the *Anti-Jacobin*'s "call for a strong national poet to rise up and take on the task of moral regeneration" (436). In some ways, the ambiguous ethical vision he presents in "The Thorn" can be understood as his attempt to present an individualized system of belief in an ultimately unknowable universe (see Ulmer). By seeing individual Christians as free agents, no longer burdened by clerics or the authoritative tradition of a Church hierarchy that controlled their beliefs or actions, Protestantism had liberated believers but at the same time also imposed a terrible responsibility on them. With no confessional or easy route like penance to assuage her sins, Martha Ray is the victim of a type of Protestantism that holds individuals accountable for their actions, and Martha is unfortunately only too willing to take that penance out on herself and, most probably, her baby. Whereas Catholicism continues to practice ritual and communal blood sacrifice every time a mass is said by a priest, there could be no such substitutive atonement for the communal Protestant imaginary. Instead, Martha was compelled to enact her own private blood sacrifice on her own body and that of her baby. There are no miraculous interventions for Martha, who almost seems to be an embodiment of Hegel's deeply troubled Protestant mind, "beset by the anguish of Christian conscience on the one hand and awareness of living in a disenchanted cosmos on the other" (Lilla, 198). In the repetition of Martha Ray's horrible refrain, "Oh misery," she enacts the terror of the Protestant conscience taking out its punishment on its own individual psyche. There would be no triumphant Hegelian "absolute knowing" for Martha, only a complete "God-forsakenness" that is a full and resigned acceptance of the reality of death.

APPENDIX

THE LASS OF FAIR WONE

Gottfried August Bürger
Translated by William Taylor of Norwich
(1796)

Beside the parson's bower of yew,
    Why strays a troubled spright,
That peaks and pines, and dimly shines,
    Thro' curtains of the night.
Why steals along the pond of toads
    A gliding fire so blue,
That lights a spot where grows no grass,
    Where falls no rain nor dew?

The parson's daughter once was good,
    And gentle as the dove,
And young and fair,——and many came
    To win the damsel's love.
High o'er the hamlet, from the hill,
    Beyond the winding stream,
The windows of a stately house
    In sheen of evening gleam,
There dwelt, in riot, rout, and roar,
    A lord so frank and free,
That oft, with inward joy of heart,
    The maid beheld his glee.
Whether he met the dawning day,
    In hunting trim so fine,
Or tapers, sparking from his hall,
    Beshone the midnight wine.
He sent the maid his picture, girt
    With diamond, pearl, and gold;
And silken paper, sweet with musk,
    This gentle message told:
"Let go thy sweethearts, one and all;

THE LASS OF FAIR WONE

From the German of Bürger
Translated by Charlotte Dacre, *Hours of Solitude. A Collection of Original Poems.* Volume II, 86–95

BESIDE the parson's dusky bow'r,
    Why strays a troubl'd sprite,
That dimly shines in lonely hour
    Thro' curtains of the night?
Why steals along yon slimy bank
    An hov'ring fire so blue,
That lights a spot both drear and dank,
    Where falls nor rain nor dew?

The parson once a daughter had,
    Fair village maids above;
Unstain'd as fair—and many a lad
    Had sought the maiden's love.

High o'er the hamlet proudly dight
    Beyond the winding stream,
The windows of yon mansion bright
    Shone in the evening beam.

A Bacchanalian lord dwelt there,
    Unworthy of his name;
He plung'd a father in despair,
    And robb'd a maiden's fame.

With wine and tapers sparkling round,
    The night flew swift away;
In huntsman's dress, with horn and hound,
    He met the dawning day.

Shalt thou be basely woo'd,
That worthy art to gain the heart
   Of youths of noble blood?
"The tale I would to thee betray,
   In secret must be said:
At midnight hour I'll seek thy bower;
   Fair lass, be not afraid.
"And when the amorous nightingale
   Sings sweetly to his mate,
I'll pipe my quail-call from the field:
   Be kind, nor make me wait.
In cap and mantle clad he came,
   At night, with lonely tread;
Unseen, and silent as a mist,
   And hush'd the dogs with bread.
And when the amorous nightingale
   Sung sweetly to his mate,
She heard his quail-call in the field,
   And, ah! ne'er made him wait.
The words he whisper'd were so soft,
   They won her ear and heart;
How soon will she, who loves, believe!
   How deep a lover's art!
No lure, no soothing guise, he spar'd,
   To banish virtuous shame;
He call'd on high God above,
   As witness to his flame.
He clasp'd her to his breast, and swore
   To be for ever true:
"O yield thee to my wishful arms,
   Thy choice thou shalt not rue."
And while she strove, he drew her on,
   And led her to the bower
So still, so dim—and round about
   Sweet smelt the beans in flower.
There beat her heart, and heaved her breast,
   And pleaded every sense;
And there the glowing breath of lust
   Did blast her innocence.

He sent the maid his picture, deck'd
   With diamonds, pearls, and gold;
Ah! silly maid, why not reject
   What on the back was told?

"Despise the love of shepherd boys;
   Shalt thou be basely woo'd
That worthy art of highest joys,
   And youths of noble blood?

"The tale I would to thee unfold
   In secret must be said;
And when the midnight hour is told,
   Fair love, be not afraid.

"And when the am'rous nightingale
   Like thee shall sweetly sing,
A stone thy window shall assail,
   My idol forth to bring."

Attired in vest of gayest blue,
   He came with lonely tread,
And silent as the beams that threw
   Their pale light o'er her head.

And did no thought affect his breast,
   Or bid his feet delay?
Ah! no! the crime but adds a zest
   To spur his guilty way.

And when the sweet-pip'd nightingale
   Sang from the dusky bow'r,
A stone her window did assail
   Just at the midnight hour.

And ah! she came;—his treacherous arms
   The trembling maid receive;
How soon do they in lover's charms
   A lover's truth believe!

But when the fragrant beans began
    Their fallow blooms to shed,
Her sparkling eyes their luster lost;
    Her cheek, its roses fled;
And when she saw the pods increase,
    The ruddier cherries stain,
She felt her silken robe grow tight,
    Her waist new weight sustain.
And when the mowers went afield,
    The yellow corn to tend,
She felt her burden stir within,
    And shook with tender dread.
And when the winds of autumn hist
    Along the stubble field;
Then could the damsel's piteous plight
    No longer be conceal'd.
Her sire, a harsh and angry man,
    With furious voice revil'd:
"Hence from my sight! I'll none of thee—
    I harbour not thy child."
And fast, amid her fluttering hair,
    With clenched fist he gripes,
And seiz'd a leathern thong, and lash'd
    Her side with sounding stripes.
Her lily skin, so soft and white,
    He ribb'd with bloody wales;
And thrust her out, though black the night,
    Thou sleet and storm assails.
Upon the harsh rock, on flinty paths,
    The maiden had to roam;

On tottering feet she grop'd her way,
    And sought her lover's home.
"A mother thou hast made of me,
    Before thou mad'st a wife:
For this, upon my tender breast,
    These livid stripes are rife:
"Behold;" and then with bitter sobs
    She sank upon the floor—
"Make good the evil thou has wrought;
    My injur'd name restore."

Lock'd in his arms, she scarcely strove,
    Seduc'd by young desire,
The glowing twin brother of Love,
    Possess'd with wilder fire.

Still struggling, faint, he led her on
    Tow'rd the fatal bow'r,
So still—so dim—while all along
    Sweet smelt each blushing flow'r.

Then beat her heart—and heav'd her breast—
    And pleaded ev'ry sense;
Remorseless the seducer prest,
    To blast her innocence.

But soon in tears repentant drown'd,
    The drooping fair bemoan'd,
And oft, when night in terror frown'd,
    Forlorn and sad she roam'd.

And when the fragile flow'rs decay'd,
    The bloom her cheeks forsook,
And from her eyes no longer play'd
    The loves with wily look.

And when the leaves of autumn fell,
    And grey the grass was grown,
Her bosom rose with lovely swell,
    And tighter grew her zone.

And when the mow'rs went a field
    The yellow corn to tend,
She felt her sorrowing bosom yield
    To all a mother's dread.

And when the winds of winter swept
    The stubborn glebe among,
In wild despair and fear she wept
    The lingering night along.
And when the fault of yielding love

"Poor soul,—I'll have
    thee hous'd and nurs'd;
Thy terrors I lament.
    Stay here; we'll have some further talk—
The old one shall repent—"
    "I have no time to rest and wait;
That saves not my good name,—
    If thou with honest soul hast sworn,
O leave me not to shame;
    "But at the holy altar be
Our union sanctified;
    Before the people and priest
Receive me for thy bride." "Unequal matches must not blot
The honours of my line;
    Art thou of wealth or rank for me,
To harbour thee as mine?
    "What's fit and fair I'll do for thee;
Shalt yet retain my love—
    Shalt wed my huntsman, and we'll then
Our former transports prove."
    "Thy wicked soul, hard-hearted man,
May pangs in hell await!
    Sure, if not suited for thy bride,
I was not for thy mate.
    "Go, seek a spouse of nobler blood,
Nor God's just judgments dread—
    So shall, ere long, some base-born wretch
Defile thy marriage-bed.—
    "Then, traitor, feel how wretched they
In hopeless shame immerst;
    Then smite thy forehead on the wall,
While horrid curses burst.
    "Roll thy dry eyes in wild despair—
Unsooth'd thy grinning wo;
    Through thy pale temples fire the ball,

No more could be conceal'd,
    She knelt, her father's soul to move,
And, weeping, all reveal'd.

But vain her tears; the ruthless sire
    In piteous voice revil'd,
And while his eye-balls flash'd with fire,
    He spurn'd his hapless child:

Spurn'd her with cruelty severe,
    And smote her snowy breast;
The patient blood, that gush'd so clear,
    Its purity confess'd.

Such are the dang'rous thorns of love,
    That strew the virgin's way,
While faithless as its roses prove,
    'Tis they that first decay.

Then drove her forth forlorn to wail
    Amid the dreary wild,
Forgets that mortals all are frail,
    But more—forgets his child!

Unhappy parent!—passion's slave!
    Had nature been thy guide,
Thy child, now sunk in hasten'd grave,
    Might still have been thy pride.

Up the harsh rock so steep and slim'd,
    The mourner had to roam,
And faint on tott'ring feet she clim'd
    To seek her lover's home.

"Alas! my blood-stain'd bosom see,
    The drooping sufferer cried;
"A mother hast thou made of me,
    Before thou mad'st a bride.

"This is thy ruthless deed—behold!"
    And sinking on the floor;

And sink to fiends below."
    Collected, then, she started up,
And, through the hissing sleet,
    Through thorn and briar, through
        flood and mire,
She fled with bleeding feet.
    "Where now," she cried, "my
        gracious God!
What refuge have I left?"
    And reach'd the garden of her home,
Of hope in man bereft.
    On hand and foot she feebly crawl'd
Beneath the bower unblest;
    Where withering leaves, and
        gathering snow,
Prepar'd her only rest.
    There rending pains and darting
        throes
Assail'd her shuddering frame;

And from her womb a lovely boy,
    With wail and weeping came.
Forth from her hair a silver pin
    With hasty hand she drew,
And prest against its tender heart,
    And the sweet babe she slew.
Erst when the act of blood was done,
    Her soul its guilt abhorr'd:
"My Jesus! what has been my deed?
    Have mercy on me, Lord!"
With bloody nails, beside the pond,
    Its shallow grave she tore;
"There rest in God,—there shame and
        want
Thou can'st not suffer more;
    "Me vengeance waits. My poor, poor
        child,
Thy wound shall bleed afresh,
    When ravens from the gallows tear
Thy mother's mould'ring flesh."—
    Hard by the bower her gibbet

"Oh! let thy love with honour hold,
    My injur'd name restore."

"Poor maid! I grieve to see thy woe;
    My folly now lament:
Go not while harsh the tempests blow,
    Thy father shall repent."

"I cannot stay," she shudd'ring cried,
    "While dubious hangs my fame.
Alas! forswear thy cruel pride,
    And leave me not to shame.

"Make me thy wife, I'll love thee true;
    High Heaven approves the deed:
For mercy's sake some pity shew,
    E'en while for thee I bleed!"

"Sure 'tis thy mirth, or dost thou rave?
    "Can I," he scoffing cried,
"Thy forfeit name from scorn to save,
    E'er wed a peasant maid?

"What honour bids I'll do for thee—
    My huntsman shall be thine;
While still our loves, voluptuous free,
    No shackles shall confine."

"Damn'd be thy soul, and sad thy life,
    May pangs in hell await!
Wretch! if too humble for thy wife,
    Oh, why not for thy mate?

"May God attend, my bitter prayer!
    Some high-born spouse be thine,
Whose wanton arts shall mock thy care,
    And spurious be thy line.

"Then traitor fell, how wretched
        those
    In hopeless shame immers'd,

stands,
Her skull is still to show;
    It seems to eye the barren grave,
Three spans in length below.
    That is the spot where grows no grass;
Where falls no rain nor dew,—
    Whence steals along the pond of toads
A hovering fire so blue.
    And nightly when the ravens come,
Her ghost is seen to glide;
    Pursues and tries to quench the flame,
And pines the pool beside.

Strike thy hard breast with vengeful blows,
    While curses from it burst!

"Roll thy dry eyes, for mercy call,
    Unsooth'd thy grinning woe;
Through thy pale temples fire the ball,
    And sink to fiends below!"

Then starting up, she wildly flew,
    Nor heard the hissing sleet,
Nor knew how keen the tempest blew,
    Nor felt her bleeding feet.

"Oh where, my God! where shall I roam?
    For shelter where shall fly?"
She cried, as wild she sought the home
    Where still she wish'd to die.

Tow'rd the bow'r, in frenzied woe,
    The fainting wand'rer drew,
Where wither'd leaves and driving snow
    Made haste her bed to strew:

E'en to that bower, where first undone,
    Now yields its bed forlorn,
And now beholds a cherub son
    In grief and terror born.

"Ah, lovely babe!" she cried, "we part
    Ne'er, ne'er to meet again!"
Then frantic pierc'd its tender heart—
    The new-born life is slain.

Swift horor seiz'd her shudd'ring soul—
    "My God, behold my crime!
Let thy avenging thunders roll,
    And crush me in my prime!"

With blood-stain'd hands the bank
    beside
  Its shallow grave she tore.
"There rest in God," she wildly cried,
  "Where guilt can stab no more."

Then the red knife, with blood imbru'd,
  Of innocence, she press'd;
Its fatal point convulsive view'd,
  And sheath'd it in her breast.

Beside her infant's lonely tomb
  Her mould'ring form is laid,
Where never flow'r is seen to bloom
  Beneath the deadly shade.

Where falls nor rain nor heavenly dew,
  Where sun-beam never shines,
Where steals along the fire so blue,
  And hov'ring spectre pines.

There, too, its blood-stain'd hand to
    wave,
  Her mournful ghost is seen,
Or dimly o'er her infant's grave,
  Three spans in length, to lean.

- CHAPTER 6 -

The Gothic Chapbook
The Class-based Circulation of the Unexplained Supernatural

> Our present situation is analogous to an eighteenth-century one. We retain a rationalistic optimism about the beneficent results of education, or rather technology. We combine this with a romantic conception of "the human condition," a picture of the individual as stripped and solitary. The eighteenth century was an era of rationalistic allegories and moral tales.
>
> —Iris Murdoch, "Against Dryness" (1961)

I.

In the passage above Murdoch appears to be suggesting that what we now recognize as "affective individualism" or modern and secularized subjectivity originated during a period that idealized isolated individuals alone with their feelings, seeking for the meaning of life by understanding the moral significance of their actions and emotions. Certainly we can see the moral evolution and psychic development of this individual in the canonical gothic novels (i.e., in the trajectories of Caleb Williams or Victor Frankenstein). But in many ways, the short gothic tales, the "rationalistic allegories and moral tales" of which Murdoch speaks, represent examples of what Charles Taylor has called cultural technologies or textual practices that serve to instantiate the agenda of ambivalent secularization. For instance, it is significant that the Minerva Press, the most successful purveyor of gothic novels in Britain and with their fingers firmly pressed to the pulse of their lower- and middle-class reading public, also promoted a variety of socially and politically conservative values in its publications. At the same time it also published a number of anti-Catholic pamphlets, like the one by Thomas Scantlebury, *The Rights of Protestants Asserted* in 1798, and its full title provides us with a glimpse of the continuing pamphlet warfare over denominational differences: "Clerical incroachment detected. In allusion to several recent publications, in defence of an exclusive priesthood, establishments, and tithes, by Daubeny, Church, and others. But more particularly in reply to a pamphlet lately published by George Markham, Vicar of Carlton, entitled, *More truth for the seekers*." On one hand, the gothic was invested in an immanent Protestant, rationalistic, and Enlightenment agenda, while on the other hand, it was riddled with ghosts, superstitions, and reanimations of the world of anima. This bifurcated subjectivity is, as we have come to see, at the heart of ambivalent secularization, and in the chapbooks we can also examine how class came to play a crucial role in defining the transformations of the gothic uncanny.

Scholars most frequently claim that the short gothic tale or chapbook grew out of the earlier tradition of cheap broadside (because printed on one side of the paper) ballads or street literature, and certainly one can see in the shorter eight-page chapbooks the residue of this direct oral to written tradition. Gary Kelly has recently observed that this early street literature is characterized by its "emphasis on destiny, chance, fortune and levelling forces such as death, express[ing] the centuries-old experience of common people ... with little or no control over the conditions of their lives. ... For these people, life was a lottery" (2002, II:x). According to Kelly, the fact that the lower classes were the target audience of these early productions is also obvious from their very heavy use of narrative repetition, their emphasis on incident and adventure, and their episodic and anecdotal structures. The other major difference between lower- and middle-class reading materials is the absence in the lower-class works of any extended depictions of subjectivity or emotions in the protagonists (II:X, xv). One example of this lower-class ideology at work can be found in Isabella Lewis's *Terrific Tales* (1804), a series of short vignettes that purport to be true, although the contents are fantastical and reveal an interesting mix of residual supernaturalism combined with rationalizing Christian moral exemplum. For instance, one tale concerns an aristocrat, "of very inordinate passions," who is kidnapped by a spirit who arrived on horseback. Obviously a prose revision and redaction of the Germanic ballad "Lenora," the homily at the conclusion remarks on his abduction as "a punishment for his excessive passions" (7). What is most interesting about these tales, besides their repetitive use of specters, devils, ghosts in chains, warnings from Purgatory, and clouds of sulphur, is their persistent assurance that the afterworld and the realm of the transcendent exists. In one tale, a dead man appears to his friend to exclaim, "Michael, Michael! Nothing is more true than what has been said of the other world" (61), and such a message is the major reason for the popularity of these works. The supernatural was not supposed to be explained away, but instead confirmed as real. Although the elite and the intelligentsia might have been willing to accept the stark lessons of materialism and the finality of death, the lower class was not able to do so, and the gothic chapbook reveals the persistence and continuing power of the supernatural in the social imaginary.

In 1800 a three-volume gothic novel could cost as much as two weeks' wages for a laborer, and we know that, for the most part, the library fees at a circulating library also would have been out of their reach. The longer (thirty-six- and seventy-two-page) prose chapbooks cost from sixpence to a shilling, or the price of a meal or a cheap theater seat (Kelly 2008, 218), and they seem to have had a written rather than a purely oral origin. The gothic chapbooks can best be understood in two ways: first, as adaptations of the extremely popular European fairy tale, and secondly, as redactions of the longer gothic novels and dramas. Circulating widely between 1750 and 1820, these tales are European culture's first "best-sellers." In fact, G. Ross Roy claims that a conservative estimate of the sale of Scottish chapbooks during this period runs to over two hundred thousand a year, a huge number given the fact that they were purchased largely by members of the working class. Originally running as twenty-four pages of single sheet, duodecimo, these truncated tales were frequently bound in coarse blue paper and sometimes illustrated with rough woodcuts and printed in a rude and unfinished style of typography (50–52).

Gothic bluebooks and chapbooks have been something of the stepchild of gothic scholarship, most frequently ignored because of their derivative nature, as well as their lack of artistic sophistication, depth, or significance.[1] Montague Summers claims that they were the reading material of "schoolboys, prentices, servant-girls, by the whole of that vast population which longed to be in the fashion, to steep themselves in the Gothic Romance." They are, in fact, commonly referred to as "the remainder trade" or "the trade Gothic" (84–85). More recently, William St. Clair has claimed that, in fact, the chapbooks were read by "adults in the country areas, and young people in both the town and the country. It would be a mistake, therefore, to regard the ancient popular print as confined to those whose education fitted them for nothing longer or textually more difficult. Many readers, whether adults or children, lived at the boundary between the reading and the non-reading nations. They were the marginal reading constituency whose numbers fell when prices rose and rose when prices fell" (343–44). Whatever the exact class of their readership, gothic bluebooks and eventually the gothic short tale's importance can be appreciated only by understanding that they carried the agenda of ambivalent secularization within their flimsy covers. It is not for nothing that Percy and Mary Shelley, along with Byron, Claire Clairmont, and John Polidori, were reading aloud from a collection of German tales of terror the night before Mary Shelley began writing *Frankenstein* (1818) and Polidori penned *The Vampyre* (1819). These German short stories began their literary life as *Das Gespensterbuch* (*The Ghost Book*), a five-volume collection of tales by Johann August Apel and Friedrich Laun that were first translated into French by J. B. B. Eyriès as *Fantasmagoriana; ou Recueil d'Histoires d'Apparitions, de Spectres* (1812), and then as *Tales of the Dead* (1813), when they were translated into English by Sarah Utterson. During the summer of 1816 the Diodati circle were very fashionably reading from the French collection.

The earlier "lottery mentality" that was operative in the lower-class chapbooks was eventually replaced during the late eighteenth century by what Kelly calls a dominant "investment mentality" that we can see evidenced in the emerging middle-class chapbooks. This "investment mentality" was characterized by the Protestant ideologies of self-improvement, self-advancement, modernization, and self-discipline, or "the middle-class discourse of merit" (II: x, xxiii). Increasingly hostile to lower-class street literature which it saw as politically subversive and at the same time spiritually reactionary, the middle class effectively displaced street literature by co-opting it. Hence Hannah More published her *Cheap Repository Tracts* (1795–98) for the lower classes, actually imitating cheap broadside and ballad chapbooks and suffusing them not with the "lottery" but with the "investment" mentality that she and her cohorts were attempting to promulgate: a disdain for immediate gratification, a focus on the disastrous consequences of moral relativism, and a stress on the accumulation of "solid and useful" knowledge for middle-class life.[2] This strategy is identical to the one that John Guillory has identified as "covert pastoralism" (124) and claimed is operating in Wordsworth's *Preface* to *Lyrical Ballads*. Sensing that they are being marginalized by a bourgeois reading public that has begun to exert power in the literary marketplace, Wordsworth and More create a binary of lower class and aristocrat and actually begin to present themselves as aristocrats in peasant dress.

But if there was a middle-class attempt to co-opt the chapbooks, there was also a concerted effort to condemn their popularity altogether. For instance, Coleridge, in his *Biographia Literaria* (1817) specifically condemned the "devotees of the circulating library" for indulging in

> a sort of beggarly day-dreaming during which the mind of the dreamer furnishes for itself nothing but laziness and a little mawkish sensibility; while the whole *material* and imagery of the doze is supplied *ab extra* by a sort of mental *camera obscura* manufactured at the printing office, which *pro tempore* fixes, reflects and transmits the moving phantasms of one man's delirium, so as to people the barrenness of an hundred other brains afflicted with the same trance or suspension of all common sense and all definite purpose. (III: 36; emphasis in original)

There is a certain amount of fear as well as class resentment expressed here about an unregulated (nonelitist) press pandering to what Wordsworth had called the "fickle tastes, and fickle appetites" of the lower-class reading public (*Preface* to the *Lyrical Ballads,* 1800).

The gothic chapbook tradition is split, then, between lower- and middle-class agendas, both of which were presenting alternative versions of the secularized uncanny to their readers. One group of tales—the middle-class variety—made claims for the powers of reason, rationality, and secularized education, while, ambivalently, it kept alive the vestiges of a belief in a mythic and sacred past of divine beings. As Kelly notes, the representation of subjectivity is much more developed in these works, but in a writer like John Aikin, a Protestant Dissenter and author of "Sir Bertrand: A Fragment" (1773), a short gothic tale that was written to demonstrate the aesthetic principles put forward in his sister Anna Barbauld's essay "On the Pleasure Derived from Objects of Terror" (1773), this subjectivity is severely "disciplined" so that the new bourgeois citizens are those who control their emotions in even the most perilous of situations (xix). The other group of tales—the lower-class variety—persisted in promulgating a "lottery" view of life, with fate, magic, or luck as the ultimate and inscrutable arbiters in all matters and with human beings still presented as "porous selves" or pawns in the hands of tyrannical forces they could not fully understand. For Kelly, the subjectivity that occasionally appears in lower-class chapbooks is

> like the simulation of richer fabrics on cheap printed cottons of the period, [it] is a form of symbolic consumption rather than ideological and cultural instruction for the text's readers. It is as if the readers of the street Gothics were aware that there was a certain model of subjectivity prized in middle-class and upper middle-class culture, but that subjectivity in itself was of

little interest, or perhaps supposed to be of little use or value, for these readers. (II:xxiii)

As I noted above, it is important to recognize that the longer chapbooks and bluebooks appear to be indebted to the earlier fairy tales as they evolved first in Italy and then in France during the 1690s. But it is also significant to recall that for the Enlightenment mentality, as Locke demonstrated, the passing on of superstitious beliefs was invariably linked to a scene in which fairy tales were read to children (*Essay* II:33, 10). *Le conte de fée* originated in France as a tale that privileged the power of women, the "fairies," in order to effect what Jack Zipes has called "a secular mysterious power of compassion that could not be explained." According to Zipes, the creative powers of the fairies should actually be understood as originating in the lost witches who were burned by the Church in an effort to eradicate religious heresy and nonconformity with the Church's male hierarchy (1991, xx). By resurrecting the specter of female creativity and power, the fairy tale effectively kept "pagan" notions alive in the public domain so that, as Zipes notes, "there was something subversive about the institutionalization of the fairy tale in France during the 1690s, for it enabled writers to create a dialogue about norms, manners, and power that evaded court censorship and freed the fantasy of the writers and readers, while at the same time paying tribute to the French code of *civilité* and the majesty of the aristocracy" (1991, xx).

In addition to developing an early canon of fairy tales that included "Cinderella," "Beauty and the Beast," "Sleeping Beauty," "Bluebeard," "Little Red Riding Hood," and other familiar tales, the French tradition was enriched first by Antoine Galland's translations of the Arabic tales *The Thousand and One Nights,* published in twelve volumes between 1704–17 in France (trans. English 1706; German 1712) and then by François Petis de la Croix (1620–75), who translated tales of the Sultana of Persia into French as *Contes Turcs* (1707). The *Arabian Nights* was, of course, favorite childhood reading for Wordsworth, Coleridge, Byron, Percy Shelley, and later De Quincey and the Brontës. Based on both written documents and oral traditions that originated in the fourteenth century, these tales began what we now recognize as the "orientalizing" tendencies in the gothic; that is, its use of a foreign and exotic setting to safely distance the actions and characters, as well as the social and political critiques from their obvious analogues in Europe. Hence a tyrannical and polygamous Caliph could be condemned as a despot rather than taking the risk of blatantly or dangerously criticizing the policies or adulteries of Louis XIV. The orientalist ideology, as we know from Edward Said's *Orientalism* (1978), was complicit in the imperialistic agenda of Europe, but it also functioned as a secularizing strategy in its implicit presentation of Christianity as just another man-made religion like Hinduism or Islam. Used by progressive writers like Thomas Paine in England, Benjamin Franklin in America, and rationalists like Wieland in Germany or Voltaire in France, orientalism in a literary text worked to normalize the practitioners of a supposedly "pagan" religion, thereby presenting all religions as equally and essentially systems of prejudice and superstition. By the time Charles Mayer published his forty-one-volume *Cabinet des Fées* (1785–89), a collection of virtually every tale published in France during the past one hundred years, these stories were an amalgam of oral traditions originating in Italy, French aristocratic legends, and orientalist pastiches (see Bottigheimer).

In many ways the gothic bluebook tradition in England is an outgrowth of the earlier situation in France.[3] Shortly after the publication of the first fairy and oriental tales in France, these French tales were reprinted in a series of cheap chapbooks called the *Bibliothèque bleue* and sold by peddlers called *colporteurs* ("chapmen" in Britain) to members of the lower classes throughout France and central Europe. As Zipes notes, the contents of the "bluebooks" were abridgments of the original tales; the language was simplified; and there were multiple versions of the tales designed specifically for different audiences: children as well as adult nonliterates who would have had the tales read aloud to them (1991, xxi). Similarly, German folk literature was also circulated in cheap, mass-produced little books that Goethe referred to as "schätzbare Überreste der Mittelzeit" or cherished remains from the Middle Ages (Buch, 38; also see Ward; Astbury). It is, of course, a short step from the *Bibliothèque bleue* to the gothic bluebooks that first showed up in England during the mid- to late eighteenth century and contained a number of abridged and vastly simplified gothic novels intended for the newly literate or, in fact, for reading aloud to a non-literate adult audience. It is also significant that by 1794 the French fairy tales of Countess D'Aulnoy were translated and published by the Minerva Press as *The Pleasing Companion: A Collection of Fairy Tales calculated to improve the heart; the whole forming a system of moral precepts and examples for the conduct of youth through life*. The title alone makes the ideological agenda explicit: the reading of fairy tales was viewed as a crucial component of the civilizing process that sought to inculcate bourgeois moral values into the often unruly lower classes.

It is also important to note that there was a strong fairy tale tradition in Germany, obviously derived from the French models that it had quickly imported. Johann Karl August Musäus (1735–87), a middle-class writer, published his collections of rude folktales, *Die Volksmärchen der*

Deutschen, between 1782–87 (translated into English in 1791 by Thomas Beddoes, father of the gothic dramatist Thomas Lovell Beddoes). Perhaps the tale with the most longevity within that collection was *Die Entführing* (The Abduction), the source for Matthew Lewis's legend of the bleeding nun. Adapted from earlier French and Germanic works, these tales also presented a number of garish and bloody scenes adapted from the chivalric tales of the medieval period. They relied heavily on German folklore and yet were clearly intended as didactic and moralistic fare for an educated bourgeois audience. Similarly, Christoph Martin Wieland (1733–1813) translated a selection of French fairy tales into German and published them in his *Dschinnistan* (1786–89), which in turn was translated and published in England in 1796. Famous for containing the source material that Mozart and his librettist Emmanuel Schikaneder adapted for *Die Zauberflöte* (*The Magic Flute,* 1791), *Dschinnistan* presents a number of tales that mock religious superstitions and reveal transcendent, antimodern beliefs to be dangerously reactionary in a newly secular society. For instance, his "The Philosopher's Stone" concerns the king of Cornwall, who falls prey to a charlatan (again, reminiscent of Count Cagliostro, the historical source for Schiller's *Ghost-Seer*) who claims that he can create a philosopher's stone if he is given all of the wealth in the kingdom. After much hocus pocus and rites in "the name of Hermes Trismegistus," the charlatan disappears with said wealth, and the king is transformed into a donkey so that he will be forced to learn yet more hard lessons about greed and wise judgments before he can return to human form, not as a king but as a simple servant. Although Mozart presents the Temple of Isis and the worship of Osiris as serious matters in *The Magic Flute,* the same cannot be said for Wieland. The use of the cult of Hermes Trismegistus in this tale as well as others in the *Dschinnistan* can be seen as not simply a mockery of the Masonic rituals that were so popular during the period, but also as a not so veiled attack on the absurdities of traditional Catholic rituals and superstitions ("The Philosopher's Stone," trans. Zipes 1991, 233–57).

Considered to be one of the most accessible writers of German fairy tales, several of Wieland's works were translated into English by at least two men who had strong ties to the gothic revival (Stockley, 100). The first, William Taylor of Norwich, translated some of Wieland's works, including the satiric tale "KoxKox and Kikequetzel," published in Taylor's anonymously issued three-volume anthology *Tales of Yore* (1810). The second English translator of Wieland's fairy tales was Robert Huish, who published *Select Fairy Tales from the German of Wieland in two volumes* (1796). Identified on the title page as "the Translator of the *Sorcerer* and the *Black Valley* of Weber," Huish clearly positioned his translated collection of fairy tales within the pulp gothic market, and in particular, the German-inflected, anti-Catholic gothics that were so popular during the 1790s. Horace Walpole's *Hieroglyphic Tales* (privately printed in 1785 in only six copies, but reprinted in his *Works,* 1798) was a fairy-tale anthology that collected Arabian, Celtic, and Oriental tales. Most "British" fairy tales, however, were actually French or German translations, with versions of Charles Perrault's tales appearing as early as 1729 and again in 1750, while an English translation of the tales of Mme d'Aulnoy was published as early as 1707.

Resolving his fairy tales with reasonable conclusions, or what we might recognize as the explained supernatural, Wieland blended Shakespearean plots, Milton, and orientalist themes and characters in a number of his works. In fact, Wieland was one of the earliest translators of Shakespeare's works, which he made accessible to German audiences in prose translations, published between 1762 and 1766. But it has long been recognized that all but one of Wieland's fairy tales ("The Philosopher's Stone") were adaptations from the earlier French fairy-tale collection, *Cabinet des Fées,* which had been translated into German and published between 1785–89 (see Farese). Certainly Wieland was well known and highly regarded by the major British romantic writers, as his most famous works were the novel *Agathon* (1766; read and admired by Mary Shelley) and the poem *Oberon* (1780; read by Wordsworth, Coleridge, Southey, and Keats, and adapted in 1826 as an opera by Carl Maria von Weber and J. R. Planché).

We do know that lending libraries developed in Germany around the same time that they did in England and that they helped to popularize the gothic novel and tale with the upper class as well as the growing middle class there (Hall, 37). We also know that fairy tales continued to be read aloud in late eighteenth-century German households, and, although we do not know the exact psychology of the inhabitants in these homes, we can make some assumptions about the continued prevalence of superstitions in their everyday lives. From the popularity of the fairy tales it seems clear that at least a large proportion of the population appears to have continued to think that "demons, spirits, sprites and a host of evil-minded forces [were] believed to influence one's existence . . . while the fairy tale reassured [its audience] that such forces can be overcome" (Buch, 45). Indeed, belief in the supernatural and fairies was so widespread in Germany at this time that the German author G. A. Keyser published a series of tales between 1785 and 1792 that sought to denounce such superstitions as dangerous (Hall, 52).

After the publication of the Grimm brothers' collection, *Kinder- und Hausmärchen* (*Children's and Household Tales,* 1812–15), the short tale was further developed by a number of German gothic writers, including most famously E. T. A. Hoffmann (1776–1822) and Ludwig Tieck (1773–1853). Hoffman's "The Sandman" and "The Mines at Falun," as well as Tieck's "The Blonde Eckbert" and "The Runenberg" (English translations by Thomas Carlyle in 1827) present the German gothic tale in its purest form. As Zipes has noted, the hero in each tale goes insane and then dies, while "the evil forces assume a social hue, for the witches and villains no longer are allegorical representations of evil in the Christian tradition but are symbolically associated with the philistine bourgeois society or the decadent aristocracy." These *Kunstmärchen* (art tales) were not intended to amuse in any simple sense, but were in fact serious philosophical attempts by these writers to conduct discussions with their culture about the nature of art, love, education, and bodily versus spiritual existence (1991, xxiii). And so in addition to presenting what we could characterize as a progressive ideology, these stories, as well as their sources in the fairy tales, explore the realm of the transcendent, the darker side of the human mind and experience, and suggest yet another manifestation of the culture's fascination with the gothic, the dream as nightmare, and the persistence and power of the folk-blood spirit, the "old ways."

Finally, the "old ways" are precisely what may be at stake in the origins and dissemination of fairy tales, and by extension, the gothic tale.[4] As Mircea Eliade has noted, myths are the tales that a culture tells itself in order to keep alive the life stories of exemplary supernatural beings. Although he goes to pains to deny the obvious, namely that fairy and folk tales are secularized or desacralized versions of myths, it is obvious that his description of myth points in that direction:

> Though in the West the tale has long since become a literature of diversion (for children and peasants) or of escape (for city dwellers), it still presents the structure of an infinitely serious and responsible adventure, for in the last analysis it is reducible to an initiatory scenario: again and again we find initiatory ordeals (battles with the monster, apparently insurmountable obstacles, riddles to be solved, impossible tasks, etc.), the descent to Hades or the ascent to Heaven (or—what amounts to the same thing—death and resurrection), marrying the princess. (196-97)

Scholars of fairy tales have long puzzled over the reasons why myths transmuted into folk and fairy tales, and Eliade himself suggests that it may have occurred when the traditional rites and cult practices were no longer believed in so that former practitioners were free to expose the formerly secret rites to public view. For Eliade, "the man of modern societies still benefits from the imaginary initiation supplied by tales. That being so, one may wonder if the fairy tale did not very early become an 'easy doublet' for the initiation myth and rites, if it did not have the role of recreating the 'initiatory ordeals' on the plane of imagination and dream" (201–2).

In a very similar manner, gothic tales also can be understood as textual practices that present abbreviated and secularized versions of the original "initiatory" story of the genre (the recovery of aristocratic property and the legitimating of the rightful heir in Walpole's *Castle of Otranto*) so that the later tales seem only to dimly remember or abruptly and crudely trace in a large scrawling hand a version of the same story. Clearly, this is a culture that had a need to continue to present narratives about the challenges faced by and conduct required of exemplary beings ("aristocrats") in extraordinarily challenging situations (the recovery of their estates or sacred places), but increasingly those "exemplary beings" became more and more "human" (middle class and subject to the immanent decay of the mortal human body) rather than "divine." What we see here is the replacement of the "lottery" worldview of the earlier works by the later middle-class "investment" mentality. In these earlier works we can see that the lower classes felt that they inhabited a world where they were "porous selves" buffeted about by inscrutable gods and giants (read: aristocrats), while in the later chapbooks the middle-class author presents a manageable society that can be mastered by the skillful individual who has practiced those virtues demanded by the bourgeoisie: control of the emotions, reason, order, good judgment, and fidelity to one's own inviolable conscience. "Religion" has moved here from "outside" of the individual to "inside" so that the line between familiar and strange, canny and uncanny, is drawn very clearly. It became the goal of the middle-class chapbooks to make the uncanny (that which is "strange" or foreign within us) modern, manageable, and secularized, as something that existed outside of us and was subject therefore to our own control.

II.

> Take—An old castle, half of it ruinous.
> A long gallery, with a great many doors, some secret ones.
> Three murdered bodies, quite fresh.
> An old woman hanging by the neck; with her throat cut.
> Assassins and desperadoes, such as suffices.
> Noises, whispers, and groans, threescore at least.
> Mix them together, in the form of three volumes, to be taken at any of the watering places, before going to bed.
>
> —*The Spirit of the Public Journals* I (1798), 224–25

Clearly delimited as a genre that flourished between 1770 and 1820, the gothic chapbook has been discussed in largely accusatory tones by earlier critics who blame it for the eventual decline of the canonical gothic novel's status and popularity. David Punter, for instance, observes that

> popular writers in the genre appear to have become increasingly able to turn out a formulaic product in a matter of weeks, and the eventual decline in Gothic's popularity was clearly at least partially to do with a flooding of the market, and also with the way in which the hold of the early Gothic masters tended to stultify originality. (1996, 114)

As there are as many one thousand chapbooks currently extant in Britain alone,[5] it is virtually impossible to provide anything other than a snapshot or freeze-frame portrait of the genre. I have chosen to look closely at a handful of representative types in order to suggest the tremendous range to be found in this mode of writing. Certainly by the time Edgar Allan Poe was writing his short tales of terror (e.g., "The Tell-Tale Heart" in 1843), he had mastered the formulae necessary to produce a taut and macabre study in gothic psychology and action. Any claim that the gothic tale was moribund by this date is patently false given the artistry that Poe brought to the genre, not to mention that developed by Maupassant in France or Hoffmann in Germany.[6] Between Sarah Wilkinson's chapbook "The Subterranean Passage: or Gothic Cell" (1803) and Poe, however, there is a considerable artistic gulf, and it is my intention to try to explain how that gap was bridged through an examination of the evolution and eventual refinement of the subjectivities presented in the gothic tale.

One cannot discuss the gothic chapbook phenomenon without also briefly addressing the development of the circulating library as a "front" so to speak for its own publishing house, William Lane's Minerva Press being the most famous example. Lane's Circulating Library opened in 1770 in London and had ten thousand items in circulation by 1794. We know that circulating libraries were widespread and viewed with more than a little class suspicion by 1775, because Sir Anthony Absolute in Richard Sheridan's comedy *The Rivals* says to Mrs. Malaprop: "Madam, a circulating library in a town is as an evergreen tree of diabolical knowledge! It blossoms through the year!—And depend on it, Mrs. Malaprop, that they who are so fond of handling the leaves will long for the fruit at last" (I:2). This interesting metaphor suggests that the chapbooks may be the "leaves," but the "fruit" is something much more valuable: the possession of a veneer of culture, class, and cultivation that cheap access to literacy provides. But just as circulating libraries were viewed with suspicion by the upper classes for the easy access they provided to gaining a modicum of culture, so were they seen as important for the role they played as moral guardians to the working class. In the how-to pamphlet *The Use of Circulating Libraries Considered* (1797), circulating libraries were specifically encouraged to avoid stocking too many chapbooks and pamphlets, but to have 79 percent of their stock in fiction. However, library proprietors were also urged to consider the following advice: "Reading and instruction should be universal—the humbler walks of life require much culture; for this purpose I would recommend to their perusal, books of authenticity, in preference to those of entertainment only." From this advice we can infer that the preferable form of fiction was of the morally didactic variety ("the novel") rather than of the "romance" (or gothic) type. The very existence of these libraries, though, was seen as playing a disruptive role in the distribution of cultural materials that were viewed by the upper classes as encouraging the working classes in their misguided and even dangerous social aspirations.[7]

As literacy rates increased among the lower classes, the demand for reading materials for them proportionally increased as well. It is difficult to know exactly what proportion of the working class purchased their own chapbooks or opted instead to obtain them through a circulating library as either a subscriber or a day-borrower (the latter option would have been the much more economical route to borrowing). Either way, through the act of reading the chapbooks, the lower classes were participating in the ideological and intellectual struggles of their culture. If they could not afford to attend the opera or theater productions in even the "illegitimate" theaters of London, they could read highly condensed redactions and much simplified abridged versions of Walpole, Reeve, Radcliffe, or Lewis's long novels. Doing so allowed the working classes, they thought, to have the same reading experience that the elite experienced and therefore the same access to and ownership of their culture's luxury items. By the early to mid-nineteenth century, however, the tales were being collected into longer anthologies that frequently contained up to five previously published stories, while the popular Ladies' periodicals began to reprint them in a bid to shore up their subscriptions (hence the *Lady's Pocket Magazine* reprints a two-volume collection of 136 previously published gothic tales as *Legends of Terror!* [1826; 1830]).

I have selected one representative collection of anonymously produced gothic stories as an example of a mixed lower- and middle-class manifestation of the genre, *Tales of Wonder* (1801), although any number of collections could have been selected as representative. Its title page reveals in a stark visual manner why I have claimed that there are clear fairy tale origins for a number of these tales (see fig. 7):

FIGURE 7: Title page from Anon., *Tales of Wonder* (London: 1801). Courtesy of the Huntington Library

The title story, "The Castle of Enchantment, or The Mysterious Deception" is a virtual plagiarism of Wieland's fairy tale "The Druid," published a few years earlier in *Select Fairy Tales* (above) and which Wieland himself plagiarized from *Voyages de Zulma dans le Pais des Fées* (vol. 16 of *Cabinet des Fées*). This anonymously published version of the tale changes the names and also uses a flashback device to enable the Egyptian Osmondy, a student of "Eleusinian and other mysteries" (6), to tell his life story to Claudio, a traveling stranger who has come upon his decayed gothic tower in France. The tale centers on his quest to find the real-life analogue to a full-sized statue of a "virgin" kept by his father Lasiris in a "magic cabinet." As any reader of the longer gothic novels will recognize, the virgin's description strongly recalls Antonia's famous bath scene in *The Monk*: "a virgin of most divine beauty, who was sitting on a couch and playing with a dove, that seemed to nestle in her bosom. She was dressed in a long robe, which hung from her right shoulder, and was bound beneath her half-revealed bosom with a golden zone" (6). During the festival of Isis, Osmondy becomes convinced that he sees a real-life version of this statue marching in a procession of virgins and is increasingly certain that the statue is based on an actual woman: "'My father, I am convinced that there is something extraordinary in this statue. Either it is a real virgin reduced to this state by magic or, if it be an inanimate mass, there exists somewhere the original of this beautiful form'" (9).

The recourse to orientalizing, platonic, Egytian, and Greek traditions is historically revealing, as the Rosetta Stone had been discovered in 1799 by Napoleon's armies and had come into British possession in 1801, the year that this collection was published. There had been throughout Europe for at least a decade an intense antiquarian interest in the Eleusinian Mysteries (the worship of Demeter and the Magna Mater) and, in fact, in all things Eastern, Egyptian, and Oriental. The cult of Isis had dominated the first and second centuries CE, and its popularity was thought to have been derived from the secret rituals practiced by its adherents in contrast to the public rites demanded by the earlier Osirian religion. As we saw in Wieland's "Philosopher's Stone," there is frequently in these works the presentation of "lost" religions as forms of superstition that rational and civilized Europeans should reject. For Wieland, the ostensible target was the Mysteries of Hermes, a cult popular in the Middle Ages and one that promised secret knowledge of alchemical principles that would accompany the power to transform base metals into gold. Wieland is clearly mocking the worship of Hermes, but the same attitude does not appear in "The Castle of Enchantment." The discussion of the power of Isis in this work is not ridiculed; rather, its serious presentation suggests the residual

FIGURE 8: Frontispiece to *The Tales of Wonder* (London, 1801).
Courtesy of the Huntington Library

power of myth in these chapbooks. The confused similarity between the real and its facsimile, the woman and the statue of the woman, also reveals how thoroughly these tales sought to secularize the uncanny through the device of doubling. The uncanny fully reveals itself when Claudio learns that the woman that Osmondy has been pursuing is, in fact, a statue of his own sister Matilda that his father had sent to his friend Lasiris, Osmondy's father, in Egypt. At the same time Osmondy learns that Claudio has fallen in love with his sister Naomi, whom he had seen in the forest and mistaken for the divine goddess Diana (19). This encounter between Naomi (as the supposedly divine goddess) and Claudio serves as the highly stylized and romantic frontispiece to the volume (see fig. 8).

The doubling of brother/sister pairs and the (supposedly) rational explanation provided at the end of the tale suggest a persistent pattern in the gothic imaginary: a recourse to the uncanniness of doubling, the use of a mechanical doll or virginal statue as a love object, but resolved not in tragedy (as in Hoffmann's "The Sandman"), but in comedy and the commonsense explanation of mistaken identities. What is most interesting in this story is how closely it mirrors the need to keep alive the belief that there are divinities on earth (the residual mythic component of the genre, discussed above). This is a culture where the "virgin/whore" dichotomy is just below the surface, as both male heroes profess a general contempt for all women except the virgin or divinity that each has chosen to pursue obsessively. It is indeed a short step from this position to the Victorian "Angel in the House" ideology that would become so prevalent by 1850. And in Claudio's pursuit of the goddess Diana in the forest we can certainly hear faint (albeit crude) traces of what would become Keats's *Endymion* (1816).

The second story in the collection, "The Robbers Daughter; or The Phantom of the Grotto," reads like an amalgam of "Cinderella," "Donkey-Skin," and "Sleeping Beauty." Set in the Black Forest of Germany on the "free-booter's hold" of a knight named Wilibald, we are initially introduced to his wife Matilda and their three daughters (20–21). Their "hold" also happens to possess an enchanted fountain presided over by a "white nymph" who appears to the wife in order to claim "god-mother" status to the newest daughter, also named Matilda, on whom she bestows a magical "musk-ball" (22). The mother soon dies and is replaced by a selfish stepmother and a new set of children, so that the abused daughter Matilda seeks out her nymph-godmother who tells her that the magical musk-ball will grant her three wishes. Matilda is forced to use her first wish when her father is killed and her home is assaulted by neighboring ruffians. Rather than save her family, she saves herself and passes invisibly out of the house. She next uses her musk-ball to wish for a beautiful gown in order to attend a great banquet given by the woman-hating Count Conrad, who promptly falls in love with her: "'I pledge my knightly honour, and engage my soul's salvation to boot, were you the meanest man's daughter, and but a pure and undefiled virgin, I will receive you for my wedded wife'" (29). The usual complications must occur before Conrad is reunited with Matilda in the guise of a "dark gypsy" who insists that he marry her as she is. When he consents, she magically returns to her beautiful form and they have two sons who both die mysteriously as infants. Only after returning to the magic fountain and using her last wish does Matilda learn that her mother-in-law has sought to kill her sons, who have been safely preserved by the nymph of the fountain: "[T]he marriage of her son proved a dagger to the heart of that proud woman, who imagined he had stained the honour of his house by taking a kitchen-wench to his bed" (36). Again, although we are in the realm of "fairy," we are also in the domain of reasonable solutions to apparent mysteries (class pride is the motive behind the mysterious "deaths" of Matilda's sons). Whereas the earlier tale had foregrounded the paradoxical nature of women as its theme (are they human or divine?), this tale focuses on class issues and validates the aspirations of virginal but lower-class women who marry above their class status, in fact, suggesting that they are innately superior to aristocratic women.

The third tale in the volume, "The Magic Legacy," concerns King Alindor who, on his deathbed, tells his son about a treasure that is buried in front of their palace: "an empty leather purse, a horn of metal, a girdle of coarse hair, and a roll of parchment" (38). The parchment informs Prince Alindor that the purse will supply him all the gold he needs, the horn will deliver all the soldiers he can use, and the girdle will allow him to travel instantly between distant places. His wealth quickly attracts the attention of the beautiful Zenomia, who arrives with her parents and a scheme to fleece him of said wealth. Very similar to Wieland's "Philosopher's Stone," this tale uses familiar fairy-tale and orientalist elements to instruct its readers on the values of honesty and the need to be wary of the beauty and treacherous seductions of women.

The fourth and final short tale in the collection, "The Enchanted Knight; or, Phebe," concerns a curse that has been placed on Oron, knight of the castle, by the "authority of daemons": "A young virgin alone can vanquish the daemons, and extinguish the enchanted flame of the Dead or Glorious Hand; for a good and beauteous virgin is of more power than a host of spirits" (48). Phebe is led by an "apparition" holding up "the remains of its left-arm" to a "gothic castle, surrounded by a moat" (49). Amid the sound of "clinking chains" and "painful and dismal groans," Phebe discovers the couch of Oron, where "over him hung suspended in the air the Glorious Hand; that is to say, a dead man's hand prepared by Necromancy, dipt in magical oil, and each finger lighted up" (50). By breathing on the hand, Phebe "purifies the air" and the curse is broken; she marries Oron and becomes "the lady of the castle." The volume concludes with the moral addenda: "perserverance in goodness must at last conduct to happiness" (50). One senses in this truncated tale less a plot or characters than an assemblage of stock gothic tropes: the castle, the chains, the groans, the "dead man's hand prepared by Necromancy." Telegraphing the gothic as the exotic and supernatural has become in these tales a way of conveying in a few quick strokes the larger parameters of the discourse in its most popular form: the mysterious world of fairy and folktale has been condensed to a few simple moral lessons that are applicable to the daily lives of both lower- and middle-class readers.

This particular volume of tales presents some interesting issues for the literary historian, although I would claim that any number of collections would reveal the same emphasis on the evolution of core bourgeois values: the "preservation of goodness" in the face of persecution and the emphasis on female "purity."[8] Clearly, virginity is fetishized in a blatant manner in all these tales, suggesting (as we saw in Opie's *Father and Daughter*, chap. 1) that the culture has reified the notion that the stability and indeed the very existence of bourgeois society and "human flourishing" is dependent on a wife's ability to prove the legitimacy of her children. But even when that legitimacy is certain, as in "The Robbers Daughter," yet another impediment emerges, the class-based prejudice that the middle class continues to experience in their attempts to establish themselves as the deserving heirs of fortune. The fairy-tale residue (the "evil" aristocratic mother-in-law) in these tales suggests the persistence of a "lottery" or lower-class mentality that has to be overcome before the protagonists in these works can move into the promised land of an "investment" mentality or control over the vagaries of "fate." Each of these tales has been examined fairly closely in order to demonstrate that the extended gothic tale did not originate solely in street literature or broadside ballads, but in the fairy tale traditions of France and Germany, and that such an origin suggests that unresolved class and religious issues continued to be a source of conflict and confusion for a reading audience whose allegiances were still very much in flux. Whether lower or middle class, these readers did not yet feel fully invested in the brave new world that the Enlightenment was preparing for its citizens and the tales' frequent recourse to the continuing power of "ill-fated stars" suggests as much.

III.

> It has been the fashion to make terror the order of the day, by confining heroes and heroines in old gloomy castles, full of specters, apparitions, ghosts, and dead men's bones.
>
> —"The Terrorist Novel Writing," *The Spirit of the Public Journals* I (1798), 223

Literary critics have been slighting if not downright hostile to the popularity and prevalence of the gothic chapbooks during the early nineteenth century in Britain, France, and Germany. We know, for instance, that Percy Shelley, Robert Southey, and Walter Scott read them as children (Potter, 37), and there is a certain appeal in their childlike simplicity, their distillation of plot, and their flattening of character. More interesting, however, is the confused spiritual ideology they promulgated for their reading audience: alternately advocating either a bourgeois, moralistic, and "investment" mentality (the "buffered self") or a "lottery," lower-class, and fatalistic attitude toward life (the "porous self"). By examining the works of one particular gothic chapbook author, it is possible to see the sometimes confused struggle between these two attitudes. Along with Isaac Crookenden (1777–1820), Sarah Scudgell Wilkinson (1779–1831) was one of the most prolific writers of gothic chapbooks, the author of some twenty-nine volumes of fiction and more than one hundred short works, at least half of which are gothic. Working at times as a writer (and perhaps editor) for Ann Lemoine's *Tell-Tale Magazine,* or independently trying to support her mother and (possibly illegitimate) daughter, Amelia, Wilkinson scratched along as a "scribbler" and owner of a circulating library until she was forced on more than one occasion to apply for financial assistance to the Royal Literary Fund, a form of welfare for indigent and worthy authors. This section will examine a few of her best-known works, "Albert of Werdendorff; or The Midnight Embrace" (based on Lewis's ballad "Alonzo the Brave and Fair Imogine"); "The Spectres" (an amalgamation of Reeve's *Old English Baron,* Radcliffe's *Sicilian Romance,* and Parsons's *Castle of Wolfenbach*); "The White Pilgrim" (based on Pixérécourt's drama *Le Pèlerin Blanc* [1802]); and "The Castle Spectre, An Ancient Baronial Romance" (based on Lewis's drama), as representatives of the genre. What is most interesting in these works is their confused and at times frantic heteroglossia, their parasitic grasping after every known gothic mode in the attempt to produce yet another new and marketable genre, the gothic tale of terror.[9]

Wilkinson has received a certain amount of critical attention recently, largely because of attempts to recover "lost" female writers and to place the chapbook tradition itself into its larger cultural and literary context. As one of the only female "hack" writers that we know by name, Wilkinson's works and career can be fruitfully examined as a case study of middling to lower-class female authorship during the early nineteenth century. In fact, her very prolific publishing profile recalls Bradford Mudge's observation that the development of mass culture during this period was linked to the dominance of women as the authors as well as readers of circulating library materials. But this female-inflected mass culture was increasingly figured at least by the Regency and the early-Victorian periods as a diseased, metastatic type of female reproduction because it challenged the hegemonic model of the realistic novel (1992, 92).

Wilkinson's biography is bleak reading indeed (Potter, 109–15), and it illustrates that the high point of the gothic trade occurred roughly between 1800 and 1815, its decline causing Wilkinson to turn to writing children's books by 1820 in order to survive. Within five years, however, that market had also shrunk to such an extent that she was again appealing to the Royal Literary Fund: "I need not point out to you that the depression in the Book trade and consequently scantiness of employ in Juvenile works has been great. . . . *Forsake me and I perish*" (RLF, December 12, 1825; emphasis in original). Casting herself as the gothic heroine of her own life story, Wilkinson was, unfortunately, prescient. But before the very bleak death she suffered in 1831 at St. Margaret's Workhouse, Westminster, she was determined to produce gothic chapbooks that would appeal to a growing reading audience of literate lower-class females.[10] As she herself observed in the *Preface* to her last gothic novel, *The Spectre of Lanmere Abbey; or, The Mystery of the Blue and Silver Bag: A Romance* (1820):

> Authors are, *proverbially,* poor; and therefore under the necessity of racking their wits for a bare subsistence. Perhaps, this is my case, and knowing how eager the fair sex are for something *new* and *romantic,* I determined on an attempt to *please* my fair sisterhood, hoping to profit myself thereby. If the following volumes tend to that effect, I shall be gratified; but if they meet with a rapid sale, and fill my pockets, I shall be elated. (qtd. Potter, 12; emphasis in original)

It would seem that whatever "elation" Wilkinson had as an author of gothic chapbooks was short-lived, while her claim to be producing "new" works is a bit disingenuous. Before her sad end, however, she did write a number of works that disseminated the major gothic tropes to a very wide, lower-class reading public and helped to codify the lower classes' understanding of "romantic" as "gothic."

Wilkinson's "Albert of Werdendorff, or The Midnight Embrace" (1812) is a prose adaptation of Lewis's gothic ballad "Alonzo the Brave and Fair Imogine," originally published in *The Monk* and then again in his *Tales of Wonder* (1801; Lewis's volume shares the same title as the anonymously authored collection of tales just discussed), and itself based on Bürger's "Lenora" (see chapter 5). As Potter has noted in his introduction to the reprinted edition, this bluebook "is extremely sensational, presenting unbridled supernaturalism to shock and horrify the reader; yet on the other hand, it is profoundly didactic and moral, emphasizing the necessity of honor, respect, virtue and the sanctity of the marriage contract" (6). In other words, this text presents an amalgamation of transcendent and immanent concerns, as well as an abbreviated and interesting mix of conflicted class concerns, with a seduced and abandoned lower-class heroine wreaking vengeance on her aristocratic suitor and his "haughty" bride. Wilkinson's tale is also interesting in that the female subjectivity presented in the work conforms to lower-class prejudices about the nature of women: the lower-class Josephine is "the ill-fated maiden," selfless, innocent, duped, and fated to be destroyed by her upper-class seducer, while her aristocratic rival Guimilda is persistently described as "proud," "revengeful," and capable of "haughty caprice and tyranny" (18, 19, 22, 23). The access that we have into the subjectivities of both women allows us to see the pain that the worthy Josephine suffers when she realizes that she has been betrayed and deserted by her lover of six months, the wealthy Albert.

We can also be privy to the psychic machinations that run through the mind of Guimilda when she learns that she has a discarded rival in the artless and sweet-tempered Josephine. Not content to merely win her husband, Guimilda wants Josephine dead and she demands that Albert do the deed himself or she refuses to allow him into their bridal bed. Agreeing all too readily to Guimilda's demands, Albert steals away from his own marriage feast to spread a mock wedding banquet for Josephine, poisoning her food and wine (a reversal of the wedding banquet scene that Keats was to use in "The Eve of St. Agnes"). When she naively asks when he will return to her, Albert replies "that he would return at the dark hour of midnight, and again clasp her in his arms" (22). But this thoughtless rejoinder actually functions as a binding oath in this oral-based community, and commits the two to a "midnight embrace" from which Albert will not emerge alive. Recalling J. L. Austin's theory of speech "performativity," that is, acts of speech which cannot be considered true or false but which none the less are meaningful, this oath is an example of what Austin calls "promising," a phrase that performs its own meaning (Miles 2008, 15). One breaks a promissory oath only at one's own peril in the gothic imaginary. Realizing his error too late, Albert quickly repents his deed and curses Guimilda as "an agent of infernal malice, sent to plunge his soul into an irremediable abyss of guilt" (25).

A day passes and, interestingly, we are not provided with a description of the nuptial bliss of Albert and Guimilda. This elision of their marital consummation stands in stark contrast to the descriptions we have had of the passionate affair between Albert and Josephine. In some ways, then, the two women are doubles of each other in Albert's bed, or perhaps we are intended to think that the sexual colonization of the lower-class woman occurs because of aristocratic female complicity as well as male action. Thunder and lightening flash above the Werdendorff castle as, at the stroke of midnight the next night, the ghastly Josephine appears in the guise of an avenging spirit: "In a hollow, deep-toned voice, she addressed her perjured lover: 'Thou. false one! Base assassin of her who thou lured from the flowery paths of virtue; her whom thou had sworn to cherish and protect while life was left thee. Thou hast cut short the thread of my existence: but think not to escape the punishment due to thy crimes. 'Tis midnight's dark hour: the hour by thyself appointed: delay no, therefore, thy promised embrace'" (26). Reminiscent of the dark ladies in Anne Bannerman's gothic ballads (see Hoeveler 2000), Josephine takes revenge on her aristocratic betrayer by kissing him with "her clammy lips" and holding him in a "noisome icy embrace" (27). Three times he raises his eyes to gaze on his uncanny "supernatural visitant" before he drops dead "as if [in the act] of imploring the mercy of offended heaven." Guimilda makes a hasty retreat to a convent and the castle falls into ruins that serve as a backdrop for tourists to the area. Every year on the anniversary of this awful event, the hall lights up and the same scene is enacted again "by supernatural beings": "the groans of the specter lord can be heard afar, while he is clasped in the arms of Josephine's implacable ghost" (28). The final paragraph of the text presents the reader with pious comments on the importance of virginity, the sanctity of marriage, and a simple moral: "virtue is a female's firmest protector" (29).

It is interesting that the lower-class victim, the dead Josephine, returns from the dead with the power to act as a direct agent of God, not just someone seeking her own personal revenge. The lower class, in other words, has divine sanction to seek restitution against its aristocratic oppressors, and such a sentiment would not have been lost on the lower-class readership of Wilkinson's bluebooks. We have seen other versions of this tale of betrayal and seduction throughout the gothic, and frequently we have seen it supernaturalized, as it is in Lewis's *The Monk* and here in Wilkinson's adaptation. I want to suggest, however, that this tale can be read as yet another variation on the secularization of virtue we have seen in so many earlier works in this period. From Paisiello's *Nina*, to Wordsworth's "The Thorn," to Opie's *Father and Daughter*, we have seen the virgin/whore representation privileged in uncanny ways, but increasingly in the bluebooks it is the issue of class envy and anger that begins to emerge most blatantly. Guimilda as aristocratic viper is the sort of female monster the reading public had seen earlier in Dacre's Victoria (*Zofloya*, 1806), a woman who sells her soul to the devil for power and the fulfillment of her lusts. The male aristocrat is equally corrupt and his doom, according to lower-class opinion, is justified, but note the persistence in this work of the power of orality, the privilege that is given to the oath Albert promises to his doomed mistress. By writing a tale that continues to promulgate the primacy of oral culture, the lower-class bluebook participated in preserving lower-class cultural values: the belief that the transcendent and the immanent can work together in concert, that natural elements will avenge a human crime in order to restore moral order, and that a female supernatural visitant has the ability to claim divine power in order to exact material revenge on her lover.

In addition to their origin in fairy tales, gothic tales can also be understood as rewriting *The affecting history of the Duchess of C***, the most notorious episode in the novelized "letters on education," *Adèle et Théodore* (1782; trans. English 1783), produced by the prolific French author Stéphanie-Félicité de Genlis (1746–1830). By excerpting and then focusing on the horror of a wife imprisoned by her husband for nine years, female gothic novelists found the ideal subplot for a longer novel (i.e., Radcliffe's *Sicilian Romance*, Eliza Parsons's *Castle of Wolfenbach*, and numerous others). This inset tale initially served as the source for the explained supernatural of a long gothic novel, the material cause for all the mysterious lights and noises at night. In fact, the imprisoned wife becomes in the female gothic genre the *deus ex machina*, the explanatory first cause brought back to life, much like a lost female matriarch restored to power. As the gothic chapbook evolved, it appropriated these intense episodes of suffering as its only content so that the genre, much like gothic drama, was a potent distillation of natural and supernatural, minus the more extended descriptions of scenery, characterizations, and subjectivity that the middle- or upper-class reader had come to expect in a novel identified as "gothic."

Wilkinson's "The Spectres; or Lord Oswald and Lady Rosa" advertises its connection to the "Duchess C" subplot in its own extended title: "Including an account of the Marchioness of Civetti, who was basely consigned to a Dungeon beneath her Castle. By her eldest Son, whose cruel Avarice plunged him into the Commission of the worst of Crimes, that stain the Annals of the Human Race." Using the *in medias res* device, the chapbook begins with the arrival of a young stranger, Rudolpho, to an Italian castle inhabited only by a pair of elderly servants. After an uneasy night in which he learns that he looks uncannily like the dead owner of the castle, Rudolpho persuades the pair to tell him its history. As in so many fairy/folk tales, not to mention Genesis, the original dispute is between an older brother, Francisco, who envies his younger and worthy brother Oswald because Oswald has inherited a vast estate on their mother's death (this occurrence, of course, undercuts the aristocratic practice of primogeniture and recalls Schiller's *Die Raüber*). After marriage to the beautiful Lady Rosa and the birth of their daughter Malvina, Oswald dies shortly after his brother comes to visit. Francisco inherits his brother's property and the pregnant Rosa is declared to have been a mistress, not a legal wife. Held prisoner by Francisco for sixteen years, Rosa dies swearing "retributive vengeance" on her fratricidal brother-in-law. The hints dropped to the reader are numerous and broad during this exposition, such as "Lady Rosa could never be persuaded out of an opinion that her second child was not still born; she would persist that she heard it cry" (298), or "Rudolpho started up, and the room was filled with a supernatural blaze of light, and the spirits of Lord Oswald and Lady Rosa (for as such he recognised them by the pictures he had seen) stood by his couch. They waved their hands over him, as if in the act of giving him their benediction" (298). The second passage is a virtual plagiarism from Reeve's *Old English Baron*, while the kidnapped child stolen at birth had been used in *The Castle of Wolfenbach*. The writing in "The Spectres" is not polished, nor is there control of plot devices, suspense, or motivations. With the appearance of the spirits of the dead parents, the plot quickly moves to its dénouement: Rudolpho is told by his parents to "save a sister's honor, and forgive thy father's murderer. Leave his punition [punishment] to heaven" (299). As Francisco attempts to rape Malvina, Rudolpho arrives to save her and in the process is revealed to be Oswald and Rosa's long-lost son, adopted by a Pisan apothecary who had recently disinherited Rudolpho in favor of his brother, the apothecary's biological son. On his journey to inform said brother of these events, Rudolpho had managed to stumble on the family castle just in time to save his sister from incestuous rape (also an act that is threatened in the *Castle of Wolfenbach* and *The Castle Spectre*).

Once he is exposed, Francisco begs to be allowed to make a full "confession" (302) in which he admits his crimes, begs forgiveness, and arranges a marriage between Rudolpho and Eltruda, Francisco's only daughter (thereby reuniting and preserving the family's ancestral estates) all in fairly short order. His final act is to reveal that envy and greed caused him to stage the death of his mother, so that he buried another woman in her place, and kept her prisoner in a dungeon below the castle for the past twenty years (all of this is extremely reminiscent of Radcliffe's *Sicilian Romance*). After ordering the release of his mother, Francisco promptly dies after receiving her "gracious" pardon (305). This chapbook is, as I have suggested, a virtual catalogue of female gothic clichés, but it presents an interesting mix of lower-class and bourgeois spiritual agendas. Lord Oswald and his wife, for all their aristocratic wealth and privilege, are presented as helpless victims of the scheming and evil Francisco. Like the lower-classes, they are unlucky enough to have drawn a very evil brother in the lottery of familial relations. In addition to this fatalistic subtext, the work presents a spirituality that is a mix of Catholic and Protestant tropes. On one hand, Francisco needs to relieve his conscience through the act of "confession," while prophetic dreams enable Rudolpho to see and hear the spirits of his parents. All of this residual Catholic "superstition," on the other hand, is contrasted with the bourgeois command to protect virginity at all costs. Also confused is Lady Rosa's dying prayer for "retributive vengeance," contradicted later when she and Oswald instruct Rudolpho to leave their uncle to heaven, a decidedly more modern and "civilized" attitude.

The confused and contradictory ideological issues found in chapbooks have been identified by Potter as "dual plots, the horrific and the moralistic" (84), but this distinction can also be understood as caused by unresolved class and religious issues as well. The "horrific" recalls the lower-class, transcendent, and Catholic components of the work, while the "moralistic" suggests a middle-class, immanent, Protestant agenda at work. It is revealing to note that commentators during the period recognized the persistence of the tropes and even commented on their continued power. In 1826 the editor of *Legends of Terror!* a collection of 136 tales that claimed to be "a complete collection of Legendary Tales, National Romances, & Traditional Relics of Every Country, and of the most intense interest," observed:

> A few centuries back, superstition gave rise to a general belief that the spirits of murdered persons wandered about the earth, until the perpetrator was either, by revenge or justice, punished for the foul deed he had committed; and that they would appear to their relatives and others, to point out the means by which their violent deaths might be avenged. Such superstitious feelings, though now seldom called into action, are probably not so completely extinguished, even in this enlightened era, as is generally imagined, but are yet cherished by a large portion of mankind. (210–11; qtd. Potter, 89, 83)

A chapbook like "The Spectres" gives further evidence of the fact that uncanny, animistic beliefs are not eliminated in the lower-class imaginary, but in fact are placed before the reading public as but one choice among many in the pursuit of "human flourishing."

The same ideological ambivalence can be seen in Wilkinson's "The White Pilgrim; or, Castle of Olival." Based on the earlier Pixérécourt drama as translated into English in 1817 by Henry R. Bishop as "The Wandering Boys; or The Castle of Olival," Wilkinson's version suggests that she was adapting and publishing gothic chapbooks at least as late as 1818. As the story begins we are introduced to the Count of Castelli, "the truly amiable and liberal" Horatio, living with his beautiful wife Amabel and their two sons in a castle in Berne, Switzerland (311). Devoted to their sons and the welfare of their tenants and dependents, the young couple has made their domain "a second Eden," unaware that there are serpents lurking in the guise of attendants, namely the Chevalier Roland, Seneschal of the castle, and his assistant Otho, Captain of the Guard. Pregnant again, Amabel has a "fearful dream" the night before her husband is to make a short trip to settle some legal affairs with his friend Count Vassali. When she informs her husband of her forebodings, he responds, "'What Amabel superstitious? This is indeed a novelty, for which I was unprepared'" (313). Mocking his wife's primitive "superstitions," Horatio next ignores the warning cries of "screech-owls and crows" as he begins his journey with his servant Claude, who warns him that the cries of the birds are "ill-omens" (313). The consummately rational man, Horatio ignores all of these warnings only to leave his family defenseless to the schemes of Roland.

Upon his return, Horatio is informed that his wife has fled the castle, her maid Theresa asserting that she has absconded with a paramour ("a near relation of her own, whom you had forbid the castle") seen lurking around the grounds. When all the evidence points to the truth of this story, Horatio resigns himself to caring for his sons until he grows restless for travel and a change of scene. Leaving his sons with a tutor, Horatio sets out for England, where he coincidentally discovers the missing maid Theresa, who tells him that she and her father had been bribed by Roland to stage the disappearance of Amabel during Horatio's absence. Horatio further learns that Amabel has in fact been held captive these past three years in a "subterranean cavity" (326) on the castle grounds, and so he begins to plot his revenge by letting it be known that he has perished in a shipwreck during the channel crossing. The resolution of the story occurs when the reader is informed that Roland is the illegitimate half-brother of Horatio, the son of the former Count and a woman who was "of obscure birth and illiterate manners" (325). When he learns that Horatio has died at sea, Roland now produces a will that allows him to claim all of Horatio's estates (327). At this very moment, the reading of the suspicious will, a pilgrim, "clad in white, his robes, his hat, and staff were all of that virgin hue," appears asking for refuge "after performing his vow of pilgrimage to the shrine of our Lady of Loretto" (327). The appearance of this man is almost atavistic, antediluvian, suggesting the uncanniness of the Catholic past, its ability to erupt as the not-quite repressed force that still figures on the edges of this culture. But the white pilgrim is also a melodramatic figure because he is introduced by Roland as "deaf," reminiscent of the "deaf and dumb" characters at the melodramatic core of Holcroft's gothicized adaptations (see chapter 4).

Thinking that he can safely discuss his plans in the presence of the white pilgrim, Roland reveals to Otho that he intends to poison the orphan boys and kill their mother: "she had long since become an object of disgust and hatred to her betrayer, for she had nobly resisted every attempt to despoil her of her honor and fidelity" (328). The servant Ruffo enables Amabel to escape her dungeon and she tells an abbreviated tale of abuse and misery that recalls the fate of Agnes, the pregnant and imprisoned nun in Lewis's *The Monk:* "she was delivered prematurely of a child, who died the same night; she was allowed no assistance, and having wept many days over her dear blossom, she buried it with her own hands in one corner of the damp dungeon" (334). Whereas her story recalls a literary source, the intended fates of her sons recall a particularly gothic moment in British history, the murder of the two princes in the Tower of London by Richard III in 1483. In an almost-repetition of that crime, this text instead allows the white pilgrim to save the children in the nick of time by substituting a safe potion for the intended poison. We learn later that all of these actions have been orchestrated by the white pilgrim, the avenging husband and father Horatio in disguise. Vassali brings the king's troops to storm the castle, and at the decisive moment, the white pilgrim strips himself of his robes and appears as "the real Count Olival" (335) to denounce the evil machinations of his illegitimate half-brother.

Similar to "The Spectres" in many ways, "The White Pilgrim" positions religious as well as class ideologies front and center. The lower class is pandered to in the privileging of premonitions and ill-omened birds, while bourgeois attitudes can be detected in the descent of Roland from an "illiterate" mother. There are clearly "lottery" elements in this work, as Horatio, an aristocrat, is frequently saved by the most chancelike occurrences (literally running into Theresa on a street in London). There are also bourgeois attitudes present, as Horatio rescues his family through cunning, skill, and what we would almost call omniscience. Originally written as a melodrama in France in 1801 and then recast as a British chapbook by Wilkinson in 1818, the text suggests the revenant power of Catholicism and the persistence of superstitions among lower-class readers. In fact, John Kerr's 1820 dramatic version of the work, titled "The Wandering Boys," continued to be so popular that it was performed in the British repetory and published as late as 1894.

Wilkinson's "The Castle Spectre: An Ancient Baronial Romance" (182?) is actually her second attempt to capitalize on the popularity of Lewis's 1797 drama *The Castle Spectre* (see chapter 3). The other version, called "The Castle Spectre: or, Family Horrors, a Gothic Story," had been published by Hughes in 1807. The two works are virtually identical and indicate how authors as well as publishers had no qualms about "borrowing" literary texts from others as well as themselves (in this case, was Wilkinson plagiarizing herself?). Set in Castle Conway on the border of Wales, the action once again concerns fratricidal envy, usurpation, attempted rape and murder, and vengeance by a maternal specter that appears at just the right moments to expose evil and protect virginity. A two-paragraph frame places the tale in superstitious territory when it describes the "supernatural visitants" to the Castle Conway: Lord Hubert, we are told, continues to be seen "riding over his dominions on the first of every moon, mounted on a milk white steed, clad in glittering armor," while his faithless wife, Lady Bertha, is still heard shrieking from the western tower, "where he had immured her for incontinence while he was at Palestine." The third ghost haunting this castle is the unlucky Baron Hildebrand, who stalks around the great hall "every night, with his head under his arm" (2). While the author claims that she cannot assert to the truth of these earlier legends, she does assure the reader that the tale of "the Spectre Lady Evelina and the base Earl Osmond" is indeed true. Interestingly, the frame revisits the Germanic ballad material of Bürger's "Der Wilde Jäger," made popular in England by Walter Scott's translation of it as "The Chase" or "The Wild Huntsman."

Beginning *in medias res*, we are initially introduced to two young peasants, Angela and Edwy, inhabiting a sort of pastoral idyll that is rudely interrupted when Angela is mysteriously taken to Castle Conway as the long-lost daughter of Sir Malcolm Mowbray, deceased, and now under the guardianship of his best friend, Earl Osmond. Edwy, however, is not who he seems. He is actually Lord Percy, heir to Alnwick Castle in Northumberland, who has chosen to assume the disguise of a peasant in order to court the lovely Angela and discover if she can love him for himself and not his wealth. After her disappearance he comes to realize that she also is not who she appears and is, in fact, the missing and presumed dead daughter of Earl Reginald, the lawful owner of Conway Castle and the elder brother of Earl Osmond, the usurper. The bulk of the text consists of positioning the principals in the castle in various threatened postures. Angela is twice the target of her murderous uncle's attempts at incestuous rape; Percy is imprisoned in a tower only to escape and attempt a rescue of Angela; and two black slaves, Hassan and Saib, alternately hurt or help the "white folks" (11).

Anti-Catholic markers and appeals to the lower class appear in this work in a number of ways. First, Gilbert describes Father Philip to Percy as "that immense walking tomb of fish, flesh and fowl . . . no more fit to be a monk, than I to be maid of hour to the Queen of Sheba" (12). The humorous mockery of the clergy in this work suggests the anticlericalism at the heart of so much gothic textuality, but in this work Father Philip is not a murderous, greedy, lecherous hypocrite, but merely a misogynistic meddler looking for his next meal. It is the ambivalent depiction of the characters of the black slaves, in fact, that bears the ideological ire of the lower-class reading audience. Saib is described as the "good" black, "the untutored child of nature," who balks when he is ordered by Osmond to murder Kenrick, one of Osmond's trusted henchmen (13), and the man who had delivered the baby Angela to her foster parents. Osmond does not want any witnesses to his earlier crimes against his brother and his family, so he thinks that killing Kenrick will protect his reputation. Saib instead warns Kenrick so that he does not drink the poisoned wine that Osmond has prepared for him, and he is at the conclusion of the work "rewarded with a comfortable asylum for the remainder of his days" (24). In contrast, Wilkinson presents Hassan as the "evil" black slave, a man embittered because he has been stolen from his "Samba and our infant son . . . here my sooty hue renders me an object of contempt and disdain. O memory, torturing memory! But since the tyrants forced me from Afric's valued shore, I have vowed hatred; yes, hatred eternal to all mankind!" (11). Hassan participates in the murderous assault on the Lady Evelina and remains loyal to the evil Osmond to the end, attempting to kill Reginald. Not surprisingly, we learn at the conclusion of the text that Hassan dies along with the "other blacks [who] met the fate their crimes deserved" (24).

But Earl Osmond has not been sleeping well of late, plagued with "dreams of the most appalling nature, in which he beheld the specters of the murdered persons threatening him with everlasting perdition" (18). Believing in the truth of visions, hallucinations, and supernaturally charged dreams is, according to Jan Vansina, a common characteristic of oral societies, and continued to persist in the popular imagination well into the early modern period (7). Similarly, Theo Brown has argued that the continued prevalence of ghost stories during this period actually functioned in a number of different ways: as a form of social correction, as an externalizing of a collective bad conscience about the Reformation, as nostalgia for medieval Catholicism, and as indignation at the manner of its dissolution (41; also see Aston). In a similar manner, the text shifts here from being one that had earlier laughed at ghostly legends and superstitions to one that makes increasing recourse to the reality of the transcendent realm and the unexplained supernatural. At the point when Angela is once again threatened with rape by Osmond, the specter of her mother appears: "a flowing drapery, or veil, expanding over her head and shoulders, leaving her bosom bare, on which was seen a ghastly wound, and the blood still appeared, as if flowing from it, over her white garments" (20). This is the moment that lower-class readers would have been waiting for, the horrific and supernatural reappearance of the undead bloody mother. It may be too much to ask so slight a text to bear so much ideological freight, but in this scene (as well as its source in Lewis's drama) it is possible to detect the traces of the dead/undead Virgin Mary, the "mother" of Catholicism, the spirit who will not die no matter how vehemently bourgeois Protestantism works to eradicate her image. I make this claim because Wilkinson's text clearly presents the Specter of Lady Evelina as something more than a mortal mother to Angela: "Our heroine sunk on her knees, the Spectre bended over her, and seemed to bless her, but spoke not. She then, with a slow solemn pace, and soundless footstep, returned to the Oratory, stopping a short time before the picture of Reginald, on which she seemed to gaze with interest. The doors then closed, music was heard, with a chorus of heavenly voices chaunting songs of triumph, and then silence reigned" (20).

The climax of the work occurs when Angela, assisted by Saib, is reunited with her undead father, held captive in an underground dungeon in the southern tower of the castle by Osmond these past sixteen years. In a desperate last bid to assassinate his brother, Osmond orders Hassan to do the deed, but at that very moment "thunder rolled, and all the elements seemed in commotion: a shock, as if from an earthquake, seemed to rend the building to its centre, and a part of the southern tower fell" (22). Again, we can see the continued prevalence of magical thinking in the lower-class imaginary, with the natural world believed to possess the ability to respond immediately to unnatural human designs. Amid the devastation that the earthquake has wrought, Angela finds her father stumbling out of his dungeon only to be assaulted by Hassan: "The slave lifted his dagger, when our heroine rushed forward with a loud shriek, and her father started up" (23). This scene is a virtual repetition of the earlier attempt on Reginald's life, the one that ended with the fatal blow given to Evelina. This time the scene abruptly stops as Osmond attempts to barter with Reginald for Angela's hand in marriage ("Osmond then offered his brother life and liberty, and one half of his possessions for the hand of Angela"). Reginald promptly repulses the notion of "an incestuous marriage: never shall the bosom of my child be made a pillow for the head of her mother's murderer" (23) and the fight is on yet again, with Angela on the verge of agreeing to the marriage in order to save her father's life. Just at the point when Angela would have "terminated the oath," the Specter of Lady Evelina appears again, Hassan drops his dagger in fright, and Angela plunges hers into her uncle (24).

The Specter of Lady Evelina departs to "solemn music," declaring that her work is completed. Osmond lives long enough to receive his brother's "merciful" forgiveness and Angela and Percy marry amid the strains of "the minstrel's harp" (24). Oaths and music have been foregrounded in this text in ways that suggest the continuing power of and attraction to an oral-based community. But the text closes on a discussion of what is to become of Angela's lower-class foster parents, the Allans. Angela wants to "raise them to a superior station in life," but it is their choice to remain in their humble cottage and to receive as gifts the many presents that Angela sends to them "to soothe their advanced years, and ameliorate the pains and infirmities of their old age" (24). The work concludes in validating the status and goodness of the lower classes, suggesting that their moral superiority and self-chosen rural isolation protect them from the evils that have characterized the life of the aristocratic Osmond. The work is nostalgic for a lower-class pastoral culture that was increasingly under siege by the early nineteenth century, while at the same time middle-class anxieties about the nature of marriage and religious beliefs emerge in a fairly chaotic manner.

The question that is most frequently begged in so many discussions of the gothic chapbooks is the reason for their popularity. Fred Frank claimed that they appealed to "the type of reader who had neither the time nor the taste for a leisurely Gothic experience. That there were many such readers during the Gothic craze is a well-documented fact" (1987, 420). But this is just another way of saying that you will always have the poor with you. A more important question might be to ask, why were the gothic chapbooks so fractured by both class and religious issues? One possible explanation is offered by McWhir, who notes that "in the very process of rejecting superstition, one suspects that these authors take pleasure in it, though their genre prevents them from completing the transition from shocked incredulity to imaginative suspension of disbelief. The completion of the movement towards suspension of a disbelief that can be assumed and therefore deliberately transgressed moves us from superstitious anecdote or supernatural tale to Gothic fiction" (McWhir, 36). As part of its secularizing and modernizing agenda, this culture saw a dramatic rise of literacy among the lower class, and the circulating library emerged as an important component of the public sphere in which commercial interests would ideally be complemented by secularizing and moralizing trends (see Thomas 1986). In a culture in which literacy was seen as advancing the bourgeois cause of promulgating moral and civic responsibilities and inculcating "investment" values, the library and its publication arm, even one as lowly as the Minerva Press, produced works that would attempt to accomplish important civilizing work at the same time they made a profit. But finally, the gothic chapbook presented its lower-class readers with yet another instance of ambivalent secularization. It was a literary technology that was predicated on the notion that many different belief systems could coexist, and that the mixing of traditional spirituality with newer rationalistic approaches to life would allow them to remake themselves as effective citizens of the new nation-state.

- EPILOGUE -

This feeling we call the fear of ghosts.
This spirit shows itself as The Infinite, and man prays.
—Jean Paul Friedrich Richter

Literary critics have long been puzzled by the gothic. Hyperbolic, sprawling, embarrassingly melodramatic and sentimental, ideologically bifurcated, the genre has been the unwanted stepchild of the romantic movement since its inception. For many years, in fact, the gothic was quietly ignored, tucked away like some odd family relation that was better off kept in an asylum. And when the gothic was brought into the light of day, dusted off, and scrutinized, critics were confused about exactly what they were examining. As Sade suggested, the gothic arose during a time of not simply political revolution, but of rapid intellectual, social, economic, and religious upheaval, and in many ways the new cultural practices of Sentimentality, melodrama, and gothic contained within themselves both their ostensible concerns—control over the anxieties produced by the forces of rapid change—as well as their opposites—rampant flirtation with and exploration of those fears. Foucault has observed on this issue that as a paranoid nineteenth-century middle-class imaginary attempted to control the challenges that it confronted, "these same dangers, at the same time, fascinated men's imaginations and their desires. Morality dreams of exorcising them, but there is something in man which makes him dream of experiencing them, or at least approaching them and releasing their hallucinations" (1988, 207–8). The gothic became the genre *par excellence* of alternately approaching and then fleeing from the realities of living in the world of the immanent. The gothic imaginary finally situates itself firmly on that cusp between the premodern and the modern, between endorsing a belief in the transcendent or the quotidian; as I have argued throughout, its subject matter consists, then, of various secularization scenarios presented to a populace that itself had not been able to chose definitively one worldview over the other and, indeed, never has.

Critics have traditionally explored the gothic worldview by focusing on its convoluted presentation of religion. For instance, one of the gothic's earliest modern historians, J. M. S. Tompkins, did not know quite what to make of the genre's use of religious themes. She recognized the anti-Catholic and anticlerical agendas of Radcliffe's novels even while she noted that they used the Catholic picturesque in an attractive and "seductive" manner:

> They are very conscious of the picturesque attractions of convents, vows of celibacy, confession and penance; they are seduced by the emotional possibilities of the situations that can be based on these usages; but they seldom fail to make it quite clear that they regard the usages as superstitious and irrational, and, if they did, there was not wanting a critic to blame this "attempt to gloss over the follies of popery, or to represent its absurdities as sacred." (274; Tompkins quotes the *Critical*'s review [March 1792] of Mary Robinson's *Vancenza*)

But while Tompkins concludes by seeing the demonization of Catholicism as motivated by the Protestant reading public's attraction to the "lurid" (274), the devoutly Catholic Montague Summers (1880–1948) boldly pronounces that the gothic should be read as a nostalgically romantic "revival" of the supernatural beliefs of Catholicism: "There is no true romanticism apart from Catholic influence and feeling" (390).[1] This attempt to situate the gothic clearly within the confines of a spiritual aesthetic does seem to have inspired the work of Devendra Varma, who claimed that the gothic took its impetus from a "new recognition of the heart's emotions and a reassertion of the numinous," as well as a craving for "other-wordly gratification" (1957, 210–11), and this sort of approach led to the "numinous" school of gothic criticism as practiced by G. Richard Thompson and S. L. Varnado during the 1980s. Indeed, apart from the dissertation of M. M. Tarr (1946), the genre's actual investment in anti-Catholicism seems to have been largely ignored for at least two decades. It was not until 1960, for instance, that Leslie Fiedler was quite explicit about the religious ideologies of the gothic novel, declaring: "Like most other classic forms of the novel, the gothic romance is Protestant in its ethos; indeed, it is the most blatantly anti-Catholic of all, projecting in its fables a consistent image of the Church as the Enemy." Like Tompkins, though, Fiedler is also forced to admit that there is a fair amount of aesthetic ambivalence in the gothic's presentation of religion: "Yet the gothic imagination feeds on what its principles abhor, the ritual and glitter, the politics and pageantry of the Roman Church" (138).

The "ritual and glitter" that Tompkins and Fiedler see as so seductive, however, can best be read not simply aesthetically, but historically and ideologically, as manifestations of the continuing presence of the uncanny traces of an older religion, while the anti-Catholic strain in so many of the texts is only one face of an ambivalently realized secularization process. More recently, Baldick and Mighall argue that it is necessary to situate the genre within its fuller "whiggish" context: its need to condemn "the twin yoke of feudal politics and papal deception, from which [Protestants] had still to emancipate themselves" (219):

> Gothic novels were set in the Catholic south because, "without great violation of truth," Gothic (that is, "medieval") practices were believed still to prevail there. Such representations drew upon and reinforced the cultural identity of the middle-class Protestant readership, which could thrill to the scenes of political and religious persecution safe in the knowledge that they themselves had awoken from such historical nightmares. (219; internal quotation from Walter Scott)

While there is no question that many of the period's gothic texts conform to this pattern, there is also, as I have suggested throughout, a concurrent residue of looking backward to the era in which transcendent beliefs were unquestioned, where the "porous self" found itself still inhabiting the world of magic and anima, and where authority structures like the Church were unquestioned in their power. The desire to hold onto these lost traditions of the past with nostalgia (νόστος = nostos = returning home, and άλγος = algos = pain/longing), or with "the pain a sick person feels because he wishes to return to his native land, and fears never to see it again," was only half of the ambivalent secularization story. The other half was, as we have seen, the need to embrace the agenda of immanence, the growing sense that we live in a world that can also be explained through science, reason, and controlled through individual efforts and responsibility. There would seem to be something of an impassable divide between these positions: either the gothic is seen as nostalgic and "romantic" in its invocation of transcendence and the trappings of supernaturalism, or it is viewed as a manifestation of Enlightenment values such as reason and the "explained supernatural." This "either/or" approach would be better served by being replaced by a "both/and" stance because of the contradictory nature and complexity of the issues that were being negotiated by these cultures.

To not recognize that cultural productions contain both strands, that is, nostalgia and reform, is to fail to recognize how easy it is to be haunted by that which we have supposedly left behind. To recall the Preface, it is as difficult to repudiate the power of past belief systems as it was for Orson to embrace Valentine and leave the forest home of his "bear" mother. Indeed, it would seem that one of history's most vital lessons is that cultures require hundreds of years to absorb radical change into their social imaginaries, and the changes that western Europe underwent, moving from the world of Brueghel's painting (see cover) to the "modern" society of the 1848 revolutions, were traumatic indeed. From the religious and intellectual upheavals that occurred during the reign of Henry VIII to the "Glorious Revolution" of 1688, England entered the eighteenth century in the grip of both scientific rationalism and spiritual uncertainty and anxiety. France and Germany went through similar, although certainly not identical, reformations, revolutions, and transformations. As Maurice Lévy has observed, the 1688 Revolution by which the Protestant ascendancy was finally established was much more important for the development of the gothic than was the French Revolution because "in some sense the fantastic is a compensation that man provides for himself, at the level of the imagination, for what he has lost at the level of faith" (1968; qtd. Porte, 43). The gothic is not, however, a simple textual substitution for discredited religious beliefs for Lévy, but instead "a genuine expression of profound religious malaise" (1968; qtd. Porte, 43).

Hans Blumenberg (1920–1996) makes much the same point about the interrelation of religion, science, and psychoanalysis. For him, it was Ludwig Feuerbach (1804–1872) who was able to define the connection between transcendence and immanence by focusing on the spiritual concept of immortality and human curiosity about the natural world manifested as "science": curiosity was simply immortality that had come to understand itself; while for Freud, immortality was curiosity about understanding the mechanisms of the inner psychological world.[2] The Feuerbachian vision, though, holds that the powers we attribute to God are actually our own human potentialities. Summarizing these positions, Peter Homans notes that "secularization is a process of individuation, and . . . religion is the primary or archetypal monument which constitutes and undergirds Western culture" (269).[3]

The gothic arose at a time when this culture was attempting to school

EPILOGUE

Figure 9: Frontispiece, M. E. L. D. L. Baron De Langon, *L'Hermite de la Tombe Mystérieuse, ou le Fantôme du Vieux Château*, vol. 1 (Paris, 1816). Courtesy Maurice Lévy

itself in a variety of empiricist protocols and repudiate a long-standing system of "magical" beliefs, superstitions like ghosts, witches, the mysterious powers of saints, the Virgin Mary, confessions, bread and wine, and perhaps for the most radical, the existence of God and the soul itself. While Hogarth's famous print *Credulity, Superstition, and Fanaticism* (1762) satirizes the notoriety of a number of contemporary superstitions (i.e., the case of Mary Toft who claimed to have given birth to rabbits, the popularity of the Cock-Lane ghost, the ghost of Mrs. Veal, and the drummer William

Drury), it also reveals that reforming Protestant sects were as invested in a variety of superstitions or, as Hume famously defined them, "enthusiasms," as Catholicism had been (74).

Hogarth's widely reprinted engraving represents one side of the secularized mind's disdain for antiquated beliefs of the past, in this case Methodist enthusiasts, but it clearly does not represent the full range of the European imaginary, as witnessed by any number of popular and widespread gothic illustrations and performances that suggest that the purely scientific Enlightenment worldview was not a psychic space that everyone was quite so quick to embrace. Indeed, there were no talismans against that ultimate embodiment of the uncanny, our consciousness of our own eventual deaths, and it was this realization that emerged so clearly in the majority of gothic works (fig. 9).

Although the suddenly awakened victim grasps a sword in his defense, the terrified look in his eyes conveys the fact that he knows his struggle will be fruitless. In some ways this illustration reverses Goya's *The Sleep of Reason Produces Monsters* (fig. 1 in the Introduction), because what it suggests is that, whether we are sleeping or waking, we will all finally be confronted by our inescapable uncanny double, the very thing-ness of death, or what Slavoj Žižek calls "the forbidden domain of the Thing" from which all human beings recoil (1991, 25). *L'Hermite* also conveys one of the central points that Freud makes in "The Uncanny." One may continue to dream of one's dead parents as alive and well because the unconscious mind refuses to accept their deaths, and so it was out of those returns every night to the land of the living dead that human beings created the transcendent realm: ghosts, totemic ancestors in disguise so that sometimes when they appear we can recognize them as our parents (as Hamlet did) and sometimes we cannot. Dreams express our unconscious and irrational beliefs, that is, that there is no death, and so in a variety of ways gothic textuality and performativity explored both the latent and manifest content of that dream: that death could be negotiated with somehow, through religion, or politics, or science, or finally fantasy-formations of all these ideologies. The rationalist may claim that only savages or the uneducated (i.e., Catholics or Protestant enthusiasts) continue to believe in primitive and animistic superstitions such as ghosts or demons, but for Freud as well as the majority of gothic authors, all human beings are irrational in their attempts to continue to believe on some level in the specters that they visit nightly in their dreams.

So cue the master trope: Death. Recent critics like Baldick and Mighall (211–21) bemoan the recourse to death as the final explanatory paradigm in so much gothic criticism, but as this examination of "gothic riffs" indicates, death would appear to be the ultimate embodiment of the uncanny, that aspect of our environment that we cannot control through the use of charms, omens, or some sort of magic or a simple secularized belief in "human flourishing." For Freud, the uncanny is located in the residue of an "infantile belief," and in fact the most infantile of beliefs is in our own immortality. Ghosts and all the other paraphernalia of supernaturalism employed through the gothic arose because the ego cannot grasp the fact of its own eventual extinction. Like the startled man in *L'Hermite* (fig. 9) who may or may not be dreaming, all of us will ultimately find death standing at the end of our beds, beckoning us to join him. Consumers of the popular and performative gothic needed to confront and at the same time repress, contain, or deny (like Baldick and Mighall) their realization that death was the ultimate uncanny visitant that no scientific advance would ever eradicate. Writing in 1759, Adam Smith actually anticipated Freud when he declared that ghosts are the natural offspring of sensibility, taking "their origin from . . . natural sympathy with the imaginary resentment of the slain" (289).

But it is less sympathy with the already dead than anxiety about our own fates that motivates so much of the ambivalent secularizing process of the gothic imaginary. This was a culture in which science had successfully provided many answers to questions that had been mysterious or inexplicable in the past, but the Enlightenment project could not explain the ultimate conundrum: how to live with the knowledge of our own eventual demise. That question, as Freud and more recently Ernest Becker have shown, haunts the psyche to such an extent that there is no escape from it except through repression, rationalization, and finally demonization of others who threaten the "death-denying" ideologies that we have created to repress our knowledge of death.[4] The gothic aesthetic arose when the plausibility and explanatory force of magic and superstitious beliefs declined and no clearly consistent or satisfactorily definitive system arose to answer the questions and anxieties that inevitably continued to persist. In its repetitive recourse to unresolved spiritual issues, the gothic mediates immanence and transcendence, present and past, living and dead, Protestant and Catholic, modern and antiquated. In fact, in some ways it is possible to view the entire European gothic corpus as a "cryptic space," an aesthetic and uncanny "archive" in the Derridaean sense: "If there is no archive without consignation in an *external place* which assures the possibility of memorization, of repetition, of reproduction, or of reimpression, then we must also remember that repetition itself, the logic of repetition . . . remains indissociable from the death drive" (11–12; emphasis in original). And recognizing the persistence of performative gothic "riffs" is another way of talking about those repetitions and textual recourses to the uncanniness of death.

There is a danger in reading human consciousness as universal, similar across time and space, and certainly it has been politically incorrect to do so for many years. But bear with me: textual evidence produced by the gothic imaginary forces us to consider the possibility of a universal tendency to cower in the face of death. The population of Europe in 1800 appears at least imaginatively to be not so radically different from the inhabitants of Northumbria of whom Bede (?672–735) writes. As Bede recorded, King Edwin and his tribe were converted to Christianity because the missionary Paulinus was able to provide a plausible answer when asked by Coifi, the chief Druidic priest, two simple questions: where were we before we were born and where do we go after we die?[5] The gothic emerged and flourished not so much as a religious explanation that provided definitive answers to these questions, but as one complex and contradictory textual response to the free-floating anxieties that occurred when the lower and middle classes of Europe were expected to participate in a rationalistic, scientific culture that they did not yet fully understand or trust.[6] It is perhaps not far-fetched to claim that the gothic continues to prosper today because many of the same anxieties continue to exist; indeed, they always will.

- NOTES -

Preface and Acknowledgments

1. Dibdin's melodrama was produced at Sadler's Wells (1794) and Covent Garden (1804). The popular British chapbook version appeared in 1804. There are some thirty pre-1804 chapbooks of *Valentine and Orson* in English listed in the British Library catalogue, one dating to 1505. For further background on *Valentine and Orson,* see Bratton (2007, 123-24), Newton, and Cooper. Should viewers of the painting on the book cover not be able to see clearly the *Valentine and Orson* play being enacted, they should consult Klein, who has reproduced and analyzed "The Masquerade of Valentine and Orson" (64-65), a woodcut based on just this section of the larger painting and signed with the name and date "Brueghel, 1566." Ingmar Bergman's film *The Seventh Seal* (1957) includes a scene in which the hero, Joseph, is forced to play Orson's bear mother, while the film's theme, the secularization of the Nativity and the flight into Egypt in order to escape the uncanny presence of death, presents in filmic terms the larger thesis of this book.

2. There are numerous theoretical, religious, sociological, and historical approaches to the carnival, but I am most interested in using Charles Taylor's discussion (45-54) of the phenomenon as the source for secularizing early European public space and providing an opportunity for displaying a new antistructural "public imaginary" in theatrical productions.

3. Britain, France, and Germany have long been seen as equally important "sources of Romanticism": "For it is in these relatively developed countries that Romanticism arose earliest, in the second half of the eighteenth century, most intensely and in the most pronounced manner. . . . [W]e agree with [Karl] Mannheim that Romanticism appeared at roughly the same time in all three European nations" (Löwry and Chapman, 49). For the most wide-ranging survey of romanticism as a form of "modernizing anticapitalism" (29), and the gothic as an offshoot of romanticism throughout Europe, see Löwy and Sayre.

NOTES TO PREFACE AND ACKNOWLEDGMENTS

4. See Varnado. In addition, G. Thompson has argued that the "numinous" (the nonrational or suprarational component of religion) characterizes much of the gothic aesthetic: "a nameless apprehension that may be called religious dread in the face of the wholly other" (1979, 6–7).

5. Freud's classic statement of "The Uncanny" ties it to religious impulses:

> Let us take the uncanny associated with the omnipotence of thoughts, with the prompt fulfilment of wishes, with secret injurious powers and with the return of the dead. The condition under which the feeling of uncanniness arises here is unmistakable. We—or our primitive forefathers—once believed that these possibilities were realities, and were convinced that they actually happened. Nowadays we no longer believe in them, we have *surmounted* these modes of thought; but we do not feel quite sure of our new beliefs, and the old ones still exist within us ready to seize upon any confirmation. As soon as something *actually happens* in our lives which seems to confirm the old, discarded beliefs we get a feeling of the uncanny; it is as though we were making a judgement something like this: "So, after all, it is *true* that one can kill a person by the mere wish!" or, "So the dead *do* live on and appear on the scene of their former activities!" and so on. Conversely, anyone who has completely and finally rid himself of animistic beliefs will be insensible to this type of the uncanny. The most remarkable coincidences of wish and fulfilment, the most mysterious repetition of similar experiences in a particular place or on a particular date, the most deceptive sights and suspicious noises—none of these things will disconcert him or raise the kind of fear which can be described as "a fear of something uncanny." The whole thing is purely an affair of "reality-testing," a question of the material reality of the phenomena. (From "The Uncanny" [1919]; *Standard Edition of the Complete Psychological Works of Sigmund Freud [SE]*, trans. James Strachey, 24 vols. [London: Hogarth Press, 1953–74], 17: 219–56; emphasis in original)

Morris analyzes Burke via Freud, concluding that "repetition is the essential structure of the uncanny. Borrowing Freud's language, we might describe Gothic sublimity as drawing its deepest terrors from a return of the repressed" (1985, 307), while Dolar sees the uncanny as that which "constantly haunts" modernity "from the inside":

> There was an irruption of the uncanny strictly parallel with bourgeois (and industrial) revolutions and the rise of scientific rationality—and, one might add, with the Kantian establishment of transcendental subjectivity, of which the uncanny presents the surprising counterpart. Ghosts, vampires, monsters, the undead, etc., flourish in an era when you might expect them to be dead and buried, without a place. They are something brought about by modernity itself. (7)

Similarly, Castle argues that the uncanny originated during the Enlightenment: "the very psychic and cultural transformations that led to the subsequent glorification of the period as an age of reason or enlightenment—the aggressively rationalist imperatives of the epoch—also produced, like a kind of toxic side effect, a new human experience of strangeness, anxiety, bafflement, and intellectual impasse" (1995, 8).

6. Clery has observed about Ann Radcliffe's gothic novels that they "strike the enlightened reader as uncanny [because] the reader progressively moves from the sense of mystery that encourages fearful, false ideas to full knowledge of the facts, intelli-

gibility of causes, means and ends, and confirmation of the truth of reason: in other words, reliving the passage from gothic to modern times" (1995, 107) and thereby reenacting the history of the Enlightenment itself. This may be true for the novels of Radcliffe, but it does not explain the ideological trajectory of those gothic works that move backward, to an evocation and seeming endorsement of earlier modes of belief and superstition. Similarly, Canuel sees the gothic as investigating the mechanisms of power, the deceptive practices of "priestcraft," by which Catholic nations enforce a uniformity of belief on subjects; the gothic novel seeks to "expose what it deemed to be a terrifying logic of confessional government and then to assume—precisely as a remedy to the anxieties about Catholicism it generated—a more tolerant relation to religious belief" (56).

7. See Garside, Raven, and Schowerling for tables concerning translations of English novels into French and German, and the publication of gothic novels, 1800–29 (I:68–69; II:41; II:56).

8. My sense of the oscillation and ambiguity inherent in the gothic aesthetic is described somewhat analogously by Hogle, who has observed that early gothics are:

> torn between the enticing call of aristocratic wealth and sensuous Catholic splendor, beckoning toward the Middle Ages and the Renaissance, on the one hand, and a desire to overthrow these past orders of authority in favour of a quasi-equality associated with the rising middle-class ideology of the self as self-made, on the other—but an ideology haunted by the Protestant bourgeois desire to attain the power of the older orders that the middle class wants to dethrone. Such a paradoxical state of longing in much of the post-Renaissance Western psyche fears retribution from all the extremes it tries to encompass, especially from remnants of those very old heights of dominance which the middle class now strives to grasp and displace at the same time. (2002, 4)

The most extended discussions of the gothic and religion/the supernatural can be found in Tarr, Varma, Geary, Carter, Porte, Sage, Lévy, Cavaliero, and Voller. Indeed, Varma concludes that "the Gothic novelists strike a union between our spiritual curiosities and venial terrors, and mediate between the world without us and the world within us. . . . The Gothic novel appeals to the night-side of the soul" (212). As far as evolving definitions are concerned, the "gothic" as a literary concept originally suggested the barbarous, then the medieval, and only much later the ghostly and supernatural (Frankl, 259–60).

Introduction

1. C. Taylor also notes, "Modernity brings about secularity in all its three forms [secularized public spaces; the decline of belief and practice; and new pluralistic conditions of belief]. This causal connection is ineluctable, and mainline secularization theory is concerned to explain why it had to be. Modern civilization cannot but bring about a 'death of God'" (21). Mark Taylor has observed that "secularity is a religious phenomenon. . . . Throughout the history of the West, God has repeatedly disappeared by becoming either so transcendent that he is irrelevant or so immanent that there is no difference between the sacred and the secular" (xvi). Earlier, D. Bell distinguished between secularization, or the loss of religious influence on political and economic

aspects of life, and profanation, and the more general rejection of religious belief. Secularization for him is a product of specialization and the rationalistic techno-economic order, but no such principle for change exists in the cultural sphere: "Culture by its nature confounds historicism" (425). Numerous works on secularization have taken both sides of the issue, ranging from Bruce to Owen. Stark and Bainbridge reject the secularization paradigm, while C. Brown takes a sociological view of the subject. Most recently McKelvy has argued that what he calls the "new vernacular literary culture" of the late eighteenth century came to occupy a "frontier once policed by religious forces, so too did that upstart literary culture adopt a religious habit and evince a longing to participate in the most sacred rites—this at a time, moreover, when an embattled religious culture often saw its promising future in literary terms" (4).

2. Thomas cites Bronislaw Malinowski, for instance, who attributes the use of magic to an attempt to "ritualize man's optimism," to give him a sense of control over an environment that he knows is indifferent if not hostile to him (647). David Hume's "Of Superstition and Enthusiasm" claimed that ignorance, melancholy, weakness, and fear were the causes of superstitious beliefs, while he observed that "in proportion as any man's course of life is governed by accident, we always find that he increases in superstition" (74).

3. Habermas has argued that "the far-reaching uncoupling of system and lifeworld was a necessary condition for the transition from the stratified class societies of European feudalism to the economic class societies of the early modern period; but the capitalist pattern of modernization is marked by a deformation, a reification of the symbolic structures of the lifeworld under the imperatives of subsystems differentiated out via money and power and rendered self-sufficient" (1984, 283). Habermas's underutilized role in the field of romantic studies has been analyzed most perceptively by Scrivener, while his theories have been best defended recently by Miles (2008, 13–18).

4. See Zagorin, as well as Nelson, who has examined pulp fiction in order to claim that the supernatural encodes elements of spirituality that can no longer be expressed in forms of public belief (2001). Saler has provided a historical overview of the issue of modern entertainment's relation to "disenchantment," claiming that we can discern three related discourses: a "binary model" that suggests that enchantment does not disappear in the nineteenth century but could be accounted for by rationalism; a "dialectical model" that claims that modernity is inherently irrational itself; and an "antinomial" position that claims that disenchanted reason coexists with the enchanted imagination, causing viewers to be entertained but not duped (693–94). The "antinomial" position is closest to Charles Taylor's argument, as well as mine. Viswanathan provides an overview of the recent secularization debates, concluding that literary critics need to recognize "the oblique processes of secularization" (468) and that the "central paradox" of secularization is that, "despite being perceived as opposed to religion in the public sphere, [it actually] preserves religious elements in its self-definition" and in art (474).

5. A number of earlier critics have been "tempted to see Modernism as a resurgence of Romanticism, though conceivably in a more extreme and strained form of pure irrationalism" (Bradbury and McFarlane, 46). See, for instance, Kermode, Hartman, Thornburn and Hartman, Bloom (1970), Langbaum, Peckham (1962), and to some extent J. H. Miller. The controversies over the definition of "modernism" or "modernity" are extensive. Most recently, Gay has claimed that modernism is a revolt against the European bourgeoisie through the cultivation of a Freudian-inflected subjectivity in which artists and intellectuals relied on their feelings or intuitions to depict the

external world.

6. Some of the early theorists on the highly contested issue of secularization include Max Weber, MacIntyre, Pratt, and Chadwick. Weber, for instance, declared that modern intellectualization had caused "the world [to be] disenchanted." With the disappearance of "mysterious incalculable forces, one need no longer have recourse to magical means" (139), a condition he found particularly hollow. Casanova chooses to forego the notion of secularization in favor of "differentiation": "If before it was the religious realm which appeared to be the all-encompassing reality within which the secular realm found its proper place, now the secular sphere will be the all-encompassing reality to which the religious sphere will have to adapt" (15). Similarly, Jager sees secularization as "multiple, as an ongoing process of creating and reforming a plethora of cultural programs. Once modernization is rendered a more parochial and local affair, secularization can be freed from the linear and teleological assumptions that hover in the background whenever it is invoked" (29).

7. Coleridge attacked *The Monk* by observing, "We trust, however, that satiety will banish what good sense should have prevented; and that, wearied with fiends, incomprehensible characters, with shrieks, murders, and subterraneous dungeons, the public will learn, by the multitude of the manufacturers, with how little expense of thought or imagination this species of composition is manufactured" (*Critical Review* 19 [1797]: 194). He also attacked Lewis's *Castle Spectre* (Drury Lane, 1797) as "Schiller Lewisized," and Maturin's *Bertram* (Drury Lane, 1816) as "modern jacobinical drama" in his *Biographia Literaria*, II:200, but his criticisms of the drama need to be understood in light of the fact that Drury Lane had recently refused to stage a revival of his own gothic drama *Remorse*. For an overview of Coleridge's ambivalence toward the gothic, see Mudge (1991) and Christensen. Wordsworth's gothic-inflected drama, *The Borderers*, was rejected by Covent Garden in 1798 just as Matthew Lewis's *Castle Spectre* was enjoying a hugely profitable run at Drury Lane (in fact, it was so popular that it was being parodied in 1803 by a three-act romance entitled *The Tale of Terror; or a Castle without a Spectre!*). Trott calls Wordsworth's "antipathy" to the gothic "pathological," while Siskin sees his early poems like the gothic "Vale of Esthwaite" as "an expression of his lifelong desire to explore the human mind and heart by integrating the natural and supernatural" (1979, 161–73).

8. Voller has noted that the "'major' Romantics did not spurn the Gothic so much as they responded to it, revised it, adapted it to their own purposes, not so much to domesticate it as to appropriate its emotional power and metaphoric capacity" (ix). The most recent attempt to analyze the fraught relationship between gothicism and romanticism can be found in Miles (2008), who argues that there was a persistent tension between the canonical romanticists and those who wrote "in obedience to the profit motive, 'trash'" (5). Similarly, Gamer has claimed that "the gothic perpetually haunts, as an aesthetic to be rejected, romanticism's construction of high literature culture" (7), while Hogle argues that "the Walpolean Gothic is thus the arena to which Western symbol-makers, including Romantic poets, most explicitly consign this simultaneous overcoming of *and* dissolution back into the restrictive past, this paradoxical desire that holds the modern middle-class person in a fearful conflict at the very foundations of his or her self-fashioning" (2003, 212; emphasis in original). Earlier attempts to compare and contrast the two genres can be found in R. Hume (1969; 1974).

9. See Jacqueline Howard for the fullest use of Bakhtinian theories in relation to the gothic as a discourse system.

10. On trauma, scars, and healing in the romantic period, particularly in the work of Wordsworth, see Goodman. Scholarly discussions of the oral residue of earlier literary works and the development of literacy can be found in Goody and Graff.

11. Using Berlin's concept of romanticism as integral to a Counter-Enlightenment movement, Miles has recently argued that "Romanticism should not be thought of as a set of 'ideological commitments,' a kind of poetic hermeneutic struggle or as a flight from georgic to lyric, but as a period in the long history of modernity's emergence in which two formations first come to be set in dialectical opposition to each other: a radical Enlightenment and its reactionary counter" (2008, 8–10).

12. Also see Habermas 1987; 1974. As for the controversy about Habermas's concept of the "public sphere" and the New Left's endorsement of a "counter-public sphere," see Mellor, who notes that "if women participated fully in the discursive public sphere and in the formation of public opinion in Britain by the late eighteenth century, then the assumption that there existed a clear distinction in historical practice between a realm of public, exclusively male activities and a realm of private, exclusively female activities in this period is also erroneous" (2000, 7).

13. Walpole's sexual preferences, as well as those of Matthew Lewis, were the subject of gossip during their lifetimes. See Macdonald, Haggerty, and Mowl. A. Williams argues that Walpole's sexual preferences were not the major "haunting" or trauma of his life as Mowl and Haggerty have claimed, but rather that he was much more anxious about his illegitimacy and it was this sense of being a fraud that had the major effect on his writings (2009, 15).

14. For a collection of French gothic tales, see Hale 1998. This book assembles twenty-four tales, nineteen of which have never before been published in English. Lévy has published a listing of translations and plagiarisms of British gothic novels into French (1974), while Grieder provides a listing of even more "borrowings" (65–73). Also see Hall for the most extensive discussion of the influence of British gothics on both French and German gothics during the 1790s.

15. See Nelson, who has defined what she calls the "Faux Catholic," a "sub-genre from Monk Lewis to Dan Brown" (2007). The "faux Catholic," however, had its origins much further back, in fact, according to Wagner, in the early anti-Catholic pornographic polemic of Pietro Aretino (1492–1556), and then in early anticlerical French works such as *The History of Madamoiselle de St. Phale, giving a full account of the miraculous conversion of a noble French lady and her daughter, to the reformed religion. With the defeat of the intrigues of a Jesuite their confessor. Translated out of French* (London, 1691), cited by Godwin as an influence on his *Caleb Williams* (1794); or *The Case of Mary Catharine Cadiere, against the Jesuit Father John Baptist Girard* (London, 1731), itself the basis for Henry Fielding's *Old Debauchees: A Comedy* (1732).

16. Several critics of the gothic have made similar observations. For example, Punter claims that the bourgeois readers of the gothic were attracted to the genre because it "displaces the hidden violence of present social structures, conjures them up again as past, and promptly falls under their spell" (1980, 418). Hogle asserts that the "ghost of the counterfeit in the Gothic" has "become so removed from its earliest reference points and so widely circulated as a hollow figure waiting to be filled up by its re-users, even as it keeps calling us back to lost origins, that it can serve perfectly as a useful, but also self-obscuring, locus for what is terrifyingly or even horrifically non-identical in the West and for the Western sense of 'identity' at the time a particular 'Gothic' work is produced" (2008, 219).

Chapter 1

1. Dixon has traced the evolution of and emphasis on the "psychology of the emotions" to what he calls the "newer and more secular network" (289) of meaning that began to emerge in the early nineteenth century. Both Sheriff and Bredvold have analyzed aspects of the debate over Sentimentality's indebtedness to Latitudinarianism, arguing that a tension exists between traditional Christian emphases on a system of active virtue and the sentimental self-absorption in one's own "good nature" as an end in itself. In contrast, Branfman attempts a psychoanalytical analysis of Sentimentality as a "magic gesture in reverse," a "wistful observation [in which the audience] passively views" the sufferings and "sadness without pleasure" of the opera's participants (624–25).

2. Markley reviews the literary and critical controversies surrounding Shafesbury's role in defining Sentimentality as "the affective spectacle of benign generosity" (211) as well as its contested religious origins in Latitudinarianism and deism. Also see J. Howard, Solomon, Barker-Benfield, D. Marshall, and Mullan (1997).

3. The June 15, 1787, British playbill for *Nina* states that the opera is "a translation from the French Opera of that name, now performing at Paris with universal applause. The principal Characters by Mr. Johnstone, Mr. Hull, Mr. Thompson, Mr. Daley, Miss Wilkinson, and Mrs. Billington. With the original Music and an additional song by Piccini" (Gabrielle Enthoven Collection, Blythe House, London). The basis of Sentimentality's physical appeal has been variously analyzed. Also see Bartlet who very usefully distinguishes between the *Théâtre-Italien,* founded to perform Italian *opera buffa* and *opera semiseria* and directed at one point by Paër, and the earlier *Théâtre-Italien* or *Comédie Italienne* (the name of the *Opéra-Comique* until 1793), whose repertoire included Italian plays in Italian, French plays, and *opéras-comiques,* but not Italian opera (123).

4. Stefano Castelvecchi 2 analyzes the striking similarities between *Nina* and the early psychological treatments developed by the founder of psychiatry, Philippe Pinel (1745–1826), that advocated "shocking the patient's imagination through what amounts to the staging of a theatrical scene" or reenactment of the original trauma in order to restore her to sanity (96). Pinel's follower Esquirol saw monomania as a hybrid of melancholia (which he called lypemania) and mania, a condition in which the sufferer is aware that he is depressed (L. Davis, 69).

5. Wiltshire asks, "Can the attentive reader of [*Mansfield Park*] fail to detect the text's allusion to *Lear* here?" (151n27). Also see Ford for an extended discussion of five period illustrations of Lear and Cordelia, including Thurston.

6. In her own comments on the writing of *A Thousand Acres,* Jane Smiley observed: "I imagined Shakespeare wrestling with the 'Leir' story and coming away a little dissatisfied, a little defeated, but hugely stimulated, just as I was. As I imagined that, I felt that I received a gift, an image of literary history, two mirrors facing each other in the present moment, reflecting infinitely backward into the past and infinitely forward into the future" (173). For other contemporary adaptations, see Feinstein, "*Lear's Daughters*" (215–32), and Margaret Atwood's novel *The Cat's Eye* (1988). Freud in his essay "The Theme of the Three Caskets" (1913) writes:

> Lear is not only an old man: he is a dying man. . . . But the doomed man is not willing to renounce the love of women; he insists on hearing how much he is

loved. Let us now recall the moving final scene, one of the culminating points of tragedy in modern drama. Lear carries Cordelia's dead body on to the stage. Cordelia is Death. If we reverse the situation it becomes intelligible and familiar to us. She is the Death-goddess who, like the Valkyrie in German mythology, carries away the dead hero from the battlefield. Eternal wisdom, clothed in the primaeval myth, bids the old man renounce love, choose death and make friends with the necessity of dying. (12:301)

Chapter 2

1. A. Williams (2006) states that "The idea that the operatic is 'Gothic' and that the Gothic is 'operatic' has not seriously been discussed in the growing body of Gothic studies and the equally thriving field of opera and literature" (126). For her, Gaetano Donizetti's *Lucia di Lammermoor* (1835) is "the only 'Gothic opera' established in the nineteenth-century canon" (127). Lindenberger points out that the natural affinity between opera and gothic can be located in their tendency to maintain "the high style" (61). In contrast to these views, Schmidgall sees the distinction between the operatic and the realistic as located in its tendency to "seek moments of expressive crisis" (11).

2. Addison observed that the "absurdity of opera shows itself at the first sight"; he went on to note that "nothing is capable of being well set to music, that is not nonsense." Samuel Johnson called opera "an exotic and irrational entertainment," while Jonathan Swift spoke of "that unnatural Taste for Italian Music among us, which is wholly unsuitable to our Northern Climate, and the Genius of the People, whereby we are overrun with Italian Effeminacy and Italian Nonsense" (qtd. Schmidgall, 32–33). Also see White for an overview of the challenges faced by "Romantic Operas" in Britain during this period (79–107); and Baumann for a discussion of German opera as "a special idiom which blended musical and literary values under the compelling imperatives of the region's distinctive theatrical institutions" (1).

3. Contrast this definition of music with that proposed by Claude Lévi-Strauss, who claimed that music is primarily an expression of the emotions, while Roland Barthes has stated that music is "inactual," that is, abstract and difficult to speak about because "language is of the order of the general, [while] music is of the order of difference." And in his meditation about the meaning of opera, W. H. Auden echoes this definition:

> Opera in particular is an imitation of human willfulness; it is rooted in the fact that we not only have feelings but insist upon having them at whatever cost to ourselves. Opera, therefore, cannot present character in the novelist's sense of the word, namely, people who are potentially good *and* bad, active and passive, for music is immediate actuality *and* neither potentiality nor passivity can live in its presence. (qtd. Schmidgall, 20; emphasis in original)

So while Barthes emphasizes the inactual quality of music, Auden asserts the opposite. These theoretical issues are further analyzed in depth by the philosopher Peter Kivy, who argues that music does not *express* emotion, but is rather *expressive of* emotion, in the way that a St. Bernard's face or a clenched fist may be taken, apart from their actual emotions, to *represent* sadness or anger (Kivy, 14–15).

4. The success of *Richard coeur-de-lion* raised the *opéra-comique* to new levels and

led to Sédaine's long-sought acceptance in the Académie française (Ledbury 1, 284). Beaumarchais and Sédaine became collaborators and the latter advised Beaumarchais on the *Mariage de Figaro* (Ledbury 2, 13–38).

5. Pixérécourt's *Final Reflections on Melodrama* in *Pixérécourt*, 316. Also see Marcoux for a full discussion of his works.

6. This tale is reminiscent of François Thomas du Fossé's life story as recounted by Helen Maria Williams in her *Letters from France* (1790; 8 vols.). Fossé was not tested by his lover's father but by his own father, Baron du Fossé, who could not accept that his heir would marry the daughter of a local farmer and who issued a *lettre de cachet* with the aim of imprisoning him to prevent the marriage (see Mellor 1992, 261–62).

7. The name "Camille" begins to function as a talisman from this time forward, with a beautiful, victimized woman named Camille rescued from a cavern in no fewer than four versions of the same rescue opera: Marsolier's *Camille ou le souterrain* (1791), Dalayrac's *Camille* (1791), Le Sueur's *La caverne* (1793), and Paër's *Camilla, ossia Il sotterraneo* (1799). Later, the female victim becomes a courtesan and by 1852 Alexandre Dumas *fils* had composed the first version of his famous *La dame aux camélias,* adapted yet again by the American Matilda Heron, who translated Dumas and starred in the title role of *Camille; or, the Fate of a Coquette* (1856).

8. Lord Mount Edgcumbe was in the audience in Covent Garden for the premiere of the work in London: "The French stage, once the pattern of decency and propriety, is now become a school for profanes and immorality, the most sacred subjects are exhibited, the most indecent exposed, almost without disguise in opera, melodrames and ballets; of this perverted type is *Robert le Diable;* yet I am sorry to say it had been translated and produced at our theatres. I saw it acted at Covent Garden, and never did I see a more disagreeable or disgusting performance, the sight of the resurrection of a whole convent of nuns, who rise from their graves, and begin dancing like so many bacchantes is revolting, and a secret service in a church, accompanied by an organ on the stage, not very decorous" (215–16).

Chapter 3

1. Ghosts entered the stage through trapdoors as early as 1700, when Colley Cibber produced *Richard III*, and the device was widely used until David Garrick's productions later in the century. In 1797 the ghost walked on and offstage at the Theatre Royal, Edinburgh, while gauze became the more typical device for introducing a ghost by the early nineteenth century. The theater historian Arthur C. Sprague observed about the production of *Julius Caesar* in the late eighteenth century that "the treatment of the Ghost follows a now familiar pattern . . . trapwork—gauzes—nothing at all" (103, 165, 325).

2. Lewis, *The Castle Spectre*, rpt. *Seven Gothic Dramas*, ed. Jeffrey Cox, 149–224. All quotations from the play taken from this edition, with act, scene, and page number in parentheses. Production information for *Fontainville Forest, The Castle Spectre,* and *The Sicilian Romance* can be found in Hogan. Burwick discusses the drama at length, analyzing the various actors who played Osmond and claiming that the use of the African henchmen in the work "effectively speaks for the anti-slavery movement of the 1790s" (2009, 170–78).

3. Boaden, *Fontainville Forest.* All quotations from this edition. On Boaden's drama,

see Saggini. Reno has observed that part of the conundrum of the continuing appearance of dramatic ghosts was their ambivalent status as signifiers: "while the supernatural had been rationalized into nonexistence by the end of the eighteenth century, it had not yet been animated fully with the symbolic or psychological reality so familiar to twentieth-century audiences. Unwilling to believe in ghosts as an objective reality and unable to describe them as a psychosymbolic reality, the late eighteenth-century critic rejected them absolutely" (97).

4. The most pertinent analyses of the literary sublime during this period include the classic study by Monk, as well as works by Mishra, Weiskel, and Morris (1972). Mishra has observed: "What marks off the various versions of the primary precursor text are levels of uncanny duplication at work in the Gothic. Read as the recognition that nothing ever happens, that all history has always already been played out and that the subject is simply locked into an incessant series of repetitions, the Gothic rewrites the sublime and prefigures its theorization as the 'Uncanny'" (71).

5. Boaden, *The Cambro-Britons*. All quotations will be from this edition.

Chapter 4

1. Holcroft's *Preface* to *Seduction*, as well as the play itself, rpt. *The Novels and Selected Plays of Thomas Holcroft*, ed. Philip Cox, 5: 65–125. All quotations from Holcroft's works from this edition, page numbers or act and scene in parentheses.

2. Nicholl downplays Pixérécourt's role in the development of melodrama, noting that "the fundamental features of the *mélodrame* were in existence in the French theatres long before 1798, and secondly, that the same features can be traced in English plays from 1770 onwards" (98). Similarly, Philip Cox downplays the melodramatic "turn" in Holcroft's career, arguing that "what might appear to be a new departure informed by continental influences is, in fact, part of an ongoing generic experimentation within the constraints of what could be performed on the late eighteenth- and early-nineteenth-century stage. And such generic experimentation is intimately linked with a desire to communicate a consistent political morality" (viii–ix). As Mortensen and others have noted, British critics have a tendency to minimize the importance of "continental" influences on the development of the British literary tradition in order to construct a national literature built on supposedly pristine and nativist works.

3. *Deaf and Dumb: or, The Orphan Protected: An Historical Drama*, 5:339–93; and *A Tale of Mystery—A Melo-Drame*, 5:395–423. I have examined the original playbill for *A Tale of Mystery* (November 18, 1802) and there was no mention of Holcoft's name as author of the work anywhere on it (Gabrielle Enthoven Collection, Blythe House, London).

4. George Taylor identifies *Inkle and Yarico* by George Colman the Younger as the first "mixed" work, with thirteen songs, a comic tone, and based on the potentially tragic subject of the slave trade. He cites Alan Sinfield's definition of a "cultural faultline" to explain the genre: "Faultline stories are the ones that require most assiduous and continuous reworking; they address the awkward, unresolved issues, the ones in which the conditions of plausibility are in dispute [and which] comprise within themselves the ghosts of the alternative stories they are trying to exclude" (40).

5. Simpson has noted that "fifteen of Kotzebue's plays were translated into English in 1799 alone, some of them by more than one hand. At least ten of these adaptations were

performed" (90). The English translation of Kotzebue's adaptation of Bouilly's *L'Abée de l'Epée* can be found in Thompson, vol. 3. Also see J. Cox's discussion of the play as "a trans-European drama of subversion and seduction, a jacobinical drama that arises in England, is transported to Germany, and that returns to England filled with notions borrowed from revolutionary France" (2007, 122).

6. Pixérécourt's two theoretical essays, *Melodrama* and *Final Reflections on Melodrama*, are available in *Pixérécourt*. Holcroft's musical collaborator, Dr. Thomas Busby, defined melodrama as "a modern species of Drama in which the powers of instrumental music are employed to elucidate the action, and heighten the passion of the piece" (qtd. Garlington, 59n33).

7. Consider by way of contrast the popular Irish melodramatist, Dion Boucicault (1820–1890), whose *The Shaughraun* (ca. 1858) presents the title character as a traditional trickster figure, at one point laid out in his coffin while the community mourns his death. Con, the Shaughraun, is only pretending to be dead in order to expose the traitors who are in league with a corrupt magistrate and British soldiers in an attempt to capture the Fenian hero. The climax occurs when the Irish villagers close in on the villains intending to kill them, and the local priest confronts them, "Are you Christians or heathens?" They pause for an extended period of time, considering the question, before putting their knives and axes aside to allow the police to make the arrest. Apparently religious faith in Ireland still functioned in a powerfully disciplinary manner that it had not in England for over fifty years. For very different attitudes toward traditional religious values, see the examples of melodramas written by British women writers collected in Franceschina.

8. Also see Jameson. Moody observes that "what fascinates Holcroft about melodrama is the genre's capacity to encode such contradictions [condemnation and forgiveness for the villain]. For whereas the conventions of sentimental comedy demanded that benevolence should reign triumphant, melodrama helps to make possible a more dynamic and nuanced view of human nature" (91). Watkins argues that all romantic drama should be read in the context of political change, noting that there is "a conflict between the content of surface structure and a deeper political unconscious [which] registers one of the key features of the Romantic historical moment: namely the difficult struggle that marked the transition from an aristocratic to bourgeois worldview" (8). G. Taylor claims that melodrama is a reactionary legacy of the Revolution, while the subtext of *Coelina* is that "trust must be restored—even if it is an irrational trust in the nobility of the aristocrats and the benevolence of the bourgeoisie" (204).

Chapter 5

1. Studies of the gothic ballad as a genre include those by Friedman, Laws, and Fulford. In discussing the broadside or stall ballad, Groom has characterized it as relying on "perpetually recycled patterns of bloody or salacious plots, treacly sentimental trash" tainted by the pretensions and commercial motives of literary print culture (22). Wordsworth's conflicted attraction to the gothic has been the subject of any number of studies. Hartman (1966) notes that the British romantic poets "toyed with the forbidden fire (with the 'Eastern Tale,' the Gothic romance, the Sublime Ode) and called up the ghosts they wished to subdue" (57). In a later article (1975; reprinted in 1987), Hartman contrasts English and German literary traditions by seeing English Romanticism as a

form of mediation between the imaginative power of the past and the present, while the German tradition requires an "art which at once organizes and organicizes a past so discontinuous with the present, that, but for it [art], only volcanic (storm-and-stress) historicism or a new religious incarnation could re-present it" (1987, 69).

2. By way of background, see McKelvy for a discussion of Percy's *Reliques* in the context of the Ossian debate (70–92), and for a discussion of William Taylor of Norwich as "the founder of the Anglo-German school in England," and the highly regarded first translator of Goethe's drama *Iphegenia in Tauris* (1793), see Herzfeld. Perhaps Wordsworth's most famous denunciation of the seductive powers and popularity of the gothic can be found in his 1800 *Preface* to the *Lyrical Ballads*:

> The human mind is capable of excitement with the application of gross and violent stimulants. . . . A multitude of causes unknown to former times are now acting with a combined force to blunt the discriminating powers of the mind, and unfitting it for all voluntary exertion to reduce it to a state of almost savage torpor. The most effective of these causes are the great national events which are daily taking place, and the encreasing accumulation of men in cities, where the uniformity of their occupations produces a craving for extraordinary incident which the rapid communication of intelligence hourly gratifies. To this tendency of life and manners the literature and theatrical exhibitions of the country have conformed themselves. The invaluable works of our elder writers, I had almost said the works of Shakespeare and Milton, are driven into neglect by frantic novels, sickly and stupid German Tragedies, and deluges of idle and extravagant stories in verse. When I think upon this degrading thirst after outrageous stimulation I am almost ashamed to have spoken of the feeble effort with which I have endeavoured to counteract it. (*Prose Works*, I:128–30)

3. Voller claims that the "departure from Gothic convention forms the foundation of Wordsworth's anti-supernaturalism" and "the beneficence of nature permits Wordsworth to abandon his Gothic landscapes" (131, 135). Swann sees Wordsworth's flirtation with German romances as a "characteristic double strategy of re-articulation and displacement, deflection and reform . . . to breach and then reinforce a distinction between their projects and popular sensational literature. . . . It flaunts its affinities with sensational literature and a feminized culture in order to establish its difference" (1993, 138–39). Also see Primeau.

4. Jacobus explores Southey's extensive "plagiarisms" of *Lyrical Ballads* (1971, 20–36). Of particular interest to me is Southey's poem "The Mad Mother," which is a crude appropriation of "The Thorn." But the "borrowings" worked both ways, which Jacobus does not acknowledge. Fulford is fairer in recognizing Wordsworth's use of Southey's earlier ballads.

5. For a detailed analysis of the use of tautology in the ballad, see Russell. She ties Wordsworth's use of the principle of repetition to his responses to Robert Lowth's *Lectures on the Sacred Poetry of the Hebrews* (1787) and Hugh Blair's *Lectures on Rhetoric and Belles Lettres* (1783). In a similar vein, Rzepka examines the protoarcheological content of the poem as evidenced by Wordsworth's readings in Druid history and the barrow excavations undertaken by William Stukeley at Stonehenge and Avebury.

6. Martha Ray's suspected crime of infanticide and infanticide in general has been dealt with in a number of studies: Symonds, Hoffer and Hull, Kord, and Cheesman. Miles presents a summary of the scandalous murder of Martha Ray (Basil Montagu's

mother) at the hands of her lover (27–30), and connects the broadside publications that ensued in the aftermath of the scandal to "gossip": "Martha Ray is transformed into a shrunken, smothered shrub beneath the public's Medusa-like gaze.... If the narrator unknowingly Gothicizes Martha, burying her alive in gossip, the reader certainly ought not to" (2008, 82).

7. For a provocative psychoanalytical reading of the baby's reflected face in the pond, see Collings 1994, 91–99; and for an overview of Wordsworth's ambivalent attitude in dealing with "sensational" material such as infanticide, see Swann (1997, 60–79).

Chapter 6

1. One of the earliest scholarly attempts to discuss the genre can be found in W. Watt, who argues that "shilling shockers" are the transitional link between the late eighteenth-century gothic novels and the short tales of terror as developed by Poe, Maupassant, and LeFanu. Varma deplored the development of the genre, seeing it "as an index of the sensation-craze into which the Gothic vogue degenerated in its declining years," also observing that the gothic bluebook "catered to the perverted taste for excitement among degenerate readers" (189). Charles May has argued that the romantic short tale was an attempt to "demythologize folktales, to divest them of their external values, and to remythologize them by internalizing those values and self-consciously projecting them onto the external world. They wished to preserve the old religious values of the romance and the folktale without their religious dogma and supernatural trappings" (5). For a history of the earlier street literature, see Collison.

2. Frank (1998) presents a survey of the 297 gothic chapbooks held in the Sadleir-Black Collection at the University of Virginia Library. Additional bibliographical information about 217 titles in the Corvey Collection and various British libraries can be found in Koch, who concludes that, in contrast to the full-length gothic novels by Lewis where horror is a manifestation of moral ambivalence and there is an unrestrained use of the supernatural, "the sentimental and rationalized contents of the bluebooks reveal them as a reactionary mode of the gothic" that reassures general readers that their own concepts of reality are "stable."

3. Bottigheimer argues for the Italian and Sicilian origins of the fairy tale, while more detailed discussions of the French and German fairy-tale traditions can be found in Zipes (2007). Other critics have commented on the fairy-tale content of gothic tales, but have not attempted to examine the issue in any detail. For instance, Frank writes: "Why were the Gothic writers so often drawn to the use of fairytale and folklore motifs of the kinds found throughout the chapbooks? The answer may be that the grotesque motifs and violent patterns of action of these primitive stories provided the distortions of reality and amoral disorientation that the Gothic writers depended upon for rendering their powerful effects. The motifs themselves are variations of the malignant sublime" (1987, 415).

4. Also see the discussion in Zipes 1994, 1–3. More recently, Zipes (2006) has explored the psychological staying power of the fairy tale by examining the theory of genre as a "selfish gene" that seeks indiscriminately to reproduce and thereby perpetuate itself ("genericity" or the relation of genetics, memetics, and material culture) as developed by Jean-Michael Adams and Ute Heidmann.

5. Potter (2005) provides two appendices that list some 650 titles for gothic chap-

books and tales published between 1799 and 1835. The catalogue of the Lauriston Castle chapbooks lists 4,080 holdings there. St. Clair claims that the height of the "chapbook gothic" craze occurred around 1810 (349). Scholarly sources on the earlier phase include Birkhead, who argues that "in these brief, blood-curdling romances we may find the origin of the short tale of terror" (186).

6. Mayo was the first critic to recognize the essentially bourgeois moralizing tone of the gothic tale as published in the periodicals, while he asserted that the gothic bluebook was too crude to appeal to the rising middle-class reader (1942, 448). In a later article (1950), he focused on the chilly reception given the bluebooks by "many critics, editors, and members of the general reading audience in whose eyes *romance* was the hallmark for barbarous superstition, unreason, moral depravity, and bad taste" (787; emphasis in original). Killick provides a broad history of the early British short story and its publication venues, while Potter distinguishes between gothic tales and gothic fragments, arguing that both "contain an abbreviated form of the gothic novel including conventional motifs and characteristics. There is no difference between the two terms except that of length, the tale being the longer of the two; consequently, the term 'Gothic tale' applies equally to Gothic short stories, tales of terror, novelettes, fragments and serialized romances" (2005, 79). Richter has claimed the "Gothic is to all intents and purposes dead by 1822" (1996, 125), while Mayo asserts that "from 1796 to 1806 at least one-third of all novels published in Great Britain were Gothic in character" (1950, 766); earlier he had observed that "the popular vogue for romances of terror was over in 1814, but their appeal was still fresh in the minds of readers" (1943, 64). Baldick claims that Poe's tales are distinctly different from the earlier gothic tales, which he sees as inferior and merely redactions of the longer gothic novels (xvi).

7. *The Use of Circulating Libraries Considered,* an anonymous how-to manual for proprietors of circulating libraries (195–203). The Edmonton Circulating Library (England) stated its terms for subscription as five shillings a quarter; nine shillings for six months; sixteen shillings a year. Extremely detailed discussions of the evolution, economics, and patronage of circulating libraries in Britain can be found in a number of sources: Blakey, 111–24; Jacobs, 157–235; Potter 2005, 114–36; and R. Hume (2006). Richter connects the rise of circulating libraries with the increase in more naïve readers (1988, 126), while Punter argues the opposite, claiming that the "confidence trick" that gothic authors play on their readers (making them believe in phantoms only to sneer at the belief) actually "demands a type of discrimination largely unnecessary in the reading of earlier realist fiction" (1996, 96).

8. I have examined a variety of gothic chapbooks throughout England and found a remarkable consistency in them. Another very representative volume is the *New Collection of Gothic Stories.* The first page of the collection states that the contents have been reprinted from the *Monthly Cabinet,* and they include "Rodolph; or the Banditti of the Castle," a faux-Germanic "robber" tale set during the Crusades in which a murdered father and daughter appear as spirits to avenge their deaths; "The Story of Frederico; or the Ruin of the House of Vilaineuf," a faux-French story also set during the Crusades concerning rival dynastic claims. Its final sentence reads: "Virtuous actions meet with their own reward in the end." "The Story of Ethelbert" is a Walpolean pastiche, a faux-Saxon tale about a portrait that sighs, a haunted tower, and a suit of armor that walks through the castle seeking revenge. The other two tales concern a monk who murders his brother and a castle besieged by Danish invaders. Gothic chapbooks and gothic tales have been reprinted fairly sporadically over the past thirty years. See Haining; Baldick;

and Potter (2003; 2009).

9. Frank characterizes Wilkinson's writings as "plundering" (1987, 412) and "automatic Gothicism produced and marketed for the reader's fee of six pence" (1987, 413). James discusses the authors of gothic chapbooks as "hack writers" and "lower-class writers . . . [who] had not enough skill to create through atmosphere a suspension of disbelief" (80–81). More recently, Kelly has stated bluntly, "Wilkinson was a hack" 2002, II:xxi).

10. A bibliography and analysis of the critical reaction to gothic romances can be found in Gallaway and Haworth.

Epilogue

1. For an assessment of Summers as a gothic scholar, as well as a rumored demon worshiper, pederast, and *faux* Catholic priest, see Jerome. Bostrom claims that the gothic "owed its protracted vogue" to the fact that it "reinforced old prejudices against Catholicism" (155). The Victorian gothics (the neo-gothic novels of the 1890s and the sensation novels) and their continued investment in anti-Catholic discourse and "sexual deviance" are best examined in O'Malley, who argues that "the work of nineteenth-century Gothic is the reworking of history itself, the distortion of the past produced as the anxiety of the present. . . . The gothic is the thematic or discursive eruption of a traumatic past into the present, distorted into a suggestion of the supernatural. . . . The gothic is the representation of the terror and fascination produced by the refusal of the past to remain in the past" (12). The earlier, post-Reformation anti-Catholic tradition is examined in Marotti. Also see Wright for a very useful overview of the history of the gothic and anti-Catholicism.

2. Blumenberg is regarded as the most radical of the secularization theorists in his attempts to dismantle secularism from its Christian explanatory structure. For him, history is contingent, cyclic, mechanical, and purposeless, while human actions are mechanistic and random, and devoid of any religious principle or spiritual promise.

3. A similar observation has been expressed astutely by Geary: "Much of Gothic fiction can thus be seen as a stage in a process of cultural and literary secularization, a literary mode whose procedures respond to the weakening of the theological matrix of providential beliefs containing the numinous but which do not fully coalesce into a new paradigm of completely naturalized or psychologized supernaturalism" (12). The cultural longevity of the gothic can be seen in films, television, and the works of any number of contemporary novels (the *Twilight* phenomenon being one). In commenting on this longevity, Lovecraft noted that the appeal of the gothic could be found in "the oldest and strongest kind of fear, the fear of the unknown": it is a "plain scientific fact that man's very hereditary essence, . . . [contains] an actual psychological fixation of the old instincts in our nervous tissue, [which] has become saturated with religion and superstition, [a condition] as virtually permanent as far as the subconscious mind and inner instincts are concerned" (13–15).

4. Becker has critiqued Freud's theory of the "death-instinct," arguing that "consciousness of death is the primary repression, not sexuality," and that humanity's "protest against death is a built-in instinctive urge" that causes it to create religions or political parties, which he calls "culturally standardized hero systems and symbols" or "death-denying ideologies" (1973, 99, 96). For another critique, see Levin.

5. In yet another manifestation of anti-Catholic sentiment by a gothic balladeer, Robert Southey connects Catholicism to Druidism when he relates the conversion of King Ethelbert of Kent to Christianity by St. Augustine (597 CE), rewriting history in order to assert a long-standing distinction between a more liberal Protestant tradition and Roman Catholic tyranny (1824, I:31). Southey continued rewriting the history of Christianity in his *Vindiciae Ecclesiae Anglicanae* (1826), in which he "exposed this baneful system [Roman Catholicism] in its proper deformity."

6. As Hutton has observed, a "privitisation" of worship (96–98) arose among the common people because the new, official Anglican religion no longer offered the services that they had come to expect, for example, Candlemas or prayers for the dead on All Souls' Day. As I suggested in the Preface, attendance at carnival performances and theatrical Christmas harlequinades—and by extension, gothic theatricals—also functioned as one means by which these popular, "older" religious traditions survived in transmuted forms.

WORKS CITED

Abrams, M. H. *The Mirror and the Lamp: Romantic Theory and Critical Tradition.* Oxford: Oxford University Press, 1953.

———. *Natural Supernaturalism: Tradition and Revolution in Romantic Literature.* New York: Norton, 1971.

Addison, Joseph. *The Spectator.* Ed. D. F. Bond. 4 volumes. Oxford: Clarendon Press, 1965.

Alexander, Boyd. *England's Wealthiest Son: A Study of William Beckford.* London: Centaur, 1962.

Althusser, Louis. *Lenin and Philosophy and Other Essays.* Trans. Ben Brewster. New York: Monthly Review Press, 2001.

Altick, Richard. *The Shows of London.* Cambridge, MA: Harvard University Press, 1978.

Anderson, Benedict R. *Imagined Communities: Reflections on the Origin and Spread of Nationalism.* London: Verso, 1983. Rev. 1991, 2006.

Anon. *Julius or the Deaf and Dumb Orphan; A Tale for Youth of Both Sexes: Founded on the Popular Play of Deaf and Dumb.* 3rd ed. London: Harris, 1806.

Anon. *New Collection of Gothic Stories.* London: S. Fisher, 1804.

Anon. *Tales of Wonder: Containing The Castle of Enchantment or The Mysterious Deception. The Robbers Daughter or The Phantom of the Grotto. The Magic Legacy &c.* London: Ann Lemoine, 1801; sold by T. Hurst, Paternoster Row.

Anon. *The Use of Circulating Libraries Considered.* Reprinted as *The Evergreen Tree of Diabolical Knowledge,* ed. Devendra Varma, 195–203. Washington, DC: Consortium Press, 1972.

Astbury, Katherine. *The Moral Tale in France and Germany 1750–1789.* Oxford: Voltaire Foundation, 2002.

Aston, Margaret. "English Ruins and English History: The Dissolution and the Sense of the Past." *Journal of the Warburg and Courtland Institutes* 36 (1973): 231–55.

Atwood, Margaret. *Cat's Eye.* 1988. Reprinted New York: Anchor, 1998.

Auerbach, Erich. "Odysseus' Scar." In *Mimesis: The Representation of Reality in Western*

Literature. Trans. Willard R. Trask. 1946. Reprint, Princeton, NJ: Princeton University Press, 1953. 3–43.
Averill, James. *Wordsworth and the Poetry of Human Suffering*. Ithaca, NY: Cornell University Press, 1980.
Backsheider, Paula. *Spectacular Politics: Theatrical Power and Mass Culture in Early Modern England*. Baltimore: Johns Hopkins University Press, 1993.
Bakhtin, Mikhail. *The Dialogic Imagination*. Ed. Michael Holquist. Trans. Caryl Emerson and Michael Holquist. Austin: University of Texas Press, 1981.
———. *Rabelais and His World*. Trans. Helene Iswolsky. Cambridge, MA: MIT Press, 1968.
Baldick, Chris, ed. *The Oxford Book of Gothic Tales*. 1993. Reprint, Oxford: Oxford University Press, 2001.
Baldick, Chris, and Robert Mighall. "Gothic Criticism." In *Companion to the Gothic*, ed. David Punter, 209–28. Oxford: Blackwell, 2000.
Ballin, Rosetta. *The Statue Room*. 2 vols. London: Symonds, 1790.
Balthazar, Scott. "Ferdinand Paër"; "Lenora"; "I Fuorusciti di Firenze"; and "Rescue Opera." In *The New Grove Dictionary of Opera*, ed. Stanley Sadie, 816–18; 1150; 316; 1293–94. London: Macmillan, 1992.
Barker-Benfield, G. J. *The Culture of Sensibility: Sex and Society in Eighteenth-Century Britain*. Chicago: University of Chicago Press, 1992.
Barrell, John. *Imagining the King's Death: Figurative Treason, Fantasies of Regicide, 1793–96*. New York: Oxford University Press, 2000.
Bartlet, Elizabeth. "Archival Sources for the Opéra-Comique and Its *Registres* at the Bibliotèque de l'Opera." *Nineteenth-Century Music* 7 (1983): 119–28.
Bate, Jonathan. *Shakespearean Constitutions: Politics, Theatre, Criticism 1730–1830*. Oxford: Clarendon Press, 1989.
Baumann, Thomas. *North German Opera in the Age of Goethe*. Cambridge: Cambridge University Press, 1985.
Becker, Ernest. *The Denial of Death*. New York: Free Press, 1973.
Bede. "The Conversion of Northumbria." In *Ecclesiastical History of the English People*, ed. Leo Shirley-Price. Book 2: chapter 13, 129–30. London: Penguin, 1990.
Behrendt, Stephen C. *Royal Mourning and Regency Culture: Elegies and Memorials of Princess Charlotte*. New York: St. Martin's Press, 1997.
Bell, Catherine. *Ritual Theory, Ritual Practice*. New York: Oxford University Press, 1992.
Bell, Daniel. "The Return of the Sacred? The Argument on the Future of Religion." *British Journal of Sociology* 28 (1977): 419–49.
Bentley, Eric. *The Life of the Drama*. New York: Atheneum, 1964.
Berlin, Isaiah. *The Roots of Romanticism*. Ed. Henry Hardy. Princeton, NJ: Princeton University Press, 1999.
Bewell, Alan. "A 'Word Scarce Said': Hysteria and Witchcraft in Wordsworth's 'Experimental' Poetry of 1797–1798." *ELH* 53 (1986): 357–90.
"Birchall, Robert." *Grove Online*. http://www.oxfordmusiconline.com (March 1, 2009).
Birkhead, Edith. *The Tale of Terror: A Study of the Gothic Romance*. London: Constable, 1921.
Blakemore, Steven. "Matthew Lewis's Black Mass: Sexual, Religious Inversion in 'The Monk.'" *Studies in the Novel* 30 (1998): 521–39.
Blakey, Dorothy. *Minerva Press 1790–1830*. London: Oxford University Press, 1939.
Bloom, Harold. *Shakespeare: The Invention of the Human*. New York: Riverhead, 1998.

———, ed. *Romanticism and Consciousness: Essays in Criticism*. New York: Norton, 1970.
Blumenberg, Hans. *The Legitimacy of the Modern Age*. Trans. Robert Wallace. Cambridge, MA: MIT Press, 1983.
Boaden, James. *The Cambro-Britons*. In *The Plays of James Boaden*, ed. Steven Cohan, n.pag. New York: Garland, 1980.
———. *Fontainville Forest*. London: Hookham and Carpenter, 1794.
———. *Memoirs of the Life of John Philip Kemble, esq., Including a History of the Stage, from the Time of Garrick to the Present Period*. 2 vols. London: Longman, 1825.
Bolton, Betsy. *Women, Nationalism, and the Romantic Stage: Theatre and Politics in Britain, 1780–1800*. Cambridge: Cambridge University Press, 2001.
Bostrom, Irene. "The Novel and Catholic Emancipation." *Studies in Romanticism* 2 (1963): 155–76.
Bottigheimer, Ruth B. *Fairy Tales: A New History*. Albany: State University of New York Press, 2009.
Botting, Fred. *Gothic*. London: Routledge, 1996.
Bradbury, Malcolm, and James McFarlane, eds. *Modernism 1890–1930*. New York: Penguin, 1976.
Branfman, Theodore. "The Psychology of Sentimentality." *Psychiatric Quarterly* 28 (1954): 624–34.
Bratton, Jacky. *New Readings in Theatre History*. Cambridge: Cambridge University Press, 2003.
———. "Romantic Melodrama." In *The Cambridge Companion to British Theatre, 1730–1830*, 115–27. Cambridge: Cambridge University Press, 2007.
Bredvold, Louis I. *The Natural History of Sensibility*. Detroit: Wayne State University Press, 1962.
Brewer, James Norris. *A Winter's Tale*. 4 vols. London: Minerva, 1799.
Bridgwater, Patrick. *DeQuincey's Gothic Masquerade*. Amsterdam: Rodopi, 2004.
Brooks, Peter. *The Melodramatic Imagination*. New Haven, CT: Yale University Press, 1976.
Brown, Callum G. *The Death of Christian Britain: Understanding Secularization in England, 1800–2000*. London: Routledge, 2001.
Brown, Marshall. *The Gothic Text*. Stanford, CA: Stanford University Press, 2005.
Brown, Theo. *The Fate of the Dead*. Cambridge: Brewer, 1979.
Bruce, Steve. *God is Dead: Secularization in the West*. Oxford: Blackwell, 2002.
Buch, David J. "Fairy-Tale Literature and *Die Zauberflöte*." *Acta Musicologica* 64 (1992): 30–49.
Buchen, Irving H. "Wordsworth's Gothic Ballads." *Genre* 3 (1970): 85–96.
Buldrini, Yonel. "Un Opéra 'Gothique' Oublié: *La Nonne Sanglante* de Charles Gounod." http://www.forumopera.com (September 1, 2008).
Bürger, Gottfried August. "Lenora." In *The Literary Ballad*, ed. Anne Henry Ehrenpreis, 67–76. London: Edward Arnold, 1966.
Burke, Edmund. *A Philosophical Enquiry into the Origins of our Ideas of the Sublime and Beautiful and Other Pre-Revolutionary Writings*. London: Penguin, 1998.
Burwick, Frederick. *Romantic Drama: Acting and Reacting*. Cambridge: Cambridge University Press, 2009.
Busby, Thomas. *The Overture, Marches, Dances, Symphonies and Songs in the Melo-Drame, called A Tale of Mystery now Performing with Universal Applause at the*

Theatre Royal, Covent Garden. London: T. Riley, 1802.
Butler, Marilyn. *Romantics, Rebels and Reactionaries: English Literature and Its Background 1760-1830.* Oxford: Oxford University Press, 1981.
Canuel, Mark. *Religion, Toleration and British Writing, 1790-1830.* Cambridge: Cambridge University Press, 2002.
Carter, Margaret. *Specter or Delusion? The Supernatural in Gothic Fiction.* Ann Arbor, MI: UMI, 1986.
Casanova, José. *Public Religions in the Modern World.* Chicago: University of Chicago Press, 1994.
Castelvecchi, Stefano. "From *Nina* to *Nina:* Psychodrama, Absorption and Sentiment in the 1780s." *Cambridge Opera Journal* 8 (1996): 91-112. Cited as Castelvecchi 1.
———. "Sentimental Opera: The Emergence of a Genre, 1760-1790." PhD diss., University of Chicago, 1996. Cited as Castelvecchi 2.
Castle, Terry. *The Female Thermometer: Eighteenth-Century Culture and the Invention of the Uncanny.* Oxford: Oxford University Press, 1995.
Catalogue of the Lauriston Castle Chapbooks, now held in Edinburgh: National Library of Scotland. Boston: G. K. Hall, 1964.
Cavaliero, Glen. *The Supernatural and English Fiction.* Oxford: Oxford University Press, 1995.
Chadwick, Owen. *The Secularization of the European Mind in the Nineteenth Century.* Cambridge: Cambridge University Press, 1975.
Chancellor, Paul. "British Bards and Continental Composers." *Musical Quarterly* 46 (1960): 1-11.
Chandler, David. "Southey's 'German Sublimity' and Coleridge's 'Dutch Attempt.'" *Romanticism on the Net* 32-33 (2003). http://id.erudit.org/iderudit/009257ar (March 15, 2009).
Charlton, David. *French Opera 1730-1830: Meaning and Media.* Aldershot, UK: Ashgate Publishing, 2000.
———. "On Redefinitions of Rescue Opera." In *Music and the French Revolution,* ed. M. Boyd, 169-88. Cambridge: Cambridge University Press, 1992.
Cheesman, Tom. *The Shocking Ballad Picture Show: German Popular Literature and Cultural History.* Oxford: Berg, 1994.
Christensen, Merton. "*Udolpho, Horrid Mysteries,* and Coleridge's Machinery of the Imagination." *Wordsworth Circle* 2 (1971): 153-59.
Clery, Emma J. "The Genesis of Gothic Fiction." In *The Cambridge Companion to Gothic Fiction,* ed. Jerrold Hogle, 21-40. Cambridge: Cambridge University Press, 2002.
———. "Horace Walpole's *The Mysterious Mother* and the Impossibility of Female Desire." In *The Gothic, Essays and Studies,* ed. Fred Botting, 23-46. Woodbridge: Brewer, 2001.
———. *The Rise of Supernatural Fiction, 1762-1800.* Cambridge: Cambridge University Press, 1995.
Cohen, Margaret, and Carolyn Dever. Introduction to *The Literary Channel: The International Invention of the Novel,* ed. Cohen and Dever, 1-34. Princeton, NJ: Princeton University Press, 2002.
Cohen, Ralph. "A Propaedeutic for Literary Change." *Critical Exchange* 13 (1983): 11-12.
Coleridge, Samuel Taylor. *Biographia Literaria.* 1817. Reprint, New York: Leavitt, 1834.
———. *The Notebooks of Samuel Taylor Coleridge.* Ed. Kathleen Coburn et al. 5 vols.

Princeton, NJ: Bollingen, 1957-2007.

———. Review of *The Monk*. *Critical Review* 19 (1797): 194-200. Reprint, *Gothic Documents: A Sourcebook 1700-1820*, ed. E. J. Clery and Robert Miles, 185-89. Manchester: Manchester University Press, 2000.

Collings, David. "Romanticism, Religion, and the Secular." Paper presented at MLA Convention, Chicago, December 2007.

———. *Wordsworthian Errancies: The Poetics of Cultural Dismemberment*. Baltimore: Johns Hopkins University Press, 1994.

Collison, Robert. *The Story of Street Literature, Forerunner of the Popular Press*. London: Dent, 1973.

Commons, Jeffrey. *100 Years of Italian Opera*. London: Opera Rara, 1982.

Conger, Syndy M. *Matthew G. Lewis, Charles Robert Maturin and the Germans: An Interpretive Study of the Influence of German Literature on Two Gothic Novels*. Salzburg: Institut für Englische Sprache und Literatur, 1977.

Cooper, Helen. "The Strange History of *Valentine and Orson*." In *Tradition and Transformation in Medieval Romance*, ed. Rosalind Field, 153-69. Woodbridge, Suffolk: Brewer, 2001.

Cornwell, Neil. "European Gothic." In *A Companion to the Gothic*, ed. David Punter, 27-38. Oxford: Blackwell, 2000.

Cox, Jeffrey. "British Romantic Drama in a European Context." In *British and European Romanticisms*, ed. Christoph Bode and Sebastian Domsch, 115-30. Trier: Wissenschaftlicher Verlag, 2007.

———. *In the Shadows of Romance: Romantic Tragic Drama in Germany, England, and France*. Athens: Ohio University Press, 1987.

———. *Seven Gothic Dramas 1789-1825*. Athens: Ohio University Press, 1992.

Craciun, Adriana. *Fatal Women of Romanticism*. Cambridge: Cambridge University Press, 2003.

Crary, Jonathan. *Techniques of the Observer: On Vision and Modernity in the Nineteenth Century*. Cambridge, MA: MIT Press, 1990.

Dacre, Charlotte. "The Lass of Fair Wone." *Hours of Solitude: A Collection of Original Poems*. 2 vols. London: Shury, 1805. Vol. 2; 86-96. http://digital.lib.ucdavis.edu/projects/bwrp/Works/DacrCHours2.htm (April 1, 2009).

Davis, Lennard J. *Obsession*. Chicago: University of Chicago Press, 2008.

Davis, Natalie Zemon. *Society and Culture in Early Modern France*. Stanford, CA: Stanford University Press, 1975.

Dean, Winton. *Handel's Dramatic Oratorios and Masques*. Oxford: Clarendon, 1959.

De Genlis, Stéphanie-Félicité. *Adelaide and Theodore, or Letters on Education*. 1783. Ed. Gillian Dow. London: Pickering & Chatto, 2007.

Dennis, John. "The Grounds of Criticism in Poetry." 1704. In *The Critical Works of John Dennis*, ed. E. N. Hooker. 2 vols. Vol. 1: 325-73. Baltimore: Johns Hopkins University Press, 1939.

Dent, Edward J. *The Rise of Romantic Opera*, ed. Winton Dean. Cambridge: Cambridge University Press, 1976.

Dercy, P., and Jean Marie Deschamps. Libretto. *Ossian ou Les Bardes*. Music by Jean-François le Sueur. 1804. Reprint, *Early Romantic Opera*, vol. 37. New York: Garland Publishing, 1979.

Derrida, Jacques. *Archive Fever: A Freudian Impression*. Trans. Eric Prenowitz. Chicago: University of Chicago Press, 1996.

De Sade, Marquis. "An Essay on Novels." Trans. David Coward. In *The Crimes of Love*, 3–20. Oxford: Oxford University Press, 2005.

Dibdin, Thomas. *Valentine and Orson; a romantic melodrama, in two acts*. London: Barker, 1804.

Didier, Béatrice. "Beaumarchais aux origines du melodrama." In *Mélodrames et romans noirs 1750–1890*, ed. Simone Bernard-Griffiths and Jean Sgard, 115–26. Toulouse: Mirail, 2000.

Dixon, Thomas. "The Psychology of the Emotions in Britain and America in the Nineteenth Century: The Role of Religious and Antireligious Commitments." *Osiris* 16 (2001): 288–320.

Dobson, Michael. *The Making of the National Poet: Shakespeare, Adaptation and Authorship, 1660–1769*. Oxford: Clarendon, 1992.

———, and Nicola Watson. *England's Elizabeth: An Afterlife in Fame and Fantasy*. Oxford: Oxford University Press, 2002.

Dolar, Mladen. "'I shall be with you on your wedding-night': Lacan and the Uncanny." *October* 58 (1991): 5–23.

Drake, Nathan. *Literary Hours, or Sketches Critical and Narrative*. 2 vols. 1800. Reprint, New York: Garland, 1970.

During, Simon. *Modern Enchantments: The Cultural Power of Secular Magic*. Cambridge, MA: Harvard University Press, 2002.

Edgcumbe, Richard. *Musical Reminiscences of an Old Amateur, the Earl of Mont Edgcumbe, containing an account of the Italian Opera in England from 1773 to 1834*. 4th ed. 1834. Reprint, New York: De Capo Press, 1973.

Eliade, Mircea. *The History of Religions*. Chicago: University of Chicago Press, 1959.

———. "Myths and Fairy Tales." In *Myth and Reality*. Trans. Willard R. Trask. New York: Urizen, 1978.

Elias, Norbert. *The Civilizing Process*. Trans. Edmund Jephcott. Cambridge: Blackwell, 1994.

Ellis, Frank H. *Sentimental Comedy: Theory and Practice*. Cambridge: Cambridge University Press, 1991.

Ellison, Julie. *Cato's Tears and the Making of Anglo-American Emotion*. Chicago: University of Chicago Press, 1999.

Evans, Bertrand. *Gothic Drama from Walpole to Shelley*. Berkeley: University of California Press. 1947. Reprinted as *The Origins of the Modern Study of Gothic Drama*. Ed. Frederick Frank. Lewiston, NY: Edwin Mellen Press, 2006.

Farese, Carlotta. "The Translator and the Fairies: Christoph Martin Wieland's *Oberon* and the British Romantics." *European Romantic Review* 20 (2009): 629–36.

Fay, Elizabeth. "The 'Honourable Characteristic of Poetry': Two Hundred Years of *Lyrical Ballads*." *Wordsworth's Balladry: Real Men Wanted*. Romantic Circles Praxis Series, November 1999. http://www.rc.umd.edu/praxis/lyrical/fay/balladry.html (March 1, 2009).

Feinstein, Elaine. "Lear's Daughters: The Women's Theatre Group." In *Adaptations of Shakespeare: A Critical Anthology of Plays from the Seventeenth Century to the Present*, ed. Daniel Fishlin and Mark Fortier, 215–32. London: Routledge, 2000.

Fenner, Theodore. *Opera in London: Views of the Press, 1785–1830*. Carbondale: Southern Illinois University Press, 1994.

"Ferdinando Paër." http://www.ferdinandopaer.ch/index.php?p=home (March 1, 2009).

Festa, Lynn. "Sentimental Bonds and Revolutionary Characters: Richardson's *Pamela* in England and France." In *The Literary Channel,* ed. Margaret Cohen and Carolyn Dever, 73–105. Princeton, NJ: Princeton University Press, 2002.

Fiedler, Leslie A. *Love and Death in the American Novel.* New York: Criterion, 1960. Reprint, New York: Dell, 1966.

Fielding, Henry. *Tom Jones.* Ed. Sheridan Baker. New York: Norton, 1973.

Fillette-Loreaux, Claude François. Libretto. *Lodoïska.* 1791. Music by Maria Luigi Cherubini. Reprint, *Early Romantic Opera.* Vol. 33. New York: Garland, 1978.

Filmer, Robert. *Patriarchia and Other Writings.* Ed. Johann P. Sommerville. Cambridge: Cambridge University Press, 1991.

Ford, Susan Allen. "'Intimate by Instinct': *Manfield Park* and the Comedy of *King Lear.*" *Persuasions* 24 (2002): 177–97.

Foster, J. R. "The Abbé Prévost and the English Novel." *PMLA* 42 (1927): 443–64.

Foucault, Michel. *Discipline and Punish: The Birth of the Prison.* Trans. Alan Sheridan. New York: Pantheon, 1977.

———. *Madness and Civilization: A History of Insanity in the Age of Reason.* Trans. Richard Howard. New York: Vintage, 1988.

———. *The Order of Things: An Archeology of the Human Sciences.* New York: Pantheon, 1970.

Fowler, David C. *A Literary History of the Popular Ballad.* Durham, NC: Duke University Press, 1968.

Franceschina, John, ed. *Sisters of Gore: Seven Gothic Melodramas by British Women, 1790–1843.* New York: Garland, 1997.

Frank, Frederick. *The First Gothics: A Critical Guide to the Gothic Novel.* New York: Garland, 1987.

———. "François Thomas Marie de Baculard d'Arnaud." In *Gothic Writers: A Critical and Bibliographical Guide,* ed. Douglass Thomson, Jack Voller, and Fred Frank, 48–52. Westport, CT: Greenwood, 2002.

———. "Gothic Gold: The Sadleir-Black Collection of Gothic Fiction." *Studies in Eighteenth-Century Culture* 26 (1998): 287–312.

Frankl, Paul. *The Gothic: Literary Sources and Interpretations through Eight Centuries.* Princeton, NJ: Princeton University Press, 1960.

Freud, Sigmund. "The Theme of the Three Caskets." In *The Standard Edition of the Complete Psychological Works [SE],* trans. James Strachey, vol. 12, 289–302. London: Hogarth Press, 1953–74.

———. "The Uncanny" [1919]. In *Standard Edition of the Complete Psychological Works of Sigmund Freud [SE],* trans. James Strachey, vol. 17, 218–56. London: Hogarth Press, 1953–74.

Friedman, Albert B. *The Ballad Revival: Studies in the Influence of Popular on Sophisticated Poetry.* Chicago: University of Chicago Press, 1961.

Fulford, Tim. "Fallen Ladies and Cruel Mothers: Ballad Singers and Ballad Heroines in the Eighteenth Century." *Eighteenth Century* 47 (2007): 309–31.

Gaillard, Françoise. "Aux limites du genre: Melmoth réconcilié." In *Balzac ou la tentation de l'impossible,* ed. Raymond Mahieu and Franc Schuerewegen, 121–32. Paris: SEDES, 2001.

Gallaway, W. F. "The Conservative Attitude toward Fiction, 1770–1830." *PMLA* 55 (1940): 104–59.

Gamer, Michael. *Romanticism and the Gothic: Genre, Reception, and Canon Formation.* Cambridge: Cambridge University Press, 2000.

Gann, Andrew G. "Théophile Gautier, Charles Gounod, and the Massacre of *La Nonne Sanglante*." *Journal of Musicological Research* 13 (1993): 49–66.

Garlington, Aubrey S. "'Gothic' Literature and Dramatic Music in England, 1781–1802." *Journal of American Musicological Society* 15 (1962): 48–65.

Garside, Peter, James Raven, and Rainer Schowerling, eds. *The English Novel 1770–1829*. 2 vols. Oxford: Oxford University Press, 2000.

Gautier, Gary. "Ann Radcliffe's *The Italian* in Context: Gothic Villains, Romantic Heroes, and a New Age of Power Relations." *Genre* 32 (1999): 201–24.

Gay, Peter. *Modernism: The Lure of Heresy*. New York: Norton, 2007.

Geary, Robert. *The Supernatural in Gothic Fiction*. Lewiston, NY: Edwin Mellen Press, 1992.

Genest, John. *Some Account of the English Stage*. 10 vols. Bath: Carrington, 1832.

Gentile, Kathy Justice. "Anxious Supernaturalism: An Analytic of the Uncanny." *Gothic Studies* 2 (2000): 23–38.

Gilmartin, Kevin. "Romanticism and Religious Modernithy: From Natural Superaturalism to Literary Sectarianism." In *The Cambridge History of English Romantic Literature*. Ed. James Chandler, 621–47. Cambridge: Cambridge University Press, 2009.

Girdham, Jane. *English Opera in Late Eighteenth-Century London: Stephen Storace at Drury Lane*. Oxford: Clarendon, 1997.

Goldberg, Rita. "Voltaire, Rousseau, and the Lisbon Earthquake." *Eighteenth-Century Life* 13 (1989): 1–20.

Goldoni, Carlo. *The Memoirs of Carlo Goldoni*. Trans. John Black. 2 vols. London: Hunt and Clarke, 1828.

Gonslaves, Joshua. "Reading Idiocy: Wordsworth's 'The Idiot Boy.'" *Wordsworth Circle* 38 (2007): 121–30.

Goodman, Kevis. "Making Time for History: Wordsworth, the New Historicism, and the Apocalyptic Fallacy." In *The Wordsworthian Enlightenment: Romantic Poetry and the Ecology of Reading*, ed. Helen Regueiro Elam and Frances Ferguson, 158–71. Baltimore: Johns Hopkins University Press, 2005.

Goody, Jack. *The Interface between the Written and the Oral*. Cambridge: Cambridge University Press, 1987.

Gossett, Philip, and Charles Rosen, eds. *Eliza ou le Voyage aux glaciers du Mont St. Bernard*. Reprint, *Early Romantic Opera: Bellini; Rossini; Meyerbeer; Donizetti & Grand Opera in Paris*. Vol. 34. New York: Garland, 1979.

Graff, Harvey, ed. *Literacy and Social Development in the West*. Cambridge: Cambridge University Press, 1981.

Graham, Gordon. *The Re-enchantment of the World: Art versus Religion*. Oxford: Oxford University Press, 2007.

Graham, John. "Lavater's Physiognomy in England." *Journal of the History of Ideas* 22 (1961): 561–72.

Gregory, Allene. *The French Revolution and the English Novel*. 1914. Reprint, New York: Haskell, 1966.

Grieder, Josephine. *Anglomania in France 1740–89*. Geneva: Droz, 1985.

Groom, Nick. *The Making of Percy's 'Reliques.'* Oxford: Oxford University Press, 1999.

Guest, Ann Hutchinson, and Knud Arne Jurgensen. *Robert le Diable: The Ballet of the Nuns*. Amsterdam: Gordon and Breach, 1997.

Guillory, John. *Cultural Capital: The Problem of Literary Canon Formation*. Chicago:

University of Chicago Press, 1993.
Habermas, Jürgen. "Modernity: An Unfinished Project." *The Theory of Communicative Action*. Trans. Thomas McCarthy. London: Beacon, 1981.
———. *The Philosophical Discourse of Modernity: Twelve Lectures*. Trans. Frederick Lawrence. Cambridge, MA: MIT Press, 1987.
———. *Post-metaphysical Thinking*. Cambridge: Polity Press, 1992.
———. "The Public Sphere: An Encyclopedia Article." *New German Critique* 3 (1974): 49–55.
———. *The Structural Transformation of the Public Sphere: An Inquiry into a Category of Bourgeois Society*. Trans. Thomas Burger with the assistance of Frederick Lawrence. Cambridge, MA: MIT Press, 1989.
———. "The Theory of Modernity." In *The Theory of Communicative Action*. Vol. 2: *Lifeworld and System: A Critique of Functionalist Reason*. Trans. Thomas McCarthy. Boston: Beacon Press, 1984.
Hadley, Michael. *The Undiscovered Genre: A Search for the German Gothic Novel*. Bern: Peter Lang, 1977.
Haggerty, George. "Literature and Homosexuality in the Late Eighteenth Century: Walpole, Beckford, and Lewis." *Studies in the Novel* 18 (1986): 341–52.
Haining, Peter, ed. *Gothic Tales of Terror*. New York: Taplinger, 1972.
———, ed. *The Shilling Shockers: Stories of Terror from the Gothic Bluebooks*. London: Victor Gollancz, 1978.
Hale, Terry, ed. *The Dedalus Book of French Horror: The Nineteenth Century*. Cambridge: Dedalus, 1998.
———. "French and German Gothic: The Beginnings." In *The Cambridge Companion to the Gothic*, ed. Jerrold Hogle, 63–84. Cambridge: Cambridge University Press, 2002.
Hall, Daniel. *French and German Gothic Fiction in the Late Eighteenth Century*. Oxford: Peter Lang, 2005.
Hartman, Geoffrey. *Beyond Formalism: Literary Essays, 1958–1970*. New Haven, CT: Yale University Press, 1970.
———. "False Themes and Gentle Minds." *Philological Quarterly* 47 (1966): 55–68.
———. "Wordsworth and Goethe in Literary History." *New Literary History* 6 (1975): 393–413. Reprinted in *The Unremarkable Wordsworth*, 58–74. London: Methuen, 1987.
Haworth, H. E. "Romantic Female Writers and the Critics." *Texas Studies in Literature and Language* 17 (1976): 725–36.
Hayles, N. Katherine. *Writing Machines*. Cambridge, MA: MIT Press, 2002.
Hegel, G. W. F. *Hegel on Tragedy*. Ed. Anne Paolucci and Henry Paolucci. 1962. Reprint, New York: Harper & Row, 1974.
Heilman, Robert. *Tragedy and Melodrama*. Seattle: University of Washington Press, 1968.
Herzfeld, Georg. *William Taylor of Norwich: A Study of the Influence of Modern German Literature in England* (1897). Trans. Astrid Wind. Ed. David Chandler. *Romantic Circles*. http://www.rc.umd.edu/reference/chandler_herzfeld/chandler_herzfeld.pdf (March 1, 2009).
Hibberd, Sarah, and Nanette Nielsen. "Music in Melodrama: 'The Burden of Ineffable Expression.'" *Nineteenth-Century Theatre & Film* 29 (2002): 30–39.
Hobbes, Thomas. *Leviathan*. Ed. C. B. Macpherson. Harmondsworth: Penguin, 1968.
Hoeveler, Diane Long. "Gendering the Gothic Ballad: The Case of Anne Bannerman's

Tales of Superstition and Chivalry." *Wordsworth Circle* 31 (2000): 97–101.

———. "Joanna Baillie and the Gothic Body: Reading Extremities in *Orra* and *De Monfort*."

Gothic Studies 3 (2001): 117–33.

———. *Romantic Androgyny: The Women Within*. University Park: Pennsylvania State University Press, 1990.

Hoffer, Peter C., and N. E. H. Hull. *Murdering Mothers: Infanticide in England and New England, 1558–1803*. New York: New York University Press, 1981.

Hoffman, François. Libretto. *Euphrosine ou Le Tyran Corrigé*. Music by Etienne Nicolas Mehul. Reprint, *Early Romantic Opera*. Vol. 38. New York: Garland Publishing, 1980.

Hogan, Charles B., ed. *The London Stage, 1776–1800: A Critical Introduction*. Carbondale: Southern Illinois University Press, 1968.

Hogle, Jerrold. "Afterword: The 'Grounds' of the Shakespeare-Gothic Relationship." In *Gothic Shakespeares*, ed. John Drakakis and Dale Townshed, 201–20. Oxford: Routledge, 2008.

———. "The Gothic-Romantic Relationship: Underground Histories in 'The Eve of St. Agnes.'" *European Romantic Review* 14 (2003): 205–23.

———. Introduction to *Cambridge Companion to Gothic Fiction*, 1–20. Cambridge: Cambridge University Press, 2002.

Holcroft, Thomas. *Deaf and Dumb: or, The Orphan Protected: An Historical Drama*. Drury Lane, 1801. In *The Novels and Selected Plays of Thomas Holcroft*, vol. 5, ed. Philip Cox, 339–93. London: Pickering & Chatto, 2007.

———. *The Life of Thomas Holcroft, written by Himself. Continued to the time of his death from his diary notes and other papers by William Hazlitt*. 1925. 2 vols. Ed. Elbridge Colby. Reprint, New York: Bloom, 1968.

———. Preface to *Seduction*. In *The Novels and Selected Plays of Thomas Holcroft*, vol. 5, ed. Philip Cox, 65–125. London: Pickering & Chatto, 2007.

———. *A Tale of Mystery—A Melo-Drame*. Covent Garden, 1802. In *The Novels and Selected Plays of Thomas Holcroft*, vol. 5, ed. Phip Cox, 395–423. London: Pickering & Chatto, 2007.

Homans, Peter. *The Ability to Mourn: Disillusionment and the Social Origins of Psychoanalysis*. Chicago: University of Chicago Press, 1989.

Hopes, Jeffrey. "Staged National Identities: The English Theater Viewed from France in the Mid-Eighteenth Century." In *"Better in France?": The Circulation of Ideas across the Channel in the Eighteenth Century*, ed. Fréderic Ogée, 203–30. Lewisburg, PA: Bucknell University Press, 2005.

Howard, Jacqueline. *Reading Gothic Fiction: A Bakhtinian Approach*. New York: Oxford University Press, 1994.

Howard, June. "What Is Sentimentality?" *American Literary History* 11 (1999): 63–81.

Hughes, Derek. *Culture and Sacrifice: Ritual Death in Literature and Opera*. Cambridge: Cambridge University Press, 2007.

Hume, David. "Of Superstition and Enthusiasm." In *Essays, Moral, Political, and Literary*. Reprint, *Essays Moral, Political, and Literary*, ed. Eugene F. Miller, 73–79. Indianapolis, IN: Liberty Classics, 1987.

Hume, Robert D. "The Economics of Culture in London, 1660–1740." *Huntington Library Quarterly* 69 (2006): 487–535.

———. "Exuberant Gloom, Existential Agony, and Heroic Despair: Three Varieties of

Negative Romanticism." In *The Gothic Imagination: Essays in Dark Romanticism,* ed. G. Richard Thompson, 109–27. Spokane: Washington State University Press, 1974.

———. "Gothic versus Romantic: A Revaluation of the Gothic Novel." *PMLA* 84 (1969): 282–90.

Hutcheon, Linda. *Opera: The Art of Dying.* Cambridge, MA: Harvard University Press, 2004.

Hutton, Ronald. "The English Reformation and the Evidence of Folklore." *Past & Present* 148 (1995): 89–116.

Hyslop, Gabrielle. "Pixérécourt and the French Melodrama Debate: Instructing Boulevard Theatre Audiences." *Themes in Drama* 14 (1992): 61–85.

Jackson, J. R. de J., ed. *Coleridge: The Critical Heritage.* New York: Barnes and Noble, 1970.

Jackson, Rosemary. *Fantasy: The Literature of Subversion.* New York: Methuen, 1981.

Jacobs, Edward. *Accidental Migrations: An Archaeology of Gothic Discourse.* Lewisburg, PA: Bucknell University Press, 2000.

Jacobus, Mary. "Southey's Debt to *Lyrical Ballads.*" *Review of English Studies* 22 (1971): 20–36.

———. *Tradition and Experiment in Wordsworth's Lyrical Ballads (1798).* Oxford: Clarendon, 1976.

Jager, Colin. *The Book of God: Secularization and Design in the Romantic Era.* Philadelphia: University of Pennsylvania Press, 2007.

James, Louis. *Fiction for the Working Man: 1830–1850.* London: Oxford University Press, 1963.

Jameson, Fredric. *The Political Unconscious: Narrative as a Socially Symbolic Act.* Ithaca, NY: Cornell University Press, 1981.

Jarrells, Anthony. *Britain's Bloodless Revolutions: 1688 and the Romantic Reform of Literature.* New York: Palgrave, 2005.

Jerome, Joseph. *Montague Summers: A Memoir.* London: Cecil & Amelia Woolf, 1965.

Johnston, Kenneth R. *The Hidden Wordsworth.* New York: Norton, 2000.

Johnstone, Nathan. *The Devil and Demonism in Early Modern England.* Cambridge: Cambridge University Press, 2006.

Jones, Ann. *Ideas and Innovations: Best Sellers of Jane Austen's Age.* New York: AMS, 1986.

Jordan, John E. *Why the Lyrical Ballads?* Berkeley: University of California Press, 1976.

Kahane, Martine. *Catalogue de L'Exposition: Robert Le Diable.* Paris: Bibliothèque Nationale Théâtre de L'Opéra de Paris, 1985.

Kallich, Martin. *Horace Walpole.* New York: Twayne, 1971.

Kaplan, Benjamin. *An Unhurried View of Copyright.* New York: Columbia University Press, 1967.

Kavanaugh, Peter. *The Irish Theatre.* Tralee, Ireland: Kerryman, 1946.

Keane, Angela. *Women Writers and the English Nation in the 1790s.* Cambridge: Cambridge University Press, 2000.

Kelly, Gary. *The English Jacobin Novel 1780–1805.* Oxford: Clarendon, 1976.

———. "Fiction and the Working Classes." In *The Cambridge Companion to Fiction in the Romantic Period,* ed. Richard Maxwell and Katie Trumpener, 207–33. Cambridge: Cambridge University Press, 2008.

———. Introduction to *Varieties of Female Gothic. Vol. 2: Street Gothic: Female Gothic*

Chapbooks, ed. Gary Kelly, . i–xxv. London: Pickering & Chatto, 2002.

Kennedy, Emmet, Marie-Laurence Netter, James P. McGregor, and Mark V. Olsen. *Theatre, Opera, and Audiences in Revolutionary Paris: Analysis and Repertory. Contributions in Drama and Theatre Studies 62.* London: Greenwood Press, 1996.

Kermode, Frank. *Romantic Image.* London: Routledge and Paul, 1957.

Kessler, Joan C. Introduction to *Demons of the Night: Tales of the Fantastic, Madness, and the Supernatural from Nineteenth-Century France,* ed. Joan C. Kessler, xi–li. Chicago: University of Chicago Press, 1995.

Kiessling, Nicolas. "Demonic Dread: The Incubus Figure in British Literature." In *The Gothic Imagination: Essays in Dark Romanticism,* ed. G. R. Thompson, 22–41. Spokane: Washington State University Press, 1974.

Killen, Alice Mary. *Le roman terrifiant ou roman noir: de Walpole à Ann Radcliffe et son influence sur la littérature française jusqu'en 1840.* 1920. Rpt. Slatkine Reprints, 1984.

Killick, Tim. *British Short Fiction in the Early Nineteenth Century.* Aldershot, UK: Ashgate Publishing, 2008.

Kimbell, David. *Italian Opera.* Cambridge: Cambridge University Press, 1991.

King, Alec Hyatt. "Music Circulating Libraries in Britain." *Musical Times* 119 (1978): 134–48.

Kistler, Mark. *Drama of the Storm and Stress.* New York: Twayne, 1969.

Kivy, Peter. *Sound Sentiment: An Essay on the Musical Emotions.* Philadelphia: Temple University Press, 1989.

Klancher, Jon. *The Making of English Reading Audiences, 1790–1832.* Madison: University of Wisconsin Press, 1987.

Klein, H. Arthur. *The Graphic Worlds of Peter Bruegel the Elder.* New York: Dover Publications, 1963.

Koch, Angela. "'The Absolute Horror of Horrors' Revised: A Bibliographical Checklist of Early-Nineteenth-Century Gothic Bluebooks." *Cardiff Corvey: Reading the Romantic Text* 9 (December 2002). http://www.cardiff.ac.uk/encap/journals/corvey/articles/printer/cc09_n03.html, (April 9, 2008).

Kord, Suzanne. "Women as Children, Women as Childkillers: Poetic Images of Infanticide in Eighteenth-Century German." *Eighteenth-Century Studies* 26 (1993): 449–66.

Lamb, Charles. *The Letters of Charles and Mary Lamb.* Ed. Edwin W. Marrs Jr. 3 vols. Ithaca, NY: Cornell University Press, 1975–78.

———. "On Garrick, and Acting; and the Plays of Shakespeare, considered with reference to their fitness for Stage Representation." In *Charles Lamb: Selected Writings,* ed. J. E. Morpurgo, 241–59. London: Routledge, 2003.

Langbaum, Robert. *The Poetry of Experience.* London: Chatto and Windus, 1957.

Lanone, Catherine. "Verging on the Gothic: Melmoth's Journey to France." In *European Gothic: A Spirited Exchange,* ed. Avril Horner, 71–83. Manchester: Manchester University Press, 2002.

Laws, Malcolm. *The British Literary Ballad.* Carbondale: Southern Illinois University Press, 1972.

Leask, Nigel. "'A degrading species of Alchymy': Ballad, Poetics, Oral Tradition, and the Meanings of Popular Culture." In *Romanticism and Popular Culture in Britain and Ireland,* ed. Philip Connell and Nigel Leask, 51–71. Cambridge: Cambridge University Press, 2009.

Ledbury, Mark. "Sédaine and the Question of Genre." In *Michel-Jean Sédaine (1719–1797):*

Theatre, Opera, Art, ed. David Charlton and Mark Ledbury, 13–38. Aldershot, UK: Ashgate Publishing, 2000. Cited as Ledbury 1.

———. *Sédaine, Greuze and the Boundaries of Genre. Studies on Voltaire and the Eighteenth Century, 380.* Oxford: Voltaire Foundation, 2000. Cited as Ledbury 2.

LeTellier, Robert I. *Kindred Spirits: Interrelations and Affinities between the Romantic Novels of England and Germany.* Salzburg: Salzburg Studies, 1982.

Levin, A. J. "The Fiction of the Death Instinct." *Psychoanalytic Quarterly* 25 (1951): 257–81.

Lévy, Maurice. "English Gothic and the French Imagination: A Calendar of Translations, 1767–1828." In *Gothic Imagination: Essays in Dark Romanticism,* ed. G. Richard Thompson, 150–76. Pullman: Washington State University Press, 1974.

———. *Le Roman 'Gothique' Anglais 1764–1824.* Toulouse: Association des publications de la Faculté des lettres et sciences humaines de Toulouse, 1968.

Lewis, Isabella. *Terrific Tales.* London: Hughes, 1804.

Lewis, Matthew. *The Castle Spectre.* In *Seven Gothic Dramas,* ed. Jeffrey Cox, 149–224. Athens: Ohio University Press, 1992.

———. *The Monk.* 1796. Reprint, London: Oxford University Press, 1992.

———. *Tales of Wonder.* 1801. Reprint. Ed. Douglass H. Thomaon. Peterborough, ON: Broadview Press, 2009.

Le Yaouanc, Moïse. "Melmoth et les romans du jeune Balzac." In *Balzac and the Nineteenth Century,* ed. Donald Charlton et al., 35–45. Leicester: Leicester University Press, 1972.

Lilla, Mark. *The Stillborn God: Religion, Politics, and the Modern West.* New York: Knopf, 2007.

Lindenberger, Herbert. *Opera: The Extravagant Art.* Ithaca, NY: Cornell University Press, 1984.

Locke, John. *An Essay Concerning Human Understanding.* 4th ed. 1700. Ed. Peter Niddich. Oxford: Clarendon Press, 1975; rpt. 1979.

Lovecraft, H. P. *Supernatural Horror in Literature.* New York: Dover, 1973.

Löwy, Michael, and Robert Sayre. *Romanticism against the Tide of Modernity.* Trans. Catherine Porter. Durham, NC: Duke University Press, 2001.

Macdonald, D. L. *Monk Lewis: A Critical Biography.* Toronto: University of Toronto Press, 2000.

MacDonald, Hugh. *Hector Berlioz.* New York: Oxford University Press, 2000.

Macgregor, Margaret E. *Amelia Opie, Wordling and Friend.* Northampton, MA: Smith College Studies in Modern Languages, 1933.

MacIntyre, Alasdair. *Secularization and Moral Change.* London: Oxford University Press, 1967.

Mannheim, Karl. *Conservatism: A Contribution to the Sociology of Knowledge.* Trans. David Kettler and Volker Meja. Ed. David Kettler, Volker Meja, and Nico Stehr. London: Routledge and Kegan Paul, 1986.

Marcoux, J. Paul. *Guilbert de Pixérécourt: French Melodrama in the Early Nineteenth Century.* New York: Lang, 1992.

Marder, Louis. *His Exits and His Entrances: The Story of Shakespeare's Reputation.* Philadelphia: University of Pennsylvania Press, 1963.

Markley, Robert. "Sentimentality as Performance: Shaftesbury, Sterne, and the Theatrics of Virtue." In *The New Eighteenth Century,* ed. Felicity Nussbaum and Laura Brown, 210–30. London: Methuen, 1987.

Marotti, Arthur. *Religious Ideology and Cultural Fantasy.* Notre Dame, IN: University of Notre Dame Press, 2005.
Marsden, Jean I. "Daddy's Girls: Shakespearian Daughters and Eighteenth-Century Ideology." *Shakespeare Survey* 51 (1998): 17–26.
———. *The Re-Imagined Text: Shakespeare, Adaptation, & Eighteenth-Century Literary Theory.* Lexington: University of Kentucky Press, 1995.
Marshall, David. *The Figure of the Theater: Shaftesbury, Defoe, Adam Smith, and George Eliot.* New York: Columbia University Press, 1986.
Martin, Xavier. "The Paternal Role and the Napoleonic Code." In *Paternity and Fatherhood: Myths and Realities,* ed. Lieve Spass, 27–39. London: Macmillan, 1998.
Mathias, T. J. *The Pursuits of Literature: A Satirical Poem in Four Dialogues.* 4th ed. London: Owen, 1797. Reprint, *Gothic Documents: A Sourcebook 1700–1820,* ed. E. J. Clery and Robert Miles, 189–91. Manchester: Manchester University Press, 2000.
Maxwell, Richard. *The Historical Novel in Europe, 1650–1950.* Cambridge: Cambridge University Press, 2009.
May, Charles. *The Short Story: The Reality of Artifice.* New York: Twayne, 1995.
Mayo, Robert D. "Ann Radcliffe and Ducray-Duminil." *Modern Language Review* 36 (1941): 501–5.
———. "The Contemporaneity of the *Lyrical Ballads.*" *PMLA* 69 (1954): 486–522.
———. "Gothic Romance in the Magazines." *PMLA* 65 (1950): 762–89.
———. "The Gothic Short Story in the Magazines." *Modern Language Review* 37 (1942): 448–54.
———. "How Long Was Gothic Fiction in Vogue?" *Modern Language Notes* 58 (1943): 58–64.
McCalman, Iain. "The Virtual Infernal: Philippe de Loutherbourg, William Beckford and the Spectacle of the Sublime." *Romanticism on the Net.* http://www.erudit.org/revue/ron/2007/v/n46/016129ar.html (March 1, 2009).
McGann, Jerome. *The Poetics of Sensibility: A Revolution in Literary Style.* Oxford: Clarendon Press, 1996.
McKelvy, William R. *The English Cult of Literature: Devoted Readers, 1774–1880.* Charlottesville: University of Virginia Press, 2007.
McLane, Maureen. *Balladeering, Minstrelsy, and the Making of British Romantic Poetry.* Cambridge: Cambridge University Press, 2008.
———. "Ballads and Bards: British Romantic Orality." *Modern Philology* 98 (2001): 423–43.
McWhir, Ann. "The Gothic Transgression of Disbelief: Walpole, Radcliffe, and Lewis." In *Gothic Fictions: Prohibition/Transgression,* ed. Kenneth W. Graham, 29–48. New York: AMS Press, 1989.
Mellor, Anne. "English Women Writers and the French Revolution." In *Rebel Daughters: Women and the French Revolution,* ed. Sara Melzer and Leslie W. Rabine, 255–72. Oxford: Oxford University Press, 1992.
———. *Mothers of the Nation: Women's Political Writing in England, 1780–1830.* Bloomington: Indiana University Press, 2000.
Micale, Mark S., and Roy Porter, eds. *Discovering the History of Psychiatry.* New York: Oxford University Press, 1994.
Mighall, Robert. "History as Nightmare." In *A Geography of Victorian Gothic Fiction: Mapping History's Nightmares,* 1–26. Oxford: Oxford University Press, 1999.

Miles, Robert. "Europhobia: The Catholic Other in Horace Walpole and Charles Maturin." In *European Gothic: A Spirited Exchange,* ed. Avril Horner, 84–103. Manchester: Manchester University Press, 2002.

———. "Gothic: The New Romanticism." Paper delivered at North American Association for the Study of Romanticism (NASSR) conference, Fordham University–NYC, August 2003.

———. *Gothic Writing 1750–1820: A Genealogy.* London: Routledge, 1993.

———. "Romanticism, Enlightenment, and Mediation: The Case of the Inner Stranger." In *This Is Enlightenment,* ed. Clifford Siskin and William Warner. Chicago: University of Chicago Press, 2010.

———. *Romantic Misfits.* New York: Palgrave, 2008.

———. "The 1790s: The Effulgence of Gothic." In *The Cambridge Companion to Gothic Fiction,* ed. Jerrold E. Hogle, 41–62. Cambridge: Cambridge University Press, 2002.

Miller, J. Hillis. *Poets of Reality.* Cambridge, MA: Harvard University Press, 1965.

Mishra, Vijay. *The Gothic Sublime.* Albany: State University of New York Press, 1994.

Money-Kyrle, Roger E. *Superstition and Society.* London: Hogarth, 1939.

Mongan, Agnes. "Ingres and the Antique." *Journal of the Warburg and Courtauld Institutes* 10 (1947): 1–13.

Monk, Samuel. *The Sublime: A Study of Critical Theories in XVIII-Century England.* 1935. Reprint, Ann Arbor: University of Michigan Press, 1960.

Monod, Jean-Claude. *La Querelle de la secularization de Hegel à Blumenberg.* Paris: Librairie Philosophique J. Vrin, 2002.

Moody, Jane. *Illegitimate Theatre in London, 1770–1840.* Cambridge: Cambridge University Press, 2000.

Morris, David B. "Gothic Sublimity." *New Literary History* 16 (1985): 299–319.

———. *The Religious Sublime: Christian Poetry and the Critical Tradition in Eighteenth-Century England.* Lexington: University of Kentucky Press, 1972.

Mortensen, Peter. *British Romanticism and Continental Influences: Writing in an Age of Europhobia.* New York: Palgrave, 2004.

———. "The Englishness of the English Gothic Novel: Romance Writings in an Age of Europhobia." In *"Better in France?": The Circulation of Ideas across the Channel in the Eighteenth Century,* ed. Fréderic Ogée, 269–97. Lewisburg, PA: Bucknell University Press, 2005.

Mowl, Timothy. *Horace Walpole: The Great Outsider.* London: Murray, 1996.

Mudge, Bradford K. "'Excited by Trick': Coleridge and the Gothic Imagination." *Wordsworth Circle* 22 (1991): 179–84.

———. "The Man with Two Brains: Gothic Novels, Popular Culture, Literary History." *PMLA* 107 (1992): 92–104.

Mullan, John. "Feelings and Novels." In *Rewriting the Self: Histories from the Renaissance to the Present,* ed. Roy Porter, 119–34. New York: Routledge, 1997.

———. *Sentiment and Sociability: The Language of Feeling in the Eighteenth Century.* Oxford: Clarendon Press, 1988.

Mulvey-Roberts, Marie, ed. *The Handbook to Gothic Literature.* New York: New York University Press, 1998.

Murphy, Agnes C. *Banditry, Chivalry, and Terror in German Fiction, 1790–1830.* Chicago: University of Chicago Press, 1935.

Myrone, Martin, and Mervyn Heard. "The Phantasmagoria." In *Gothic Nightmares: Fuseli, Blake and the Romantic Imagination,* ed. Martin Myrone, 146–49. London:

Tate Publishing, 2006.
Nairn, Tom. *The Break-Up of Britain: Crisis and Neo-Nationalism.* London: New Left Books, 1977.
Napier, Elizabeth. *The Failure of the Gothic.* Oxford: Oxford University Press, 1987.
Nelson, Victoria. "Faux Catholic: A Gothic Subgenre from Monk Lewis to Dan Brown." *boundary 2* 34 (2007): 87–107.
———. *The Secret Life of Puppets.* Cambridge, MA: Harvard University Press, 2001.
Newman, Gerald. *The Rise of English Nationalism: A Cultural History, 1740–1830.* New York: St. Martin's, 1997.
Newman, Steve. *Ballad Collection, Lyric, and the Canon: The Call of the Popular from the Restoration to the New Criticism.* Philadelphia: University of Pennsylvania Press, 2007.
Newton, Michael. *Savage Girls and Wild Boys: A History of Feral Children.* London: Faber and Faber, 2002.
Nicholl, Allardyce. *A History of English Drama, 1660–1900. Volume IV: Early Nineteenth-Century Drama 1800–1850.* Cambridge: Cambridge University Press, 1955.
Nodier, Charles. "Critique Litttéraire: Le Petit Pierre, traduit de l'allemand, de Speiss (I)." *Annales de la Litterature et des Arts,* 16e livraison (1821).
Oergel, Maike. "The Redeeming Teuton: Nineteenth-Century Notions of the 'Germanic' in England and Germany." In *Imagining Nations,* ed. Geoffrey Cubitt, 75–91. Manchester : Manchester University Press, 1998.
Okun, Henry. "Ossian in Painting." *Journal of the Warburg and Courtauld Institutes* 30 (1967): 327–56.
O'Malley, Patrick R. *Catholicism, Sexual Deviance, and Victorian Gothic Culture.* Cambridge: Cambridge University Press, 2006.
Otto, Rudolf. *The Idea of the Holy: An Inquiry into the Non-Rational Factor in the Idea of the Divine and Its Relation to the Rational.* Trans. John W. Harvey. New York: Oxford University Press, 1950.
Owen, Alex. *The Place of Enchantment: British Occultism and the Culture of the Modern.* Chicago: University of Chicago Press, 2004.
Paisiello, Giovanni. *Nina, o sia, La pazza per amore.* DVD videorecording. Munich: Arthaus Musik, 2002. 1 videodisc (166 min). Opera buffa in prose and verse in 2 acts (1790 version). Libretto by Giuseppe Antonio Carpani, expanded by Giovanni Battista Lorenzi.
Parreaux, André. *The Publication of "The Monk": A Literary Event 1796–1798.* Paris: Didier, 1960.
Parrish, Stephen. *The Art of the "Lyrical Ballads."* Cambridge, MA: Harvard University Press, 1973.
Pascal, Roy. *The German Sturm und Drang.* Manchester: Manchester University Press, 1953.
Paz, Denis G. *Popular Anti-Catholicism in Mid-Victorian England.* Stanford, CA: Stanford University Press, 1992.
Peck, Louis F. *A Life of Matthew G. Lewis.* Cambridge, MA: Harvard University Press, 1961.
Peckham, Morse. *Beyond the Tragic Vision: The Quest for Identity in the Nineteenth Century.* New York: Braziller, 1962.
———. "Toward a Theory of Romanticism." *PMLA* 66 (1951): 5–23.
Pecora, Vincent. *Secularization and Cultural Criticism: Religion, Nation, & Modernity.*

Chicago: University of Chicago Press, 2006.
Pfau, Thomas. *Romantic Moods: Paranoia, Trauma, and Melancholy, 1790–1840.* Baltimore: Johns Hopkins University Press, 2005.
Pinch, Adela. *Strange Fits of Passion: Epistemologies of Emotion, Hume to Austen.* Stanford, CA: Stanford University Press, 1996.
Pixérécourt, René-Charles Guilbert de. *Coelina.* In *Théâtre Choisi.* Introduction by Charles Nodier. 4 vols. Paris: 1841.
———. "Melodrama" and "Final Reflections on Melodrama." In *Pixérécourt: Four Melodramas,* trans. and ed. Daniel Gerould and Marvin Carlson, 311–18. New York: Segal Theater Center, 2002.
Pocock, J. A. G. *Virtue, Commerce, and History: Essays on Political Thought and History, Chiefly in the Eighteenth Century.* Cambridge: Cambridge University Press, 1985.
Porte, Joel. "In the Hands of an Angry God: Religious Terror in Gothic Fiction." In *The Gothic Imagination,* ed. G. R. Thompson, 42–64. Spokane: Washington State University Press, 1974.
Porter, Dennis. *The Pursuit of Crime.* New Haven, CT: Yale University Press, 1981.
Potter, Franz. *The History of Gothic Publishing, 1800–1835: Exhuming the Trade.* New York: Palgrave, 2005.
———. *Romances and Gothic Tales.* Crestline, CA: Zittaw, 2003.
———, ed. *Literary Mushrooms: Tales from the Gothic Chapbooks,* Crestline, CA: Zittaw, 2009.
Pratt, Vernon. *Religion and Secularisation.* London: Macmillan, 1971.
Primeau, John K. "The Influence of Gottfried August Bürger on the *Lyrical Ballads* of William Wordsworth: The Supernatural vs. the Natural." *Germanic Review* 58 (1983): 89–96.
Punter, David. *The Literature of Terror: A History of Gothic Fictions from 1765 to the Present Day.* London: Longman, 1980, rpt. 1996.
———. "The Uncanny." In *The Routledge Companion to the Gothic,* ed. Catherine Spooner and Emma McEvoy, 129–36. London: Routledge, 2007.
———, and Elizabeth Bronfen. "Violence, Trauma, and the Ethical." In *The Gothic,* ed. Fred Botting, 7–21. Cambridge: Boydell and Brewer, 2001.
Purves, Maria. *The Gothic and Catholicism: Religion, Cultural Exchange and the Popular Novel, 1785–1829.* Cardiff: University of Wales Press, 2009.
Pye, Henry James. "Advertisement." In *Lenore, A Tale: From the German of Gottfried Augustus Bürger.* Trans. Henry James Pye. London: Sampson Low, 1976.
Rabkin, Eric S. *The Fantastic in Literature.* Princeton, NJ: Princeton University Press, 1976.
Radcliffe, Ann. "The Supernatural in Poetry." *New Monthly Magazine and Literary Journal* 7 (1826): 145–52. Reprinted in *Gothic Documents: A Sourcebook 1700–1820,* ed. E. J. Clery and Robert Miles, 163–72. Manchester: Manchester University Press, 2000.
Rahill, Frank. *The World of Melodrama.* University Park: Pennsylvania State University Press, 1967.
Railo, Eino. *The Haunted Castle: A Study of the Elements of English Romanticism.* 1927. Reprint, New York: Humanities, 1964.
Ranger, Paul. *'Terror and Pity reign in every Breast': Gothic Drama in the London Patent Theatres, 1750–1820.* London: Society for Theatre Research, 1991.
Reed, Edward. *From Soul to Mind: The Emergence of Psychology from Erasmus Darwin*

to William James. New Haven, CT: Yale University Press, 1997.

Rees, Terence. *Theatre Lighting in the Age of Gas*. London: Society for Theatre Research, 1978.

Reno, Robert P. "James Boaden's *Fontainville Forest* and Matthew Lewis' *The Castle Spectre*: Challenges of the Supernatural Ghost on the Late Eighteenth-Century Stage." *Eighteenth-Century Life*, n.s., 9 (1984): 94–106.

Richards, Graham. *Mental Machinery: The Origins and Consequences of Psychological Ideas, Part I: 1600–1850*. Baltimore: Johns Hopkins University Press, 1992.

Richardson, Alan. *British Romanticism and the Science of the Mind*. Cambridge: Cambridge University Press, 2001.

Richter, David. *The Progress of Romance: Literary Historiography and the Gothic Novel*. Columbus: Ohio State University Press, 1996.

———. "The Reception of the Gothic Novel in the 1790s." In *The Idea of the Novel in the Eighteenth Century*, ed. Robert Uphaus, 117–37. East Lansing, MI: Colleagues Press, 1988.

Robbins, Bruce. *The Servant's Hand: English Fiction from Below*. New York: Columbia University Press, 1986.

Robinson, Michael. *Giovanni Paisiello: A Thematic Catalogue of His Works*. Stuyvesant, NY: Pendragon Press, 1991.

Root-Bernstein, Michele. *Boulevard Theater and Revolution in Eighteenth-Century Paris*. Ann Arbor, MI: UMI Research Press, 1984.

Roy, G. Ross. "Some Notes on Scottish Chapbooks." *Scottish Literary Journal* 1 (1974): 50–60.

Royle, Nicholas. *The Uncanny*. Manchester: Manchester University Press, 2003.

Russell, Corinna. "A Defense of Tautology: Repetition and Difference in Wordsworth's Note to 'The Thorn.'" *Paragraph* 28 (2005): 104–18.

Ryan, Robert. *The Romantic Reformation: Religious Politics in English Literature, 1789–1824*. Cambridge: Cambridge University Press, 1997.

Rzepka, Charles. "From Relics to Remains: Wordsworth's 'The Thorn' and the Emergence of Secular History." In *Romanticism on the Net* 31 (2003). http://www.erudit.org/revue/ron/2003/v/n31/008696ar.html (March 1, 2009).

Sage, Victor. *Horror Fiction in the Protestant Tradition*. London: Macmillan, 1988.

Saggini, Francesa. "Radcliffe's Novels and Boaden's Dramas: Bringing the Configurations of the Gothic on Stage." http://www.unipr.it/arpa/dipling/GT/Saggini/saggini.html (March 1, 2009).

Saler, Michael. "Modernity and Enchantment: A Historiographic Review." *American Historical Review* 3 (2006): 692–716.

Scantlebury, Thomas. *The Rights of Protestants Asserted*. London: Lane, 1798.

Schiller, Friedrich. *The Ghost Seer; or, Apparitionist: an interesting fragment, found among the papers of Count O***** From the German of Schiller*. New-York: T. and J. Swords, 1796.

Schmidgall, Gary. *Literature as Opera*. New York: Oxford University Press, 1977.

Schmidt, Giovanni. Libretto. *Elisabetta, Regina D'Inghileterra*. Music by Gioachino Rossini. Reprint, *Early Romantic Opera*. Vol. 7. New York: Garland, 1979.

Schoch, Richard W. *Victorian Theatrical Burlesques*. Aldershot, UK: Ashgate Publishing, 2003.

Scholes, Percy A. *The Oxford Companion to Music, Self-Indexed and with a Pronouncing Glossary and over 1,100 Portraits and Pictures*. 9th ed. London: Oxford University

Press, 1955.

Scott, Walter. "Essay on Imitations of the Ancient Ballad." 1830. In *Minstrelsy of the Scottish Border,* 4 vols. Reprint, Edinburgh: Oliver and Boyd, 1932.

———. "Mrs. Ann Radcliffe." In *The Lives of Eminent Novelists and Dramatists,* 337–89. London: Frederick Warne, 1834.

Scribe, Eugene, and Germain Delavigne. Libretto. *Robert Le Diable.* Music by Giacomo Meyerbeer. Reprint, *Early Romantic Opera.* Vol. 19. New York: Garland Publishing, 1980.

Scrivener, Michael. "Habermas, Romanticism, and Literary Theory." *Literature Compass* 1 (November 2004). http://www.blackwell-compass.com/subject/literature/article_view?article_id=lico_articles_bs1127 (March 1, 2009).

Scull, Andrew. *The Most Solitary of Afflictions: Madness and Society in Britain 1700–1900.* New Haven, CT: Yale University Press, 1993.

Sedgwick, Eve. *The Coherence of Gothic Conventions.* New York: Arno, 1980.

Shawe-Taylor, Desmond. "Performance Portraits." *Shakespeare Survey* 51 (1998): 107–23.

Shell, Alison. *Oral Culture and Catholicism in Early Modern England.* New York: Cambridge University Press, 2007.

Shepherd, Simon. "Melodrama as Avant-garde: Enacting a New Subjectivity." *Textual Practice* 10 (1996): 507–22.

———, and Peter Womack, eds. *English Drama: A Cultural History.* Oxford: Blackwell Publishing, 1996.

Sherbo, Arthur. *English Sentimental Drama.* East Lansing: Michigan State University Press, 1957.

Sheriff, John K. *The Good-Natured Man: The Evolution of a Moral Ideal, 1660–1800.* Tuscaloosa: University of Alabama Press, 1982.

Siebers, Tobin. *The Romantic Fantastic.* Ithaca, NY: Cornell University Press, 1984.

Simpson, David. *Romanticism, Nationalism, and the Revolt against Theory.* Chicago: University of Chicago Press, 1993.

Siskin, Clifford. *The Historicity of Romantic Discourse.* New York: Oxford University Press, 1988.

———. "Wordsworth's Gothic Endeavor." *Wordsworth Circle* 10 (1979): 161–73.

———. *The Work of Writing: Literature and Social Change in Britain, 1700–1830.* Baltimore: Johns Hopkins University Press, 1998.

Smiley, Jane. "Shakespeare in Iceland." In *Transforming Shakespeare: Contemporary Women's Re-Visions in Literature and Performance,* ed. Marianne Novy, 159–80. New York: St. Martin's, 1999.

Smith, Adam. "The Theory of the Moral Sentiments" (1759). In *British Moralists.* 1897, ed. L. A. Selby-Bigge. Reprint, Indianapolis, IN: Bobbs-Merrill, 1964.

Smith, Christopher. "*Ossian, ou Les Bardes:* An Opera by Jean-François Le Sueur." In *From Gaelic to Romantic: Ossianic Translations,* ed. Fiona J. Stafford and Howard Gaskill, 153–63. Atlanta: Rodopi, 1998.

Smith, Christopher. "Robert Southey and the Emergence of Lyrical Ballads." *Romanticism on the Net* 9 (1998). http://www.erudit.org/revue/ron/1998/v/n9/005792ar.html (March 1, 2009).

Smith, James. *Melodrama.* London: Methuen, 1973.

Smith, Jonathan Z. *To Take Place: Toward Theory in Ritual.* Chicago: University of Chicago Press, 1987.

Smith, Ruth. *Handel's Oratorios and Eighteenth-Century Thought*. Cambridge: Cambridge University Press, 1995.

Solomon, Robert C. "In Defense of Sentimentality." *Philosophy and Literature* 14 (1990): 304–23.

Southey, Robert. *The Book of the Church*. 2 vols. London: Murray, 1824.

———. "The Old Woman of Berkeley." 1802. In *The Poetical Works of Robert Southey, Collected by Himself*. 10 vols. London: Longman, 1838.

Spacks, Patricia Meyer. *The Insistence of Horror: Aspects of the Supernatural in Eighteenth-Century Poetry*. Cambridge, MA: Harvard University Press, 1962.

Sprague, Arthur C. *Shakespeare and the Actors: The Stage Business in His Plays, 1660–1905*. Cambridge, MA: Harvard University Press, 1944.

St. Clair, William. *The Reading Nation in the Romantic Period*. Cambridge: Cambridge University Press, 2004.

Stafford, Barbara, and Frances Terpak. *Devices of Wonder: From the World in a Box to Images on a Screen*. Los Angeles: Getty, 2001.

Stark, Rodney, and William Bainbridge. *The Future of Religion: Secularization, Revival and Cult Formation*. Berkeley: University of California Press, 1985.

Staves, Susan. "British Seduced Maidens." *Eighteenth-Century Studies* 14 (1980): 109–34.

Stephanson, Raymond. "Richardson's 'Nerves': The Physiology of Sensibility in *Clarissa*." *Journal of the History of Ideas* 49 (1988): 284.

Stewart, Susan. *Crimes of Writing: Problems in the Containment of Representation*. Durham, NC: Duke University Press, 1994.

Stockley, Violet. *German Literature as Known in England: 1750–1830*. London: Routledge, 1929. Reprint, Port Washington, NY: Kennikat Press, 1969.

Stone, Lawrence. *The Family, Sex and Marriage in England 1500–1800*. New York: Harper and Row, 1977.

———. "Literacy and Education in England, 1640–1900." *Past & Present* 42 (1969): 109–25.

Stones, Graeme. Introduction to *Parodies of the Romantic Age*. Ed. Graeme Stones and John Strachan. 5 vols. London: Pickering and Chatto, 1999.

Summers, Montague. *The Gothic Quest: A History of the Gothic Novel*. London: Fortune, 1938.

Swann, Karen. "'Martha's Name,' or the Scandal of 'The Thorn.'" In *Dwelling in Possibility: Women Poets and Critics on Poetry*, ed. Yopie Prins and Maeera Shreiber, 60–79. Ithaca, NY: Cornell University Press, 1997.

———. "Public Transport: English Romantic Experiments in Sensation." *American Notes and Queries* 6 (1993): 136–42.

Sweet, Nanora. "Felicia Hemans's *A Tale of the Secret Tribunal*: Gothic Empire in the Age of Jeremy Bentham and Walter Scott." *European Journal of English Studies* 6 (2002): 159–71.

Symonds, Deborah. *Weep Not for Me: Women, Ballads, and Infanticide in Early Modern Scotland*. University Park: Pennsylvania State University Press, 1997.

Tarr, S. Mary Margaret. *Catholicism in Gothic Fiction*. Washington, DC: Catholic University Press, 1946.

Taylor, Charles. *A Secular Age*. Cambridge, MA: Harvard University Press, 2007.

Taylor, George. *The French Revolution and the London Stage, 1789–1805*. Cambridge: Cambridge University Press, 2000.

Taylor, Mark C. *After God*. Chicago: University of Chicago Press, 2007.
Thomas, Keith. *Religion and the Decline of Magic*. New York: Scribner's, 1971.
Thompson, Benjamin. *The German Theatre*. 6 vols. London: Vernor, Hood and Sharpe, 1811.
Thompson, G. Richard. Introduction to *Romantic Gothic Tales: 1790–1840*. New York: Harper & Row, 1979.
———. "Introduction: Romanticism and the Gothic Tradition." In *The Gothic Imagination: Essays in Dark Romanticism*. Pullman: Washington State University Press, 1974.
Thornburn, David, and Geoffrey Hartman, eds. *Romanticism: Vistas, Instances, Continuities*. Ithaca, NY: Cornell University Press, 1973.
Todorov, Tzvetan. *The Fantastic*. Trans. Richard Howard. Cleveland, OH: Case Western Reserve University Press, 1973.
Tompkins, J. M. S. *The Popular Novel in England, 1770–1800*. 1932. Reprint, London: Methuen, 1969.
Trainer, James. *Ludwig Tieck: From Gothic to Romantic*. The Hague: Mouton, 1964.
Travitsky, Betty S. "'A Pitilesse Mother'? Reports of a Seventeenth-Century English Filicide." *Mosaic* 27 (1994): 55–76.
Trott, Nicola. "Wordsworth's Gothic Quandry." *Charles Lamb Bulletin* 110 (2000): 49–59.
Trumpener, Katie. *Bardic Nationalism: The Romantic Novel and the British Empire*. Princeton, NJ: Princeton University Press, 1997.
Turner, Victor. *The Ritual Process: Structure and Anti-Structure*. Ithaca, NY: Cornell University Press, 1969.
Ty, Eleanor. *Empowering the Feminine: The Narratives of Mary Robinson, Jane West, and Amelia Opie*. Toronto: University of Toronto Press, 1998.
Van Gennep, Arnold. *Rites of Passage*. London: Routledge, 1960.
Vansina, Jan. *Oral Tradition as History*. Madison: University of Wisconsin Press, 1985.
Varma, Devendra P. *The Gothic Flame: Being a History of the Gothic Novel in England: Its Origins, Efflorescence, Disintegration, and Reisduary Influences*. London: Arthur Barker, 1957.
Varnado, S. L. *Haunted Presence: The Numinous in Gothic Fiction*. Tuscaloosa: University of Alabama Press, 1987.
Viswanathan, Gauri. "Secularisim in the Frameword of Heterodoxy." *PMLA* 123 (2008): 466–76.
Voller, Jack G. *The Supernatural Sublime: The Metaphysics of Terror in Anglo-American Romanticism*. DeKalb: Northern Illinois University Press, 1994.
Voloshinov, V. N. *Marxism and the Philosophy of Language*. New York: Seminar Press, 1973.
Wagner, Peter. "Anti-Catholic Erotica in Eighteenth-Century England." In *Erotica and the Enlightenment*, ed. Peter Wagner, 116–92. Frankfurt: Secker & Warburg, 1991.
Walpole, Horace. *The Castle of Otranto: A Gothic Story* and *The Mysterious Mother: A Tragedy*. Ed. Frederick S. Frank. Peterborough, ON: Broadview, 2003.
Ward, Albert M. *Book Production, Fiction and the German Reading Public 1740–1800*. Oxford: Clarendon Press, 1974.
Ward, Bernard. *The Dawn of the Catholic Revival in England, 1781–1803*. London: Longmans, Green, 1909.
Warner, Marina. *Phantasmagoria: Spirit Visions, Metaphors, and Media into the Twenty-

first Century. Oxford: Oxford University Press, 2006.
Watt, James. *Contesting the Gothic: Fiction, Genre and Cultural Conflict, 1764-1832.* Cambridge: Cambridge University Press, 1999.
Watt, William. *Shilling Shockers of the Gothic School: A Study of Chapbook Gothic Romances.* New York: Russell & Russell, 1932.
Weber, Max. "Science as a Vocation." 1919. In *From Max Weber: Essays in Sociology,* trans. and ed. H. H. Gerth and C. Wright Mills, 129-56. New York: Oxford University Press, 1958.
Weiskel, Thomas. *The Romantic Sublime: Studies in the Structure and Psychology of Transcendence.* Baltimore: Johns Hopkins University Press, 1976.
Wells, Susan. *Sweet Reason: Rhetoric and the Discourses of Modernity.* Chicago: University of Chicago Press, 1996.
White, Eric Walter. *The Rise of English Opera.* London: Lehmann, 1951.
Whyte, Samuel. *A Miscellany, Containing . . . A Critique on Bürger's Lenora.* Dublin: Whyte, 1799.
Wilkinson, Sarah Scudgell. *Albert of Werdendorff, or, The Midnight Embrace: A Romance from the German.* 1812. Reprint. Ed. Franz Potter. Crestline, CA: Zittaw, 2003.
———. "The Castle Spectre: An Ancient Baronial Romance." London: Bailey, n.d.
———. "The Spectres." In *Varieties of Female Gothic.* London: Langley, 1814. Reprint. Ed. Gary Kelly, vol. 2, 273-305. London: Pickering and Chatto, 2002.
———. "The White Pilgrim." In *Varieties of Female Gothic.* London: Dean and Munday, 1818. Reprint. Ed. Gary Kelly, vol. 2, 307-36. London: Pickering and Chatto, 2002.
Williams, Anne. "Ghostly Voices: 'Gothic Opera' and the Failure of Gounod's *La Nonne Sanglante.*" In *Operatic Migrations: Transforming Words and Crossing Boundaries,* ed. Roberta M. Marvin and Downing A. Thomas, 125-44. Aldershot, UK: Ashgate Publishing, 2006.
———. "Monstrous Pleasures: Horace Walpole, Opera, and the Conception of the Gothic." *Gothic Studies* 2 (2000): 104-18.
———. "Reading Walpole Reading Shakespeare." In *Shakespearean Gothic,* ed. Christy Desmet and Anne Williams, 15-47. Cardiff: University of Wales Press, 2009.
Wilson, Lisa. "Monk Lewis as Literary Lion." *Romanticism on the Net* 8 (1997). http://www.erudit.org/revue/ron/1997/v/n8/005775ar.html (April 1, 2009).
Wiltshire, John. *Recreating Jane Austen.* Cambridge: Cambridge University Press, 2001.
Wood, Gillen D'Arcy. *The Shock of the Real: Romanticism and Visual Culture.* Basingstoke: Palgrave, 2001.
Wordsworth, William. *Essay, supplementary to the Preface.* In *The Prose Works of William Wordsworth,* ed. W. J. B. Owen and Jane W. Smyser. 3 vols. Oxford: Oxford University Press, 1974.
———. *The Letters of William Wordsworth.* Ed. Philip Wayne. London: Oxford University Press, 1954.
———. *The Prose Works of William Wordsworth.* Ed. W. J. B. Owen and Jane W. Smyser. 3 vols. Oxford: Clarendon, 1974.
———. "The Thorn." In *The Poetical Works of William Wordsworth,* ed. Ernest de Selincourt and Helen Darbishire. 5 vols. Oxford: Clarendon, 1940-49.
———. "Written on a Blank Leaf of Macpherson's *Ossian.*" In *Sonnet Series and Itinerary Poems, 1820-1845, by William Wordsworth,* ed. Geoffrey Jackson, 610-12. Ithaca, NY: Cornell University Press, 2004.
Wright, Angela. "'The Sanctuary is Prophaned': Religion, Nationalism and the Gothic."

In *Gothic Fiction*, 74–96. New York: Palgrave, 2007.
Wu, Duncan. *Wordsworth's Reading, 1770–1799*. Cambridge: Cambridge University Press, 1993.
Young, Edward. Introduction to *The Complaint, or Night Thoughts on Life, Death and Immortality*. Ed. Stephen Cornfold. Cambridge: Cambridge University Press, 1989.
Zagorin, Perez. "The Idea of Religious Toleration in the Enlightenment and After." In *How the Idea of Religious Toleration Came to the West*, 289–312. Princeton, NJ: Princeton University Press, 2003.
Zipes, Jack. *Fairy Tale as Myth: Myth as Fairy Tale*. Lexington: University of Kentucky Press, 1994.
———. *When Dreams Came True: Classical Fairy Tales and Their Tradition*. 2nd ed. New York: Routledge, 2007.
———. *Why Fairy Tales Stick: The Evolution and Relevance of a Genre*. New York: Routledge, 2006.
———, ed. *Spells of Enchantment: The Wondrous Fairy Tales of Western Culture*. New York: Viking, 1991.
Ziter, Edward. *The Orient on the Victorian Stage*. Cambridge: Cambridge University Press, 2003.
Žižek, Slavoy. "I Hear You with My Eyes." In *Gaze and Voice as Love Objects*, ed. Renata Alecl and Slavoj Žižek, 90–127. Durham, NC: Duke University Press, 1996.
———. *Looking Awry: An Introduction to Jacques Lacan through Popular Culture*. Cambridge, MA: MIT Press, 1991.

- INDEX -

Abbé, L de l'Epée (Bouilly), 137, 141, 144, 247n5
Abrams, M. H., 112
"Abduction, The" (Lewis), 203
Addison, Joseph, 42, 129, 170
Adèle et Théodore (Genlis), 81, 96
Adorno, Theodore, 48
Adventures of King Richard Coeur-De-Lion, The (White), 82
"Affecting History of the Duchess of C**, The" (Genlis), 81, 96, 219
Agathon (Wieland), 204
Agnese di Fitzhenry (Paër), 42–43, 47, 68–70
Aikin, John, 200
"Albert of Werdendorff; or The Midnight Embrace" (Wilkinson), 215–19
Alexander, Boyd, 107
Alexis; ou La Maisonnette dans les bois (Ducray-Duminil), 151
All's Well That Ends Well (Shakespeare), 35
"Alonzo the Brave and the Fair Imogene" (Lewis), 106, 215, 217
Alonzo the Brave, or The Spectre Bride (Milner), 106
Althusser, Louis, 10

Ancient and Modern Scottish Songs (Herd), 181–82
L'Amour conjugal (Mayr), 98
Amours du Chevalier de Faublas, Les (Courvray), 82
Anderson, Benedict, 101, 122
"Andrea Vesalius the Anatomist" (Borel), 22
anti-Catholic, and gothic. *See* Gothic and anti-Catholic.
anti-clerical French dramas, 122–23; French novels, 242n15
Apel, Johann August, 199
Aretino, Pietro, 242n15
Argens, Jean Baptiste, 122
Arnold, Samuel, 62
Atwood, Margaret, 70, 243n6
Auden, W. H., 244n3
Auerbach, Erich, 143
Austen, Jane, 46, 58
Austin, J. L., 217
Averill, James, 185
Avison, Charles, 77

Backsheider, Paula, 105, 112, 143
Baillie, Joanna, 107, 116
Bakhtin, Mikhail, xiv, 14, 183
Baldick, Chris, 231, 234–35

INDEX

ballads, Germanic *volk,* 165–66, 174–75; Gothic, 12, 17, 163; of infanticide, 180–82, 248–49n6. *See* Gothic and ballads.
Ballin, Rosetta, 85
Balthazar, Scott, 100
Balzac, Honoré de, 29
Banditti, or Love's Labyrinth, The (Arnold), 78
Bannerman, Anne, 165
Barbauld, Anna Letitia, 110, 164, 200
"Bard, The" (Gray), 121
Barthes, Roland, 244n3
Bartoli, Cecilia, 52
Battle of Carnival and Lent, The (Brueghel), xiii, 17
Baudrillard, Jean, 145
Baumann, Thomas, 244n2
Beattie, James, 77
Beaumarchais, Pierre, 80, 138, 245n4
Beckford, William, 107
Becker, Ernest, 235, 251n4
Bede, The Venerable, 236
Beddoes, Thomas, 203
Beddoes, Thomas Lovell (son of Thomas Beddoes), 203
Beethoven, Ludwig von, 79, 98–100
Beggar's Opera, The (Gay), 63
Behrendt, Stephen, 134
Bell, Charles, 45
Bell, Daniel, 239n1
Berlioz, Hector, 73
Bergman, Ingmar, 237n1
Berton, H.-M., 94
Bertram; or the Castle of St. Alodbrand (Maturin), 6, 20, 241n7
Bewell, Alan, 175
Bible, 46, 71, 73
Bibliothèque bleue, 202
Bickerstaffe, Isaac, 47, 62
Biographia Literaria (Coleridge), 172–73, 200, 241n7
Biographien der Selbstmörder (Spiess), 23
Birchall, Robert, 67
Bishop, Henry, 222
Blackwood's Edinburgh Magazine, 72
Blair, Hugh, 248n5

Blake, William, 72, 95, 155, 166
Bleeck, Pieter van, 61, 66
"Blonde Eckbert, The" (Tieck), 205
Bloom, Harold, 44
Blue Beard (Colman), 83, 94
Blumenberg, Hans, 232, 251n2
Boaden, James, 22, 114, 118, 123, 126, 129–32, 134, 137, 143, 245n2, 245–46n3
Bolton, Betsy, 139
Booth, W., 68
Borderers, The (Wordsworth), 12, 118, 169, 171, 241n7
Borel, Pétrus
Boucicault, Dion, 247n7
Bouilly, Jean-Nicolas, 94, 98–99, 144, 137, 141, 144, 149
Brewer, James Norris, 128
Brewster, David, 111
"Bride of Corinth, The" (Goethe), 180–81
Bronfen, Elizabeth, 184
Brontë, Charlotte, 26, 201
Brontë, Emily, 201
Brooks, Peter, xv, 161
Brown, Marshall, xvii, 19
Brown, Theo, 225
Brueghel, Pieter, xiii–xvi, 17, 147, 232, 237n1
buffered self. *See* porous vs. buffered self
Buonavoglia, Luigi, 69
Bürger, Gottfried August, 24, 164–68, 172, 178–79, 186, 189–94, 217, 224
Burke, Edmund, theories of the sublime, 20, 93, 116–18, 129, 161, 169, 170, 174, 246n4
Burns, Robert, 165, 168
Burwick, Frederick, 83, 245n2
Busby, Thomas, 159, 247n6
Butler, Marilyn, 169
Byron, Lord (George Gordon), 12, 26, 72, 78, 119, 199, 201

Cabinet des Fées, Les (Mayer), 202
Cagliostro, Count, 22, 111, 203
Cambro-Britons, The (Boaden), 118, 132–34
camera obscura, 109, 113, 200

Camilla, o sia Il sotterraneo (Paër), 96, 254n7
Camille; or, the Fate of a Coquette (Heron), 245n7
Camille, ou le Souterrein (Marsollier des Vivetières), 81, 245n7
Campavert: Contes Immoraux (Borel), 21
Canuel, Mark, 239n6
Carlyle, Thomas, 24, 78, 205
Casanova, Jose, 241n6
Castelvecchi, Stefano, 51–52
Castle of Otranto, The (Walpole), 19, 38, 50, 75–76, 80, 119, 144–45, 206
Castle of Wolfenbach, The (Parsons), 82, 215, 219–20
Castle Spectre, The (Wilkinson), 215, 224–27
Castle Spectre, The (Lewis), 6, 20, 83, 114–17, 123–29, 132, 143, 153, 220, 224, 226, 241n7, 245n2
Castle, Terry, 36, 111, 238n5
Catherine of Aragon, 85, 125
Catholic, and gothic. *See* Gothic as Catholic genre
Cat's Eye, The (Atwood), 70, 243n6
Cazotte, Jacques, 6, 21–22
chapbooks, gothic
Characteristics of Women, Moral, Poetical, and Historical (Jameson), 58
Charlotte, Princess, 134–35
Charlton, David, 79–80, 92, 99
Chateaubriand, René, 16
Château des Appenins ou le fantôme vivant, Le (Pixérécourt), 84
Château du diable, Le (Loaisel-Tréogate), 87–88
Cheap Repository Tracts (More), 199
Cherubini, Luigi, 79, 82, 94
"Christabel" (Coleridge), 31, 173, 180
Cibber, Colly, 245n1
Cibber, Susannah, 61
Cimetière de la Madeleine (Regnault-Warin), 21
Cimetière de Mousseaux (Villemain d'Abancourt), 21
circulating libraries, and chapbooks, 207–8, 228, 250n7

Clairmont, Claire, 199
Clarissa (Richardson), 41, 50, 62, 66
class anxieties. *See* Gothic and class anxieties.
Clery, Emma J., 38, 44, 112, 129, 238n6
Coelina ou l'Enfant du mystère (Pixérécourt), 97, 137–38, 140, 151–62, 247n8
Cohan, Steven, 132
Cohen, Margaret, xvi–xvii, 101
Cohen, Ralph, 163
Coleridge, Samuel Taylor, xiii, 1–2, 1, 9, 12, 24, 31, 59, 72, 86, 122, 164–65, 167–70, 172–75, 177, 180, 200–1, 204, 241n7
Coligny; ou La Saint Barthelemi (D'Arnaud), 122
Collings, David, 33
Colman, George, 83, 246n4
Complaint, The, or Night Thoughts (Young), 21, 39
Comte d'Albert (Sédaine), 100
Condillac, Étienne Bonnot de, 113
Confessions of a Justified Sinner, The (Hogg), 20, 31
Contes Turcs (Croix), 201
Corinne; or Italy (de Staël), 83
Cornfold, Stephen, 39
Corvey Castle Library (Germany), xvi, 249n2
Couvray, Jean Baptiste, 82
Couvent, ou les voeux forcés, Le (de Gouges), 122
Cowper, 168
Cox, Jeffrey, 126, 153, 247n5
Cox, Philip, 154, 246n2
Crary, Jonathan, 109, 113
Crimes of Love (Sade), 21
Croix, François Petits de la, 201
Crookenden, Isaac, 215
Cruelty, Superstition, and Fanaticism (Hogarth), 233–34
Cruikshank, George, 62

Dacre, Charlotte, 180, 189–95, 219
Dalayrac, Nicolas, 50–51, 84, 94, 100
Dame aux camélias, La (Dumas fils), 245n7

INDEX

D'Arnaud, François Thomas Marie de Baculard, 47, 50, 116, 122–23, 137, 151
Darwin, Erasmus, 45
Das Petermännchen (Spess), 23
D'Aulnoy, Countess Marie-Catherine, 202, 204
Davis, Lennard, 66
Davis, Nathalie, xiv
Dean, Winton, 49, 67, 79
Deaf and Dumb; or, The Orphan Protected (Holcroft), 137–38, 140, 144–50, 154, 157–58
Deborah (Handel), 66–67
De l'Allemagne (de Staël), 22, 101
Délassements de l'homme sensible (D'Arnaud), 50
Dennis, John, 74–75, 129
DeQuincey, Thomas, 23, 201
Derrida, Jacques, 235
Descartes, René, 113
Deserted Daughter, The (Holcroft), 137, 140
Deux journées, Les (Bouilly), 94
Dever, Carolyn, xvi–xvii, 101
Devil, demonic, beliefs in, 5–6, 28–29, 43, 89–91, 97, 104, 142, 165–67
Devil's Elixir, The (Hoffman), 24–25; versions of, 25
Diable amoureux, Le (Cazotte), 6
Dibdin, Thomas, xiii, 237n1
Diderot, Denis, 44, 48, 122
Dobson, Michael, 58
Dolar, Mladen, 238n5
Don Giovanni (Mozart), 69
Donizetti, Gaetano, 56
Dr. Jekyll and Mr. Hyde (Stevenson), 20
Dracula (Stoker), 20
Drake, Nathan, xviii
Dramatic Sketches of the Ancient Northern Mythology (Sayers), 164
"Druid, The" (Wieland), 210
Dryden, John, 119, 129, 165
Dschinnistan (Wieland), 203
Ducray-Duminil, François-Guilllaume, 151–52
Duff, William, 45–46
Dumas, Alexandre, *fils*, 245n7

Durkheim, Emile, 177–78, 186–87
During, Simon, 108

Edgcumbe, Lord Mount, 245n8
Edgeworth, Maria, 155
Eliade, Mircea, 205
Elias, Norbert, 141
Elisabetta, Regina D'Inghilterra (Rossini), 85
Elizabeth I (Queen of England), 85–86
Eliza ou le Voyage aux glaciers du Mont St. Bernard (Reveroni, Saint-Cyr), 78–79
Ellison, Julie, 43–44, 63
Empson, William, 116
Endymion (Keats), 212
"Entail, The" (Hoffman), 24
Entführung, Die (Musäus), 205
Esquirol, Jean-Étienne, 64, 243n4
Essay on Original Genius (Duff), 45
Essay on Taste (Gerard), 45
"Essay on the Operas after the Italian Manner, An," 74
Essays on Physiognomy (Lavater), 154–55
Euphémie: ou, le triomphe de la réligion (D'Arnaud), 123
Euphrosine ou le Tyran Corrige (Méhul), 94
Euripides, 119
Eyriès, J. B. B., 199
"Eve of St. Agnes, The" (Keats), 31, 217

fairy tales, as influence on chapbooks, 198, 201–2, 214, 220, 249n3; and myth, 205–6
Fantasmagoriana; ou Recueil d'Histoires d'Apparitions, de Spectres (Eyriès), 199
Father and Daughter, The (Opie), 41, 47, 57–63, 72, 214, 219
Faust (Goethe), 39, 97
Fawcett, Joseph, 172
Fay, Elizabeth, 187
Fayel (D'Arnaud), 116
Feinstein, Elaine, 70, 243n6
Feuerbach, Ludwig, 232
Fidelio (Beethoven), 79, 98–100, 144

INDEX

Fiedler, Leslie, 230–31
Fielding, Henry, 103
Filmer, Robert, 55
Fish, William, 68
Five Sermons on the Errors of the Roman Catholic Church (Maturin), 28–29
Fliegende Holländer, Der ("The Flying Dutchman," Wagner), 98
Follies of a Night, The (Holcroft), 138
Ford, John, 119
Fordyce, James, 59
Forêt périlleuse des brigands de la Calabre, La (Loaisel-Tréogate), 88
Fossé, François Thomas du, 245n6
Foucault, Michel, 30, 56, 113, 121, 229
Fountainville Forest, The (Boaden), 114–17, 123, 129–31, 133
Fouqué, Friedrich de la Motte, 97
Fowler, David, 168
"Fragments of a Gothic Tale" (Wordsworth), 170
Fragoletta, ou Naples et Paris en 1799 (Latouche), 21
Frank, Frederick, 119, 227, 249n2, 249n3, 251n9
Frankenstein (Shelley), 116, 196, 199
Franklin, Benjamin, 108, 111, 202
Frederick II, 137
Freud, Sigmund, xv, 2, 24, 27, 30, 37, 59, 70, 232, 234–35, 238n5, 243n6, 251n4
Friedman, Albert, 168

Galland, Antoine, 201
Gamer, Michael, 168, 175, 241n8
Garlington, Aubrey, 75, 83, 126
Garrick, David, 44, 61–63, 69, 106–7, 129, 245n1
Gaskell, Elizabeth, 26
Geary, Robert, 251n3
Geisterbanner, Der (Kahlert), 22, 78
Geisterseher, Der (Schiller), 22
Genest, John, 128
Genlis, Stéphanie-Félicité de, 81, 96, 138, 219
Gennep, Arnold van, xiv
George III (King of Great Britain), 62, 69, 120, 134
Gerard, Alexander, 45
Ghost Book, The (Apel and Laun), 199
Ghost-Seer, The (Schiller), 22–23, 203
Gleich, Joseph Alois, 24
Godwin, William, 121, 137, 155
Goethe, Johann Wolfgang von, 22, 24, 39, 113, 138, 165, 180–81, 202, 248n2
Goldoni, Carlo, 50
Goldsmith, Oliver, 137
"Goody Blake and Harry Gill" (Wordsworth), 170
Gordon, Lord George, and Gordon Riots, 26
Gothic, as aesthetic, xv–xvi, xviii, 5, 27, 30, 38, 40, 45–47, 58, 93, 116, 121, 135, 181; as anti–Catholic, xvii–xviii, 21, 28–29, 119–20, 122, 148, 197, 225, 230, 251n1, 252n5; ballads, 163–95, history of, 247n1; as Catholic genre, xvi–xviii, 2, 23, 26–31, 86, 91–92, 98, 109, 118–20, 123, 125–26, 128, 134, 180, 188, 221, 223. 226, 230, 234; chapbooks, 196–228, history of, 249n1, 250n5, 250n6; and class anxiety, 14–15, 19, 36, 80, 136–37, 139, 145–46, 157, 214, 217–27; conflicted religious agenda in, 229–36; drama, 103–35, 143; as hybrid genre, 8, 10–11, 14–15, 139; opera, 40–41, 43–44, 74–76, 98; as public ritual or ritual practice, 9–10, 13, 15, 18, 27, 32–33, 48, 56, 70–71, 76, 92, 115, 160, 180–81, 184–85, 188, 210; as Protestant genre, xvi–xvii, 6, 8, 18, 23, 26–28, 30, 46, 86, 101, 109, 180, 187–88, 197, 199, 221, 226, 230, 233, 234
Götz von Berlichingen (Goethe), 22
Gouges, Olympe de, 122
Gounod, Charles, 85
Goya, Francisco, 8, 107, 234
Gradiva (Jensen), 59
Graham, Gordon, 4
Graham, John, 155
Gray, Thomas, 121, 165

{ 281 }

Gretry, André-Ernest-Modeste, 48
Grimm, Jacob Ludwig Carl and Wilhelm Carl, xv, 204
Guillory, John, 199
"Guilt and Sorrow" (Wordsworth), 169

Habermas, Jürgen, 8, 17–18, 177–78, 186–87, 242n12
Hamlet (Shakespeare), 59, 129
Handel, George Frideric, 66–69, 71, 77, 101
"Hart-Leap Well" (Wordsworth), 170
Hartman, Geoffrey, 247–28n1
Haunted Tower, The (Storace), 82–83
Hayles, Katherine, 6
Hazlitt, William, 23, 59, 163
Headlong Hall (Peacock), 57
Hegel, Georg William Friedrich, 10, 162, 188
Heidegger, Martin, 3
Heine, Heinrich, 74
Hemans, Felicia, 22
Henry VIII (King of England), 85, 125, 232
Herd, David, 181
Herder, Johann Gottfried, 165
"Her Eyes Are Wild" (Wordsworth), 170
L'Hermite, de la Tombe Mystérieuse (Langon), 233–34
Hermann von Unna (Naubert), 22
Hervey, Rev. James, 87
Hieroglyphic Tales, The (Walpole), 204
Hill, Aaron, 44
Hoare, Prince, 57
Hobbes, Thomas, 154–56
Hoffman, E. T. A., 24, 59, 97, 205, 207, 212
Hoffman, François B., 84
Hogarth, William, 233–34
Hogg, James, 20, 28, 112
Hogle, Jerrold, 145, 239n8, 241n8, 242n16
Holcroft, Thomas, 12, 136–62, 223, 246n1, 246n2, 246n3
Homans, Peter, 232
"House of Aspen, The" (Scott), 22
Howard, June, 42

Hughes, Derek, 92
Huguenots, Les (Meyerbeer), 92
Huish, Robert, 203
Hume, David, 28, 45, 240n2
Humphreys, Samuel, 66
Hunter, Henry, 155
Hurd, Richard, 45
Hussey, Dyneley, 79
Hutcheon, Linda, 97
Hutcheson, Frances, 42
Hyslop, Gabrielle, 146

"Idiot Boy, The" (Wordsworth), 179, 186
I Fuorusciti de Firenze (Paër), 96
Imogen (Godwin), 121
Inchbald, Elizabeth, 49, 122, 137, 140
"Incipient Madness" (Wordsworth), 169
Ingres, Jean, 95
Inkle and Yarico (Colman), 246n4
Intrigues monastiques ou l'amour encapuchonné (Argens), 122
Italian, The (Radcliffe), 22, 122–23, 152

Jacobin Espagnol, Le (Prévost), 85
Jacobus, Mary, 168
Jager, Colin, 241n6
Jameson, Anna, 58
Jameson, Fredric, 14, 72
Jane Eyre (C. Brontë), 31, 162
Jean Shogar (Nodier), 20
Jensen, Wilhelm, 59
Jentsch, Ernst, xv
Jesuits, 25–26, 29, 109, 242n15
Julie, ou la religieuse de Nîmes (Pougens), 122
Julius Caesar (Shakespeare), 245n1
Julius, or the Deaf and Dumb Orphan (anonymous), 150
Johnson, Samuel, 59, 75, 244n2
Johnston, Kenneth, 187
Johnstone, Nathan, 6
Jonson, Ben, 165
Joyce, James, 1

Kahlert, Karl Friedrich (Lorenz Flammenberg), 22, 78
Kant, Immanuel, 113

Kauffmann, Angelica, 54
Kean, Edmund, 112
Keane, Angela, xvi
Keats, John, 1, 16, 31, 122, 204, 212, 217
Kelly, Gary, 140, 197, 199–200, 251n9
Kelly, Michael, 83, 125–26
Kemble, Marie Therese, 69
Kerr, John, 224
Keyser, G. A., 204
Kiessling, Nicolas, 179
Kivy, Peter, 244n3
King Lear, The Tragedy of (Shakespeare), 46, 57–58, 60–63, 67–68, 70–73, 94, 243n5, 243n6
Kircher, Athanasius, 109
Klob, Karl M., 79
Knave, or Not? (Holcroft), 140
Koch, Angela, 249n2
"KoxKox and Kikequetzel" (Wieland), 203
Kotzebue, August Friedrich Ferdinand von, 141, 162, 246–47n5
Kreutzer, Rodolphe, 82

Lacan, Jacques, 10–11
Lamb, Charles, 59, 113, 175
Lane, William, 207
"Lass of Fair Wone, The" (Bürger), 180, 182, 189–94
"Lass of Fair Wone, The" (Dacre), 180, 182, 189–95
Latouche, Henri de, 21
Laun, Friedrich, 199
Lavater, Johann Caspar, 138, 154–55
Laws, Malcolm, 168
Lear's Daughters (Feinstein), 70, 243n6
Lear of Private Life, The (Moncrieff), 69
LeBrun, Charles, 44
Lectures on Rhetoric and Belles Lettres (Blair), 248n5
Lectures on the Philosophy of Religion (Hegel), 10
Lectures on the Sacred Poetry of the Hebrews (Lowth), 248n5
Lee, Harriet, 114
Lee, Sophia, 21, 41, 85
Legends of Terror! (anonymous), 221
Lemoine, Ann, 215

"Lenora" (Bürger), 172, 178–79, 197, 217
Lenora, ossia l'amore conjugale (Paër), 98, 100
Lenore, oder der triumph der ehelichen liebe (Beethoven), 99
Léonore ou l'amour conjugal (Bouilly), 98–99, 144
Léon, ou Le Château de Montenero (Hoffman and Dalayrac), 84
L'Éppe, Charles-Michel de, 144
Le Sueur, Jean-François, 94, 245n7
Letters from France (Williams), 245n6
Letters on Chivalry and Romance (Hurd), 45
Lévi-Strauss, Claude, 244n3
Leviathan (Hobbes), 155
Lévy, Maurice, 232
Lewis, Isabella, 197
Lewis, Matthew, 6, 13, 18, 22, 24, 26, 78, 81, 83–84, 91–92, 106, 114–17, 122–30, 132, 137, 143, 145, 153, 155, 164–65, 173–74, 180, 187, 203, 208, 215, 217–18, 220, 223–24, 226, 241n7, 242n13, 245n2
Life of John Philip Kemble, The (Boaden), 126, 129, 132
Life of Rossini (Stendahl), 68
Life of Thomas Holcroft (Holcroft and Hazlitt), 138
Lindpaintner, Peter von, 32, 98
literacy, as secularization theme in gothic, xvi, 12, 148, 207–8, 223, 228, 242n10
Literature of Terror, The (Punter), 2
Lloyd, Robert, 123
Loaisel-Tréogate, Joseph-Marie, 87–88
Locke, John, 55, 113, 117, 201
Lodoïska, versions of, 82–83
Loret, Jean, 108
Loutherbourg, Philippe Jacques de, 106–8
Love-A-La-Mode (Inchbald), 49
Lovecraft, H. P., 251n3
Lowth, Robert, 248n5
Lucile (Gretry), 48
Lucy poems (Wordsworth), 170
Lyrical Ballads and *Preface* to (Words-

worth and Coleridge), 166–88, 199–200, 248n2

Macbeth (Shakespeare), 113, 123, 129
McGann, Jerome, 36
McKelvey, William, 240n1
Machiavelli, 40
Mackenzie, Henry, 43
Macklin, Charles, 44
McLane, Maureen, 40, 166
Macpherson, James, 39, 94–95, 168
McWhir, Ann, 171, 227
"Mad Mother, The" (Southey), 248n4
Madame Putiphar (Borel), 22
Magic Flute, The (Mozart), 203
magic lantern show, history of, 106–13, 115
Maid of the Mill, The (Bickerstaffe), 47, 62
Maine de Biran, François-Pierre-Gonthier, 113
Man of Feeling, The (Mackenzie), 43
Manon Lescaut (Prévost), 41
Mansfield Park (Austen), 58, 243n5
Mariage de Figaro, Le (Beaumarchais), 80, 138, 245n4
Marder, Louis, 72–73
Markham, George, 197
Markley, Robert, 42, 47, 56, 243n2
Marschner, Heinrich, 32, 98
Marsden, Jean, 59
Marsollier des Vivetières, Benoît-Joseph, 50–51, 81
Mary Barton (Gaskell), 26
Mary, Queen of Scots, 85–86
Massacre, The (Inchbald), 122
Mathias, T. J., xviii, 166
Maturin, Charles, 6, 20, 28, 97, 241n7
Maupassant, Guy de, 207
May, Charles, 249n1
Mayer, Charles, 202
Mayo, Robert, 168, 250n6
Mayr, Simon, 98
Meeke, Mary, 151
Méhul, Etienne, 94
Mellor, Anne, 242n12
melodrama, characteristics of, 11, 52, 86, 88–89, 94, 97, 102, 105, 136–62;

history and definition of, 140–41, 246n2, 247n6, 247n8
Melmoth Réconcilié (Balzac), 29
Melmoth the Wanderer (Maturin), 6, 20, 22, 29, 31, 97
Melville, Herman, 119
Méthode pour apprendre à dessiner les passions (Le Brun), 44
Meyerbeer, Giacomo, 89, 92, 97
Midnight Hour, The (Inchbald), 49
Mighall, Robert, 231, 234–35
Miles, Robert, xvi, 18, 26, 121, 241n8, 242n11, 249n6
Milner, Henry M., 106
Milton, John, 204
Minerva Press, 23, 151, 196, 202, 207–8
"Mines at Falun, The" (Hoffman), 205
Mishra, Vijay, 246n4
Moncrieff, Thomas, 69
Money-Kyrle, Roger, 38
Moine, Le (Camaille-Saint-Aubin and Ribie), 84–85
Moine, ou la Victime de l'Orgueil, Le (Pixérécourt), 84
Molière, Jean-Baptiste Poquelin, 137
Monk, The (Lewis), 6, 18, 20–22, 24, 78, 84, 91–92, 123, 125, 173, 210, 217–18, 223, 241n7
Monod, Jean-Claude, 9
Montagu, Basil, 182, 248n6
Montagu, Elizabeth, 46
Monvel, Jacques-Marie Boutet de, 122
Moody, Jane, 105, 144, 154, 247n8
More, Hannah, 155
Mortensen, Peter, xvii, 168
Mozart, Wolfgang Amadeus, 49, 69
Mudge, Bradford, 216
Murdoch, Iris, 196
Musäus, Johann, 202
Mysteries of Udolpho, The (Radcliffe), 84, 124
Mysterious Marriage, The (Lee), 114
Mysterious Mother, The (Walpole), 118–20

Nairn, Tom, 121
Napier, Elizabeth, 36
Napoleon, 49, 56, 84, 88, 95–96, 99,

105, 137, 151–53, 210
Naubert, Christiane, 22
Necromancer, The (Kahlert), 78
Nelson, Victoria, 242n15
Neufchâteau, François de, 47
New Collection of Gothic Stories (anonymous), 250n8
Newman, Gerald, 101
Newman, Steve, 185
Nicholl, Allardyce, 246n2
Nicholson, William, 111
Nina or the love-mad Maid (Paisiello), 42–43, 46–57, 63, 68, 154, 219, 243n3, 243n4
Nodier, Charles, 20–21, 93, 151
Nonne de Lindenberg, La (Cailleran and Coupilly), 85
Nonne Sanglante, La, versions of, 85
Nouvelle Clémentine, La (D'Arnaud), 50
Nun, The (Diderot), 122

Oedipus (Sophocles), 59, 119
Offenbach, Jacques, 24
Old English Baron, The (Reeve), 80, 215
"Old Woman of Berkeley, The" (Southey), 165
O'Malley, Patrick, 251n1
"On Garrick, and Acting; and the Plays of Shakespeare" (Lamb), 113
"On Naïve and Sentimental Poetry" (Schiller), 17, 41
"On the Pleasure Derived from Objects of Terror" (Barbauld), 200
opera, British reactions to Italian, 47, 244n2; "rescue," 74–102; Sentimental, 47–57; theories of, 244n3
Opie, Amelia, 41, 47, 57–63, 68–70, 72, 210, 219
Ordeals of Sentiment, The (D'Arnaud), 50
Orra (Baillie), 116
Ossian (Macpherson), 24, 39–40, 94–95, 102, 248n2
Ossian ou Les Bardes (Le Sueur), 75, 94–96
Otto, Rudolph, 117

Paër, Fernando, 41, 47, 68–69, 95–96, 98, 100, 243n3, 245n7

Paine, Thomas, 202
Paisiello, Giovanni, 41, 47–57, 219
Pamela (Richardson), 41, 47, 50, 62, 66; operatic versions of, 47, 62
Parrish, Stephen, 175
Parsons, Eliza, 82, 215, 219–20
Patriarchia (Filmer), 55
Peacock, Thomas Love, 57
Pèlerin Blanc, Le (Pixérécourt), 215, 222
Percy, Thomas, 164–65, 168, 248n2
Perrault, Charles, 141, 204
"Peter Bell" (Wordsworth), 170, 179
Philipsthal, Paul (Paul Philidor), 109, 111–12
Philosophe anglais, Le, ou Histoire d'un M. de Clèveland (Prévost), 41, 85
"Philosopher's Stone, The" (Wieland), 203, 210, 213
Picture of Dorian Gray, The (Wilde), 20
Pinch, Adela, 44
Pinel, Philippe, 64, 243n4
Pirates, The (Storace), 82–83
"Pitilesse Mother, A" (anonymous), 180
Pixérécourt, René-Charles Guilbert de, 80, 87, 97, 137–38, 144, 151–57, 215, 222, 245n5, 147n6
Planché, J. R., 204
Pleasing Companion: A Collection of Fairy Tales, The (D'Aulnoy), 202
Pleasures of the Imagination, The (Addison), 170
Pocock, J. A. G., 40
Poe, Edgar Allan, 207
Polidori, John, 20, 98, 199
porous vs. buffered self, theories of the, 17–19, 32, 39, 41, 43, 57, 72, 86, 103–4, 107, 109–10, 115, 119, 128, 142–43, 148, 162, 165, 200, 206, 215, 231
Pope, Alexander, 187
Porter, Dennis, 21
Potter, Franz, 217, 221, 250n6
Pougens, Charles-Joseph, 122
Preston, William, 167
Prévost, L'Abbé Antoine-François, 41, 47, 50, 85
Protestant. *See* Gothic as Protestant genre

Providential Deism, theory of, 3, 18, 28, 36–37, 42–43, 47, 63, 72, 74–76
Punter, David, xvi, 2, 184, 207, 242n16, 250n7
Purves, Maria, xvi
Pye, Henry James, 166
Pygmalion (Rousseau), 141
Pyne, W. H., 106

Radcliffe, Anne, 13, 18, 22, 82, 84, 89, 117–18, 119, 122, 124, 129–30, 132, 143, 145, 151–52, 165, 173, 208, 215, 219, 221, 230, 238n6
Railo, Eino, 116
Rais, Gilles de, 84
Ranger, Paul, 106
Raoul, Barbe bleue (Sédaine and Grétry), 83–84
Raoul, Sire de Créqui (Dalayrac), 94, 100
Raüber, Die (Schiller), 78, 123, 141, 220
Raymond and Agnes (Lewis), 114
Raymond and Agnes, or The Castle of Lindenbergh (Farley), 114
Recess, The (Lee), 41, 85
Reeve, Clara, 21, 80, 145, 208, 215, 220
Regnault-Warin, Jean Joseph, 21
Reliques of Ancient English Poetry (Percy), 164, 168, 248n2
Remorse (Coleridge), xii, 78, 241n7
Reno, Robert, 128, 131, 246n3
"Rescue" opera. *See* opera.
Ribié, César, 84–85
Richard Coeur-de-lion (Sédaine), 50, 80, 82, 244n4
Richard III (Shakespeare), 38, 129, 245n1
Richardson, Samuel, 41, 43, 47, 50, 62, 140
Richter, David, 250n6, 250n7
Richter, Jean Paul, 229
Rights of Protestants Asserted, The (Scantlebury), 197
Rigueurs du cloître, Les (Berton), 94
"Rime of the Ancyent Marinere, The" (Coleridge), 165, 168, 170, 174–75, 180
Rivals, The (Sheridan), 207

Road to Ruin, The (Holcroft), 137
Robbins, Bruce, 158
Robert, chef des brigands (Lamartellière), 78
Robert le Diable (Meyerbeer), 75, 89–92; British reaction to, 245n8
Robertson, Étienne-Gaspard, 108, 110–11
Roi Lear, Le (Berlioz), 73
Romance of the Forest, The (Radcliffe), 117–18, 129, 151
Romanticism, canonical vs. gothic, 12; theories of, 237n3, 240n5, 247–48n1
Romanticist and Novelist's Library, The (Hazlitt), 23
Romeo and Juliet (Shakespeare), 94
Rossini, Gioachino Antonio, 49, 85
Rousseau, Jean Jacques, 5, 42, 141, 154
Roy, G. Ross, 198
Ruined Cottage, The (Wordsworth), 175
"Runenberg, The" (Tieck), 205
"Ruth" (Wordsworth), 170
Ryan, Robert, 38

Sade, Donatien Alphonse François, Marquis de, 13, 21, 83, 96, 229
Sage, Victor, xvi
Sagen der Vorzeit (Wächter), 23
Saggini, Francesa, 131
Said, Edward, 57, 201
Saler, Michael, 240n4
Salon de 1765 (Diderot), 44
"Sandman, The" (Hoffman), 24, 59, 205, 212
Sayers, Frank, 164
Scantlebury, Thomas, 197
Schiller, Friedrich von, 17, 22–24, 41, 123, 181, 203, 241n7
Schlegel, Friedrich, 16
Schmidgall, Gary, 77, 244n1
Scott, Walter, 12, 19, 22, 57, 111, 119, 122, 164–65, 177, 215, 224, 231
Secret Tribunal, The (Boaden), 22; versions of, 22, 89
secularization, theories of, xv, 2–4, 6, 13, 18–19, 30, 37, 59, 102–4, 109, 114–15, 166, 171, 178, 197, 199,

228, 231, 241n6
Sédaine, Michel-Jean, 50, 80, 82–83, 94, 100, 245n4
Seduction (Holcroft), 136
Sense and Sensibility (Austen), 46
Sensibility, theories of, 40–41, 49, 52, 55, 71
Sentimental Journey, A (Sterne), 54
Sentimental opera. *See* opera.
Sentimentality, theories of, 8, 11, 35–36, 41–42, 47–49, 51–52, 56–57, 59–60, 63, 71, 243n1, 243n2
Secular Age, A (Taylor), 2
Sermons for Young Ladies (Fordyce), 59
Seventh Seal, The (Bergman), 237n1
Shaftesbury, Earl of, 42, 77, 154
Shakespeare, William, 24, 32, 35, 44, 46, 57–60, 62, 68, 71, 73, 83, 93, 101–3, 113–14, 118, 129, 131–32, 204, 243n6
Sharpe, Granville, 139
Shaughraun, The (Boucicault), 247n7
Shell, Allison, 27
Shelley, Mary Wollstonecraft Godwin, 155, 199, 204
Shelley, Percy Bysshe, 12, 16, 19, 26, 122, 199, 201, 215
Shepherd, Simon, 158, 160–61
Sheridan, Richard, 207
Shirley (C. Brontë), 26
Sicilian Romance, A (Radcliffe), 82, 89, 129, 215, 219, 221
Sicilian Romance, The, or the Apparition of the Cliff (Siddons), 116, 120, 129
Siddons, Henry, 116, 120, 129, 137
Simpson, David, 246–47n5
Sinfield, Alan, 246n4
"Sir Bertram: A Fragment" (Aikin), 200
Sir Charles Grandison (Richardson), 41, 66
Siskin, Clifford, 164, 168, 241n7
Sleep of Reason Produces Monsters, The (Goya), 8, 107
"Smarra, or The Demons of the Night" (Nodier), 21
Smiles and Tears; or, The Widow's Stratagem (Kemble), 69
Smiley, Jane, 70, 243n5

Smith, Adam, 42–43, 45, 235
Smith, Charlotte, 41
Soirées de mélancolie, Les (Tréogate), 21
Sophocles, xv, 59, 119
Southey, Robert, 24, 78, 164–64, 174–75, 178; ballads on infanticide, 181–82; 204, 215, 248n4, 252n5
Spacks, Patricia, 39
Spectre of Lanmere Abbey, The (Wilkinson), 216
"Spectres, The" (Wilkinson), 215, 219–22
Spiess, Christian, 23
Sprague, Arthur C., 245n1
Staël, Germaine de, 22, 83. 101
St. Clair, William, 198, 250n5
Staudlin, Karl, 181
Statue Room, The (Ballin), 85
Staves, Susan, 70
Steele, Richard, 42
Stendahl (Marie-Henri Beyle), 68
Stephanson, Raymond, 43
Sterne, Laurence, 42, 54
Stevenson, Robert Louis, 20, 32
Stewart, Susan, 166
Stone, Lawrence, 55–56, 148
Stoker, Bram, 20, 32
Stones, Graeme, 180
Storace, Stephen, 82–83
Sublime, theories of the. *See* Edmund Burke.
Summers, Montague, 85, 198, 230, 251n1
supernatural, explained and unexplained, xv–xviii, 2–6, 8, 10, 13, 19, 23, 25–26, 37, 127–28, 131
"Supernatural in Poetry, The" (Radcliffe), 118
Swann, Karen, 175, 248n3
Swift, Jonathan, 75

Tale of Mystery, A (Holcroft), 137–40, 149, 151–62, 246n3
Tale of Mystery, A, or Celina (Meeke), 151
Tale of the Secret Tribunal, A (Hemans), 22
Tales of the Dead (Utterson), 199

Tales of Wonder (anonymous), 208–14
Tales of Wonder (Lewis), 164, 217
Tarr, S. Mary Margaret, 128, 230
Tate, Nahum, 60–61, 68
Taylor, Charles, xiv–xv, 2–3, 4–6, 11, 13, 17–18, 32, 36–37, 42, 75, 104, 110, 114–15, 142, 196, 237n3, 239n1, 240n4
Taylor, George, 160–61, 246n4, 247n8
Taylor, Mark, 239n1
Taylor, William, of Norwich, 166–67, 180, 182, 189–94, 203, 248n2
Terrific Tales (I. Lewis), 197
Theory of Moral Sentiments, The (A. Smith), 42–43
Things as They Are; or, The Adventures of Caleb Williams (Godwin), 196
Thomas, Keith, 8, 103
Thompson, G. R., 230, 238n4
"Thorn, The" (Wordsworth), 170–71, 175–88, 219, 248n4, 248–49n6
Thousand Acres, A (Smiley), 70, 243n6
Thousand and One Nights, The (Galland), 201
"Three Graves, The" (Wordsworth and Coleridge), 169
Thurston, John, 65–66
Tieck, Ludwig, 205
Titley, Walter, 103, 107
Todorov, Tzvetan, theory of the fantastic, 5
Tom Jones (Fielding), 103
Tompkins, J. M. S., 230–31
Torch of Death, The (Gleich), 24
Tour enchantée, Le (Sade), 83
Trott, Nicola, 181, 241n7
Trenck, Baron, 138
Tréogate, Joseph-Marie Loaisel de, 21
Tristram Shandy (Sterne), 54
Trumpener, Katie, 133
Turner, Victor, xiv
Two Treatises on Government (Locke), 55
Tytler, Alexander, 78

Udo the Man of Steel (Gleich), 24
uncanny, theories of the, xiv–xv, 2, 5, 24, 27, 29–30, 37, 234–35, 237n1, 238n5, 238n6, 246n4
Undine (Fouqué), 97
Use of Circulating Libraries Considered, The (anonymous), 208, 250n7
Utterson, Sarah, 199

"Vale of Esthwaite, The" (Wordsworth), 169–70, 241n7
Valentine and Orson, versions of, xiii–xiv, 2, 232, 237n1
Vampyre, The (Polidori), 20, 199
Vampyr, Der (Lindpaintner), 32, 98
Vampyr, Der (Marschner), 32, 98
Vansina, Jan, 225
Varma, Devendra, 78, 230, 239n8, 249n1
Varnado, S. L., 230
Vathek (Beckford), 107–8
Victimes de Cloîtrées, Les (Monvel), 122–23
Victor, ou l'enfant de la forêt (Pixérécourt), 137, 151
Villemain d'Abancourt, François-Jean, 21
Viswanathan, Gauri, 240n4
Venoni (Lewis), 123
Voleurs, Les (Friedel and de Bonneville), 78
Volksmärchen der Deutschen, Die (Musäus), 202–3
Voller, Jack, 241n8, 248n3
Voloshinov, V. N., 183
Voltaire, 38, 202

Wachter, Leonard (Veit Weber), 22–23
Wagner, Richard, 98
Walpole, Horace, 19, 21, 38, 50, 75–76, 80, 118–20, 144–45, 204, 206, 208, 242n13
Walpole, Robert, 19
"Wandering Boys, The" (Bishop), 222
"Wandering Boys, The" (Kerr), 224
Warner, Marina, 110
Watkins, Daniel, 247n8
Watt, James, 82, 121
Watt, W., 249n1
Weber, Carl Maria von, 97–98, 204
Weber, Max, 4, 142, 241n6

Wells, Susan, 14
Werner (Byron), 78
White, Eric, 82
White, James, 82
White Pilgrim, The (Wilkinson), 215, 222–24
Whyte, Samuel, 166
Wieland, Christoph Martin, 202–4, 210
"Wild Huntsman, The" (Scott), 166, 167, 224
"Wilde Jäger, Der" (Bürger), 165, 167, 224
Wilde, Oscar, 20, 32
Wilde, Samuel de, 157
Wilkinson, Sarah Scudgell, 207, 215–27, 251n9
"William and Helen" (Scott), 164
Williams, Anne, 75–76, 85, 242n13, 244n1

Williams, Helen Maria, 137, 245n6
Wittgenstein, Ludwig, 3
Wollstonecraft, Mary, 137
Woman's Revenge; or the Tribunal of Blood (Wächter), 23
Wood, Gillen, 112
Wordsworth, William, 12, 24, 39, 72, 78, 88, 118, 122, 164–88, 199–201, 204, 219, 241n7, 248n2
"Written on a Blank Leaf of Macpherson's *Ossian*" (Wordsworth), 39–40
Wu, Duncan, 180
Wuthering Heights (E. Brontë), 31, 162

Young, Edward, 21, 39, 87

Zipes, Jack, 201–02, 205, 249n4
Žižek, Slavoj, 70, 234
Zofloya, of The Moor (Dacre), 78, 219

www.ingramcontent.com/pod-product-compliance
Lightning Source LLC
Chambersburg PA
CBHW021214240426
43672CB00026B/79